LIBRARY OF RELIGIOUS BIOGRAPHY

Edited by Mark A. Noll, Nathan O. Hatch,
and Allen C. Guelzo

The LIBRARY OF RELIGIOUS BIOGRAPHY is a series of original biographies on important religious figures throughout American and British history.

The authors are well-known historians, each a recognized authority in the period of religious history in which his or her subject lived and worked. Grounded in solid research of both published and archival sources, these volumes link the lives of their subjects — not always thought of as "religious" persons — to the broader cultural contexts and religious issues that surrounded them. Each volume includes a bibliographical essay and an index to serve the needs of students, teachers, and researchers.

Marked by careful scholarship yet free of academic jargon, the books in this series are well-written narratives meant to be *read* and *enjoyed* as well as studied.

LIBRARY OF RELIGIOUS BIOGRAPHY

available

The Divine Dramatist:
George Whitefield and the Rise of Modern Evangelicalism
Harry S. Stout

William Ewart Gladstone:
Faith and Politics in Victorian Britain
David Bebbington

Aimee Semple McPherson: Everybody's Sister
Edith L. Blumhofer

Sworn on the Altar of God: A Religious Biography of Thomas Jefferson
Edwin S. Gaustad

Charles G. Finney and the Spirit of American Evangelicalism
Charles E. Hambrick-Stowe

Emily Dickinson and the Art of Belief
Roger Lundin

Thomas Merton and the Monastic Vision
Lawrence S. Cunningham

The Puritan as Yankee: A Life of Horace Bushnell
Robert Bruce Mullin

"Occupy Until I Come": A. T. Pierson and the Evangelization of the World
Dana L. Robert

The Kingdom Is Always But Coming: A Life of Walter Rauschenbusch
Christopher H. Evans

The Kingdom Is Always But Coming

A Life of Walter Rauschenbusch

Christopher H. Evans

William B. Eerdmans Publishing Company
Grand Rapids, Michigan / Cambridge, U.K.

Wm. B. Eerdmans Publishing Co.
255 Jefferson Ave. S.E., Grand Rapids, Michigan 49503 /
P.O. Box 163, Cambridge CB3 9PU U.K.
www.eerdmans.com

Printed in the United States of America

09 08 07 06 05 04   7 6 5 4 3 2 1

Library of Congress Cataloging-in-Publication Data

Evans, Christopher Hodge, 1959-
The kingdom is always but coming: a life of Walter Rauschenbusch / Christopher H. Evans.
p. cm. — (Library of religious biography)
Includes bibliographical references and index.
ISBN 0-8028-4736-6 (pbk.: alk. paper)
1. Rauschenbusch, Walter, 1861-1918. 2. Baptists — United States — Clergy — Biography. 3. Theologians — United States — Biography. I. Title. II. Series.

BX6495.R3E83 2004
286'.1'092 — dc22
[B]

2004040902

All photos in this volume are from the Rauschenbusch Family Manuscript Collection, American Baptist–Samuel Colgate Historical Library, unless otherwise indicated.

To Peter and Andrew
for the grace and sanity
you bring to my life

Contents

Foreword

Toward the end of the nineteenth century, as the Western Christian churches struggled to deal with the implications of "modernity," a number of creative figures representing almost all major ecclesiastical traditions offered enduringly significant proposals in response to the pressing needs of the day. "The modern situation" was as variously understood in that era as it is in the first years of the twenty-first century, but at a minimum it entailed new confidence in scientific procedure, new awareness of the wider world, new doubts about hereditary religious certainties, and, perhaps above all, new problems of daily existence created by the emergence of industrial society. Especially where dedicated Christian leaders came face-to-face with the full consequences of modern urbanization — unprecedented wealth, unprecedented opportunities for middle-class advance, unprecedented appeal to migrants from the countryside and from other countries, unprecedented human deprivation — the result was a series of efforts to build bridges between familiar worlds of biblical discourse and new worlds of visceral human need.

In Germany, the religious community in Bad Boll that was led by Christoph Friedrich Blumhardt (1842-1919) took the lead in expanding the traditional focus of Pietism on individual spirituality to include a social definition of "the Kingdom of God." While maintaining evangelistic preaching and the traditional emphases of Württemberg pietists on personal Bible study, Blumhardt became so committed to making a difference in this world that he even served for a time as a Social Democratic representative in his state Parliament. Even broader in its impact was the effort by Wilhelm von Ketteler (1811-1877), long-time Catholic bishop of Mainz, to provide a discerning Christian response to rapidly shifting needs of workers and the rural poor. A widely discussed book from 1864, *Die Arbeiterfrage und das Christentum* (The Worker Question and Christianity) won him the title of "the workers' bishop" and propelled him into a key political, as well as religious, role during the founding years of the modern German nation.

Ketteler's application of historic Catholic dogma to modern social issues was a prelude to the great Catholic contribution of the age, which emerged especially in the pontificate of Leo XIII (1878-1903). In a series of papal pronouncements, of which the encyclical *Rerum Novarum* in 1891 was the most important, Leo brought to bear the theology of Thomas Aquinas, a sympathetic assessment of workers and their families, and a great deal of penetrating Bible study to champion notions of social solidarity, political moderation, and church involvement that have continued to inspire many branches of the Christian church, particularly Christian Democratic movements in many European countries.

The same year that Leo issued *Rerum Novarum,* Abraham Kuyper delivered in the Netherlands an important speech on "The Social Problem and the Christian Religion" that was as widely influential in its smaller Protestant orbit as the pope's encyclical was in broader Catholic circles. For Kuyper — a whirlwind of energy who inspired reforms among Dutch Protestants in ecclesiastical, educational, political, spiritual, and journalistic spheres — it was just as important as for the pope to find biblically rooted Christian guidance for steering between the Scylla of secular socialism and the Charybdis of exploitative capitalism.

In Britain one of the ablest advocates of the pope's version of social Christianity was Cardinal Henry Manning (1808-1892), who had begun life as an evangelical Protestant, passed through the Anglican Oxford Movement, and then became a Roman Catholic. As the Archbishop of Westminster, Manning felt that responding to his era's altered social conditions was one of his most important tasks. To that end, he encouraged Catholic social action and exerted an important public role in mediating the London dock strike of 1889. Manning's Anglican contemporary, Brooke Foss Westcott (1825-1901), is better known today for his scholarly works on the New Testament, but at the end of his career Westcott also became deeply committed to the task of providing Christian answers to the crisis of urban industrialism. Following as it were in the footsteps of Cardinal Manning, Westcott as the Anglican Bishop of Durham in 1892 translated theoretical commitments into action by helping mediate a turbulent strike by coal miners.

Westcott and Manning represented the efforts of ancient magisterial churches to respond to new social conditions, but efforts of similar scope were also forthcoming from Britain's dissenting Protestants. Manning, in fact, on more than one occasion commended the work of the Salvation Army as actually providing the very responses to practical social problems that (despite what from his Catholic angle he called its Protestant deficiencies) all true Christians should approve. The Army, led by William Booth (1820-1912) and Catherine Booth (1829-1890), has been underappreciated in academic assessments of the period, but its practical success in seeking out the marginalized ones whom almost no other Christian group could reach overachieved on the ground. A different sort of populist Christian presence was exerted by Keir Hardie (1856-1915) and some of his socialist colleagues who in the 1890s founded Britain's Labour Party. To Hardie, who probably was influenced as a young man toward the deep evangelical convictions of his adult life by hearing Dwight L. Moody preach, the principles of socialism, especially when leavened by Christian altruism, would advance social justice amid the era's new industrial realities.

In the United States there also appeared significant voices attempting to respond as Christians to the social distresses of "modernity." Yet it was probably even more difficult for American Christian believers to mount effective responses to the crises and opportunities of industrialism than elsewhere in Western Christendom. The Civil War, by demonstrating the inability of populist evangelical theologies to master the problem of slavery, had discredited the Christian traditions whose denominations and voluntary societies had done so much to knit American culture together in the early days of the republic. A very strong tradition of governmental laissez-faire meant that great reluctance existed on all sides to think that Congress, the courts, or the president should attempt to manage industrial change. American political life in general was so thoroughly decentralized that, once the great railroad, steel, oil, sugar, and manufacturing giants arose, there seemed little to check their multi-state and even international power.

In these circumstances, the most consequential Christian response to America's crisis of industrialization came from an unexpected quarter. Walter Rauschenbusch was a German-American who throughout his life and many trips to his family's native land remained as much at home in Germany (and German) as in America (and English). Rauschenbusch was also a Baptist, and Baptists have historically entertained serious doubts about other Christians who tried to translate their faith into social and economic action. Rauschenbusch was an observer of social crisis who came to exalt the family as key to solving industrial crises, yet he experienced strained relationships with his own parents and his own children. He chastised industrialists for their moral callousness, yet he was also a friend of John D. Rockefeller. He was liberal enough in theology to win the distrust of the great majority of American Protestants who remained conservative in their views. Yet he was also committed enough to personal piety — and even to what seemed like the social unconcern of traditional Pietism — to expend great energy in translating Ira Sankey's gospel songs into German.

Rauschenbusch came from his seminary studies in 1886 to pastor a Baptist church in an era of New York City that reflected the worst of overcrowded, undergoverned, disease-ridden, industrially blighted urban America. He left eleven years later to become professor of church history at the Baptists' Rochester Theological Seminary. In 1907 he published *Christianity and the Social Crisis.*

What Rauschenbusch, who became deaf at age 30, nonetheless learned about himself, the human condition, and the meaning of the gospel during his work in New York City's "Hell's Kitchen"; how his decisive book came to be written; why in the end its arguments did not win over his own children but lived to inspire reformers in later generations like Martin Luther King Jr.; why it is wrong to think of Rauschenbusch in simple theological terms as either a "liberal" or a "pietist"; how his Christian solution to the social crisis of mass industrialization compared to what was being proposed by such important contemporaries as William and Catherine Booth, Abraham Kuyper, Pope Leo XIII, C. F. Blumhardt, and other Christian voices — these are the important questions opened up by the thoroughly researched, judiciously argued, carefully written, and altogether engaging book by Christopher Evans that you now hold in your hands.

MARK A. NOLL

Acknowledgments

This book could not have been written without the assistance I received from numerous staff members of the American Baptist–Samuel Colgate Historical Library in Rochester. I am especially grateful to Stuart Campbell, Karen Sundland, Nancy Blostein, Betsy Dunbar, Deborah Van Broekhoven, and Sally Dodgson for giving me unlimited access to the enormous collection of materials contained in this archives, including the Rauschenbusch Family Manuscript Collection. I am also indebted to the staff of the Ambrose Swasey Library at Colgate Rochester Crozer Divinity School, under the direction of Christine Wenderoth, for access to its holdings, including several rare books. In addition, I consulted sources at the Rush Rhees Library of the University of Rochester, the Rochester Historical Society, the Boston University School of Theology Library, and the United Library of Seabury Western and Garrett-Evangelical Theological Seminary, Evanston, IL.

I am especially thankful to Walter Raushenbush, Paul Raushenbush, Irmgard Klee, Carl Baldwin, and Steven Baldwin, who took an interest in my work and provided me with hospitality and valuable information on their famous ancestor at various stages of this project. My research was greatly assisted by Naomi Annandale, a former

CRCDS student, who tracked down several rare sources, amidst the thousands of documents in the Rauschenbusch Family Papers.

When I undertook this project, I was well aware that I was writing about an individual who taught in the same institution, and in the same discipline, that I currently teach. The task of writing a balanced and engaging biography was assisted by several people who read all, or portions, of the manuscript at various stages. My gratitude is extended to Maribelle Reiss, Gary Dorrien, Ellie Stebner, Carolyn DeSwarte Gifford, and Chuck Van Hof for their detailed comments and suggestions for revision. Over the years great colleagues like Wendy Deichmann Edwards, Donald McKim, Susan Lindley, Timothy Tseng, Dianne Reistroffer, Rosemary Keller, Annie Russell, Max Stackhouse, Janet Furness, Janet Fishburn, Dale Davis, and Bob Hill provided comments on related scholarly work, coming out of a variety of academic conferences and writing projects. These wonderful friends and colleagues helped nurture this current project; I am truly grateful for their support. To Robin Olson, I offer perpetual gratitude for all the ways she supported this project for many years.

Finally, I am grateful to numerous faculty, staff, and students at Colgate Rochester Crozer Divinity School who indulged my obsession with this topic with their encouragement and engagement. In particular, I owe an enormous debt to many students whose comments in a variety of classes and conversations challenged me in my work.

One of Walter Rauschenbusch's perpetual worries concerned the kind of world his generation would pass on to their children. While he often did not agree with the choices made by his kids, they held passionately to their father's social vision. As I look at my two children, Peter and Andrew, my hope is that they might share certain values from their parents' generation, at the same time that they leave their own unique legacy. It is in honor of these two wonderful young people that I dedicate this book.

CHRISTOPHER H. EVANS

Introduction

In May 1904, an article entitled "The New Evangelism" appeared in the popular weekly magazine *The Independent.* Its author was a professor of church history at Rochester Theological Seminary, a prominent Northern Baptist seminary in Rochester, New York. At the time of the article's publication, Walter Rauschenbusch was known primarily among German-American Baptist constituencies in the United States and among liberal clergy and academics, associated with a movement in late nineteenth-century Protestantism that contemporaries referred to as "social Christianity." In the *Independent* article, Rauschenbusch took aim at those who saw Christian evangelism merely as a matter of personal conversion. What was needed in the church, Rauschenbusch argued, was a new model of evangelism that would bring persons in touch with the nation's social and economic sins caused by late-nineteenth-century industrialization. Yet he concluded his article with a conciliatory tone, insisting that in awakening America to confront its social sins, he was really invigorating an ancient Christianity. "The tongue of fire will descend on twentieth century men and give them great faith, joy and boldness, and then we shall hear the new evangel, and it will be the Old Gospel."[1]

1. Walter Rauschenbusch, "The New Evangelism," *The Independent* (May 12,

Fourteen years later, by the time of his death in July 1918, the name of Walter Rauschenbusch was inseparable from a movement that today is known as "the social gospel." In 1907, Rauschenbusch's book *Christianity and the Social Crisis* became the magnum opus of that movement, selling thousands of copies and going through multiple printings in only a few years. For the next decade, Rauschenbusch was one of the most visible Protestant leaders in the United States, his books and other writings widely read and quoted in America and worldwide. In the years since his death, numerous international church leaders and social reformers — most notably Martin Luther King, Jr. — have cited their debt to Rauschenbusch as a primary intellectual influence. Rauschenbusch would also be cited by many theologians as a foundational figure whose writings served as a link to movements associated with late-twentieth-century liberation theology.

Since his death in 1918, Rauschenbusch has been the subject of countless studies, yet few of these works have sought to interpret how he sheds light upon the historical circumstances of his own lifetime.[2] My desire is to enable the reader to understand how Walter Rauschenbusch serves as a window toward developing a more comprehensive portrait of a distinctive and misunderstood period in American religious history. In particular, the book examines Rauschenbusch's significance in relationship to the theological tradition that shaped his legacy in American Protestantism: the social gospel.

Despite the ongoing fascination with Walter Rauschenbusch's legacy, his life and his era of American religious history resist easy interpretation. He was born in Rochester, New York, in 1861, not long after the evangelical revival and social reform fires that made the city part of western New York's "Burned Over" district in the early nineteenth century had died out. Rauschenbusch's father, August, was a prominent German-American Baptist leader, who soon after immigrating to the United States broke ranks with a deeply rooted family

---

1904), 6, pamphlet in the Rauschenbusch Family Collection, box 40, located in the American Baptist–Samuel Colgate Historical Library, Rochester, New York. (All citations with a box number are from the Rauschenbusch Family Collection.)

2. While countless works have been published on various aspects of Walter Rauschenbusch's life and thought, only two full-length biographies have been written. See Dores Sharpe, *Walter Rauschenbusch* (New York: Macmillan, 1942), and Paul Minus, *Walter Rauschenbusch: American Reformer* (New York: Macmillan, 1988).

heritage of German Lutheranism to embrace a conservative Baptist pietistic tradition that took root in America during the early nineteenth century. August's son was on a path that seemed to indicate that he would follow in his father's footsteps. Although the younger Rauschenbusch professed a personal conversion experience in his teens, he struggled as a young man against the theological orthodoxy reflected in his father's conservative pietism. While he would never completely abandon the faith of his father, theological liberalism found its way into Rauschenbusch's thought from his days as a university and seminary student in the early 1880s. It was, however, his pastorate of a German-Baptist congregation in the "Hell's Kitchen" section of New York City between 1886 and 1897 that served as the greatest influence in shaping his theology and his orientation toward social reform. During his eleven years in that city, Rauschenbusch's theology went through a radical reorientation — not only due to the poverty he encountered in New York, but through his encounter with liberal ideologies that reflected the birth of the American Progressive Era. His ministry in New York also accentuated his personal suffering. By the age of thirty, Rauschenbusch was almost totally deaf, and the intense loneliness brought on by his deafness affected both his theology and his personal life in ways that inspired and discouraged him.

Although Rauschenbusch's publications were commonplace in many Baptist and academic periodicals by the mid-1890s, it wasn't until he became a professor at Rochester Theological Seminary in 1897 that he was able to disseminate his ideas on a popular scale. After the publication of his landmark *Christianity and the Social Crisis,* Rauschenbusch became one of the most sought-after religious speakers in the United States; his rise to prominence coincided with the institutional ascendency of the social gospel as a theological movement in American Protestantism. By 1912, Rauschenbusch had paradoxically come to be understood as a prophetic figure, but one who enjoyed a great deal of popularity among middle-class Americans.

After World War I began in August 1914, Rauschenbusch, although not an absolute pacifist, became identified with a minority of religious and political leaders who opposed the war. Finding himself under public suspicion because of his German ancestry and his ambivalence toward the motives of the allied cause, he found himself frequently under attack from many whom he considered his friends and allies. By the time of American intervention into the war in the spring of 1917, he was moving away from criticizing the war toward an attempt to articulate how the theology of the social gospel was America's best hope for promoting the economic reconstruction of the postwar world. Cancer, however, interfered with these plans and led to his untimely death in July 1918 at the age of fifty-six.

Like most historical figures who capture the imagination of later generations, Walter Rauschenbusch's life was marked by paradoxes. First, although he has been cited as one of the first important twentieth-century Protestant theologians, his intellectual underpinnings were firmly rooted in the cultural and social currents of the late nineteenth century. Rauschenbusch's contemporaries and later generations heard in his words a message of theological radicalism. But his social vision was at points quite conservative, showing a strong affinity for the cultural worldview characteristic of the late-nineteenth-century Protestant middle class. His conservatism, in part, was highlighted by his conflicted views toward women's rights (although he did support women's suffrage), a failure to engage systematically the evils of American racism, and a paternalistic view toward the American working class. Rauschenbusch believed that socialism represented the best political option for reforming America's economic ills. Yet his understanding of socialism was frequently more idealistic than practical. Like more politically conservative social gospel leaders such as Josiah Strong, Rauschenbusch shared a deep suspicion of the motives of many political socialists. He shared a trait common among many progressive leaders of that time who equated violent political radicalism, and its accompanying godlessness, with the massive waves of immigration that transformed America in the years between 1880 and 1920. For Rauschenbusch, socialism's power rested in the way it embodied the ethics of Jesus to American society, instructing an educated middle class to carry these values throughout the institutional life of the nation. Even as he identified concrete ways in which socialist principles could be applied to modern economic life, he never sought the wholesale dismantling of class interests in America. In fact, he depended on these interests to promote his vision of Christian socialism. During his life, he courted the friendship and patronage of some of the most powerful men in America, most notably fellow Baptist and Standard Oil tycoon John D. Rockefeller. Although Rauschenbusch believed earnestly in the need for powerful economic interests to share their wealth with the poor, the primary means to accomplish this change was not through political activism, but through moral suasion, where the teachings of Christ would appeal to the consciences of the powerful to change social structures.

Rauschenbusch's indebtedness to late-nineteenth-century intellectual sources reflects a second paradox in his career: his balancing of German and American cultural heritages. His father, August Rauschenbusch, instilled in his son a love for German intellectual culture, reflected in the fact that Rauschenbusch at critical junctures of his career made extended pilgrimages to his ancestral homeland. In addition to spending several years in Germany with his family as a boy, he received a post-secondary diploma from a German Gymnasium school in 1883. At a crisis point in his New York City pastorate in 1891, when Rauschenbusch contemplated leaving parish ministry for good, he traveled to Europe, spending the bulk of his sabbatical time in Germany immersing himself in that nation's intellectual culture. The result of that trip produced his first extensive manuscript on the topic of the church and social questions that had plagued him since he came to New York in 1886.[3] At the moment when *Christianity and the Social Crisis* was published in April 1907, he took a sabbatical leave from Rochester Theological Seminary to spend a year in Germany doing research. Unlike other leaders of the American social gospel movement, Rauschenbusch was thoroughly bi-cultural, as he saw in Germany not only a nostalgic ancestral home, but a place that epitomized all that was outstanding in Western intellectual culture. His fondness for Germany, as ancestral home and as an intellectual model, dovetailed with his own work as a church historian. His understanding of history, a critical foundation for the idealism of his theology, was rooted in prominent nineteenth-century German historians including August Neander, Philip Schaff, and especially the liberal historians Albrecht Ritschl and Adolf von Harnack. This intellectual grounding in German intellectual sources influenced his optimistic views related to social reform and his beliefs in historical progress.[4]

3. This manuscript, which remained lost for decades after Rauschenbusch's death, was later published under the title *The Righteousness of the Kingdom* (Nashville: Abingdon Press, 1968).

4. See Henry Warner Bowden, "Walter Rauschenbusch and American Church

Yet, Rauschenbusch was thoroughly American. Like other Protestants of his era he hailed the virtues of the Anglo-American heritage (despite his lifelong suspicion of Great Britain), and he praised the model of American democracy not only as a political virtue but also as an embodiment of his theological ideals. The majority of his insights on contemporary economic theory were drawn from late-nineteenth-century American economists, especially Henry George and Richard Ely, the latter considered one of the pioneers in the development of modern economics. As a professor of church history, Rauschenbusch was one of the few scholars of his day to find merit in the relatively new discipline of "American church history," seeing the providential hand of God at work, building up democratic principles in America's churches, government, and other social institutions (and, not surprisingly, with the Baptists playing a primary role in the story of God's "salvation history" in America). As much as he loved his German heritage, Rauschenbusch's passion as a writer and church leader was focused upon an American, not European, audience.

Third, Rauschenbusch's life illustrates the elusiveness of defining the social gospel as a historical and theological phenomenon in American Christianity. The most common definition for the social gospel was penned by the liberal theologian and biblical scholar, Shailer Mathews, who referred to the movement as "the application of the teaching of Jesus and the total message of the Christian salvation to society, the economic life, and social institutions . . . as well as to individuals."[5] Mathews and subsequent scholars presupposed the social gospel's linkage to late-nineteenth-century liberal Protestant theology, with its acceptance of biblical criticism and its accommodation of Christianity to the natural sciences. Focusing only on the liberal theological dimensions of the social gospel, however, obscures the movement's impact upon American culture.

The social gospel was part of a cultural and theological revolution in America. Not only did its ministers occupy prominent pulpits

History," in *Foundations* 9 (July-September 1966), 234-50, and "Church History and the Social Gospel," in *Church History in the Age of Science: Historiographical Patterns in the United States, 1876-1918* (Chapel Hill: University of North Carolina Press, 1971), 170-95.

5. Quoted from Charles Howard Hopkins, *The Rise of the Social Gospel in American Protestantism, 1865-1915* (New Haven: Yale University Press, 1940), 3.

throughout the nation, but its proponents ran for political office and engaged in political activism on both a local and national level. The movement's leaders held public forums, institutes, and lectures that repeatedly drew enormous audiences throughout the country. Its adherents wrote popular fiction, their books becoming best sellers in North America and Europe. Its proponents wrote hymns that are still sung by Christian faith communions worldwide. Most notably, its advocates wrote books by the hundreds on topics dealing with "social Christianity" that were widely read and discussed in both religious and secular circles.

Although it is likely that the average American of the early twentieth century would probably be more familiar with the old-time gospel of Billy Sunday than with the social gospel of Walter Rauschenbusch, the popularity of Rauschenbusch and the social gospel in America led to an unparalleled institutional and popular revolution. The peak years of the social gospel between 1907 and 1918 witnessed an explosion in Protestant home and foreign missions. At a time when most Protestant communions were closed to the leadership gifts of women, the theology of the social gospel provided a major impetus for women to find leadership roles in institutional Christianity. In spite of resistance from male church hierarchies, these women built schools, established and ran settlement houses, and proclaimed publicly a gospel of Christian reform to America.[6]

The social gospel was a major catalyst behind the birth of the modern ecumenical movement. When the Federal Council of Churches of Christ was formed in 1908, not only did it symbolize the spawning of the twentieth-century ecumenical movement; it symbolized as well the interconnection that existed between the drive for Christian unity and the imperative for Christian social action. While some historians view the social gospel more as a footnote to the Progressive Era,[7] leaders of the social gospel took center stage in galvanizing a powerful reform impulse in the early twentieth century, an im-

6. See, for example, John Patrick McDowell, *The Social Gospel in the South: The Woman's Home Mission Movement in the Methodist Episcopal Church, South, 1886-1939* (Baton Rouge: Louisiana State University Press, 1982).

7. The view that the social gospel was largely a peripheral movement to Progressive Era reforms has been made by many historians. See, for example, Robert H. Wiebe, *The Search for Order, 1877-1920* (New York: Hill & Wang, 1967), 207-8.

pulse that some scholars see as part of a "Third Great Awakening" in American history.[8] The social gospel's legacy not only survived among later generations of church reformers, but also contributed to a liberal social-economic philosophy that looked with greater regularity to government as the primary arbiter for social change — an ideology that

was critical to spawning the birth of the modern "welfare state" during the New Deal administrations of Franklin Roosevelt in the 1930s. Even though the social gospel as a popular movement dissipated after World War I, its proponents lived on in American churches and within various components of American secular society.

As this biography reveals, however, what historians call "the social gospel" was never a unified social or theological phenomenon. Its primary leaders were widely scattered throughout numerous networks encompassing academic, ecclesiastical, civic, and business interests. Many historians find the origins of the social gospel coinciding with the rise of industrial capitalism in the urban north, while other scholars point to the tradition of social reform embodied by early nineteenth-century evangelical Protestantism.[9] While scholars will continue to debate the origin and definition of the social gospel, the emergence of Walter Rauschenbusch as the major spokesman of the movement by 1907 signaled the social gospel's shift from the periphery to the center of American Protestant identity. At a moment when many American churches were reluctant to publicly address social

questions, Walter Rauschenbusch made it acceptable for many Protestant churches to speak out on a variety of social issues.

By the time Rauschenbusch wrote *Christianity and the Social Crisis,* he was contributing to a well-established legacy of religious and social idealism, inherited from late nineteenth-century church leaders such as Josiah Strong, Washington Gladden, Richard Ely, George Herron, and W. D. P. Bliss. Additionally, the definitive years of Rauschenbusch's influence in America, between 1907 and 1918, coincided with the apex of the social gospel, reflected in the writings of influential church leaders such as Frank Mason North, Shailer Mathews,

8. See Robert William Fogel, *The Fourth Great Awakening and the Future of Egalitarianism* (Chicago & London: University of Chicago Press, 2000).

9. Timothy L. Smith, *Revivalism and Social Reform in Mid-Nineteenth Century America* (Nashville: Abingdon Press, 1957).

Francis Peabody, Harry F. Ward, and Vida Scudder. Yet a central purpose of this study is to understand why Rauschenbusch stood out among his contemporaries (and through the verdict of later historians and theologians) as the most "satisfying exponent" of the social gospel in America.

Rauschenbusch's contemporaries used a variety of labels to identify him, among them church historian, Christian socialist, sociologist, and theologian. In reality, he was primarily a pastor whose goal was nothing short of preaching for the conversion of America. The social gospel may have produced more prominent social activists, institutional church leaders, and biblical scholars. But none of these leaders captured the Zeitgeist of the social gospel better than Walter Rauschenbusch did. With the possible exception of the fiction of Charles Sheldon, author of the widely popular novel *In His Steps,* no one in American Protestantism communicated the message of Shailer Mathews's definition of the social gospel with greater clarity, persuasion, and power than Rauschenbusch.

Like other pioneers of the social gospel, Rauschenbusch believed that he was living in a unique moment of history that required nothing less than the restoration of "primitive" Christianity, based upon the prophetic tradition of the Old Testament and a recovery of the social teachings of Jesus. What differentiated Rauschenbusch from other social gospel liberals, however, and what contributed to his popularity, was how his theology reflected a blending of social optimism *and* social crisis. Although Rauschenbusch was seen by later scholars as one of the most radical church leaders of his generation, he was in actuality more of a centrist figure within the social gospel movement. On one hand, his critique against American capitalism was more incisive than the irenic tone that characterized the work of Washington Gladden, the prominent writer and pastor of the First Congregational Church, Columbus, Ohio. Yet Rauschenbusch's work did not approach the vitriolic radicalism of George Herron, the controversial cleric and professor of practical Christianity at Iowa College in Grinnell, Iowa, in the 1890s. While Gladden was critical of American capitalism, he shunned any suggestion of social radicalism, seeing social reform as incremental and bound by preexisting institutional structures in America. Herron, on the other hand, reflected an extreme expression of the social gospel, calling for a radical political and economic restructuring of American society.[10] Although Rauschenbusch's theology shared points in common with both men, his social vision grafted a compelling prophetic Christian narrative upon the middle-class culture of his era.

Rauschenbusch stressed that social progress depended on how Americans responded to the contemporary social crisis reflected by the problems of poverty, caused by the predatory capitalism of the wealthy. His social revolution was based upon an ability to arouse the moral indignation of the middle class — in effect, to stir a religious awakening in America. Unlike the radicalism that characterized the meteoric but brief career of George Herron in the 1890s, Rauschenbusch believed that God's prophetic judgments were designed not to destroy the cultural fabric of America but to instill in the nation the moral resolve to fight social injustice and evil. As he explained in his "New Evangelism" article, the importance of evangelism was not just to bring individuals in touch with a personal conversion experience. It was designed to make sense of the social dimensions of modern society. "The powerlessness of the old evangelism is only the most striking and painful demonstration of the general state of the churches. . . . It does not lie in lack of hard work or of prayer or of keen anxiety. It lies in the fact that modern life has gone through immense changes and the Church has not kept pace with it in developing the latent moral and spiritual resources of the Gospel which are needed by the new life."[11] According to Rauschenbusch, Christianity needed to retain what was valuable within its earlier heritage related to individual regeneration. Yet he popularized in American Protestantism the language of "social salvation" that would become a hallmark for later theological discourse in the twentieth century. In order to expand the human conception of salvation, "it will have to give an adequate definition of how a Christian man should live under modern conditions, and then summon men to live so."[12] At the heart of his ministry he was a pastor who sought to help Americans make sense of contemporary society, ap-

10. For a comparison of the careers of George Herron and Walter Rauschenbusch, see Peter J. Frederick, *Knights of the Golden Rule: The Intellectual as Christian Social Reformer in the 1890s* (Lexington: University of Kentucky Press, 1976), 141-83.

11. Rauschenbusch, "The New Evangelism," 5.

12. Ibid., 6.

pealing to the moral conscience of America to use its Protestant heritage to build a just nation. In a succession of nineteenth-century Protestant ministers like Charles Finney, Henry Ward Beecher, and Washington Gladden himself, Rauschenbusch's ministry emanated out of his pastoral identity that drove his social passion and enabled him to appeal to a sizeable segment of middle-class Americans. As one scholar surmised, "Rauschenbusch was engaged in a continuous camp meeting designed to reclaim the 'sinner,' America, for the kingdom of God."[13]

Rauschenbusch's concept of social salvation was inseparable from his major contribution to American theology: his reinterpretation of the Christian doctrine of the kingdom of God. As he noted in *Christianity and the Social Crisis,* faith in the kingdom of God "is not a matter of getting individuals to heaven, but of transforming the life on earth into the harmony of heaven."[14] Unlike other social gospel liberals, Rauschenbusch struggled not to equate the ultimate realization of the kingdom of God with any earthly social order, affirming in the conclusion of *Christianity and the Social Crisis,* "At best there is always but an approximation to a perfect social order. The kingdom of God is always but coming."[15] For much of his life, however, Rauschenbusch was hopeful that signs of the kingdom were visible throughout America, especially among influential segments of white middle-class America. As the social gospel grew in popularity in the early twentieth century, he looked confidently for signs of the kingdom in government, business, churches, and in America's most important social institution: the family. In this regard, Rauschenbusch's relationship to his own family is instructive. Though he hoped that the American family would serve as a microcosm for building the kingdom of God, his own home life was often the center of dissension, plagued by Rauschenbusch's own insecurities as a husband and parent, and the inevitable rebellions of his children, who saw their lives charting a different path from their parents.

13. Stanley Hauerwas, "Walter Rauschenbusch and the Saving of America," in *A Better Hope: Resources for a Church Confronting Capitalism, Democracy, and Postmodernity* (Grand Rapids: Brazos Press, 2000), 71.

14. Rauschenbusch, *Christianity and the Social Crisis* (New York: Macmillan, 1907; reprint Louisville: Westminster/John Knox Press, 1991), 65.

15. Ibid., 421.

UNINTENDED OUTCOMES

Finally, Rauschenbusch's life accentuates many of the historical ironies of a period that the renowned historian Arthur Schlesinger, Sr., called "a critical period in American religion."[16] The period of Rauschenbusch's public ministry from the mid-1880s until his death in 1918 has been characterized by many as the last era of Protestant cultural hegemony in the United States. This era of American religious history witnessed the disintegration of a perceived Protestant theological consensus, setting the stage for the fundamentalist-modernist controversy that erupted soon after Rauschenbusch's death in 1918. Martin Marty characterizes the early twentieth century as a time when a "two-party" split occurred within American Protestantism, reflected by the use of the terms "evangelicals" for those who embraced a conservative-fundamentalist theology and "liberals" who followed a world-embracing "modernist" expression of Christian belief.[17]

In spite of the usefulness of Marty's two-party thesis, this argument alone does not grasp the complexities of the theological divisions that split American Protestantism apart in the late nineteenth and early twentieth centuries. The story of Walter Rauschenbusch suggests an era in which churches were dividing along numerous fault lines that broke Protestantism into not just two camps but into several. These divisions occurred among conservative evangelicals, but also among the heirs of the social gospel, many of whom were increasingly looking beyond the realm of America's churches for signs of the coming kingdom in the 1920s and 1930s.

What Rauschenbusch's life story reveals is that the distinction of who falls under the labels "evangelical," "liberal," "fundamentalist," or "modernist" is as much a judgment constructed by contemporary historians and theologians as it is an indicator of how Rauschenbusch and his contemporaries labeled themselves. Rauschenbusch has been characterized as an "evangelical liberal," and in many ways this biog-

16. Arthur M. Schlesinger, "A Critical Period in American Religion, 1875-1900," Massachusetts Historical Society, *Proceedings* 64 (1932): 523-47.

17. Martin E. Marty, *Protestantism in the United States: Righteous Empire* (New York: Dial Press, 1970).

raphy supports that identity.[18] As much as he was indebted to the ideas of social and theological liberalism, he never completely broke from a tradition of early nineteenth-century postmillennial evangelicalism that dreamed that the virtues of Protestant piety would lead to a redeemed society. Rauschenbusch's lifetime witnessed numerous divisions occurring within American Protestantism, including the rise of the Holiness movement, the birth of modern Pentecostalism, the emergence of premillennial dispensationalism, and the nascent origins of what would become identified in the 1920s as fundamentalism. However, even as these divisions were emerging in American Protestantism, these disparate theological identities struggled to remain united to make America a Christian (Protestant) nation.

This goal that Rauschenbusch shared with more theologically conservative Protestants illustrates Martin Marty's characterization of the late nineteenth and early twentieth centuries as an era of irony in American religious history.[19] While church leaders hoped they were working to build a more unified church and society, they witnessed the dissolution of those dreams in the face of mounting theological, religious, and cultural pluralism in America. Although Rauschenbusch would be seen by later generations of conservative Christians as an enemy to evangelicalism, one of his earliest publications was an 1888 article praising Dwight Moody's revivalist movement as "a near approach to heaven."[20] In the 1890s Rauschenbusch collaborated with Moody's partner, Ira Sankey, on a two-volume German translation of Sankey's gospel hymns. This collaboration was not an anomaly in Rauschenbusch's career, but reflects that although he held different theological suppositions from Moody and Sankey, he did not doubt that he was working with them toward the same end: to win America and the world to the cause of Protestant Christianity. Even toward the end of his life when he developed more of a vitriolic response to popular revivalists like Billy Sunday, Rauschenbusch never doubted that he possessed a theological identity that placed him squarely within a larger

18. See Kenneth Cauthen, *The Impact of American Religious Liberalism* (New York: Harper & Row, 1962).

19. Martin E. Marty, *Modern American Religion: The Irony of It All* (Chicago: University of Chicago Press, 1986).

20. Walter Rauschenbusch, "Impressions of the Northfield Meetings," in *The Christian Inquirer* (August 16, 1888).

heritage of Protestant evangelicalism. Dores Sharpe, his former secretary who wrote the first full-length biography of Rauschenbusch, noted an occasion when he and Rauschenbusch were attending a conference in Chicago. While the two took time out of their schedule to share a meal on the banks of Lake Michigan, Rauschenbusch asked Sharpe, "How do you think of me and my work?" Sharpe replied, "I think of you as an evangelist and of your work as evangelism of the truest sort." Rauschenbusch replied by hugging Sharpe and exclaimed, "I have always wanted to be thought of in that way."[21] Whatever embellishment Sharpe may have added to this account is beside the point. The fact remains that for Rauschenbusch, and for the majority of social gospel leaders of his generation, the term "evangelical" was not understood as secondary to their theological identity.[22] Yet that theological term (along with many others) would end up meaning very different things depending on who was uttering it. When Rauschenbusch wrote in 1904 about the emergence of a "new evangelism" in America, it indicated that the theological divisions that would become more easily identifiable and visible among religious leaders in the decades following Rauschenbusch's death were already well established within the tapestry of American Protestant churches.

The story of Walter Rauschenbusch reflects, in part, upon the death of a larger Protestant dream of cultural and theological unity in American religious history. Yet his biography also serves as a birth narrative for a genre of liberal Christianity that would make a distinctive contribution to twentieth-century Christian theology and ethics. Although Rauschenbusch argued that he was helping Christians rediscover the true meaning of ancient Christianity, his future identity marked him as the propagator of a new genre of Christianity that changed the way Christianity would be interpreted in America. Given the historical realities of Rauschenbusch's life, such an outcome is indeed ironic.

21. Sharpe, 393.

22. See Grant Wacker, "The Holy Spirit and the Spirit of the Age in American Protestantism, 1880-1920," *The Journal of American History* 72 (June 1985): 45-62.

1 In the Shadow of August Rauschenbusch

In July 1879, seventeen-year-old Walther Rauschenbusch arrived in Germany to begin the first phase of preparation for his chosen vocation as a Baptist minister. For the next several years that this young American would live and study in Germany, he wrestled with the fact that he was living in a country that he very much loved, but in which he was never quite at home. This was not, however, the first, nor would it be the last, time that the man who later adopted the English spelling Walter for his first name had to confront this German-American tension. As a seventeen-year-old, the young Rauschenbusch knew that he came from a unique family that centered around the life and personality of his father, August.

August Rauschenbusch stood at the culmination of a family heritage that reflected a deep-seated spirituality rooted in the German pietism of his forefathers, combined with a fierce independence that was well-suited to the religious temper of his adopted American home. As he accompanied his only son to Germany in the summer of 1879, he was reaching the climax of an American ministry that would serve his son both as a point of reference and as a point of deviation. As much as he had, and would, rebel against the theological legacy of his father, Walter Rauschenbusch's life was indebted to the intellectual and theological heritage of his father.

WESTPHALIAN PIETISTS

The earliest known Rauschenbusches labored as farmers in the Westphalia region of northwestern Germany, a region that was at the heart of the Thirty Years War between European Catholics and Protestants in the first half of the seventeenth century. According to a family saga, a young nobleman from Sweden came to the region during that war to defend the Protestant cause and, after being wounded in battle, was nursed back to health by the peasant daughter of a man named Rauschenbusch. Finding that "love could melt a hero's iron heart," the young man, Alfred, renounced his royal inheritance and family name to marry this peasant daughter. In a reverse of the prodigal son parable, it is the young man's father who comes to his senses, as years later he journeys to his son's adopted family to seek forgiveness.[1]

When August Rauschenbusch was born two centuries later in 1816, his family had moved beyond the status of being rural farmers, as August was the descendant of five generations of Lutheran ministers who prospered in Westphalia. The first to enter the ministry was Esaias Rauschenbusch, who in the mid-seventeenth century succeeded his father-in-law in a Lutheran church in Merbeck. Esaias was succeeded in his parish by his son, Hilmar Ernst, who in turn was succeeded by one of his sons, Johann Carl.

Connected as they were to the state-church Lutheranism of Prussia, these three generations of Rauschenbusches enjoyed a rising social status that came to clergy who were part of the Lutheran church establishment. Yet August's family also reflected the roots of German Pietism, a renewal movement within German Lutheranism that arose in the aftermath of the Thirty Years War. Associated with the ministry of Philip Jacob Spener in the late seventeenth century, Pietism was a movement

1. "Rauschenbusch Saga," written in 1850 by Wilhelm Fischer, with English translation by Irmgard Klee. A copy of this document is located in the American Baptist–Samuel Colgate Historical Library, Rochester, NY. Genealogical information on Rauschenbusch's family can also be found in box 143, RFC.

that stressed an individual's experiential piety as a means of promoting spiritual renewal. In juxtaposition to an insistence on creedal orthodoxy and religious rationalism, Spener's ministry stressed the importance of a strong devotional life, characterized by prayer and through small groups that fostered spiritual renewal. The fruits of Spener's ministry would not only be evident in German Lutheranism, but would take root in a number of eighteenth-century religious movements, including the Moravians and the Methodist revivalism of John and Charles Wesley.

These pietistic roots were especially evident in Johann Carl's son, and August Rauschenbusch's grandfather, Hilmar Ernst, who lived from 1745 to 1815. University trained at Göttingen and the Pietist-dominated university at Halle, Hilmar Ernst ministered to Lutheran congregations in Bunde and later in Elberfeld, in the Wupper Valley of Westphalia. Described by Walter Rauschenbusch's first biographer, Dores Sharpe, as a man possessing a "sturdy individualistic piety," Hilmar Ernst was a man who gained a reputation for his stubborn and independent actions. He wrote several Pietist tracts to keep the Lutheran rural hymnal free of "the enervating novelties of metropolitan Rationalism." He once furiously entered a tavern to drive out some of his parishioners, saving them from the sins of brandy. As one ministerial colleague noted, Hilmar Ernst was a man who "had to go in the teeth of the north wind."[2]

Hilmar Ernst's son, August Ernst, also had a distinguished career, serving for years as a pastor in Altena and as a synodal superintendent. Like his father, August Ernst displayed a talent for writing, and his work *Biblische Historien* was widely used as a school textbook. While he apparently lacked the passionate exuberance of his father, August Ernst displayed a steadfast nationalism. During the Napoleonic Wars, he served as a field chaplain; several of his patriotic poems appeared as fliers.[3] When Karl August Rauschenbusch was born in 1816, his young life took on the temperament of both his grandfather and father. At his birth, his father expressed his hope that his son would grow up fearing God, "lead a righteous life, and become a soldier."[4] Although he pos-

2. Dores Sharpe, 17.

3. Ibid., 19.

4. Carl Schneider, "Americanization of Karl August Rauschenbusch, 1816-1899," in *Church History* 24 (March 1955): 4.

sessed his father's scholarly bent, he displayed his grandfather's devotion to pietism that later took his life in ways that moved his family's legacy beyond the geographic and spiritual confines of Westphalia.

At the age of eighteen, August began his theological studies at Berlin University, an institution that was at the center of an intellectual revolution. August arrived in Berlin in 1834, the same year that the university's founder, Friedrich Schleiermacher, had died. In the decades following his death, Schleiermacher became identified as one of the great intellectual architects of liberal Protestant theology, whose legacy served as a point of departure for many German theologians and historians in the mid- and late nineteenth century. Schleiermacher set out to show how Christianity could be reconciled with post-Enlightenment rationalism, mediating between what seemed to be the competing polarities of theological orthodoxy and scientific rationalism. Although the scholars whom Schleiermacher attracted to Berlin differed widely on specific matters of theological belief, they shared a conviction that the way to understand Christianity was through the dimension of religious experience. Among the scholars emphasizing this theme who greatly influenced August Rauschenbusch was the historian Johann August Neander.

Neander displayed a penchant for making his students think of church history both as an intellectual science and as a spiritual enterprise. His strong piety compelled his students to discern how God's spirit, through Jesus Christ, was at the center of all human history and scientific knowledge. Neander was part of a rising theological movement that followed in the tradition of Schleiermacher by emphasizing the primacy of an individual's experience over the role of church creeds and dogmas. One of Neander's chief intellectual disciples, and August's contemporary at Berlin University, Philip Schaff, would say of his great teacher that he instilled in his students a deep faith in Christ, demonstrating how church history reflected a strong providential theme in which Jesus Christ always served "as the highest revelation of a holy and merciful God" and "the fountain of all salvation and sanctifying grace for a ruined world."[5] Although Neander was theologically orthodox, his teaching laid a foundation for the development of church history as a distinct theological discipline in the nineteenth

5. Henry Warner Bowden, *Church History in the Age of Science*, 53.

century. He contributed to a foundation that would be built upon by Schaff and by Albrecht Ritschl, perhaps the most influential German theologian to influence a later generation of theological liberals like Walter Rauschenbusch.

Neander's influence helped young August resolve what had been an intense struggle between the creedal dogmatism of state Lutheranism and the spirit of Pietism that permeated his family roots. He struggled between an emerging post-Enlightenment scientific rationalism and the creedal orthodoxy of Lutheranism. In 1836, Rauschenbusch settled this dilemma by undergoing a pietistic conversion experience that put him squarely in line with his grandfather's faith.

August's view of pietism would reveal itself in ways that pushed beyond those of his family. Prone to an anxious disposition reminiscent of his grandfather, he suffered a breakdown, and after a convalescence period he engaged in extended travel in Germany and Austria. Establishing a pattern to be replicated by his son, August attended university lectures in different German cities that pushed his intellectual curiosity beyond theology, especially in the areas of the natural sciences.[6] Yet, August's pietist conversion left him no doubt that all scientific knowledge was subservient to theology. While Neander attempted to show his students how Enlightenment rationalism could be reconciled to divine revelation, August would not tolerate this theological equivocation. Religious faith was an "all or nothing" proposition, and despite a lifelong love of botany and horticulture, he remained unflinching in his theological conservatism.[7]

After August's ordination, and one year after his father's death in 1840, he became pastor of his father's church in Altena. While in Altena, he supported the founding of a temperance society and his congregation supported a local deaconess society. The deaconess movement emerged out of German Lutheranism as a means for young women to pursue a religious vocation aimed at performing works of charity and mercy, especially associated with hospital ministries. Functioning as a Protestant version of a female religious order, the deaconess movement had modest successes in European and Ameri-

6. Sharpe, 21-22.
7. Schneider, 6.

can Lutheranism, before it would reemerge in the late nineteenth century in more evangelical denominations in North America, especially the Methodists and Baptists. August's ministry, however, was far from being a "social gospel." His driving passion as a minister was to save souls and to make the members of his congregation aware of their sin and accept Jesus into their lives. While August earned the respect of his congregation, the intensity of his personality raised the concern of some in his church. He was driven by the unequivocal passion to convince his flock that one's salvation was not dependent upon the recitation of creeds or church membership, but by the individual decision to surrender one's self to God. This conviction led August to a second traumatic conversion experience. In 1844, his exhaustive energy brought on a serious illness. Although he recovered fully from this, the experience left him convinced that he needed to pursue another calling in his ministry by taking up missionary service in the United States.

Germany in the 1830s and 1840s was going through intense political strife that compelled many families to seek refuge in America. Unlike other European powers, Germany for centuries was made up of a series of provinces dominated by the autocratic state of Prussia. Efforts to bring about political unity, and to resist Prussian domination, led to the outbreak of numerous protests in favor of democratic political reform that ultimately led to an ill-fated revolution in 1848. Even before the 1848 revolution, however, German immigration to the United States grew rapidly. In 1835, the German population living in the United States was just under 200,000. By 1850, the number was 1,200,000.[8] It was August's intent to create a new mission field among these immigrant communities, and his departure for America in 1846 was marked by confidence in his journey to this unknown mission field.

Yet even before arriving in America, August's penchant for argumentation displayed itself. He got into an intense theological debate with a group of theological students from Bavaria on his ship bound for America, arguing with them how the creedal dogmatism of Lutheranism often contradicted the intensely personal nature of

8. Albert John Ramaker, "The Story of the German Department," *The Rochester Theological Seminary Bulletin* (October 1927): 31.

pietistic conversion. Yet once in America, August Rauschenbusch encountered a religious environment that he found both alienating and alluring. America in the 1840s was in the aftermath of the Second Great Awakening, characterized by its emotionally charged religious revivals that erupted throughout the American frontier in the opening decades of the century. August's eyes were opened by the free-market flow of evangelical religious movements that competed with one another to save souls and to add members to their constituencies. In particular, the American religious landscape was dominated largely by two traditions: Methodists and Baptists. Largely existing as trace elements in America at the beginning of the American Revolution, by 1850 both of these churches displaced the old colonial Congregational, Presbyterian, and Anglican religious establishments as the largest churches in the nation. On one hand, Rauschenbusch thought little of the Methodists and their Arminian theology of free grace. August had inherited a deeply rooted Calvinist bent toward salvation and did not believe that a church should accept anyone into membership who was unsure of their salvation. On the other hand, August Rauschenbusch saw in American evangelicalism a spirit of vital piety that was missing from the churches in his native Germany.

He was especially drawn to the Baptists. When August first arrived in America in 1846, he accepted a position with the American Tract Society, one of many Protestant voluntary societies born out of the revival fires of the early nineteenth-century Great Awakening. Soon after his arrival, Rauschenbusch headed to the western frontier of Missouri to distribute religious tracts to German immigrants. The following year, he moved to New York City, where he became the director of the society's program aimed at disseminating evangelistic literature to German immigrants. It was during his tenure in New York that he experienced a final conversion: his decision to become a Baptist. August saw in the Baptists not only the spirit of evangelical piety that was so vital to him but also a tradition that honored the fidelity of the individual's experience. In the Baptists, he found a tradition that seemed to exemplify what his great teacher Neander had emphasized about true Christianity: its redemptive power came not through church dogma but through the power of Christian experience. For August, the Baptists embodied a New Testament model of primitive

Christianity, a church that had the ability to approximate in its fellowship a godly fellowship of righteousness.

The Baptist emphasis on the importance of the individual believer seemed to fit August's own peripatetic nature. In May 1850, August was baptized by immersion in the Mississippi River, and much to the consternation of his Lutheran kin back in Germany, August Rauschenbusch's career as a paragon of German Baptist Christianity in the United States had begun. In the years following his baptism, August served as an evangelist and church planter among German-Baptist immigrant communities, traveling widely in the United States and lower Canada. In 1855, he accepted a call to serve as the pastor of a German Baptist congregation in Pine Oak Creek, Missouri. He had moved a long way from his days as a university student in cosmopolitan Berlin, finding himself in the heart of the American western frontier where members of his church were often separated by miles. In later years, he was fond of telling of his encounter with a settler from Kentucky who claimed that he moved to Missouri to give himself more space — in Kentucky there had been only five miles between himself and his neighbors.[9] Despite the rustic conditions of his ministry, August adapted himself to his surroundings and prospered. Like many Baptist ministers of that era, Rauschenbusch farmed to supplement his income and also taught children in his home during the week. In subsequent years, the rigor of August's work ethic was not lost on other family members, especially on his son, who in his own life regarded physical labor as a means of drawing closer to God.

By the time Rauschenbusch settled in Pine Oak Creek in 1854, he had married a young woman named Caroline Rump. Twelve years younger than August, Caroline had been a former confirmand in August's parish in Altena. Despite concerns from his family that he was marrying someone beneath him in social standing, Caroline appeared to share her husband's passion to build a regenerate church of the faithful on the American frontier. However, August Rauschenbusch was soon drawn away from the role of frontier evangelist toward a career that better reflected the intellectual underpinnings of his ancestors.

9. Reprint of Walter Rauschenbusch address in *Christian Work* (January 23, 1913), box 94.

THE SEMINARY IN A HOTEL

Around the time of August's baptism, a group of Baptist clergy and laity established the Rochester Theological Seminary in Rochester, New York. At a time when theological education was a rarity among American evangelical churches, Rochester Theological Seminary was founded with a clear mission of training an educated Baptist ministry for the unique challenges of ministry in America. Concurrently established with the University of Rochester in 1850, the new university and seminary were initially housed in a Rochester hotel and were considered little more than second-rate schools that hardly approached the caliber of the nation's leading universities and theological seminaries. Ralph Waldo Emerson allegedly remarked that the two schools served "as an illustration of Yankee enterprise, saying that a landlord in Rochester had an old hotel which he thought would rent for more as a university — so he put in a few books, sent for a coach load of professors, bought some philosophical apparatus, and by the time green peas were ripe, had graduated a large class of students." Emerson's comment was not far from the truth. In their first year of operation, the university had sixty-six students with five professors and the seminary twenty-four students and two professors.[10]

But the new seminary was situated in a unique area of the country. When the Erie Canal created an east-west thoroughfare through New York state to Lake Erie, it paved the way for massive migrations westward in the 1820s and 1830s. Increasingly, the city of Rochester, founded on an area largely made up of swampland, was transformed into what historians have called the first American boomtown. With only a few thousand residents in the early 1820s, the city grew to over 40,000 residents by 1850, including many recent immigrants from Germany. Significantly, Rochester was at the heart of the "Burned Over" district, an area that had been at the center of the revival fervor of the Second Great Awakening. The religious climate of the area fostered an eclectic assortment of churches, sectarian movements, and social re-

10. Conrad Henry Moehlman, "The Ambrose Swasey Library" (Rochester, NY: The Rochester Historical Society, 1937), 136. (A copy of the article was provided to the author courtesy of the Ambrose Swasey Library of Colgate Rochester Crozer Divinity School.)

form movements. In the early 1830s, Joseph Smith in nearby Palmyra, New York, led a small group of followers west after establishing what became popularly known as the Mormons. In the 1840s, the Fox sisters of Rochester brought national attention to the phenomenon of Spiritualism, one of the precursors in American religious history of what would be known in the late twentieth century as the "New Age" movement. Over the years, the famed revivalist and abolitionist Charles Finney used Rochester as a staging area for many of his revivals, and the city would soon become the home for two of the nation's most prominent activists for abolitionism and women's suffrage, Frederick Douglass and Susan B. Anthony.

In the context of the population boom taking place in western New York, especially in response to the increase in German immigration to the United States in the 1840s, a German department of Rochester Theological Seminary was established in 1851. The Rev. Zenas Freeman, its principal founder, saw the department as a means both to train German pastors in their native language and to enable these immigrants to preserve their native culture in America. "Those who are to hold an influential standing among them as Gospel Ministers must be men speaking their tongue and be so skilled in it as to secure to themselves the reputation of intelligence as well as piety."[11]

Yet the new school was hardly a success in its early years. In addition to precarious funding and a small number of students, the school's founders had difficulty finding a faculty of German Baptist scholars who were sufficiently orthodox theologically and who possessed the intellectual acumen to provide students with the rudiments of a liberal arts education. August Rauschenbusch was considered a logical choice for heading up the department, not only because of his growing reputation as a Baptist missionary in the United States but also because he was one of a small number of German Baptist ministers who possessed a university education.

August initially declined offers to join the German department and opted for his ministry on the Missouri frontier. While August clung to his conservative pietism, he was outraged by the reality of American chattel slavery. In the 1850s, Missouri was at the center of the slavery controversy that was tearing the nation apart. With his

11. Ramaker, 33.

strong sense of personal freedom and a fundamental belief that slavery impeded the ability of African slaves to experience the power of grace, August became a supporter of the abolitionist movement. Like many northern evangelicals, he viewed the impending Civil War as a divine judgment upon the nation and, like many Protestants of that era, as a form of moral cleansing for America.[12]

As August wrestled over issues of his future ministry, he found himself dealing with the realities of fatherhood. In September 1855, a daughter, Frida, was born and a son, Winfried, followed in April 1857. August could not repress his joy at having a son to carry on the Rauschenbusch name. "You may well imagine that we look upon this son as a welcome and worthy gift from God," he wrote soon after Winfried's birth. "If you would show me a kindness, then pray . . . only once that God might bless my son, who has inherited nothing from me but sin, death and damnation, and allow him to inherit life and salvation in Christ. . . ."[13] With a family to support, he was tempted to resume his work with the American Tract Society in New York City, which offered him an attractive salary to come back east. Despite the precarious financial state of the German department in Rochester, Rauschenbusch finally accepted the position to head up the department in 1858. Even though the seminary was less than ten years old, it was already going through a rapid expansion. Rauschenbusch was especially impressed by the seminary's library, which had secured in 1857 the personal library of his mentor, August Neander, a collection of 4,600 volumes.

Yet as the Rauschenbusch family headed east in the summer of 1858, Winfried fell ill and died. In spite of the family's grief, August began his teaching duties at Rochester Theological Seminary that fall, and he quickly brought his passion to the new position and displayed a providential vision that this enterprise would not, and could not, fail. His first priority was to stabilize the financial conditions of the department and concurrently to build up the faculty. When at the end of his second year he was told by representatives of the board of trustees that the department would have to close, he replied, "Gentlemen, that

12. Minus, 4.

13. Donovan E. Smucker, *The Origins of Walter Rauschenbusch's Social Ethics* (Montreal and Kingston: McGill–Queen's University Press, 1994), 24.

I cannot and will not do."[14] For almost three decades afterwards, Rauschenbusch made good on his word and the German department, along with the seminary's English department, grew and expanded its facilities, academic resources, and students. Not only was August skilled at raising money for the school, but he also was an adroit teacher who taught botany, history, Latin, Greek, astronomy, and psychology, in addition to teaching courses in Bible and theology. Students in the classroom were impressed not only by his intellectual dexterity but also by his skill as a communicator. His peripatetic existence during his first decade in America had instilled in him an ability to make difficult and obtuse ideas understandable to an audience of generalists. It was a gift that would be passed on to his second son.

In the years that followed his appointment in Rochester, August Rauschenbusch became a revered figure among German Baptists in the United States and in the fledgling Baptist movement in his native Germany. Although the German department's enrollment remained small, compared to that of the English department, its graduates went on to distinction as pastors of influential Baptist churches throughout the country and many returned to found Baptist churches in their native Germany. Although August was granted little time to delve into original research, he established himself as a historian of the sixteenth-century Anabaptists. August viewed the Anabaptists as the closest incarnation of the primitive church in church history and, like many Baptists of his generation, tended to view modern-day Baptists as a direct outgrowth of the continental Anabaptist movements of the Reformation. For many German Baptists in both Europe and the United States, August Rauschenbusch became a symbol of an orthodox-pietistic Christianity that approximated the Christianity of the primitive church. Augustus Strong, the future president of Rochester Theological Seminary who would become one of the great exponents of Protestant theological orthodoxy in the late nineteenth century, wrote of August, "Had he been born in England he would have become a Puritan of the most rigid kind. . . . He was a great man, a man of God."[15]

Yet there was another side to August's life that appeared to some publicly in glimpses, but more frequently emerged only to his family.

14. Ramaker, 35.
15. Ibid., 35.

Always a high-strung person, August had periodically displayed outbursts of temper with members of his congregations in Germany and Missouri. In Rochester, Caroline became the chief brunt of his anger. Despite the birth of a second daughter, Emma, in 1859 and the fact that Caroline was expecting another child in 1861, a rift was growing between the couple that grew increasingly acrimonious. Over the next several years, August's relationship with his family would be characterized both by his prolonged absences and persistent anger when he was in his family's presence.

On October 4, 1861, at the Rauschenbusch's home, a healthy baby boy was born to Caroline and August. "Time will show which kind of aptitudes small Walther has," August noted in a letter to his brother, Wilhelm, in Germany. "Presently his strong voice indicates that one day he will be heard in the world. My hope is that God will make a Christian and preacher out of him, a Rauschenbusch and a man of deeds."[16] In an autobiographical narrative that Walter Rauschenbusch presented to his wife Pauline in 1900, he reminisced about his early life. "Doubtless we were kept rather strictly," he noted. He recalled snapshots from his youth — playing at home, passing recollections of childhood tantrums, his father's sternness, a family excursion to Niagara Falls, and an incident when he was asked by his father what he wanted to be when he grew up; he answered, John the Baptist.[17]

Yet one incident in his early childhood stood out in his memory and it occurred on April 15, 1865, the day that President Abraham Lincoln died from an assassin's bullet. He recalled his family's reaction of pain and anger, and their neighborhood's response to Lincoln's death. "The neighbors are winding black around the pillars of their porch. We too are displaying some sign of mourning, but not as much as our neighbors. We children feel that we ought to have more and ask Father, but he refuses."[18]

Two months after Lincoln's death, Walther, his sisters, and their mother left Rochester in what would turn into a four-year family residency in Germany. For most of the time that the family lived in Ger-

16. Letter August Rauschenbusch to Wilhelm Rauschenbusch (English translation), box 139.

17. "Reminiscences of My Life," written by Walter Rauschenbusch in December 1900, box 139.

18. Ibid.

many, the Rauschenbusches would be separated from August. Although August hoped that life in Germany would enable his children to establish family ties with their German relatives, it also reflected the deterioration of his marriage. By 1865, the relationship between August and Caroline had reached a point of irreconcilability. Although the family's neighbors in Rochester recalled August as a man of polite manners who became noted for the beauty of his flower gardens, August increasingly viewed his relationship with Caroline as a curse. Years later Walther gave his family and friends only glimpses of his parents' relationship; however, the picture that emerges of August and Caroline's marriage is one that was volatile and, at the minimum, verbally violent. Walther later wrote to his oldest daughter that the estrangement between his mother and father was one of "the great sorrows in my life."[19]

The four years that young Walther spent in Germany by contrast were largely happy ones. With German spoken regularly in his home, the children were bilingual and easily adapted to life in Germany. Initially the family stayed in an upstairs apartment of a dry-goods merchant in Neuwied, a town on the Rhine River. While his older sister Frida was sent to live with August's sister Maria, Walther Rauschenbusch entered school and enjoyed the opportunity to develop friendships with German children. He recalled getting in trouble in school for carrying a small American flag, joking that the incident marked the "first memorable sin" of his life.[20]

In the fall of 1866, the family relocated to Barmen, where they settled once again in austere accommodations, this time in the upstairs suite of a bakery. Walther attracted a group of friends from several prominent local families, and spent hours with his cadre of friends playing. His recollections of Barmen and its surrounding environs were hardly favorable, as he commented on the pollution in that industrial region of Germany. He recalled also how he witnessed a confrontation between Catholic and Protestant schoolchildren and how he joined his Protestant friends as they taunted the Catholic youth with the slogan "Fried in butter, rolled in flour, and led to the devil." Rauschenbusch gave a hint of the family's deeply rooted anti-Catholicism when he reflected, "I think we really felt that these chil-

19. Walter to Winifred Rauschenbusch, November 4, 1916, box 144.
20. "Reminiscences of my Life," box 139.

dren were bad and dangerous, quite different from us, who were good and altogether on the way of righteousness."[21]

In particular, Rauschenbusch relished the contact with his German relatives. Although the Lutheran Rauschenbusches were dismayed by August's decision to become a Baptist, it did not rupture the family bond. Walther especially loved visits with his Aunt Maria and his Grandmother Rauschenbusch. The widow of August's father, Walther's grandmother was completely deaf and could communicate only by writing on a slate board. One aspect that Walther did not enjoy, however, was going to church. He recalled an incident when he begged his mother to let him play with a neighbor's child instead of having to go to church. Although his mother appeared to relent to his demands, he was soon fetched from his playmate's home and sent off to church. As he later joked, "the pretense of liberty of worship" was short-lived in this case.[22]

In June 1868, after a three-year absence, August joined the family in Barmen. Although Walther recalled enjoyable activities with his father, including berry picking, swimming, and hiking, the young boy was constantly aware of his father's sternness, if not outright judgment of his behavior. His father challenged him to swim across a deep pond, and although Walther accomplished this, it was at the expense of choking on the water. He also received warnings from his father concerning the evils of sexual immorality, lectures that perhaps adversely affected Walther in his later dealings with members of the opposite sex. By the same token, August made it clear to his family that his primary reason for being in Germany was not to be a doting parent and husband. He spent intermittent time away from his family, conducting research on the Anabaptists in a number of German universities.

In the absence of his father, Walther sought close relationships with his siblings. However, he largely felt estranged from his sister Frida. Although she rejoined the family in Barmen, Frida struck her brother as more of an adult figure than a child. "She was always a sober and serious girl," he recalled years later. While August loved her because of her "seriousness and absence of childish folly," her demeanor did not lend itself to developing a close bond with her brother.

21. "Reminiscences of My Life," box 139.
22. Ibid.

In contrast, Walther and his sister Emma grew inseparable. He described his sister as "a wild bumble bee" and very much a tomboy. "She was active physically, up to mischief, with an inclination to insist on her rights, and with a capacity for friendship and also for jealousy of others."[23] The two siblings, separated by only two years and similar in disposition, developed a close bond that carried into their young adulthood. It would not be until he was in his thirties that Walther would develop a close bond with his oldest sister.

ROCHESTER COMING OF AGE

In July 1869, the Rauschenbusches finally left Germany and returned to their Rochester home. The four years away from Rochester grafted upon Walther a lifelong love for his ancestral homeland that carried over into matters of religion and the intellect. At the center of that love was his father's influence. "I think one of the best things he did for me was to keep alive the family feeling and tradition," Rauschenbusch wrote to a friend years later. While he noted that his father was "exceedingly democratic in his intercourse with people," he "made me feel that I must live up to the traditions of education and religion which had been set for our family by our forefathers."[24] Rauschenbusch's reaction gives a subtle hint to the fact that as a boy he was not immune from what he termed "the meaner and baser things" in life.[25] On one hand the Rauschenbusches quickly readapted themselves to being an American family. Their neighborhood in Arnold Park was in a growing English-speaking middle-class section of the city and the family was well thought of by their neighbors. "We all loved the old 'Professor.' He was so kind and genial," wrote a former neighbor. At the same time, the family was perceived by their neighbors as somewhat exotic. When a number of large snails appeared on their street, neighborhood kids became convinced that the species either came from Mars or the Rauschenbusches' backyard.[26]

23. Ibid.

24. WR to D. C. Vandercook, February 23, 1917, box 31.

25. Ibid.

26. Letter Lola Baldwin to Winifred [Rauschenbusch] Rorty, January 24, 1944, box 117.

Walther often visited his father on the Rochester Theological Seminary campus, now located only a few blocks from the family's home, and even sat in on August's classes. These experiences deepened his appreciation for his father's intellectual acumen and the young boy was taken by the respect and reverence in which his father was held. For his part, Walther appeared to be living up to his father's expectations to strive for intellectual excellence. He was an excellent student in primary school and when he enrolled in high school at Rochester Free Academy, he continued his high academic performance.

Yet Rauschenbusch's movement toward adolescence was not without its troubles. "Wallie," as many neighborhood children and friends called him, tended to social shyness, especially around girls. Tall for his age and with light red hair, many girls found him attractive. However, Walther found interaction with girls difficult, if not downright painful. Some girls on his street, sympathetic to his shyness, attempted to "educate him along more social lines," including how to go about carrying a young girl's books to school.[27] Despite these efforts, Walther's shyness remained intact and served as a barrier in his social relationships with women as an adult.

There are dimensions of Rauschenbusch's childhood and adolescence between 1869 and 1879 that reflect an almost idyllic view of post–Civil War middle-class American life. August Rauschenbusch had moved away from his days as a bi-vocational farmer-preacher and settled his family into a secure and, by the standards of the day, comfortable existence in one of Rochester's most prosperous middle-class neighborhoods. Rochester during the 1860s and 1870s continued to grow rapidly, as more immigrants moved into the city and its economic base expanded rapidly with the addition of several new industries and a population of just under 80,000 by 1880. Although the Rauschenbusch children were surrounded by a network of their father's German colleagues and students from the seminary, they remained largely isolated from these larger social changes taking place in the city. As his son matured into adolescence, August intentionally focused Walther's attention not on the city, but the country. Walther spent many summers in the 1870s living and working on farms owned

27. Ibid.

by many of August's German immigrant friends and colleagues. These summer experiences, where he often engaged in rigorous physical labor, reinforced in Walther his father's emphasis upon the virtues of physical work. Many Protestant leaders who came of age at the time often spoke of the virtues inherent in hard work, frequently placing that labor in the context of the idyllic image of a rural small town — an image that was increasingly under siege in the face of late nineteenth-century industrialization. Although Rauschenbusch was technically a city dweller, his worldview was consistent with many future social gospelers, who often equated the kingdom of God with the virtues of hard work associated with rural America.

Yet Walther's world had a far less idyllic side. Even before his teen years, Rauschenbusch found occasions to rebel against his father's authority. On one occasion, the boy was whipped by his father for preaching skepticism to the other boys in his Sunday school class.[28] The rebellions against August's authority periodically earned the boy a similar fate at home. These outbursts from his son caused added tension with Caroline, as August often used her as a scapegoat when Walther and his siblings went through various adolescent rebellions. Repeatedly Caroline endured numerous accusations from her husband, not the least being that she mistreated and neglected her children. Most severe, August confessed in a letter to his sister in Germany that he prayed at times for his wife's death.[29] Caroline countered her husband's abusive accusations with her own resolute stubbornness and voiced her own suspicions about her husband's fidelity to their marriage. Clearly, Caroline was her husband's match in terms of possessing an uncompromising nature. Years later Rauschenbusch wrote to his sister Frida that their mother was a woman who possessed an unfortunate "faculty for seeing things distorted out of their proper proportions."[30]

The constant fighting between his parents increasingly took its toll on Walther and his siblings. As a teenager, many of his parents' ar-

28. Biographical statement by Winifred R. Rorty, no date, box 143.

29. Gary Dorrien, "Walter Rauschenbusch and the Legacy of the Social Gospel," in *Reconstructing the Common Good: Theology and the Social Order* (Maryknoll: Orbis, 1990), 17, and Minus, 14-15.

30. Walter Rauschenbusch to Frida Rauschenbusch Fetzer, September 12, 1913, box 36.

guments centered over the suitability of young men to court Frida and Emma. In 1877, after initial opposition from both her parents, Frida at age 22 married Georg Fetzer, a student in the German department at the seminary, and the couple left for Germany, where they became leaders among the Baptists in Germany. Around the same time, August succeeded in breaking up the courtship between Emma and a German Baptist pastor in Buffalo.[31]

These tensions between his parents and siblings were not lost on Walther. Never close to Frida and struggling to maintain his bond with Emma, he rebelled more openly. For a brief period of time he joined a gang, although there is no evidence to suggest that beyond some public mischief and swearing, his experience with these youths would lead him astray from the faith of his parents. And yet, the tension that Rauschenbusch experienced as a teenager concerning his faith was intensely serious. Given his family history, there were only two choices — accept his father's evangelical pietist Christianity or reject it. During the 1870s, liberal Christianity was still in its nascent stages, and although more Americans were becoming familiar with the work of the theology of Horace Bushnell, and many middle-class Americans were captivated by the published sermons of Henry Ward Beecher, these forms of Christianity were not an option for the young Rauschenbusch. His official exposure to the liberal Christian option lay in his future.

August's seriousness with Walther stemmed from his own hope that his son, the heir to the Rauschenbusch name in America, would in good Baptist fashion profess his saving faith in Christ and be baptized. The circumstances that led to Walther's baptism in the spring of his senior year in high school remain unclear. When he spoke of having a religious experience years later, he did so with a combination of fondness and ridicule.

> Now, that religious experience was a very true one, although I have no doubt there was a great deal in it that was foolish. . . . And yet, such as it was, it was of everlasting value to me. It turned me permanently, and I thank God with all my heart for it. It was a ten-

31. Minus, 15.

> der, mysterious experience. It influenced my soul down to its depths. Yet, there was a great deal in it that was not really true.[32]

Rauschenbusch's equivocation about his conversion experience was made years after the fact, yet at the time it moved him deeply into an acceptance and embrace of much of his father's faith, even as he avoided discussing the specific circumstances behind it. Paul Minus points out that Rauschenbusch's account of his conversion experience took on the form of the prodigal son parable, and the language of his inner struggle reflects how the seventeen-year-old Rauschenbusch was being called to give an account of his life before both his earthly father and his heavenly Father. "This was my way of saying: 'I am out in the far country and I want to get home to my country, and I don't want to tend the hogs any longer.' And so I came to my Father, and I began to pray for help and got it."[33]

It is unclear to what extent Walther yearned to follow in his father's footsteps before having this religious experience. Yet it is clear that Rauschenbusch's desire to serve God in ministry would deepen in the years after this experience — as did his sense of his own unique gifts for ministry. As he noted, "I felt that every Christian ought to in some way or other participate in the dying of the Lord Jesus Christ, and in that way help to redeem humanity. And it was that thought that gave my life its fundamental direction in the doing of Christian work."[34] Thus Rauschenbusch resolved that he "ought to be a preacher, and help to save souls."[35]

Rauschenbusch's newfound purpose found expression in his intellectual abilities, reflected in his stellar high school academic record. Walther enjoyed a close fraternity of high school friends that included Ed Hanna, a Roman Catholic youth who years later become an archbishop in the Roman Catholic Church in the United States. He also displayed an intensely competitive side in his work and he excelled in public speaking, literary elocution, and language study. One of his earliest surviving essays revealed a deep-seated mistrust of England, call-

32. WR, "The Kingdom of God," *Cleveland Young Men* (January 9, 1913), box 39.

33. Ibid.; Minus, 17.

34. "The Kingdom of God," box 39.

35. Minus, 17.

ing that nation a place of "greed and selfishness," in contrast to American freedom.[36] When he graduated from high school in June 1879, he was second in his class behind his friend Ed Hanna.

With barely enough time to say good-bye to his friends, Walther accompanied his father to Germany. For a consequence of the decision to enter the ministry was to be shaped by the will of his father. August Rauschenbusch had a plan for his son, and in accompanying him to Germany he was leading his son on a path that would not only make him a saver of souls but also allow him one day to follow in August's footsteps in building upon a great family destiny. Neither August nor his young son could have foreseen, however, that Walther's rebellions were far from over.

36. Ibid., 13.

2 The Energetic American

The years between 1879 and 1886 were critical years for the ascendency of liberal theology in the United States. The writings of Horace Bushnell, a New England Congregational minister who had died in 1876, were developing an audience among a critical mass of American clergy. In many cities in the Northeast and Midwest, liberal Protestant pulpiteers styled after the models of Henry Ward Beecher in New York City and Phillips Brooks in Boston were drawing large middle-class audiences into their churches. In the early 1880s, liberal theologians Theodore Munger and Newman Smyth picked up where Bushnell had left off, advocating the need for a Christianity that could be reconciled to the modern forces of the natural sciences and post-Enlightenment reason. And in 1882, Washington Gladden, later to be identified as the "father" of the American social gospel, began his long-term pastorate at the First Congregational Church in Columbus, Ohio, after stints as a Congregational pastor in Pennsylvania and Massachusetts, and as an editor for Henry Ward Beecher's influential periodical, the *Independent.*

During much of this time when liberalism was starting to gain a small but influential audience within the institutional fabric of American Protestantism, Walther Rauschenbusch was miles away from these currents both in terms of physical location and theological environment. Through his father's arrangements and personal wishes, Rauschenbusch began a four-year sojourn as a student in a German Gymnasium school located in the small Westphalia city of Gütersloh. August Rauschenbusch had two motivations for sending Walther to Gütersloh. First, he wanted his son exposed to the German system of higher education, which he believed was superior to the American one. Second, he wanted Walther nurtured in the religious and cultural environment that would reinforce the values of August's own theological orthodoxy. This school, which had an established tradition for preparing young men for university studies, embodied the conservative Lutheran pietism that reflected the Rauschenbusch family heritage. The plan was for Walther to receive a diploma from Gütersloh and then return to Rochester, where he would undertake his theological studies.

Years later, Rauschenbusch commented that his years in Germany, while intellectually challenging, brought to him no altered purpose, except that to engage in a ministry of soul saving, noting, "I had no outlook except the common evangelicalism."[1] He made similar allusions toward his theological orthodoxy and his mission as a church leader when he became a full-time parish minister after graduating from Rochester Theological Seminary in 1886. Yet his years of formative theological education, in Germany and in Rochester, provided him with indispensable experiences educationally and culturally that sowed the seeds of Walther's burgeoning theological liberalism and, in some ways, his future social outlook.

AN AMERICAN IN GERMANY, 1879–1883

The model of the German Gymnasium was analogous to an American university education, and in many instances the curriculum was far more rigorous. After spending several weeks with Frida and her young family, Walther arrived at Gütersloh in early September. His immediate impressions of the town and the area were not favorable, and he found the town drab, dirty, and smelly. More immediately, how-

1. Walter Rauschenbusch to John Phillips, May 24, 1909, box 39.

ever, Walther had to worry about his placement in the school. While no stranger to the curriculum model of the time that emphasized language study and classical literature, Walther soon realized his deficiencies in certain areas, especially his inadequate preparation in Greek, Latin, and French. Although he was not yet 18, he was also older than his classmates and that added to his insecurity. Nevertheless the school chose to place him in a higher class that exempted him from remedial work. "I nearly stood on my head," he wrote his high school friend Munson Ford in Rochester, "for that means: one year less in Germany."[2]

For the next year, Rauschenbusch went through an intellectual baptism by fire. Although he was used to the authoritarian disposition of his father, the atmosphere surrounding teacher authority at Gütersloh at times intimidated Rauschenbusch. "At first I was like a plant that is taken and transplanted to a soil . . . , and is kept alive only by plenty of water," he wrote to Ford. Not only did the weight of the academic work put pressure on Rauschenbusch, but the demands of his regimented schedule were a far cry from what he had known in high school. Classes began early in the morning and extended through most of the day. Students were allowed off campus only a few hours each day, and a curfew was maintained that for all intents and purposes kept students confined to the campus.

During his first year, Rauschenbusch won over the Gütersloh faculty, both by his work ethic and by his academic performance. After initial difficulty with his schoolwork, by the end of his first year Rauschenbusch had moved toward the top of his class, earning him the nickname "the energetic American." The bulk of his first year curriculum revolved around the study of Latin, Greek, French, and Hebrew. "We also have 2 lessons a week in 'religion,'" he noted to Ford, "something like a bible class only that we have to learn very many verses and songs by heart. And that is the way in all these studies, we have to learn a horrible pile of Latin and Greek by heart."[3] In his second year, his curriculum broadened somewhat as

2. Walther Rauschenbusch to Munson Ford, November 30, 1879, box 23. A summary of Rauschenbusch's extensive correspondence with Ford between 1879 and 1886 can be found in Winthrop S. Hudson, ed., *Walter Rauschenbusch: Selected Writings* (New York: Paulist Press, 1984), 49-59.

3. WR to Munson Ford, November 30, 1879, box 23.

he studied (Roman) history, mathematics, natural philosophy, and by the middle of his second year, Rauschenbusch stood second in his class of 35.

Rauschenbusch's experience in his first two years at Gütersloh ranged from exhilaration to loneliness. Not only did he miss his friends in America, but the fact that he was not allowed to speak English unnerved him. At the end of his first year, he started to keep a journal of poetry, where he included verses of favorite poems by Byron and Longfellow, as well as indulge himself in a love he had started to cultivate in Rochester, by writing poetic verse. Many of the numerous poems that Walther wrote in German and English reflect some of his ambivalence about his experience in Germany, as he reflected in part of a poem from the summer of 1880:

> And in the varied landscape
> Are hamlets strewed around
> And higher mount the chimneys
> Of factories around.
> And in the hamlets peasants
> Enjoy their frugal meal
> Content to have that little
> Which makes their woe and weal . . .

Yet as Rauschenbusch continues the poem, he makes it clear that he has in mind for himself a loftier plan for his life, one that would never be content with the simplicity that comprised much of what he saw of German life outside of the Gymnasium.

> Would you not also number
> Among that humble throng,
> Unheeded passing over
> Ambition's siren-song?
> And taking unto your bosom
> Some faithful simple wife,
> To raise a flock of children
> And live an obscure life?
> No! ne'er would I surrender
> The joys of intellect,

The lofty walks of knowledge,
Ne'er could I them reject.[4]

Rauschenbusch's poems covered a number of themes, and also included several that reflect his sense of patriotism and love for America. In a poem entitled "My Country" written on July 4, 1881, he struck a decidedly jingoistic tone, typical of many American youth of that era.

Safe while we trust in God,
Bow to his mighty rod. . . .
. . . .
Raise high the beacon-light,
Pierce through the world's black night
Show her the noble sight of liberty.[5]

Yet the majority of poems are very introspective, and in particular display Walther's romantic passions and dreams of sexual fantasy, written for imaginary lovers. Many of Rauschenbusch's "love poems" display the contemporary passion for liberal romanticism associated with numerous German and English poets of the nineteenth century. Despite the lectures he had received from his father as a young boy concerning sexual morality, his poems reflect a deep eroticism, echoing the style of one of Walther's favorite poets, Lord Byron.

How I long thy lips to press
On thy mouth, oh sweet caress,
That would all my sorrows chase;
Could I hold thy rosy charms
Fast within my loving arms
Call thee ever mine!
Yes, I hope the sun will rise
That I look into your eyes
So my own and lawful prize,
Press you to my side

4. Poem by Walther Rauschenbusch, August 16, 1880, box 100.
5. Poem by Walther Rauschenbusch, July 4, 1881, box 100.

As my own dear bride,
And be ever thine.[6]

For all his academic accomplishments and future promise, Walther was lonely and, in ways that he could express only in private, yearned to find someone with whom he could experience the ecstacy of physical intimacy.

. . . To be by her caressed and teased
By that sweet darling to be pleased, . . .
. . . .
Stroke your hot forehead, call you dear,
And with her rosy mouth creep near,
And then to have the greatest bliss,
From her sweet lips the sweetest kiss.[7]

Amidst his times of loneliness, his years in Germany afforded him unprecedented breaks of leisure and adventure. In addition to the opportunities to spend holidays with Frida and her family, Walther used blocks of his winter and summer vacations to travel throughout Europe. Supplied with a generous allowance from his father, Walther made excursions through Germany, Switzerland, and Italy. For many Americans living in the middle and late nineteenth century, European travel was seen not only as an opportunity to be exposed to the cultural graces of Europe but also as a rite of intellectual passage. August himself realized this, as Walther noted to Munson Ford that his father viewed travel as "a chief source of instruction" and "a splendid opportunity for the study of human nature."[8] Indeed, Walther drank up the physical beauty of many areas of Germany and Switzerland that he visited, fueling further his romantic imagination. "I believe in America we don't cultivate the perception of the beautiful enough, at least I have learned to appreciate it only in Europe. I feel so intensely happy when I can drink in with full draughts the beauty that God has poured with a prodigal hand over

6. Poem "To G," October 31, 1880, box 100.
7. Poem "Her Eyes," May 15, 1880, box 100.
8. WR to Ford, June 24, 1881, box 23.

this earth of ours."[9] But he also relished the opportunities to observe human nature, especially among the lower classes of Germany. He was especially fascinated by the opportunities to travel by train and observe the peasants with their livestock, who rode with him in fourth-class train compartments. These excursions would stoke his literary imagination years later, when he would reflect back on his travels as a young American in Europe. On occasions, Rauschenbusch "clubbed" and "loafed" on excursions with his Rochester friends, Ed Hanna and Charles Strong, the son of Rochester Theological Seminary president Augustus Strong. Rauschenbusch was delighted when Strong joined him as a classmate at Gütersloh during Walther's third year, and though their vocations would take very different paths, their friendship with one another would be lifelong. (Charles went on to become a distinguished American philosopher. His brother, John, would later be a faculty colleague of Rauschenbusch's at Rochester Theological Seminary.)

He also developed bonds of friendship with many of his German classmates at Gütersloh, and upon occasion was not immune from joining his comrades in social revelry. Yet he continued to bemoan the lack of meeting female companions. "Poor fellow that I am, I hardly get a glimpse of young ladies here," he observed to Ford.[10] The shyness around young girls that had been a joke in his neighborhood growing up had not dissipated with age. In a show of humor that would be commonplace over the years, he remarked, "I have been buried in our small town so long and so entirely, that I look all green, when a girl only looks at me, which you probably know is the most violent kind of blushing."[11]

Rauschenbusch had a degree of indifference about the faith that was being imparted upon him and his fellow students at Gütersloh. Although he thought highly of the school's Lutheran chaplain, and displayed warm affection for many of the Lutheran clerics he met, he expressed a bemused curiosity toward the church's annual festivals, and he also felt that Lutheranism impeded the ministry of the laity.[12] His gentle paternalism toward the Lutherans was a reflection of how much

9. WR to Munson Ford, August 20, 1882, box 23.
10. WR to Munson Ford, June 19, 1881, box 23.
11. WR to Munson Ford, March 18, 1883, box 23.
12. WR, "Reflections on Germany," typed manuscript, January 1913, box 39.

Walther rooted himself in the democratic theological ethos of the Baptists. He loved the tradition of Lutheran hymnody that emerged out of the Pietist movement, but his Baptist heritage caused him to be inherently suspicious of state-church authority. In later years, he would judge the evangelical traditions of Europe and America, particularly the Baptists and the Methodists, as the churches that most approximated primitive Christianity because they focused on a democratic equality of clergy and laity. From an early age, Rauschenbusch carried a degree of suspicion toward more sacramental Protestant traditions, in particular the Lutheran and Anglican communions, and he shared an even deeper suspicion, if not outright hostility, toward the Roman Catholic Church. This hostility was expressed by Walther's dismay over Ed Hanna's decision to enter the priesthood as he bemoaned to Munson Ford: "I wish I could take the Jesuit spectacles off his nose and take him around the world and make him see life as it is, instead of the caricatured image his teachers show him."[13]Although Walther sought to maintain his friendship with Hanna, his correspondence reveals how he increasingly viewed his Catholic friend with a mixture of consternation and pity. Not long after he returned to Rochester in 1883, he commented tersely to Ford, "I should be glad to see him again to make a psychological study of him."[14] In this regard, Rauschenbusch's perspective was hardly unique for American Protestants of the late nineteenth century, who castigated the Catholic Church for its secretive nature, its foreign rituals (the Latin mass), and, most especially, its undemocratic-authoritarian (and non-American) hierarchy.

By the end of his second year at Gütersloh, Walther had clearly mastered the intellectual regimen. His "dint of working like an American" had paid off in his academic performance. Although he continued to struggle with Greek and French, he had developed fluency in Latin, the language that alternated with German lectures and his written examinations. Often students were given several weeks to complete essay assignments, but Rauschenbusch had grown confident enough in his intellectual acumen to start and complete many of these assignments the day before they were due.[15] In his final two years, he was delighted

13. WR to Ford, May 27, 1883, box 23; Minus, 29.
14. WR to Munson Ford, September 22, 1883, box 23.
15. See, for example, WR to Ford, June 19, 1881, box 23.

to take up course work in German and classical literature and developed a special fondness for the writings of Plato, Sophocles, German literature, and Scandinavian mythology. Yet as he prepared for his final examinations at Gütersloh, he confessed that he was growing tired of his regimen. "I have come hither, grown quite lazy in fact and haven't been able to rally enough to go to work in earnest even with the exams confronting me like the jaws of lions."[16] He needn't have worried. In March 1883, Walther Rauschenbusch graduated at the top of his class, with the designation "Primus Omnium." Just prior to his graduation, the young man had entered the final phase of his European education. With an itinerary largely put together by his father, and reflecting a pattern that had become typical for many Americans of his generation, Walther attended lectures at several German universities, including Dresden, Leipzig, Halle, and his father's university, Berlin. Rauschenbusch expressed a spirit of ecstasy in hearing "all the big men" at these universities. He showed, however, little interest in the intellectual ideas being discussed, placing more emphasis on the experience of travel as opposed to the content of the lectures he attended. His romantic nature was taken in by the fine art he saw in museums, and as he confessed to Ford, he eagerly "sat at the feet of the teachers . . . , drank in their words eagerly, soon to forget them in boating parties" with friends.[17] He clearly viewed his experience of educational touring as a fitting conclusion to his four years in Germany, and, not without a degree of self-confidence, he expressed his conviction that he saw a great part of his future devoted to the development of his intellect. The whimsical way that he spoke of his travels was not so much a manifestation of a spirit of bohemianism as it was his belief that he was living the life of a cultured late nineteenth-century American. "You see I believe I owe mankind a full development of all that my brain contains the 'potentia' of and that I can do more good with that than with my muscles."[18]

Before he returned to America, Walther had a decision to make. Although he was clear that he wanted to enter seminary at Rochester, and that the seminary would accept his Gymnasium diploma as the equivalent of an American university degree, he also wanted to receive

16. WR to Ford, November 12, 1882, box 23.
17. WR to Ford, May 27, 1883, box 23.
18. WR to Ford, March 18, 1883, box 23.

a college degree. In part he didn't want to be the first Rauschenbusch in several generations not to receive a university degree and, in particular, he wanted to fill in the gaps in his education in Germany. As he made plans to resume his education that fall, he admitted to Ford that he was looking forward to doing work in "political economy" and English literature, "as such things I know perfectly nothing."[19]

Before he finalized his plans, however, he made one final stop in his itinerary, by returning to America through England, where he spent a few weeks in London with visits in Oxford and finally Liverpool. Walther came to lament that he had reserved only a few weeks of travel in England, which he enjoyed more than he had imagined. Rauschenbusch's brief odyssey in England did not give him the chance to notice two disparate faith traditions that would figure prominently in his later social awakening: the evangelical pietism of the Salvation Army and the tradition of Christian socialism that arose out of the Church of England.

Nineteenth-century Christian socialism represented an important, but in some ways brief, chapter in the history of Western Protestant thought. In the context of increased industrialization in England during the 1840s and 1850s, a small coterie of Anglican priests launched a critique against the prevailing patterns of industrialization, citing in particular the problems of poverty and disease brought on by these developments. These priests stood in a tradition of Anglican social protest, with roots going back to the eighteenth-century revival movements that led to the birth of Methodism. By the mid-nineteenth century, priests such as Charles Kingsley, Frederick Denison Maurice, and Frederick W. Robertson, influenced by the romantic idealism of British writers like Samuel Taylor Coleridge, crafted a distinctive theological orientation that appealed to the ministry and death of Jesus as the essence of Christian discipleship. The way that these Anglicans considered themselves "socialists" was not as such in a political sense, but in the way that the ideals of Christ's teachings gave to the modern church a distinctive mission to reach out and transform the personal and social ills of society. By the early 1880s, the ideas of these "Christian socialists" were soon to gain renewed impetus through a variety of "Christian socialist" societies

19. WR to Ford, May 27, 1883, box 23.

that formed in both Great Britain and North America in the 1880s and 1890s. It could be argued that mid-nineteenth-century Anglican priests like Maurice and Robertson were the first representatives of what came to be known as the social gospel.[20]

In discussing his intellectual pilgrimage in later years, Rauschenbusch was somewhat vague and contradictory about where he first received the theological impetus for his "social gospel." Yet Frederick Robertson, a young priest who had died in 1853 while serving the poor in his Brighton, England, parish, might very well have been the first catalyst for Rauschenbusch's social awakening. In the years immediately following his return to America, Rauschenbusch devoured Robertson's published sermons. Rauschenbusch later wrote that he "absorbed the idea of the law of the cross as the obligatory and distinctive thing in Christianity" from Robertson.[21] In some way when Rauschenbusch later spoke about his own religious experience in the 1870s as giving him the desire to "die with Christ," he was expressing in an anachronistic fashion his own early embrace of Robertson's theological liberalism.

In late July 1883, Rauschenbusch's voyage home brought him back to Rochester by way of the St. Lawrence River and Lake Ontario. Being home with his parents again at 10 Arnold Park was rewarding, but also somewhat lonely. His close friend, Munson Ford, had recently moved away from Rochester to enter business in Illinois and other high school friends had also moved from Rochester. He also had to make some quick decisions as to the future of his education. August was insistent that if Walther intended to receive a university degree, he needed to attend to that task before enrolling in seminary. As it turned out, the University of Rochester gave him three years of standing, so he would need only one more year to receive his undergraduate degree. Walther was able to convince both his father and administrators at the University of Rochester and the seminary that he could undertake both degree programs concurrently, and in September 1883, he began studies at both institutions.

20. A strong case for the influence of British social Christianity upon the American social gospel is made by Paul T. Phillips, *A Kingdom on Earth: Anglo-American Social Christianity, 1880-1940* (University Park: Pennsylvania State University Press, 1995); see especially 1-47.

21. Minus, 44.

SEMINARIAN

In just over thirty years, both the University of Rochester and Rochester Theological Seminary had come a long way from the schools' humble origins. While neither school was considered at the vanguard of American higher education, each school had been the beneficiary of excellent administrative leadership that had seen growth in the physical resources of both institutions. Both the university and seminary were closely linked together through their Baptist piety and, in particular, Rochester Theological Seminary's library and scholarly resources were unprecedented compared to many North American theological schools. With a faculty of 10 and student body of 87, Rochester was one of the largest Baptist seminaries in the country at the time.[22] More significantly, the school had established itself as a defender of a distinctive blend of evangelical Calvinism.

The individual who captured the ethos of Rochester Theological Seminary more than any other was the school's president and father of one of Walther's best friends, Augustus Hopkins Strong. Born in 1836, Strong was a product of one of Rochester's most prominent families. His father Alvah was the editor of a Rochester newspaper and devout Baptist who was converted to evangelical Christianity through the influence of Charles Finney, during Finney's first revival in the city of Rochester in 1830. In 1853, Strong headed to Yale University, where he was exposed to the atmosphere of the New England "new light" Calvinist heritage of New Haven. Yet in 1856, while home on vacation, he too fell under the spell of Charles Finney, who conducted a revival in Rochester that spring. Like his father, Augustus felt that his life had been transformed by the great revivalist. Unlike his father, Augustus saw his future vocation in the ordained ministry, not as a journalist. After graduating from Rochester Theological Seminary (of which his father was a co-founder), Strong served as pastor of the First Baptist Church in Haverhill, Massachusetts, before accepting the call in 1865 of the prestigious First Baptist Church of Cleveland. His parishioners in Cleveland were some of the nation's wealthiest men, including John D. Rockefeller, who in subsequent years became one of Rochester Theological Seminary's chief benefactors. When Strong accepted the presi-

22. Minus, 38.

dency of the seminary in 1872, he also began a prolific period of theological scholarship. His first edition of *Systematic Theology* published in 1878 immediately established him as a champion of theological Calvinist orthodoxy and, in the minds of many Protestants in subsequent years, a defender of the timeless truths of Christian doctrine. Yet Strong also possessed a degree of ecumenical openness that was a result partly of his own evangelical pietism, and also a reflection of an irenic quality in his personality that in the distant future would compel him to make some fateful decisions related to the seminary's future.[23]

Walther's first semester in both schools was strenuous, with courses that included Greek, homiletics, and theology at the seminary, and English literature and zoology at the university. He developed a close relationship with a professor of natural science, Harrison Webster. Although the University of Rochester, like many denominationally sponsored colleges of that era, carefully toed the line on matters of faith and evolution, Webster was the scholar who primarily convinced Rauschenbusch that the foundations of natural science were not incompatible with the claims of an evangelical Christianity. Webster enabled his student to see that science and religion were compatible with one another. In many respects, Webster's consistent counsel and friendship helped Rauschenbusch reconcile the claims of evolutionary science and religion in a manner that was not overly traumatic for the young seminarian.

The influence of Webster also exposed Rauschenbusch to the inevitable pitfall that faced many evangelicals of that generation — what did it mean to say that Scripture was infallible? In his training in Germany Walther had learned from scholars who dismissed emerging arguments of biblical higher criticism, and, in many ways, his seminary teachers reinforced this conservatism. In theology, he read Strong's own systematic theology textbook and did Hebrew exegesis with Howard Osgood, a learned biblical scholar who went to great lengths in his classes to refute the misguided arguments of German higher criticism. At the same time, the spirit of Johann Neander was alive and

23. For biographical information on Strong and his significance, see LeRoy Moore, Jr., "The Rise of American Religious Liberalism at the Rochester Theological Seminary, 1872-1928" (Ph.D. dissertation, Claremont Graduate School, 1966); see especially chapter 2. See also Grant Wacker, *Augustus H. Strong and the Dilemma of Historical Consciousness* (Macon, GA: Mercer University Press, 1985).

well at the seminary. Like his father, Walther became fascinated by study of the Anabaptists and was drawn to the teachings of the seminary's church historian, Benjamin True. True emphasized how the Anabaptists both epitomized the spirit of early Christianity and manifested a distinctive vision of the kingdom of God that influenced the subsequent development of the English Baptists. In a similar vein, Rauschenbusch was equally drawn to the teaching of Thomas Pattison, who taught homiletics.

As Walther drank deep from the intellectual resources of the seminary, he nevertheless felt a degree of melancholy. Although he did join a fraternity at the university, his involvement in it was truncated, due to living with his parents. He still wrote regularly to Munson Ford, and reconnected with another old high school friend, Joe Gilbert, who now worked on a farm in nearby Palmyra. Yet Walther found himself back in a home environment with two acrimonious parents and no older siblings to rely on for support. Frida was now living in Hamburg, Germany, where her husband had become a professor of theology at a Baptist seminary. Emma had also left Rochester far behind. In the early 1880s, she had relocated briefly to Germany and then headed to India as a missionary at the Telugu Baptist mission.

Rauschenbusch still had the close friendship of Charles Strong, who was now enrolled at the university. He also became friends with another senior at the university, a young Methodist named George Albert Coe. Coe would later become a major figure in the social gospel, both in terms of his social activism and for his writings on Christian education, which had a major impact on numerous Protestant denominations in the period between 1900 and 1920.

Yet Rauschenbusch's focus was on his studies, which often carried him into a disparate stream of intellectual and theological sources. In addition to reading English literature and poetry, as well as the work of Frederick Robertson, he read the religious writings of mathematician and philosopher Blaise Pascal, the sermons of Phillips Brooks, and the work of the seventeenth-century Anglican theologian Jeremy Taylor, whose "holy living" theology of sanctification would be instrumental in shaping the eighteenth-century evangelical pietism of John Wesley.

Walther graduated from the University of Rochester in the spring of 1884 and immediately embarked on his first experience in Christian ministry. He had received an opportunity to pastor a small German

Baptist congregation in Louisville, Kentucky, over the summer. "I deliberated a while whether it were better for me to stay at Roch. and make love to our librarian at the Sem., or to go off and do some active work," he joked to Ford.[24] Rauschenbusch clearly approached this first parish high in self-confidence, even though he found himself serving a congregation racked by internal dissent. The routine of preaching four services a week agreed with him and he immensely enjoyed living in the Louisville environs. "I began with the determination to raise the spiritual standard of every Christian among them as far as he or she would let me," he wrote. "I worked a great deal from house to house, poo-pooed and frowned on their backbiting stories, reconciled those who hated each other, and tried everywhere to awaken in their hearts the love of Christ as the only sure cure for their love of self and sin."[25] Rauschenbusch's ministry in Louisville was apparently very successful. When he returned to Rochester for his second year of seminary, he was gratified by the fact that his ministry had brought about several conversions and apparently a changed attitude in the congregation. Walther would be invited back by the congregation and return to Louisville for the following summer.

Rauschenbusch clearly recognized that he had a bit of a reputation of being a bookworm. Although he didn't mind the reputation, he seemed to acknowledge that his intended calling in the ministry took precedence over his social life. Walther matured into an attractive young man, clean shaven with light red hair and standing just over 5′11″. While displaying a confidence in his intellectual acumen that might very well have struck some of his fellow students as arrogant, he continued to display a degree of public awkwardness. After describing his visits with two young women friends from his high school days to Munson Ford, he quickly added, "Don't imagine, however, because I have mentioned several calls to young ladies that I have any habits tending in that line. I enjoy them when I do [meet] them but on the whole I find myself better without."[26] Rauschenbusch's bravado is likely an indication that he had not overcome his earlier shyness around members of the opposite sex.

24. Quoted in Hudson, 50.

25. Hudson, 6.

26. Hudson, 54. Information on Rauschenbusch's physical appearance was taken from a copy of his passport, box 38.

Now free of obligations at the University of Rochester, Rauschenbusch concentrated on his seminary studies when he returned from his summer pastorate in Louisville. Despite his father's standing in the German department, the majority of his classes and interests were shaped by faculty in the English department. He continued to read widely, yet as he did further course work with Strong, he showed a certain disdain for the intense philosophical speculation centered upon the discipline of systematic theology. His academic work was being put through his own theological prism, which made him "look more for the great thoughts that shake mankind than for certainty in regard to a disputed date in Acts or an obscure root of a Hebrew verb."[27] As he had sought to do in his Louisville church, he was clearly driven by a desire to share his passion for Christ with his friends and colleagues. He counseled his friend Joe Gilbert through his own spiritual uncertainty, even as Gilbert admonished Rauschenbusch for supporting Grover Cleveland in the 1884 presidential election.[28] Gilbert's observation that his friend was turning his back on the reform politics of the Republican Party is a small indication that Rauschenbusch's emerging theological perspective had still not been grafted to a coherent social vision. A collection of Rauschenbusch's papers from his middler and senior years in seminary however, indicate that many aspects of Rauschenbusch's later theology were already solidifying.

Walther's lifelong passion for Anabaptism was evident in many of his papers. In an essay on "The Donatists" written during his middler year, he defended this group of third- and fourth-century Christians for their insistence that righteous living was an essential component if the church was to become a community of "regenerate saints." Yet he criticized the movement for what he saw as its motivation to convert its opponents by hatred, rather than love. "They sought their religion not in righteousness and love, but in soundly hating the Samaritan." What was worse for Rauschenbusch was that the Donatists had fallen victim, like the later Catholic Church, of trying to use the state to enforce the movement's beliefs. State control of religion "became the germ of the whole system of spiritual despotism, of intol-

27. Hudson, 54.

28. See, for example, Joe Gilbert to WR, August 3, 1884, October 26, 1884, and March 8, 1885, box 106.

erance and persecution, and was the watchword in the very courts of the inquisition."[29] Rauschenbusch would use a variation of this argument in many of his later writings. For him, part of the critical lesson of church history was how the model of state-church establishment brought about by the Roman Emperor Constantine in the fourth century deprived the early church of its spiritual power.

Rauschenbusch was drawn to religious movements in history that seemed to him to embody a theology of selflessness over those groups that fostered the ecclesiastical growth of the church. In his senior year, he wrote a paper on "The Waldenses," a twelfth-century sectarian Christian movement, for Prof. True's church history class. True was so pleased with the paper that he had Rauschenbusch submit it to a Missouri Baptist periodical where it was eventually published.[30] Again, Rauschenbusch used an argument that was increasingly important to his later theology, in which he viewed sectarian movements as a sign of church renewal. In juxtaposition to institutional Christianity, these movements "were true to the light they had and ready to receive more light when it came. . . . They were a salt of the church."[31] Much of Rauschenbusch's work in church history developed this theme, pointing out how the Catholic Church violated the spirit of true Christianity. Yet there were dimensions of Catholic thought that attracted him, especially the example of figures in the church who followed Thomas à Kempis's "imitation of Christ" theme. He expressed admiration for the eighteenth-century Catholic mystic, Madame Guyon, noting much in common between his own Baptist piety and her Catholic mysticism. "There are still ardent hearts, impatient of the slow, toiling ascent of a faithful, humble Christian life; hearts that long for some mighty sanctifying power to carry them, as with the sweep of eagle's pinions, out of the depressed, up-and-down life of the average Christian into the clear air of a higher life with God."[32]

The most revealing indication of Rauschenbusch's burgeoning liberalism, however, was a paper that he wrote on the atonement theory of Horace Bushnell in the fall of 1885, his final year in seminary.

29. "The Donatists," box 14.
30. Handwritten note on "The Waldenses," box 14.
31. "The Waldenses," box 14.
32. "Madam Guyon," box 14.

Bushnell's theology was anathema from the standpoint of most of the Rochester faculty. Rauschenbusch, however, found in Bushnell theological similarities to the work of Frederick Robertson.

The essay gave Rauschenbusch the opportunity to question "ransom" or "substitutionary" theologies of the atonement, that is, the deep-seated tradition that Christ's death occurred as a "payment" for the sins of humanity. He castigated these theological perspectives as nothing more than "business transactions in which human souls are the merchandise and merit earned or pain suffered is the price." He asserted, "we want something warmer, more living, something nearer to us. Attention is turning away from that which took place in ages past and which concerned God alone, and turning toward that which concerns us and takes place to-day." He argued instead for a "moral influence" view of the doctrine, whereby Christ's sacrifice did not "appease the wrath of an angry God against sinful men," but reconciled "the hearts of sinful men to their loving God." Rauschenbusch did not acknowledge in the essay the historical debt of this view of the atonement to earlier antecedents in church history, especially in medieval theology. Rather, he saw Bushnell in line with nineteenth-century Christian socialists like Robertson and Frederick Maurice for emphasizing God's love for humanity, allowing humans in a new spirit to receive the saving love of God. Using the Prodigal Son parable as justification for his argument, he asserted, "What was Christ's theology of salvation? He preached that men are sinful; that an entire change must take place in them by entering into a new and spiritual life; that God is very sorrowful over their absence from him and will be delighted to welcome them back to his love; . . . and if they do not come they will have to bear the terrible consequences of their refusal."[33]

Rauschenbusch did not completely reject the doctrine of the substitutionary atonement, noting that there were elements in Scripture that gave warrant to these teachings (although from his view, the specific teachings of Jesus did not). He ended the paper by calling on Christians to judge Scripture through knowledge and experience, affirming that ultimately "we can pray earnestly for more light and a clearer apprehension of the work of our Savior, Jesus Christ."[34]

33. "The Bushnellian Theory of the Atonement," box 14.
34. Ibid.

This essay was the source for the first of many theological controversies in Rauschenbusch's career. Rauschenbusch wrote the essay in a theology class taught by President Strong, the orthodox patriarch, who, while conceding the high quality of the writing, also thought the essay "to be subversive of scripture." Rauschenbusch took pride that Strong in subsequent lectures used his essay as a springboard to discuss the case for an orthodox Christianity.[35] Strong was not alone among the faculty in sharing a concern over Rauschenbusch's orthodoxy. Yet, there were many other occasions in which the young seminarian's lapses into theological apostasy gave way to the Baptist pietism of August Rauschenbusch. In a chapel sermon he preached just prior to his graduation from seminary, he affirmed that Christian pietism meant that one must embrace the intent of Christ in all aspects of his life. "It is the heart that God looks to; it is the Christ-like life that he wants. Any knowledge that does not operate to make the heart purer and better, is not the knowledge that belongs to the eternal life. . . . The eternal life is ours when we know the only true God through him whom he has sent, Jesus Christ."[36]

Yet Rauschenbusch's chapel sermon also showed that his theology of personal conversion was predicated on many liberal suppositions. He believed that any effort to ascertain the nature of Christian salvation was dependent upon understanding the true intent of Jesus' ministry. The question "What would Jesus do?" that Charles Sheldon raised a decade later in his famous best-selling novel *In His Steps* became a key question for most evangelical-liberals who embraced what would be called the social gospel. Rauschenbusch echoed the liberal belief that human beings could aspire to Christlike qualities in their daily living. "When God revealed himself in Christ, he revealed himself in the one way in which we can know him. The Word became *flesh* and dwelt among us. The only God we can know is a human God, with a heart that answers to our heart, who loves as we love, who is angry as we are angry, who sorrows with our griefs and rejoices with our joys."[37] This emphasis on God's love came partly from Rauschen-

35. Handwritten comments by WR written on copy of "The Bushnellan Theory of the Atonement."

36. Chapel Sermon, March 19, 1886, box 14.

37. Ibid.

busch's pietist heritage. Unlike his father, however, by 1886 Walther was less interested in talking about the human capacity to sin, emphasizing instead the human possibility to overcome sin. Rauschenbusch did not discount the reality of human sinfulness, yet as he prepared to enter full-time ministry he was converted to a theology that held that the way humans battled sin was through "moral earnestness." "As a man fights sin and draws near to God in prayer, so does this knowledge pour into his soul. And therefore it is equally within reach of all, for all can fight and all can pray."[38]

Curiously, his student writings largely lack references to the one doctrine that became the cornerstone of his later liberalism: the kingdom of God. Walther tended to think of the kingdom, much like his father, as an otherworldly culmination of Christianity. Many members of the seminary's faculty were hostile to the writings of the liberal theologian and historian Albrecht Ritschl, whose teachings at Göttingen University pushed beyond the theological boundaries of Schleiermacher and Neander. For Ritschl, a theologian whose own politics were very conservative and heavily tied to the German monarchy, the idea of the kingdom of God was not just an ideal, but it represented the sine qua non of Christianity — it was the key concept for understanding the nature and purpose of the church in this life. Rauschenbusch would later embrace the perspective of Ritschl and his disciple Adolf von Harnack concerning the centrality of the kingdom of God in Christian theology. In 1886, however, Rauschenbusch placed greater emphasis on how the religion of Jesus Christ exposed the sinner to the saving grace of God.

When Rauschenbusch graduated from seminary in May 1886, he made it clear that the vibrancy of Christian faith for the future depended not on the dogma of church tradition, but in how contemporary experience was brought to bear on that tradition. In a student oration given at his graduation, he affirmed that "honesty demands that [one] be not content with the reassuring words of tradition; that he call no doctrine the dwelling-place of Truth, till he hear her own voice from within giving answer to the call of him who seeks her. A Christly loyalty to truth and a godly trust in the Spirit of truth, will give honesty in the search for truth."[39] Rauschenbusch may have viewed his mission after seminary as

38. Ibid.

39. "The Ethics of Thinking," May 19, 1886, box 14.

being a soul-saving evangelist, but he was clearly on the road to becoming a theological liberal. Although his theology would go through major developments over the years, by 1886 he had in place some of the chief convictions that grounded his future theological liberalism.

Despite some concerns over his liberalism, the seminary faculty looked with pride to Rauschenbusch's academic record and many saw great things in his future. Any theological rift between Rauschenbusch's nascent liberalism and the orthodoxy of the seminary faculty has to be viewed with some caution. Although theological heresy trials between liberals and conservatives were becoming increasingly common by the 1880s, the theological climate of that time was still largely characterized by a spirit of common purpose among American Protestants. The nation was still decades away from using terms like "Fundamentalists" and "Modernists" to describe the theological divisions that became less permeable by the 1920s and 1930s. In the 1880s, "new theology" liberals competed with "orthodox" Protestants to define the theological contours of American Protestantism. Yet each movement saw itself as drinking from the well of an earlier tradition of evangelical Protestantism. The 1880s represented the heyday for the revivalist Dwight L. Moody, a businessman turned preacher who carried on a tradition of earlier nineteenth-century revivalism epitomized by evangelists like Charles Finney. Moody preached a persuasive message of personal salvation through Christ, whereas he spoke less than earlier generations of evangelicals about the need for social reform. Nevertheless he advocated a "big tent" theology when it came to matters of Christian cooperation. It is indeed ironic that over the next thirty years of American Protestant history, church leaders who later identified themselves as conservative fundamentalists and as social gospel liberals would claim Moody as their spiritual mentor. As Grant Wacker surmises about the state of late nineteenth-century Protestantism, "the relationship between liberals and evangelicals in the 1880s and 1890s is best understood, not as a confrontation between aliens, but as a contest — albeit a deadly serious contest — between siblings who perceived and defined the issues in remarkably similar ways."[40]

40. Grant Wacker, "The Holy Spirit and the Spirit of the Age in American Protestantism, 1880-1910," 59; see also Heinz D. Rossol, "More Than a Prophet," *American Baptist Quarterly* 29 (June 2000): 147.

The argument that liberals and conservatives were, in a sense, spiritual bedfellows can be seen in a series of events that would have a profound impact on Rauschenbusch's future. At the end of his senior year, Walther remained somewhat uncertain about his future. He had received feelers from several Baptist churches, and one particularly attractive offer from a German Baptist church in Springfield, Illinois. Yet he was also compelled by the possibility of going into missionary service and emerged as a candidate for a post as the president of the Telugu Baptist Seminary in Ramapatnam, India. The fact that Rauschenbusch surfaced as a candidate for the position was likely due to the influence of the head of the Telugu mission, John Clough.[41] Clough had met Rauschenbusch during a speaking engagement at Rochester Seminary in 1884, and was a colleague of his sister Emma, who had served as a teacher at the mission since 1881.

When Rauschenbusch graduated at the top of his class in May 1886, he was clearly held in highest regard by the faculty of the seminary and it would not have been inconceivable to them that a young man of his intellectual promise would be offered such an attractive position. Yet some on the faculty were concerned that Rauschenbusch's liberal leanings needed to be excised from his theology before he could truly carry the seminary's theological mantle into his public ministry. In particular, Howard Osgood, the Old Testament patriarch at the seminary, expressed his worries over Rauschenbusch's liberalism in a letter he sent to the American Baptist Missionary Union, citing that his former student denied the divine authority of the Old Testament. Largely due to Osgood's concerns, Rauschenbusch was suddenly informed by J. N. Murdock of the missionary union in mid-September that despite his excellent recommendations, Rauschenbusch was being dropped as a candidate for the Telugu position. Murdock cited the missionary union's (and Howard Osgood's) belief that although Rauschenbusch's qualifications were excellent, he needed a few years of pastoral experience, "in order to acquire experience and the settled convictions which come from it."[42] Although Osgood is not mentioned in Murdock's letter (and Rauschenbusch would not learn for some time the identity of the individual who had raised concerns over his

41. See J. N. Murdock to WR, August 12, 1886, box 23.
42. J. N. Murdock to WR, September 18, 1886, box 23.

theology), the conciliatory tone of the letter makes it evident that those who were concerned about Rauschenbusch's liberalism believed that pastoral experience would stabilize his beliefs and bring him back into a more orthodox fold. In many ways, this incident reflects the theological temper of the era and although Rauschenbusch's liberalism was a concern to men like Osgood, it was an aberration that did not, as yet, reflect an irreconcilable chasm.

Whatever misgivings the Baptist Missionary Union may have had about Rauschenbusch's theological convictions soon dissipated when in April 1887 Murdock renewed the invitation to Rauschenbusch to reapply for the seminary presidency.[43] By this time, however, Walther Rauschenbusch was immersed in a new venture that now precluded the possibility of taking up foreign missionary service.

43. J. N. Murdock to WR, April 19, 1887, box 23.

3 Beneath the Glitter

When Walther Rauschenbusch began his pastoral ministry at the Second German Baptist Church of New York City on June 1, 1886, he did so at an important juncture in the history of American social Christianity. Years later, Rauschenbusch remarked that the few advocates of social Christianity before 1900 were lone prophets, "and we shouted in the wilderness."[1] The cultural and theological climate of American Protestantism before 1900, and in the early years of the twentieth century, seemed to affirm Rauschenbusch's assessment. Although the final quarter of the nineteenth century marked the ascendency of theological liberalism in American Protestantism, the acceptance of liberalism was confined largely to a small coterie of ministers and seminary professors in the northeastern United States. Few of these individuals who identified with the "new theology" of liberalism translated their faith in ways that resembled what would later be called "the social gospel."

Amidst an era of perceived theological and missional virility, the final quarter of the nineteenth century was a time when several fault lines emerged in the facade of American Protestantism. These fault lines would lead to the creation of distinctive movements of American

1. WR, *Christianizing the Social Order* (New York: Macmillan, 1912), 9.

Protestantism by the early twentieth century. In the spring of 1886, when Rauschenbusch was first approached by the Second German Baptist Church of New York City about the prospect of becoming their pastor, there appeared little chance that this tiny congregation could attract such a promising ministerial candidate. Yet Rauschenbusch perceived that the church would give him the opportunity to live out many of his faith convictions as a preacher and as an evangelist. He did not realize, however, that he was entering a cultural and theological epicenter that would in a short time radically alter many of his core convictions.

THE KINGDOM OF GOD IN AMERICA: 1886

American Protestantism in the early nineteenth century reflected a polyglot of theological currents. Major streams of influence before 1850 included the New England Unitarianism of William Ellery Channing, the evangelical Calvinism of Lyman Beecher, and, most especially, the Arminian "free grace" theology of Charles Finney and hosts of nascent evangelical churches born amidst the revival fires of the Second Great Awakening. As much as Protestant leaders and churches squabbled and fought passionately over matters of theological doctrine, the years before the Civil War reflected a fairly sanguine continuity in purpose among these disparate theological traditions. Most took for granted the divinity of Christ (even initially many of the Unitarian disciples of William Ellery Channing), and that Christ's divinity served the purpose of leading the sinner to experience firsthand the saving grace of God. While the caretakers of American Protestantism disagreed passionately over specific matters of doctrine and the means to impart the gospel message to the masses, there was a strong unanimity that the chief purpose of Protestantism was to save sinners from the wrath of hell.

Yet the consequence of this personal faith led to an amazing social virility among American Protestants prior to the Civil War. The theological orientation of this Protestant evangelicalism was postmillennial. These Christians believed that the more people were converted, social conditions would improve, thus setting the stage for the second coming of Christ and fulfilling the prophecy in Revelation 21:1,

"And I saw a new heaven and a new earth: for the first heaven and the first earth were passed away." In the decades prior to the Civil War, evangelical Protestants welded their efforts into ecumenical voluntary societies directed to promote the causes of temperance, educational reform, campaigns for women's rights, and especially the abolitionist movement. These reform efforts would continue to manifest themselves in American Protestantism in the second half of the nineteenth century, especially through the efforts of organizations like the Woman's Christian Temperance Union and the various woman's home and foreign missionary societies that came into existence after the Civil War.

By the 1870s and 1880s, the earlier sense of Protestant unity was beginning to break apart. In 1867, the National Camp Meeting Association for the Promotion of Holiness was formed. This was a largely Methodist enterprise designed to encourage people to seek "the second blessing" of entire sanctification, a state of divine grace in which the individual would be made free from the power of sin. Derived from the theology of John Wesley, the doctrine of sanctification had been a source for Wesley's own social concern that had translated itself seamlessly into the American evangelical context of early nineteenth-century social reform. During the time Rauschenbusch studied in seminary, however, Holiness adherents had become increasingly distressed by what they saw as the wealth and prosperity of many of the nation's Protestant churches, who put wealth and status ahead of personal conversion. Increasingly, they called upon the faithful to "come out" of these churches to form more Christlike fellowships. The result was the creation of a number of independent camp meeting associations in the 1880s that ultimately led to the founding of several independent Holiness denominations in the 1890s and early 1900s such as the Church of the Nazarene and the Church of God. Ultimately, the rise of the Holiness movement spawned the birth of the Pentecostal movement in the early twentieth century.

Another division that emerged during the final quarter of the century was the movement that would become known decades later by the term "fundamentalism." In 1886, however, "fundamentalism" was not a movement but a disparate range of orthodox theologies from the rigid Calvinism taught at Princeton Theological Seminary to the popular evangelicalism of the famed revivalist Dwight L. Moody, who like Charles Finney before him captured the imagination of many Americans from the 1870s until his death in 1899. In 1886, Protestants did not use the term "fundamentalist" as a title of self-designation. Nevertheless, the chief theological concepts associated with the later twentieth-century fundamentalist movement were hotly contested during the mid 1880s. Debates over biblical inerrancy, personal salvation only through the atoning death of Jesus Christ, and a hostility toward modern science that was epitomized in those years by the debate over Charles Darwin's theory of evolution put many Christians of the late nineteenth century at odds with church leaders like Rauschenbusch, who adhered to the teachings of liberalism.

The final quarter of the nineteenth century also saw the emergence of a new millennial fervor that simmered in the theological caldron of American Protestantism: premillennialism. In juxtaposition to the optimistic assessment of the future carried by postmillennialists, premillennialists crafted a far more apocalyptic scenario. Building on the example of groups like the Millerites, an 1840s sectarian movement that believed that the end of the world was foretold by Scripture to occur in 1843 or 1844, the British minister John Nelson Darby taught that Christ would not return after the millennium, when social conditions had improved. Rather, through his study of Scripture, Darby believed that history was divided into a series of "dispensations" that indicated that Christ's return would occur suddenly and without warning. This coming would signal the "rapture" of the faithful, both past and present, into the kingdom of heaven, whereas those who remained on earth, consistent with the prophecies in the books of Daniel and Revelation, would be "left behind" to face terrible tribulation and ultimately, for most, the perils of eternal punishment. Only after this tribulation would come the millennium of a thousand years of Christ's reign on a purified earth. Thus the important distinction is that the postmillennialist believed that Christ would return *after* a (metaphorical) thousand years of universal Christian peace, while the premillennialist believed that Christ would come *before* the establishment of his millennial kingdom on earth.

Although the birth of modern fundamentalism is often associated with the Niagara Bible Conferences that were inaugurated in 1878 and continued throughout the nineteenth century, what came to be known as fundamentalism by the 1920s represented variations of theological orthodoxy of the late nineteenth century. While many late nineteenth-century Protestant ministers may have believed in biblical inerrancy and rejected the teachings of Charles Darwin, their orientation toward millennialism might very well have been toward a version of postmillennialism. (This was largely the case with many of the American theological caretakers of the Calvinist legacy that included, in the 1880s, Rochester Theological Seminary.) At the same time, a representative figure of that era who embodied the qualities of modern fundamentalism, Dwight Moody, tended to place his specific premillennial beliefs in the background of his theology. What was important to Moody was that the sinner came to Christ, and whether one was a pre- or postmillennialist was of secondary importance.

The final fracture to emerge in the late nineteenth century was over what contemporaries called "the new theology," or theological liberalism. Although historians have tended to draw a distinction between the rise of liberalism and the social gospel, in many ways the two movements were interconnected, if not inseparable. Already by 1886, theological liberalism had bequeathed two qualities that became indispensable to the rise of the social gospel in America: an acceptance, if not an outright embrace of, the natural sciences and a belief that the nature of Christian salvation did not rest solely upon the atoning death of Christ, but in the character of Jesus' earthly ministry that enabled one to understand the reasons behind Christ's death on the cross. As a pastor in New York City, Rauschenbusch would not only digest a huge scope of theological influences, both liberal and orthodox; he would assimilate numerous intellectual sources that sketched out his convictions that the social order, for all its sins, could be made over to reflect the true intent and purpose of primitive Christianity.[2]

2. Donovan Smucker's *The Origin of Walter Rauschenbusch's Social Ethics* remains a definitive investigation into the theological sources of Rauschenbusch's social thought. Yet as the next two chapters reveal, it is evident that Rauschenbusch drew on an eclectic assortment of intellectual influences during his early years in New York City. Frederick W. C. Meyer, a classmate of Rauschenbusch's at RTS and a later colleague on the seminary's faculty, recollected that Rauschenbusch drew most heavily in his early pastorate on Henry George, Edward Bellamy, Giuseppe Mazzini, Karl Marx, Leo Tolstoy, Josiah Strong's *Our Country* "and maybe Washington Gladden." See F. W. C. Meyer to Mrs. James Rorty [Winifred Rauschenbusch], September 17, 1929, box 39.

What became known in the early twentieth century as "the social gospel" may have lacked large numbers of adherents in the 1880s and 1890s. At the same time, liberal theology moved a number of influential clergy, academicians, and popular writers to reinterpret the social significance of the gospel in ways that moved beyond an earlier heritage of American Protestant evangelicalism.

THE SOCIAL GOSPEL IN 1886

Although the term was not used in the mid-1880s, the theological and social contours of what became known by the second decade of the twentieth century as "the social gospel" were taking hold in American Protestantism. What defined the contours of the social gospel in America in the late nineteenth century was the way that its leaders shared a common concern with the social, economic, *and* cultural problems caused by the rise of capitalism. Throughout church history, a variety of reformers engaged the issue of the Christian's relationship to wealth, most visibly evident in the writings by a wide range of Catholic and Protestant theologians in the late medieval and early modern period against the sins associated with usury. Most, if not all, evangelical Protestants in the eighteenth and nineteenth centuries emphasized the need for Christians to support the poor. However, social conditions in American society after the Civil War, especially the meteoric growth of the nation's cities, witnessed discernible changes in the ways that some Christian leaders viewed the issues of economic wealth.

America in the years between 1865 and 1900 went through an unprecedented population explosion, rising from just over 31 million on the eve of the Civil War to almost 76 million by 1900. America's economic base shifted away from farming and agriculture toward the industrial base of the nation's cities. In just twenty years, between 1870 and 1890, the country's urban population more than doubled from under 10 million to over 22 million.[3] New York was not only the nation's largest city but also was a point of entry for thousands of immigrants

3. Statistics cited from Heinz D. Rossol, "Walter Rauschenbusch as Preacher: The Development of His Social Thought as Expressed in His Sermons from 1886 to 1897" (Ph.D. dissertation, Marquette University, 1997), 34.

who arrived in ever increasing numbers after the Civil War. By the mid-1880s the nation averaged over 500,000 new immigrants per year, and that percentage of new arrivals continued to increase dramatically well into the early twentieth century.[4] What many caretakers of Protestant America found so alarming about this second great wave of immigrants, however, was they largely came from non-Protestant nations in eastern and southern Europe. In addition to massive numbers of Roman Catholic immigrants, the nation received an unprecedented number of orthodox Jews who started coming to America after 1880 to escape persecution in Russia and Poland.

The rise of industrial monopolies on the one hand and of a workforce made up of poor immigrants on the other created a perplexing psychological dilemma for the caretakers of American Protestantism. Many of the business moguls who rose to prominence in the late nineteenth century, most notably John D. Rockefeller, were deeply religious men who shared a faith that Christ's message of salvation would unite the nation under the banner of evangelical Protestantism. Many Protestant ministers, however, were concerned that the problems of immigration were creating urban social problems that were unprecedented in scope and could not simply be solved through personal conversion. Many Protestants, following the lead of groups like the Salvation Army and the reform efforts of Dwight Moody's Chicago-based Evangelization Society (later the Moody Bible Institute), continued to subscribe to a belief that the best way to engage in social reform was through a continuation of the Protestant evangelical efforts of the early nineteenth century. These evangelical ministries were instrumental in the creation of vigorous social ministries that reached out to the nation's urban poor.

At the same time, a small number of Protestant clergy in the 1870s and 1880s, while vigorous supporters of the efforts undertaken by men like Moody and the hands-on evangelism of the Salvation Army, expressed a growing belief that these efforts of social charity on their own were inadequate. As a result, the first generation of social gospel leaders in the United States was born, represented primarily in the work of two men: Washington Gladden and Josiah Strong. Gladden and Strong were instrumental in shaping the outlook of social

4. See Mark A. Noll, *The Old Religion in a New World: The History of North American Christianity* (Grand Rapids: Eerdmans, 2002), 124.

Christianity in the period between 1880 and 1900, and both men later developed warm and close professional relationships with Christian social reformers of the next generation, including Walter Rauschenbusch. In his later accounts of the history of social Christianity in the United States, Rauschenbusch showered high praise on these two Christian reformers. "These men had matured their thought when the rest of us were young men, and they had a spirit in them which kindled and compelled us."[5] In his early years in New York, Rauschenbusch latched on to other intellectual sources that influenced him more than Gladden and Strong. However, the fact that Rauschenbusch spoke so effusively of both men as unique pioneers of social Christianity was not false praise.

There had been American clergy as far back as the early 1870s who sought to translate the Christian socialism of Frederick Maurice and Frederick Robertson into the context of American society. Yet these efforts were confined to very small cadres of clergy in the northeastern United States.[6] The writings of Gladden and Strong, however, were instrumental in grafting an older postmillennial vision of Protestant evangelicalism upon the social context of the late nineteenth century. For all the ways that Rauschenbusch moved beyond the moralism of Gladden and Strong, their writings in the 1880s defined the theological and cultural contours in which Rauschenbusch defined his own ministry during his years in New York.

In 1886, fifty-year-old Washington Gladden had emerged as the leading proponent of American social Christianity. Born in 1836 and raised in the upstate New York village of Owego, Gladden went through a series of short-term pastorates in the 1860s and a stint as an editor for the *Independent* in the early and mid-1870s. During his years at the *Independent,* he wrote a series of editorials attacking the political corruption of Boss Tweed's political ring in New York City. In 1875, he was called to the North Congregational Church in Springfield, Massachusetts, where in 1876 he published his first major work on the church and social issues entitled *Working People and Their Em-*

5. WR, *Christianizing the Social Order,* 9.

6. The classic discussion of the social gospel's rise in the urban Northeast remains Charles Howard Hopkins, *The Social Gospel in American Protestantism, 1865-1915;* see especially chapter 2.

ployers, a book that Rauschenbusch acknowledged years later as one of the classic texts on social Christianity. In 1882, Gladden was called to the pastorate of the First Congregational Church in Columbus, Ohio, where for the next thirty years as senior pastor he would publish over thirty books, mostly based upon sermons preached in his Columbus pulpit and in addresses given throughout the United States.

Gladden was one of the early representatives of theological liberalism in American Protestantism. Unlike his mentor, Horace Bushnell, and his contemporary Theodore Munger, he was one of the first liberals whose writings focused primarily on how the Christian church might ethically and prescriptively address the growing chasm in America between capitalist owners and wage earners. While highly sympathetic to the plight of labor, his writings throughout much of his career reflected a lukewarm endorsement of labor unionism. Like many Americans of his generation, he was terrified by the outbreak of violence that occurred in many labor strikes in the 1870s and 1880s, culminating in the Chicago Haymarket riot in 1886 in which several persons were killed by a bomb believed to be the work of anarchists. The interconnection in the public's mind between political anarchy and immigration was prevalent in the minds of many Protestant leaders of Washington Gladden's generation, including Gladden himself. While he castigated the way that the capitalist wage system affected the nation's workingmen, he decried equally the dangers of political socialism and insisted that enlightened men of the business classes would be able to spread the true social meaning of Jesus' teachings to the workingmen of the nation. To counteract the threat of political socialism, Gladden prescribed personal responsibility, along with very modest government regulation, as the best means to ensure that the imbalance between rich and poor would be corrected. He advocated revenue sharing between employers and their workers, as an alternative to the violence inherent within political socialism. As he noted in his 1886 book *Applied Christianity,* the nation's wealthy were under a special obligation to reach out in a Christian spirit to the nation's laborers. "The great inequalities arising from the present defective methods of distribution will only be corrected through a deepening sense of the obligations imposed by the possession of wealth. The economic law, like the moral law, can never be fulfilled without love."[7] This moderate stance likely reflected Gladden's desire not to alienate the powerful business and political leaders who made up his upper-class Columbus congregation. Nevertheless, Gladden was the prototype for future generations of prominent liberal Protestant "pulpiteers" in the early decades of the twentieth century like Ernest Fremont Tittle, Henry Sloane Coffin, Ralph Sockman, and most especially Harry Emerson Fosdick — men whose reform liberalism sought to appeal to the consciences of their upper-middle-class congregations.

Gladden was one of the first Protestant leaders to articulate a theology that became popularly known as "social salvation." He believed that the message of Christianity needed to be applied in a systemic fashion to address the social-economic problems facing America. However, his articulation of this concept did not signal an abandonment of the idea of an individual conversion experience, or the importance of individual salvation. If anything, Gladden's understanding of social salvation was a means of strengthening, not weakening, the message of personal salvation. The difference between Gladden and an earlier generation of Protestant evangelicals was that the ancient truths of Christianity needed to be reappropriated and adapted to the conditions of modern industrial society. "We must make men believe that Christianity has a right to rule this kingdom of industry, as well as all the other kingdoms of this world; that her law is the only law on which any kind of society will rest in security and peace; that ways must be found of incorporating good-will as a regulative principle, as an integral element, into the very structure of industrial society."[8] The goal of Christianity for Gladden was nothing short of the creation of a just society, a society that manifested fully the teachings of Christianity in all areas of life.

If Washington Gladden represented the first clear articulation of a liberal theology for the social gospel in the 1880s, then Josiah Strong symbolized the cultural ideals that many later social gospel leaders sought to defend. For all of Gladden's rising stature as a writer and preacher of social Christianity in the 1880s, it was Strong who in one

7. Washington Gladden, *Applied Christianity: Moral Aspects of Social Questions* (Boston and New York: Houghton, Mifflin and Company, 1886), 37.

8. Ibid., 173.

book captured the ethos of the early social gospel. In the early 1880s, Strong was a little-known congregational minister in Cincinnati. However, with the publication of his 1885 book *Our Country,* Strong emerged as one of the major intellectual voices in American Protestantism. *Our Country* represented a concrete blueprint for social amelioration that put the nation's Protestant churches at the center of the struggle for the soul of the nation. Strong was far less attracted to theological liberalism than Gladden, but like Gladden was influenced by Horace Bushnell's understanding of Christian nurture, whereby the significance of Christian conversion was not defined in terms of a singular conversion experience. Rather Strong and Gladden saw the litmus test of Christianity reflected in how Christian values imparted themselves to individuals and consequently upon the rest of society. Strong's belief in Christian nurture resonated with Gladden's liberal view that Jesus' teachings needed to be translated ethically to address contemporary social problems. His narrative painted a portrait of late nineteenth-century America as a nation in crisis, and a series of chapters laid out the problems posed to the nation by immigration, Catholicism, intemperance, socialism, and the growth of sectarian religious movements like the Mormons. For Strong, these problems accentuated how the values and religious heritage of America Protestantism were under siege in a nation that was increasingly becoming urbanized and dominated by non-Protestant immigrants.

Strong believed that America's future rested upon reinvigorating the virtues of old-stock Puritanism, manifested in his belief that the Anglo-Saxon heritage needed to "Christianize" the nation. Strong's ethnocentrism was expressing a popular sentiment held by many middle-class Protestants in the 1880s, and he was guilty more of cultural chauvinism than of overt racism based upon biological superiority. He believed that America and Great Britain made the greatest contributions to world history, embodied in particular by the United States. America was not only the greatest democratic power in the world but also a nation whose customs and culture in the arts, education, and government made America a distinctive exemplar of Christianity to the rest of the world. Reflecting an outlook that blended various Darwinian theories with Bushnell's arguments on Christian nurture, Strong believed that the spirit of Anglo-Saxon American Protestantism would, with the passing of time, subdue all alien social and religious forces in America and throughout the world. "In my own mind, there is no doubt that the Anglo-Saxon is to exercise the commanding influence in the world's future; but the exact nature of that influence is, as yet, undetermined. How far his civilization will be materialistic and atheistic, and how long it will take thoroughly to Christianize and sweeten it, how rapidly he will hasten the coming of the kingdom wherein dwelleth righteousness, or how many ages he may retard it, is still uncertain; but is *now being swiftly determined.*"[9] More than any book of religious nonfiction up to that time, *Our Country* caught a wave of popular sentiment, selling over 100,000 copies in its first few editions.

The writings of Strong and Gladden provided a critical context for the emerging social thought of Rauschenbusch. He largely embraced the cultural paradigm of Strong, with the difference that he substituted the cultural tradition of Germany for Great Britain because of his lifelong suspicion of Great Britain. Although Gladden's writing appears less culturally elitist than Strong's, he shared a common concern that the values of an Anglo-European Protestantism, embodied by the nation's Puritan religious heritage, were going to waste in the religious and secular climate of the late nineteenth century. Picking up where Horace Bushnell had left off, Strong and Gladden warned that the nation's Protestant heritage was in peril of being overrun by "alien" religious and secular forces. Years later, Rauschenbusch would echo repeatedly a concern articulated by both men that the social problems of urbanization, intemperance, and the excesses of socialism (epitomized by the godless utopian society of Karl Marx) could only be countered by an increase in the religious and cultural virtues of American life that were reflected in the values of an old-stock Protestantism. For Rauschenbusch, as with Strong, "Christianization" was a term synonymous with Americanization.

Washington Gladden and Josiah Strong had a strong impact upon Rauschenbusch's thinking. These men would be surpassed in their theological analyses by more incisive Protestant social Christians, yet throughout their lengthy careers, they epitomized the late nineteenth-century cultural context that gave birth to the social gospel.

9. Josiah Strong, *Our Country* (reprint; Cambridge: Belknap Press of Harvard University Press, 1963), 217.

The staging ground for this social reinterpretation was America's major cities, and the battle was enjoined in the 1880s by a growing number of clergy and social scientists, some of whom, like Gladden, Strong, and the economist Richard Ely, reached wide audiences through national lectureships like the Lyceum movement and later in the 1890s through the Chautauqua movement.

For all the ways the writing of the early social gospel seemed to transcend the parameters of earlier Protestant evangelicalism, theirs was a social vision that seized upon, and reinterpreted for a new generation, an earlier Protestant postmillennial vision to realize the kingdom of God in America: to create "a new heaven on earth." The writings of Gladden and Strong gave the kingdom doctrine a new concreteness that paved the way for a younger generation of Protestant leaders like Rauschenbusch. The kingdom of God was synonymous for all of these men with a belief that the virtues of Christianity would gradually make America a more Christianized, democratic society.

When Rauschenbusch began his ministry in New York City, he may not have been clear about the means to achieve this vision of a Protestant America. But the goal of striving after the kingdom of God quickly became the focal point of his ministry.

EARLY SOCIAL AWAKENING

In many respects, the world that Walther Rauschenbusch entered in June 1886 came right from the pages of *Our Country.* For all of Rauschenbusch's unique educational background, and his own self-confidence about his ministry gifts, he stepped into a world completely alien from the one he had known in Rochester and Germany. New York in the mid-1880s was the nation's largest city, consisting of almost three million residents and on the front line of immigration and social-economic unrest. Rauschenbusch was 24 when he began his ministry, and he found himself in a setting that was a far cry from the German Baptist church that courted him in Springfield or the seminary presidency that eluded him. His church consisted of 125 working-class German-immigrant parishioners in one of the poorest sections of New York, located on West 45th Street just off of the "Hell's

Kitchen" section of New York's Bowery district. The building's physical structure was far from impressive, as he noted to Munson Ford soon after his arrival in the city, observing tersely that his church was "old-fashioned, inconvenient and rather ugly."[10] His new congregation was part of a larger working-class, tenement-dwelling population that included carpenters, shoemakers, butchers, grocers, as well as a variety of skilled and unskilled laborers.[11] In juxtaposition to his congregation, Rauschenbusch's annual salary of $600 (in addition to a $300 stipend for apartment rent) was far from austere.

Yet Rauschenbusch came to his new pastorate brimming with self-confidence, in spite of the social barriers that separated him from his congregation. As he noted to Ford, he was determined to bring his congregation "into living and personal relations with our Lord Jesus Christ."[12] Even as he settled into his parish responsibilities during his first summer that centered upon preaching two Sunday services and visiting members of his church, he was faced with a major obstacle — he needed to prepare himself for a public ordination examination that fall. Rauschenbusch received several pleas from his parents who worried that their son's liberal tendencies in seminary reflected bad tidings for the future. However, Walther reassured his family that his faith was cut from the same stock as his parents. As he noted in a letter to his mother, "This is all the consolation I am able to offer you: I believe in the gospel of Jesus Christ, with all my heart." Yet his parents might very well have been unsettled by Rauschenbusch's added comment, "What this gospel is, everyone has to decide for himself, in the face of his God."[13] Was he making a pledge to uphold the Baptist principle of individual freedom or was he making a declaration of independence from the chains of theological orthodoxy?

In spite of any misgivings held by his parents, Rauschenbusch sailed through his ordination exams and was ordained into the Baptist

10. WR to Munson Ford, June 30, 1886, reprinted in Dores Sharpe, 59-60.

11. Data on the occupational makeup of Rauschenbusch's parishioners is implied from wedding registries kept by Rauschenbusch throughout his ministry in New York., in which he frequently listed the grooms' occupations. Rauschenbusch's wedding record is in box 97.

12. Hudson, 7.

13. Klaus Juergen Jaehn, *Rauschenbusch: The Formative Years* (Valley Forge: Judson Press, 1976), 12.

ministry at Second German Baptist Church on October 21, 1886. One of the examiners congratulated Rauschenbusch on his handling of the examination, noting, "during the years past I have attended the examination of not a few young men for the ministry; but none have given, to me, so satisfactory a statement of truth." The letter gives no impression of any theological irregularities and affirms the doctrinal soundness of Rauschenbusch's theology, especially his views on "the God consciousness of man, and of the necessity of man." The letter extolled this young minister as one who "will be a great help to men, in their struggles, to realize righteousness as a life and character; and to know God as He wants to be known i.e. the Father God, who loves them."[14]

In his first year at Second German, one side of Rauschenbusch's ministry gave little hint of any concern other than the traditional evangelical nurture of his congregation. Heinz Rossol observed that Rauschenbusch's early sermons supported the pietistic thrust of his parents' theology. He preached two Sunday services, almost exclusively in German, emphasizing the holiness of God, the sinfulness of humanity, and the importance of personal conversion.[15] Rauschenbusch's sermons in his first year mostly centered upon New Testament Scriptures, with heavy emphasis on John and the Pauline texts, somewhat ironic given Rauschenbusch's later ambivalence toward these sources.[16]

While the young pastor emphasized a pietistic message that called upon his congregation to turn away from sin, he also displayed a warm pastoral side in his everyday relationships with his parishioners. Rauschenbusch made frequent pastoral calls upon members of his church, and also formed friendships with members of the larger German-immigrant community. His pastoral presence, along with his sermons, reflect how he saw his ministry as a means to cultivate a quality of Christlike discipleship within his congregation. This emphasis in his ministry was enhanced after he read William Arthur's *The Tongue of Fire* early in his New York City pastorate. Arthur was an Irish Methodist minister who published his seminal work in 1856. The

14. Rev. H. Charles, Jr., to WR, October 14, 1886, box 23.

15. See Heinz D. Rossol, "More than a Prophet," in *American Baptist Quarterly* 29 (June 2000): 129-153.

16. See sermon notebooks in box 150.

book's widespread popularity in America after the Civil War has been cited as an influence in the rise of the Holiness movement in the late nineteenth century and Pentecostalism in the early twentieth century. Arthur was an adherent of John Wesley's belief in entire sanctification, an understanding that human beings could be made free of sin. Using the imagery of Pentecost from the book of Acts, Arthur insisted that a new era was dawning in the church, where the miracle of the first Pentecost would ignite in the souls of humanity a renewed moral strength that could be used to convert the modern world.

> A tongue of fire — man's voice, God's truth; man's speech, the Holy Spirit's inspiration; a human organ, a superhuman power. Not one tongue, but cloven tongues. As the speech of men is various, here we see the Creator taking to himself the language of every man's mother, so that in the very words wherein he heard her say, "I love thee," he might also hear the Father of all say, "I love thee."[17]

References to William Arthur would emerge in many of Rauschenbusch's later writings. Pastorally, Arthur's sanctification theology complemented Rauschenbusch's pietism, in fostering a belief that one's old sinful nature could be made over to approximate that more perfect character of Christlike love. A letter that Rauschenbusch received from a parishioner not long after he completed his second year in New York is revealing in this regard.

> I feel as if I owe it to you to let you know, how much my heart and soul was strengthened yesterday. O what a blessing to have a sinless, holy, loving Jesus to go to with all faults and mistakes and to know that he is always ready . . . to help us to be more like him, and not to be satisfied untill *[sic]* we are. May God bless you and keep his loving wing around you, and protect you from all that might hinder you in the work that he has put you to.[18]

17. William Arthur, *The Tongue of Fire or The True Power of Christianity* (original publication, 1856), quoted in John Brittain, "William Arthur's *The Tongue of Fire: Pre-Pentecostal or Proto Social Gospel?*" in *Methodist History* (July 2002): 248-249.

18. Mrs. E. Kaiser to WR, July 2, 1888, box 23.

The sentiment appears to be a common one among his congregation, as the church experienced significant growth during his first two years in New York. By 1888, forty-six new adult members were added to the church rolls.[19] Rauschenbusch's ministry was likely aided by his mother, who left Rochester and her husband in the fall of 1886 to live with her son in New York for the next four years. The extent of Caroline's involvement in her son's parish is not fully known. However, it is probable that in the absence of a spouse, she served as a surrogate minister's wife, who doubled as both a housekeeper and parish assistant, similar to Lydia Niebuhr, who twenty-five years later served the same role in her son Reinhold's German-immigrant parish in Detroit.

At the same time that Rauschenbusch served his congregation as a doting pastor and evangelist, the foundation for his social passion was being laid. The conditions of tenement poverty that he encountered in the city were a completely new experience for the young man. In the context of urban America's explosive growth after the Civil War, cities like New York devised the tenement as a means to house a number of persons in a relatively small space. While tenement buildings often reflected an aesthetically pleasing appearance on the outside, what one saw upon entering was another matter. These multistory buildings usually had four or more families living on one floor, were poorly ventilated, and frequently inhabitants had no access to windows and outside lighting. Rauschenbusch was appalled by the unsanitary living conditions in these houses, as the tenements of New York and other cities were the breeding grounds for numerous contagious and fatal diseases, including typhoid fever and cholera.

The conditions that his parishioners faced in their tenement dwellings reflected the dire economic conditions that many of the immigrants in New York faced daily. "I saw how men toiled all their life long, hard, toilsome lives, and at the end had almost nothing to show for it; how strong men begged for work, and could not get it in the hard times?" he reminisced years later.[20] Nothing impacted him more than the funerals he had to conduct. His first in New York, on Febru-

19. See Heinz D. Rossol, "Walter Rauschenbusch as Preacher: The Development of His Social Thought as Expressed in His Sermons," Appendix B, 324; *New York State Baptist Annual* (New York: The State Missionary Convention, annually 1887-98).

20. WR, "The Kingdom of God," box 39.

ary 24, 1887, happened to be a funeral for a young child. Rauschenbusch's message revealed little affinity with orthodox Calvinism's tendency to use funerals to speak of God's divine sovereignty in the face of human sin and death. Rather, he spoke passionately about the reality of God's presence and love for humanity in the face of death. After giving his assurance that the parents would see their child again in heaven, he reassured his audience that God would take away the pain of those who mourned. "Dear friends, when you talk to God about this loss you do not speak to one who cannot be touched with a feeling [for] our infirmities. . . . Tell God your pains, He alone fully understands you." While Rauschenbusch used the refrain "He doeth all things well" to speak of God's presence with the mourning family, such theological assertions did little to comfort him.[21] He felt an agony over the number of funerals he had to conduct, especially for children who died as a result of poverty-induced disease. "Oh, the children's funerals! They gripped my heart — that was one of the things I always went away thinking about — why did the children have to die?"[22]

By the same token, Rauschenbusch was clearly energized by the newness of his new social environment. During his first summer in New York, he wrote at length to a relative in Germany indicating that the acquired faith of his parents was inadequate to meet the needs of modern society. "Here one feels the waves of human life all around, as it really is, not as it ought to be according to the *decretum absolutum* of an old theology. Here one can test for oneself whether the people have needs which cannot be satisfied by the almighty dollar, whether the Gospel of Jesus Christ contains a real power which could save a certain man who opens up to its influences." In an assertion that reveals that Rauschenbusch's thought was already going through a major shift, he noted that since his arrival in the city less than two months earlier, "I have not read anything except newspapers and yet, I have learned more than in a long time before."[23]

As Rauschenbusch pondered the context of the working poor in

21. Funeral notes, dated February 24, 1887, sermon book 4, box 150.

22. WR, "The Kingdom of God."

23. Quoted in David Roy Harry, "Two Kingdoms: Walter Rauschenbusch's Concept of the Kingdom of God Contrasted with the Theology of Revivalism in Early Twentieth Century America" (Ph.D. dissertation, Southwestern Baptist Theological Seminary, 1993), 32.

his church, he also pondered a question that ate away at the consciences of men like Washington Gladden and Josiah Strong: how should the Christian understand the relationship of wealth to different economic classes in America? Like these two men, he quickly found an answer in Henry George's 1879 book, *Progress and Poverty*. George's social analysis struck a nerve for many Protestant reformers who emerged in the years between 1880 and 1900. Like his Protestant contemporaries, George worried that immigration coupled with the practices of big-money capitalism was creating a massive economic gulf between the rich and the poor. He was especially alarmed by the fact that many rich Americans were earning exorbitant profits from land that they acquired not through merit, but by wealth. This problem was especially evident in large urban centers like New York, where absentee landlords garnered exorbitant profits at the expense of the poor. Wealthy proprietors often owned blocks of tenements, charging high rents, with few or no legal measures to protect the rights of the tenants. George's solution was to require landowners to pay a set tax that could be used by municipal authorities to support a spate of public initiatives to benefit the poor, such as the creation of municipal parks and better housing. George's tax proposal, or "the single tax" as it became known, was one of the most talked-about reform initiatives throughout the 1880s and 1890s. He instilled in Rauschenbusch a conviction that would remain one of his primary concerns throughout his life: all unearned income on the part of the wealthy was inherently parasitic and needed to be benevolently overseen by the state.

It was more than George's single-tax solution that attracted Rauschenbusch, however. In a fashion that would be picked up more systematically by social scientists like Richard Ely later in the 1880s, George insisted that his solutions for redistributing wealth were not only economically prudent, but were grounded upon the ethics of Jesus. "The religion which allies itself with injustice to preach down the natural aspirations of the masses is worse than atheism," he wrote.[24] Rauschenbusch's arrival in New York coincided with the crest of George's popularity as an American reformer, one of several who helped establish a foundation for the Progressive Era in the United States. During Rauschenbusch's first fall in New York City in 1886,

24. Quoted in Hopkins, 60.

George was a third-party candidate for mayor of New York and Rauschenbusch was among his most enthusiastic supporters. For all of the ways that he would later embrace an understanding of social reform that would wed the languages of evangelical postmillennialism to democratic socialism, the practical thrust of Rauschenbusch's reform initiatives derived heavily from the work of George. As he wrote in 1912, "I owe my own first awakening to the world of social problems to the agitation of Henry George in 1886, and wish here to record my lifelong debt to this single-minded apostle of a great truth."[25]

Rauschenbusch's interest in social questions was also stoked toward the end of his first year in the city when he befriended two young New York City clergymen: Nathaniel Schmidt and Leighton Williams. Schmidt, like Rauschenbusch, was a recent seminary graduate, completing his studies at Rochester Theological Seminary's sister institution, Hamilton Theological Seminary, located in central New York. In early 1887, Schmidt became pastor of a nearby Swedish Baptist church and, like Walther, shared a deep interest in both liberal theology and the reform proposals of George. By contrast, Leighton Williams was older than the other two men, but also new to the ministry. A graduate of Columbia Law School, Williams chose to give up his law practice to assume the pulpit of his esteemed father, William R. Williams, at the Amity Baptist Church, also located just blocks away from Second German.

Williams shared his father's passion for the development of personal spirituality that displayed a deep interest in the resources and practices stemming from both Catholic and Protestant sources. At the same time, Williams's friendship appears to have pushed Rauschenbusch into a more detailed investigation into matters of social reform. While Williams shared Rauschenbusch's fondness for George, he brought to his friend's attention the work of an individual who became another institutional catalyst for the social gospel in its early years: Richard Ely. Years later, Rauschenbusch cited Ely, along with Gladden and Strong, as the third major pioneer of American social Christianity before 1900. Seven years older than Rauschenbusch, and a friend and classmate of Williams at Columbia University, Ely was one of the first Americans of his generation to receive a Ph.D. in economics

25. *Christianizing the Social Order,* 394.

at a German university (Heidelberg). Upon his return to America, Ely embarked on a lengthy career as a professor of economics at Johns Hopkins University and the University of Wisconsin. Ely was a cofounder of the American Economic Association in 1885 (along with Washington Gladden) and he emphasized a theme that would be embraced by many influential economists and sociologists during the late nineteenth and early twentieth centuries: Jesus' message should be utilized to solve the nation's economic problems.

In the years that he lived in New York, Rauschenbusch devoured Ely's books. Although Ely shared Gladden and Strong's suspicion of socialism, he went beyond these two men in his effort to outline concrete proposals for how the spirit of Jesus might translate itself into social reform efforts. A devout Episcopalian, Ely repeatedly affirmed his belief that being a Christian was inseparable from one's "public" identity, and that the task to love one's neighbor was not an abstract concept, but required a reassessment of public values and priorities. Castigating the popularity of social Darwinism associated with British philosopher Herbert Spencer, Ely believed that the teachings of Jesus provided modern Christianity a key toward the development of a just economic order. As he commented in one of his most famous books, *Social Aspects of Christianity,* published in 1889, the nature of Christianity was not just to lead one to the study of theology, but also of sociology, "the science of society."

> The church has in recent years, for the most part, contented herself with repeating platitudes and vague generalities which have disturbed no guilty soul, and thus she has allowed the leadership in social science to slip away from her. It can, then, scarcely excite surprise that communism has become infidel, and socialism materialistic. Has she not, indeed, without any careful examination of their claims hastened to condemn them to please the rich?[26]

By the end of Rauschenbusch's first year in New York, he, Williams, and Schmidt had formed a tightly knit fellowship, centered upon weekly meetings when the three men gathered for study and

26. Quoted in Robert Handy, ed., *The Social Gospel in America* (New York: Oxford University Press, 1966), 189.

prayer. They modeled their fellowship as a modern day "society of Jesus," a term adapted from the sixteenth-century Jesuit movement and from an address given by Leighton Williams's father at Brown University in 1838, when he called upon his audience to emulate those characteristics of piety and scriptural knowledge that would lead to the creation of men who "belong, in the highest sense of the words, to 'the Society of Jesus.'"[27] Rauschenbusch and his new colleagues immersed themselves in the pursuit of this ideal. Not only did they engage each other in the study of Scriptures, but also in various spiritual disciplines of prayer, fasting, and upon occasion, sharing communion. As Williams later described the group's purpose, the friends sought to be "a new society of Jesus," bringing together "the union and combination of Catholic devotion with Protestant faith in the service of Jesus as Lord and Master."[28]

The ascetic proclivities of the three Baptist ministers, while unusual, was certainly not unprecedented in church history — and the three friends knew this. The three men turned to a variety of eclectic sources in Christian tradition for inspiration. They read Augustine's *Confessions* and Thomas à Kempis's fifteenth-century classic *The Imitation of Christ* and were driven by the desire to create a communion that was devoted to a model of Christlike servitude that built upon that book's legacy. More directly, however, the friends were inspired by diverse models of spirituality that came from the legacy of Protestant evangelism in the post-Reformation Church of England. They read the seventeenth-century Puritan classics including Richard Baxter's *The Saint's Everlasting Rest* and John Bunyan's *Pilgrim's Progress.* They were inspired by the life of Anglican clergyman John Wesley, especially the way that Wesley's understanding of Christianity was connected with the promotion of small-group piety that came out of the Methodist revivals in the eighteenth century. It was also in the vein of this tradition that the three men discovered William Arthur.

Soon, however, the reading list of the three friends extended into literature that moved beyond works of theology, exploring writings that fleshed out the relationship between religion and contemporary society. The group was especially inspired by the writings of Giuseppe

27. Hudson, 11-12.
28. Ibid., 13.

Mazzini. A mid-nineteenth-century Italian politician, Mazzini was instrumental in the campaign for Italy's political union in the 1850s and 1860s. His writings on political democracy contained a highly religious tone, and Rauschenbusch took to heart Mazzini's assertion that "the religious element" in all great reform movements was "universal, immortal."[29]

By the time Rauschenbusch entered his second year in New York City in late 1887, the young pastor was undergoing major changes in his beliefs. The close friendships with Joe Gilbert, Ed Hanna, and Munson Ford were fading not only because of the lack of proximity but also because of differences in faith temperament. In spite of the different social worlds in which Williams and Schmidt came from, they shared with Walther a common faith quest that originated from the social context of late nineteenth-century New York.

HEAVEN ON EARTH

By the end of 1887, Rauschenbusch was moving in two different worlds. On one hand there was his fellowship with Schmidt and Williams; on the other hand, there was his primary responsibility as pastor of Second German Baptist. While Rauschenbusch shied away from any preaching on social questions, the theological tenor of his sermons, emphasizing God's love and the responsibilities of his congregants to live Christlike lives, came directly out of his association with his two friends, especially evidenced by the way that Rauschenbusch appears to have been influenced by the sanctification theology of Arthur.

The stark poverty that he observed in his church and in his New York neighborhood had an indelible effect on both his theology and his personality. Increasingly, he was asked to intercede on behalf of parishioners who were confronted with a variety of problems stemming from economic deprivation. On one occasion, he was asked to assist an elderly parishioner who was cast out of a New York hospital due to lack of money, ultimately resulting in the man having a leg amputated. He was called to the homes of his congregation to be with the dying,

29. Quoted in the preface of Ray Stannard Baker, *The Spiritual Unrest* (New York: Frederick A. Stokes Company Publisher, 1910).

and, most difficult for Rauschenbusch, to preside over funerals. In a letter written in March 1887, he noted that he was obsessed with two questions: the spiritual care of his congregation and the social conditions of the city that separated the rich and the poor. "I believe that man is more than a superior kind of swine and that his situation is not very much improved by more food. . . . My real question is, how a man can be made better, what it is that has power over his soul so that his main question would not be, 'What is pleasurable?' but rather, 'What is right?'"[30] At its core, Rauschenbusch's "little society of Jesus" was devoted to this task. By the end of 1887, Rauschenbusch was nurturing a developing social theology that was welded to William Arthur's notion that the power of the Holy Spirit was leading the contemporary church to a new sense of mission in the modern world.

For all the ways he was attracted to Arthur's theology, Rauschenbusch felt alienated from the emotionalism of the American Holiness movement. During a summer vacation in 1887, he traveled to Ocean Grove, New Jersey, to one of the "camp meeting" grounds of the National Camp Meeting Association. Part of the impetus behind the Holiness movement was to reinvigorate the spirit of emotionalism and "white hot" religion that characterized the revivals of the Second Great Awakening earlier in the century. But the atmosphere of Ocean Grove left Rauschenbusch feeling ice cold, commenting that "the engine that whistles too much has no steam left to pull the train."[31] His understanding of sanctification had more in common with John Wesley than many of his nineteenth-century followers, in that Rauschenbusch understood sanctification more as a process of holy living, as opposed to a mark of instantaneous conversion or "second blessing."

By the end of his second year in New York, Rauschenbusch's social convictions had started to find an outlet beyond his small circle of friends through published writings. Rauschenbusch's early ministry coincided with an era when the denominational periodical had reached its height of influence in American culture. In an era before mass secular periodicals, Americans from a variety of backgrounds and social classes often read the news through hundreds of denominational peri-

30. Jaehn, 16.

31. WR, "Impressions of the Northfield Meetings," in *The Christian Inquirer* (August 16, 1888), 3.

odicals. Spearheaded by the Methodist Episcopal Church, which had by 1860 built one of the largest publishing empires in the world, a variety of Protestant, Catholic, and sectarian movements used the press as a means to disseminate their teachings. The Baptists were not far behind the Methodists in publishing tenacity, and by the 1880s, both northern and southern Baptists produced scores of regional periodicals that provided constituents with both denominational news and commentary on subjects ranging from temperance reform to the status of foreign missionary movements. Rauschenbusch's first "theological" publication, an article that dealt with Baptist mission work in Germany, had actually appeared in a Philadelphia Baptist publication while he was still a seminarian. Throughout the 1880s and 1890s, he wrote several articles and book reviews that appeared in both English and German Baptist publications, with much of his early work dealing with matters pertaining to the state of German Baptists in America.[32] Although he had written an unpublished essay in defense of Henry George that he delivered to a Rochester civic group in late 1887, and an essay on "the golden rule of Christ" that appeared in the German Baptist periodical *Der Sendbote* in the spring of 1888, Rauschenbusch's first publication devoted solely to his social passion was an essay that appeared in the August 2, 1888, issue of the New York Baptist periodical *Christian Inquirer* entitled "Beneath the Glitter." The fact that the article was unsigned indicated that its author feared that his views might subject him to possible repercussions from his clergy colleagues, or perhaps from his own parishioners.

"Beneath the Glitter" is a prime example of both the style and social moralism that characterized American social Christianity in its nascent stages in the 1880s and 1890s. Set as a fictitious monologue, the story's narrator gives an account to a passerby of the social misery of New York's poor, a poverty often covered up by the facade of the city's wealth. The style of the essay is an awkward imitation of the literary tradition reflective of Charles Dickens's *Christmas Carol,* in which Rauschenbusch describes the economic misery and personal suffering of the poor, whose lives remain hidden "beneath the glitter" of upscale New York.

32. See Jaehn, 49, for a bibliography of the earliest publications by Rauschenbusch.

> Fine sight, you think? Yes, the stores are bright, people well dressed mostly; they all look busy and happy, as they push by. . . . "The world is not so bad a world as some would like to make it." That's your verdict, is it, from what you see? You'll go and pooh-pooh this talk about want and degradation and the iron law, and all that. . . . Getting mad, am I? Oh, no, only a bit wild. You'd do the same if you had eyes to see.[33]

The moral vignettes that Rauschenbusch paints, including a tailor's daughter who lies home dying of consumption, while the tailor is forced to work late in the night in order to keep his job at a fashionable retail store, and the saga of a poor elderly woman who cannot afford the city's exorbitant rents and witnesses the cycle of poverty pass to her children, reflect the tone of moral indignation of the early social gospel.

> There, do you see that big clothing house on the corner there? Brilliantly lighted; show windows gorgeous; all hum and happiness. But somewhere in that big house there's a little bullet-headed tailor doubled up over the coat he is to alter, and as surely as I know that my hand is pressing your arm, I know too that he is choking down the sobs and trying to keep the water out of his eyes. Why? Because his little girl is going to die tonight and he can't be there. . . . O yes, you can say that: [he] ought to go home, permission or none; but that means throwing up a job that he has been hanging to by his finger nails. And so he has to sew away and let his little girl die three blocks off. When he gets home he can . . . sob over her corpse; what more does he want?[34]

"Beneath the Glitter" anticipated the popularity in the 1890s of the genre of the social gospel novel, in which literary heroes confront the social-economic woes of the day using the rhetorical question, "What would Jesus do?" made famous in Charles Sheldon's 1897 novel, *In His Steps.* The story was certainly a reflection of Rauschen-

33. "Beneath the Glitter," *Christian Inquirer* (August 2, 1888), quoted in Sharpe, 81.

34. Quoted in Sharpe, 81-82.

busch's actual experiences in New York City, and the tone of the story seeks to raise the reader's moral indignation to reach out to the city's poor.

What Rauschenbusch also makes clear in his vignettes, in juxtaposition to the theme sounded by Horatio Alger in his popular stories of that era, was that the poor could not be saved through the virtues of hard work. Despite all of the accoutrements of wealth and economic opportunity, New York was a city teeming in poverty and suffering — a point that the story's main character keeps emphasizing to the passerby. "Exceptional case, you think. Not a bit of it. It's the drop on the crest of the wave, but there are a million other drops underneath it, all hurled along, or that one drop couldn't be so high."[35] At the story's end, as the narrator is launching into yet another tragic vignette, the listener has had enough and clearly wants to hear no more about the suffering of the city's poor. "Do you see the girl in front of . . . got to go, eh? Bored you, didn't I? Yes, guess I am something of a crank on these things. Wish you'd trot around with me for a week; you wouldn't think so highly of things as they are."[36]

While clearly an indication of his social awakening, the publication of "Beneath the Glitter" did not signal Rauschenbusch's abandonment of his inherited evangelicalism. Two weeks after "Beneath the Glitter" appeared, the *Christian Inquirer* published another article by Rauschenbusch, consisting of an "in-the-field" account of his experience at a Dwight Moody revival in Northfield, Massachusetts. Rauschenbusch made plain in his article that his experience at Northfield was far more satisfactory than the one he had at Ocean Grove the previous summer. His article was filled with high praise for Moody and fellow revivalist J. Hudson Taylor, equating the former with the disciple Peter and the latter with John, while relating Moody's enterprise to the best attributes of middle-class Protestant religion. "There is a steady, silent current of feeling here, flowing like the water in a mill-race, which is just as strong between the sessions as during the preaching."[37] The young Baptist minister was taken both by the spirituality of the gathering and the themes of the numerous sessions and sermons

35. Ibid., 82.
36. Ibid.
37. WR, "Impressions of the Northfield Meetings," 3.

he heard, focusing on the work of the Holy Spirit (perhaps he sensed in Moody the spirit of William Arthur). Additionally, Rauschenbusch applauded what he believed was the appropriate social decorum of his two-week experience in Northfield, in juxtaposition to the emotionalism of Ocean Grove. "Indeed, life is wonderfully sweet here," he affirmed to his readers. "The green leaves and the far-away beauty of the Connecticut valley; the rambles through the glen and fields with saintly souls; the lift and rush of the spirit in the great meetings; the absence of wickedness and the simplicity and trustfulness of intercourse; and the constant turning of thoughts on God's truth and Christ's love; surely heaven cannot be very unlike this."[38]

By mid-1888, Rauschenbusch was clearly entering a period of intense theological reformulation. He rarely mentioned social questions in his early sermons, confining himself to questions of individual morality, especially centered upon matters like temperance reform. Yet his social idealism led him to rearticulate some of his earlier liberal theological leanings. At this critical theological crossroads in the spring of 1888, August Rauschenbusch concluded his teaching career at Rochester Theological Seminary and Walther was offered his father's chair in the German department.

Even as Augustus Strong extended this offer to Walther, he expressed concern that the young man's liberal proclivities had not been worked out of his system since his graduation from seminary. The two men apparently exchanged their perspectives on the doctrine of the atonement, and Strong worried that Rauschenbusch did not give enough credence to the power of the cross to forgive sinners.[39] Whatever worries Strong had about Rauschenbusch's orthodoxy, it did not deter him or his faculty colleagues from extending an invitation to the young man to join the faculty. Rauschenbusch was flattered by Strong's offer. However, with church membership expanding, and with serious conversation underway to consider the possibility of building a new church, Rauschenbusch felt no desire to move from the city, nor dissolve the bonds of Christian fellowship with his two friends, Schmidt and Williams.

By the fall of 1888, Rauschenbusch was finding success in both

38. WR, "Impressions of the Northfield Meetings," 3.

39. See, for example, WR to Strong, April 25, 1888, box 23.

his parish ministry and a growing clarity in his social vision, spurred on by his friendship with Schmidt and Williams. The next four years of Rauschenbusch's ministry inspired him in his theological quest, yet also left him with doubts concerning his role in building the kingdom of God in America.

4 Social Salvation

Between 1886 and 1892, Walther Rauschenbusch went through a profound change in his identity as a Christian. In part, this transformation was intellectual. While he did not completely renounce the faith of his parents, his reading list was peppered with an eclectic assortment of books that took up matters of Christianity and contemporary social problems. He read many sources on British socialism, including the works of the Fabian socialists, Sidney and Beatrice Webb. He was captivated by Edward Bellamy's 1888 utopian novel, *Looking Backward,* which depicted a twenty-first-century society of social equality, free of the sins of wealth and poverty. He was inspired by the evangelical piety of William Booth's book *In Darkest England* and the social commentary of Jacob Riis's famous 1890 expose *How the Other Half Lives,* which depicted the social misery of urban tenement poverty in New York. He also read the works of Karl Marx and Frederick Engels, and was compelled by the social analysis of the two men despite their hostility toward Christianity. He also absorbed numerous volumes by John Ruskin, a prominent nineteenth-century English fine arts critic, whose writings welded together aesthetic romanticism and Christian morality.[1]

1. These sources are taken directly from a reading list on social Christianity that Rauschenbusch composed around 1900. Box 90.

As much as he borrowed his ideas from a variety of thinkers, Rauschenbusch's intellect and imagination was taken over not by an author or a book, but by an ideal: the kingdom of God. His father had taught him that the ideals of Christianity were not perpetuated through the ecclesiastical perpetuation of the church, but in the way that the church manifested itself as a godly assembly of the converted, living in the midst of a sinful world. By 1892, Walther Rauschenbusch had taken this heritage and used it to craft a new vision of the kingdom — a view far less sectarian than his father's — that made the quest for the kingdom of God the primary purpose for living as a Christian disciple. It would be a nine-month sojourn in his ancestral homeland that enabled Rauschenbusch to hone his theological conceptualization of the kingdom.

THE CONSEQUENCES OF SERVANTHOOD

At the same time that Rauschenbusch was singing the praises of Dwight Moody, he had discovered another outlet to express his views on matters dealing with religion: the Baptist Congress. Founded in 1882, the Baptist Congress was an organizational link for Baptist constituencies throughout the Northeast and Midwest, serving as a forum for Baptist leaders to address a host of questions concerning the faith and life of Baptists in the United States. Beginning in 1888, and extending over the next several years, Rauschenbusch, along with his colleagues Leighton Williams and Nathaniel Schmidt, became regular fixtures at meetings of the Baptist Congress, using these meetings as an opportunity to air their ideas to a wider national audience. Additionally, Rauschenbusch spoke regularly at various Baptist association meetings throughout New York state and contributed to a number of projects related to the larger mission of German Baptists in America. He covered many themes in his addresses, from higher education, to the role of Baptists in America's future, to the virtues of American democracy, to the church and social questions.

The tone of Rauschenbusch's early speeches and writings was not atypical of other Protestant leaders of his era. Like Josiah Strong, Rauschenbusch believed that the virtues of Western Protestantism represented the highest standards of religious and cultural advancement, and like most Protestants he held a deep-seated suspicion of the Roman Catholic presence in America. In an address to the Southern New York Baptist Association in October 1888, he castigated Catholic parochial schools for not giving a balanced education that would prepare future leaders in the nation. Articulating a theme that would become the cornerstone of his later theology, Rauschenbusch argued that the great gift of the country's Protestant churches was to build up American democracy. "The Gospel of Christ means life, light, liberty, knowledge, and where the people are too ignorant to educate themselves, those who bear the Gospel must do it for them."[2] Significantly, Rauschenbusch cast his eye toward the problems of racial inequality in the American south in the same address, calling upon churches to fund denominational schools to educate impoverished African-Americans. He asserted, "when unjust laws or the inequality of social conditions in a civilized people has deprived some classes of the educational facilities to which they are theoretically entitled, organized Christianity feels bound to enter the breach and to make up for the sins of the body politic. So the secular education of the colored people in the South and the industrial training of the poor in our manufacturing cities are rightly regarded as eminently proper functions of Christian organizations."[3]

The most common critique leveled against the major proponents of the social gospel has been their astigmatism on the issue of race, and in many respects that critique is justified. Like most white, middle-class social reformers of his generation, Rauschenbusch largely saw the question of race as a southern problem, and only later in his career did he work directly with African-Americans as students in Rochester and in his lectures in the south. At the same time, Rauschenbusch's vision of the church's role in building up the fiber of democratic society early in his ministry was not confined only to the educated white middle class: "And whenever a fuller justice and wider humanity shall have secured for all, black and white, poor and rich, the actual opportunity, as well as the theoretical right, to develope *[sic]* whatever is in them; whenever the State and civil community shall do for them fully

2. WR, address to Southern N.Y. Baptist Association, unpublished manuscript, October 10, 1888, box 17.

3. Ibid.

and ably, what individual Christians are now feebly striving to do, then the Christian church may lay down that work and go forth in quest of other wrongs to be righted."[4]

Despite the social passion that emanated from his speeches and early writings, Rauschenbusch's social and theological moorings were still in a state of flux. Although he hoped that his involvement in the Baptist Congress would enable him to gain a hearing on social questions, his pastoral ministry treaded lightly on the general topic of social Christianity. Most of his social sermons were on the evils of intemperance and included prophecies that the closing of the city's saloons would result in the uplifting of individual virtue and character.[5] He preached mostly in German, although he did occasionally preach in English for the church's Sunday evening worship service.[6] He also promoted the ministry of German Baptist pastors in America through periodic speaking appearances in English-speaking Baptist churches in New York. By the second anniversary of his New York ministry, Rauschenbusch was clearly relishing both his work and the independence of living in that city. As he joked to a friend about his lack of housekeeping skills, "I am piling all the dirty [dishes] in a big pan and when my mother comes, she will find the accumulations of centuries. But you haven't any idea how nice it is to be your own master."[7]

Yet Rauschenbusch's mood was also clouded by the realization that he was losing his hearing. Beginning in his seminary years in Rochester, he experienced some difficulty with his hearing. At the time of this early hearing loss, he was well aware of his family's history of deafness, and he recalled his boyhood visits to his grandmother in Germany, who could communicate only through writing. During his first summer in New York, he had minor ear surgery, which only worsened his condition. In successive years, Rauschenbusch continued to lose his hearing, although he was often able to mask it to his congregation and his friends. But the strain of his pasto-

4. Ibid.

5. See, for example, sermon on August 19, 1888, sermon book 11, box 150.

6. The assessment that the majority of Rauschenbusch's sermons were in German is the judgment of Minus, 208 (note 12) and Heinz D. Rossol, "Walter Rauschenbusch as Preacher: The Development of His Social Thought as Expressed in His Sermons from 1886 to 1897"; see especially chapter 4.

7. WR to "Mrs. Munger," June 23, 1888, box 50.

ral responsibilities took its toll on his physical health and ultimately his hearing. During the winter of 1888, in which many poor froze to death in the streets of New York, Rauschenbusch became ill and was confined to a sickbed for several weeks. This illness further exacerbated his hearing loss.

Rauschenbusch never became totally deaf. Yet with the passing of years, he reached a point where it was impossible for him to hear unless he stood directly in front of people. What also distressed him was that he lost the ability to pick up on the nuances of daily life, the ability to interpret social gatherings in ways that hearing people took for granted. Church meetings became more strenuous for him, and even preaching was made difficult due to his inability to adequately assess the inflection and tone of his voice.

His deafness had a profound impact not only on his pastoral ministry, but on his social outlook. By the late 1880s, he had discovered the writings of Leo Tolstoy, and was especially compelled by his book *My Religion.* The great Russian author's Christian asceticism, which emphasized a radical sectarian separation from the corruption of society, resonated with Rauschenbusch's own Anabaptist and sanctification beliefs. Tolstoy's new interpretation of the Sermon on the Mount, and the radical obligation that Christians had to put Jesus' teachings into practice, further piqued Rauschenbusch's belief (learned from Henry George) that men who lived by the comforts of unearned wealth were in direct violation of the teachings of Jesus. By the end of the 1880s, Russell Conwell, a prominent Baptist minister in Philadelphia, picked up where Henry Ward Beecher had left off, by articulating a therapeutic gospel to the American middle class. Conwell's "acres of diamonds" sermon became one of the most popular addresses of the late nineteenth century and was widely reprinted and spawned a genre of therapeutic Christianity that boomed in the twentieth century. For Conwell, and for future generations of Protestant preachers who followed his example, Christianity represented the key to a prosperous life, with the message of Jesus justifying the individual acquisition of wealth as a form of good Christian stewardship. For Rauschenbusch, however, such beliefs were anathema to the intent of Christianity. He believed that the message of Jesus was leading men not to a life of comfort, but as Tolstoy described, to a demand that a Christian embrace an existence of voluntary self-sacrifice.

By the spring of 1889, Rauschenbusch's sermons began to hint at his burgeoning social awakening. In a sermon from May 1889, Rauschenbusch echoed themes that were hinted at in his "Beneath the Glitter" article, attacking the rich for their "vainglory" and castigating Christians for obscuring their faith through ritual and doctrine, as opposed to seeking justice. The same sermon also made reference to the problem of American racism, denouncing what he saw as Christianity's caste system, where a "white man [was] treated one way and [a] black man another."[8]

What increasingly marked Rauschenbusch's sermons was his emphasis on vicarious suffering. For centuries Christian thinkers had dwelt on the theme of human suffering, and the relationship of suffering to the doctrine of the atonement. A generation earlier, Horace Bushnell sought to modify this doctrine by emphasizing the way that an individual's suffering was analogous to Christ's sacrificial death on the cross. Although most late nineteenth-century liberals ignored the fine points of Bushnell's atonement theory, he bequeathed to the liberal tradition a belief that suffering, in some form, served as a vehicle toward ultimate redemption and reconciliation through Christ. This emphasis would gradually emerge in the social gospel movement by the early twentieth century, and Rauschenbusch was in the vanguard of a generation that took this theme to heart, believing that a just society would emerge largely through personal sacrifice and, if necessary, death. As he noted in a sermon, "justice never shines so brightly as when [there is] suffering."[9] A later generation of neo-orthodox theologians, such as H. Richard Niebuhr, attacked components of the liberal theological tradition for removing the themes of divine judgment and human suffering from their theology.[10] For Rauschenbusch, however, these themes were central to his theological imperative to work for the kingdom of God.

For all of Rauschenbusch's fascination with the asceticism of Tolstoy, he recognized the practical realities that faced him as a pastor. Second German as a congregation had its share of parishioners who quali-

8. Sermon preached May 12, 1889, sermon book 14, box 150.

9. Ibid.

10. See H. Richard Niebuhr, *The Kingdom of God in America* (New York: Harper, 1937).

fied by the standards of their day as "working poor." However the church also had a number of parishioners who had risen to levels of social respectability in the German immigrant community. Within the larger German community of his neighborhood, Rauschenbusch befriended grocers, merchants, carpenters, and small-business proprietors, individuals he would rely on in various ways to support his ministry. Ultimately, his vision of Christian social reform would not lead him to renounce the material world like Tolstoy, but to embrace with growing frequency the cultural worlds of the middle and upper classes.

The growth of Second German under Rauschenbusch was hardly meteoric. But the success that Rauschenbusch had with building up worship and Sunday school attendance inspired the congregation and their pastor to look to the building of a new sanctuary. Initially, the church had discussed the possibility of building an addition to the existing church, but it ultimately opted to sell the old church and purchase a lot on 43rd Street near 9th Avenue.[11] Rauschenbusch took on the chief role of fund-raising and his efforts in this direction enabled him to gain the confidence of one of America's most powerful men, John D. Rockefeller. Rauschenbusch originally met Rockefeller in Rochester years earlier, where Rockefeller served as a major financial benefactor to the seminary. In April 1889, Rauschenbusch renewed his acquaintance with him at the wedding of Rockefeller's daughter, Bessie, to Rauschenbusch's old friend, Charles Strong.

Strong must have been shocked to see the physical changes in Rauschenbusch's appearance. In addition to his hearing loss, he had lost a great deal of weight since he left Rochester and he also had grown a beard, giving him the appearance of many of the working-class men in his congregation. "My full beard has grown to be a permanent institution of this land, because I do not want to become a martyr of the barbershop like a modern," he joked earlier to a friend.[12]

Soon after the wedding, Rauschenbusch made his first pitch to Rockefeller for financial assistance toward building a new sanctuary. Rockefeller was quick to respond that he could make no promises, but would consider the request. Undaunted, Rauschenbusch was able to convince Rockefeller in a matter of months to provide an $8,000 grant

11. Jaehn, 25; Minus, 59-60.
12. Jaehn, 21.

toward the new building. Showing strong administrative acumen, Rauschenbusch secured an additional $8,000 from the Baptist City Mission of New York. The final $11,000 came from the sale of the old building; the congregation broke ground on the building in October 1889, and in April 1890 the new church was dedicated.[13]

The paradox that developed between Rauschenbusch's growing social vision and his patronage of a rich benefactor like John Rockefeller was not an anomaly. Indeed, the dawning of the Progressive Era in the 1880s witnessed the launching of numerous reform initiatives that often were financed through the wallets of the rich. Social gospel leaders like Washington Gladden and Rauschenbusch sought to appeal to the consciences of the rich, in hopes that their hearts would be moved to change their views. By the second decade of the twentieth century, part of the success of the social gospel was the coalition that existed between middle-class liberal clergy, leaders in higher education, and a small but significant number of business leaders who helped finance the growth of what historians would call "the Protestant establishment." As Protestant churches were dividing along theological lines by the early twentieth century, liberal Protestants, for better or worse, became increasingly identified with the interest of preserving the values of middle-class Christianity. As opposed to the growing premillennialist movement, liberals sought the "perfecting" of the social order through the expansion of higher education, civic improvement projects, and the creation of charitable endowments. Business leaders who supported these projects felt they were playing their role to promote the victory for a long-standing Protestant vision to Christianize America, symbolized by the hope shared by Protestant clergy and laity alike that America would one day be a land in which all (Protestant) churches were united.[14] It was not until the aftermath of World War I that increasing radicalism among certain Protestant leaders brought this alliance to an end. Yet the remnant of this alliance extended well into the twentieth century,

13. Ibid., 25.

14. See, for example, William R. Hutchison, ed., *Between the Times: The Travail of the Protestant Establishment in America, 1900-1960* (Cambridge: Cambridge University Press, 1989); see especially chapter 1; Conrad Cherry, *Hurrying to Zion: Universities, Divinity Schools, and American Protestants* (Bloomington: Indiana University Press, 1995).

epitomized by the patronage of John Rockefeller's son, John Rockefeller, Jr., in the building of Riverside Church in New York, the pulpit of the famed social gospel liberal Harry Emerson Fosdick.

Amidst his activities in pursuit of a new church building, Rauschenbusch was surprised to receive yet another offer from Augustus Strong to join the German department at Rochester Theological Seminary in the fall of 1889. Rauschenbusch again declined the offer. In his correspondence with Rauschenbusch over the offer, Strong made evident his fondness for Rauschenbusch, at the same time that he expressed concern for the direction of the young man's theology. He chided Rauschenbusch to be wary of the claims of so-called "Christian socialists," asserting, "there are some panaceas for human ills which are not the gospel, but a substitute for the gospels. Let us beware of them, while we at the same time work for the Kingdom in Christ's way and in Paul's way."[15]

From his own perspective, Rauschenbusch was far from turning his back on the great Protestant tradition of American evangelicalism. One of the aspects that Rauschenbusch loved about his experience at the Northfield Conference was the revivalistic singing. After his return from that summer conference, he collaborated with a Baptist colleague on a hymnal translation to be used for German Baptist congregations in the city. In late 1889, Rauschenbusch approached Ira Sankey, Dwight Moody's famed revivalist companion, about the possibility of the two men working on a collaborative German hymnal project, directed not only for German Baptists in America but also to meet the need of the growing Baptist movement in Germany. Sankey agreed to work with Rauschenbusch as a partner-consultant on the project and the result was two hymnals under the title *Evangeliums-Lieder,* the first published in 1891 and the second in 1895. The volumes contained German translations of numerous popular hymns, including "Onward Christian Soldiers," "What a Friend We Have in Jesus," "Joy to the World," and "Rock of Ages," translated by Rauschenbusch and other German-American Baptist colleagues.[16] Whatever theological differences existed between the two men were not readily apparent from their correspondence. Sankey not only agreed to allow Rauschenbusch

15. Augustus Strong to WR, October 18, 1889, box 23.

16. See Minus, 57, and WR to L. H. Biglow, January 10, 1895, box 93.

to receive the full copyright royalties for the hymnals, a financial windfall much appreciated by the young pastor, but he emphasized to the young man the importance of using simple language in order that the hymnals attract the widest possible audience.[17] Rauschenbusch's passion for hymnody would be a lifelong love, and as he would later argue, if the social gospel was to succeed, it needed to produce hymns of the same quality and simple character as those embodied in the earlier tradition of nineteenth-century evangelical revivalism.

FOR THE RIGHT

At the same time he was planning to launch his German hymnal project, two other events occurred that impacted his future. The first was in October 1889, when the inaugural issue of a small monthly newspaper, *For the Right,* was published. *For the Right* was the brainchild of Rauschenbusch and Leighton Williams, who had for months conceived of the idea of starting a citywide publication with the goal of reaching the city's working class with their vision of Christian social reform. The two men, already close friends, developed an even tighter bond during the year when their third comrade, Nathaniel Schmidt, accepted a teaching position at his alma mater at Hamilton Theological Seminary by the end of 1888. In May 1889, Rauschenbusch and Schmidt attended a conference in Boston where they met an emerging figure in the social Christian movement, an Episcopal priest named W. D. P. Bliss. Bliss's rising stature in the late 1880s represented a significant development in the history of American social Christianity. Like Rauschenbusch, Bliss was deeply influenced by the tradition of Christian socialism that had emerged earlier in Great Britain, reflected in the work of Anglican clergy like Frederick Denison Maurice. He had been a vigorous supporter in 1887 for the establishment in the Episcopal Church of the Church Association for the Advancement of the Interests of Labor, an organization that called upon the church to seek an active engagement with the interests of American labor. The C.A.A.I.L. appealed to its members to follow a number of practices that would develop the church's sympathy for the working man, including en-

17. See, for example, Ira Sankey to WR, November 22, 1890, box 96.

couraging ministers to preach sermons on labor issues, and that all members should study regularly the issues of the labor movement, "in light of the Incarnation."[18] Over the next ten years, the C.A.A.I.L. spawned several local chapters in cities in the Northeast and set a context for the more radical social vision of Bliss. Along with Richard Ely, he was an influential figure in the establishment in the 1880s within the Episcopal Church of the Christian Social Union, modeled after a parallel movement in the Church of England. In 1889, Bliss through his Boston-based Church of the Carpenter launched the Society of Christian Socialists and a periodical called *The Dawn,* symbolizing the conviction held by Bliss and his followers that America was "awakening to new light upon Social Problems."[19] In 1897, Bliss published a volume with the rather ambitious title *The Encyclopedia of Social Reform* in which he affirmed his debt to the legacy of British Christian Socialism.

Bliss's influence upon Rauschenbusch and upon other social Christian leaders of his generation was extensive. A broad-church Episcopalian, Bliss was not only ecumenical and open to the initiatives of social Christianity from colleagues in other denominations, but he courted a number of different social reformers of that era to his cause including Ely and Edward Bellamy, as well as Frances Willard, the popular president of the Woman's Christian Temperance Union. Under the moniker of "Christian socialism," Bliss not only became one of the more radical proponents of social Christianity, in terms of his calls for a redistribution of wealth, but he helped spread the cause of his gospel in the 1890s through his appearances at the Chautauqua Institute in western New York — perhaps the nation's main staging arena for Progressive Era religious and secular leaders to expose their views to an American middle-class audience. Bliss's impact also nudged Rauschenbusch to embrace the identity of "Christian socialist."

The encounter with Bliss and the apparent success of his publishing endeavor pushed Rauschenbusch and Williams to seek ways to pursue their own social Christian newspaper in New York City. They enlisted the financial backing of some sympathetic New York City pa-

18. See Charles H. Hopkins and Ronald C. White, Jr., eds., *The Social Gospel: Religion and Reform in Changing America* (Philadelphia: Temple University Press, 1976), 71.

19. Ibid.

trons, including Grace Hoadley Dodge, a New York philanthropist who was a devoted follower of Moody and would later become president of the national board of the YWCA.[20] In addition, the two men recruited J. E. Raymond, another New York City Baptist pastor, and Elizabeth Post to serve as co-editors with Rauschenbusch and Williams.[21]

The first issue of *For the Right* opened with the bold claim that the paper was "published in the interests of the working people of New York City. It proposes to discuss, from the standpoint of Christian socialism, such questions as engage their attention and affect their life. . . . The editors freely give their time and labor to this undertaking, animated solely by the hope that their efforts may aid the advancement of that kingdom in which wrong shall have no place, but Right shall reign for ever more."[22] In the eighteen months of its existence, from October 1889 until March 1891, *For the Right* was a periodical that allowed its editors a forum to articulate their vision of Christian social reform. With Williams and Rauschenbusch providing the bulk of the articles and editorials, the paper carried a combination of news and commentary on contemporary social issues, as well as lifestyle advice for working-class immigrant families. The centerpiece of the periodical, however, was its straightforward pitch of a vision for a Christian socialist society. In the April 1890 issue, the editors published a "Declaration of Principles of the Christian Socialist Society," in which they stated their convictions that the ethical principles of Jesus needed to be applied to society "so that our industrial relationships may be humanized, our economic system be moralized, justice pervade legislation, and the State grown into a true commonwealth."[23] The editorial, however, was quick to point out that the nature of what constituted Christian socialism was not specific to a particular economic doctrine, but to a way of life. "We are concerned with principle, not with methods," the editorial noted. "We believe that whatever better social order is coming in on the earth will come as an evolution. We are evolutionists, not revolutionists."[24] The periodical emphasized the necessity for

20. Hudson, 20.

21. The identity of Elizabeth Post remains a bit of a mystery. Hudson conjectures that she was the sister of Louis Freeland Post, a prominent journalist and social reformer of that era. See Hudson, 19.

22. Sharpe, 86.

23. *For the Right* (April 1890); cited in Sharpe, 91.

clergy to assume the task of educating their congregations on social issues, through the pulpit and classroom, and summoned churches to work for specific reform measures, including "shorter hours of labor, improved conditions of labor and laborers' homes, the identification of the interests of the employee and employer, more equitable taxation, control or ownership by the city and state of natural monopolies, the reassertion of the underlying right of the commonwealth over the land in the interests of the people at large."[25]

Prior to the first issue of *For the Right* in the fall of 1889, Rauschenbusch's life took another fateful turn. During his first three years in New York, he found little time for female companionship. While attending a German Baptist convention in Milwaukee in September 1889, however, he met a woman who would change his life: Pauline Rother. Three years younger than Rauschenbusch, the young schoolteacher had emigrated to the United States from Prussia after her father's death, when she was a girl. Rauschenbusch was clearly taken by the charm of the young woman, but was also likely drawn to her by her enthusiasm and support for his ideas. Pauline had a well-established reputation in her family for her independent spirit and strong will. As a school teacher, the young woman was known to defy social convention by allowing her classes to play outside on rainy days. "On fine days, she would sometimes tell her pupils to fetch their caps and hats and would conduct her classes — not in the school-room — but in a near-by city park."[26] Pauline was engaged to another man and a courtship between her and Walther seemed out of the question. Over the next year, however, the two met again when Rauschenbusch returned to Milwaukee for a meeting and a relationship, platonic at first, ensued.

It is likely, however, that for much of 1890, Rauschenbusch was thinking more of his New York activities as opposed to a possible courtship with Pauline. Although he wrote several articles for both German and English church periodicals, the bulk of his attention was as a writer/editor for his new "people's paper." Rauschenbusch's writing in *For The Right* reflects on how many of his theological convic-

24. Ibid., 91.

25. Sharpe, 92.

26. Biographical sketch by Winifred [Rauschenbusch] Rorty (no date), box 143.

tions on social salvation were coming together. Quoting William Arthur's *Tongue of Fire* in the August 1890 issue: "The most dangerous perversion of the Gospel, viewed as affecting individuals, is when it is looked upon as a salvation for the soul after it leaves the body, but not salvation from sin while here. . . . Nothing short of the general renewal of society ought to satisfy any soldier of Christ."[27] In the same issue, he elaborated on Arthur's words:

> [We] believe that every individual soul ought voluntarily to subject itself to the law of God and obey it because it loves it. . . . On the other hand, we differ from many Christian men and women in our insistence on good institutions. They believe that if only men are personally converted, wrong and injustice will gradually disappear from the construction of society. It does not appear so to us. . . . Special work and hard work has to be done in pointing out a social wrong and thinking out its remedy, before the righteous purposes of a community can be brought to bear upon it. This is essentially a function of those who profess to know and love God's will, and we raise the charge of negligence and sloth against the church of God in suffering injustice to be incorporated in the very construction of society.[28]

For all of its good intentions to reach out to the city's working class, and despite the fact that in some of the paper's columns, including an editorial published in defense of Native American land rights, the paper was ahead of its time, *For the Right* was too erudite and patronizing to attract a wide readership. Elizabeth Post's monthly columns instructed working-class women on how to emulate the lifestyles of middle-class American homes, and oftentimes Rauschenbusch and the other editors penned narratives in the form of children's short stories to advocate a particular measure like the single tax.[29] There was also dissension among the staff of *For the Right* in terms of what specific measures of reform should be advocated. Post withdrew from the paper because of what she saw as the increasing radicalism of her col-

27. *For the Right* (August 1890), cited in Hudson, 62.
28. Hudson, 60.
29. Ibid., 20.

leagues, and by the end of 1890, with fewer than 200 subscriptions sold, and with the periodical's financial backing dried up, the paper's days were numbered.

The death of *For the Right* was likely sealed before its first issue. By 1890, the American labor union movement was beginning to pick up momentum. Under the leadership of Samuel Gompers, the American Federation of Labor began to form an alliance among immigrants and various American intellectuals and the small number of political socialists in the country. Gompers was typical of many labor leaders who, while sympathetic to the ethical dimensions of Christianity, were contemptuous of how churches hypocritically preached the golden rule on Sunday and proceeded to oppress and exploit workers for the balance of the week. John Swinton, a socialist journalist of that period and a strong advocate for union rights, noted in an 1885 article in the *Independent* that although many clergy were now beginning to preach on social issues in their pulpits, "few of them appear to know anything about it."[30] While liberal clergy like Washington Gladden were respected by some labor advocates, they tended to be seen by many more as advocates of an older economic caste system, whose social solutions made the "golden rule" a mockery of the demands for worker's rights and economic redistribution. Henry George, one of the most famous political advocates for the cause of American labor in the late nineteenth century, did not share this negative view of the clergy. But even he acknowledged that often clergy focused their attention too exclusively on a gospel of kindness and generosity that made light of the just demands of American labor. "Kindness, generosity, none of these amiable virtues can narrow that widening gulf between the rich and the poor. What is needed is something higher, and something that must come first. What is needed is justice."[31]

Rauschenbusch would have agreed wholeheartedly with George's assessment. Yet few readers could hear that message through the often patronizing tone of *For the Right.* At the same time Rauschenbusch was clear in its pages that the goal of Christianity was to create a society in which all people, regardless of wealth, were equal. "Political

30. Henry May, *Protestant Churches and Industrial America* (rev. ed., New York: Harper, 1967), 219.

31. Ibid., 220.

freedom is only the means towards the real end," he noted in September 1890. "The real end is the abolition of class privilege and the establishment of social equality. Political liberty is ours and should be used to secure social equality."[32] By the time the final issue of *For the Right* was published in March 1891, however, Rauschenbusch had left New York. In this time of transition in his career he had decided to return to his ancestral home.

A SECOND CONVERSION EXPERIENCE

By the end of 1890, Rauschenbusch realized that his hearing loss was impeding his ability to fulfill all of his obligations as a pastor. To a stunned congregation, he announced in January 1891 his resignation from the church. He had contemplated taking up another form of ministry, leaning toward the possibility of a career as a writer. But first, Rauschenbusch wanted to travel to Germany where he could reconnect with his family, yet also partake of the intellectual waters of his ancestral home. In the back of his mind also was the hope that German physicians might assist him in finding some cure for his hearing loss. Rauschenbusch was equally stunned and moved when the church not only refused his resignation, but offered to contribute toward the expenses of his travels, plus pay an interim pastor in his absence.

Rauschenbusch's nine-month sojourn in Europe between March and December 1891 was an intellectual and spiritual oasis for the worn-out preacher. While his efforts to track down a cure for his hearing loss were unsuccessful, the trip jelled his growing social convictions around one central theological concept: the kingdom of God.

In the first year of his New York pastorate, most likely in the spring of 1887, Rauschenbusch attended a rally in New York in support of Henry George's "single tax" crusade. Speaking in support of George's measure was a prominent New York Roman Catholic priest, Father Edward McGlynn. In spite of Rauschenbusch's deep-seated and lifelong suspicion of all things Catholic, he was struck by how McGlynn tied his Christian faith to matters of economic reform. At the conclusion of his speech, the priest proclaimed the words of the Lord's Prayer in a fashion

32. Sharpe, 93.

that applied the prayer's meaning to contemporary society. "Thy kingdom come! Thy will be done on earth." As Rauschenbusch later recalled, the words lifted him, if not the audience, out of his seat.[33]

Rauschenbusch was not the only Protestant leader of his generation to pick up on the theme of the kingdom of God and tie its social significance to the Lord's Prayer. As the social gospel grew as a movement in the 1880s and 1890s, increasingly Protestant leaders used the language of the kingdom of God to describe their vision of a just society. Yet Rauschenbusch's fixation on this doctrine would have far-reaching consequence for the development of the social gospel in America. On one hand, Rauschenbusch's conception of the kingdom doctrine was tied to the Anabaptist/Baptist heritage of his father. Yet his vision of the kingdom of God was also a distinctively American vision, rooted both in a deep-seated tradition of evangelical postmillennialism and in the way that he increasingly tied the legacy of America's churches to the specific genius of the Baptist people. As he ruminated on the significance of Father McGlynn's words, he increasingly made reference to the kingdom of God in various addresses delivered in the period between 1888 and 1889. In the spring of 1889, Rauschenbusch brought these ideas to bear in several of his sermons at Second German. In language echoing many of the sentiments of Josiah Strong in *Our Country,* Rauschenbusch proclaimed that God had reserved for America a special mission to the world, and at the center of that mission was the realization of the kingdom of God. "The leaven is the Kingdom. It is not in Heaven but it is here."[34] His words to his congregation reflect a distinctive twist on a classic American Protestant postmillennialism: "the best way to get the self ready for Heaven . . . is to get this world ready for God."[35]

Sometime during this period, perhaps as early as the fall of 1889, Rauschenbusch began to contemplate writing an extended manuscript that would set forth his views on the church and the kingdom of God. His nine months in Europe provided him with the intellectual founda-

33. Rauschenbusch attributed this speech to a rally held for George in the fall of 1886. However, Jaehn notes that the first time McGlynn evoked the Lord's Prayer address on George's behalf was in the spring of 1887. See Jaehn, 15.

34. Max L. Stackhouse, "The Formation of a Prophet: Reflections on the Early Sermons of Walter Rauschenbusch," in *Andover Newton Quarterly* (January 1969): 153.

35. Ibid., 153.

tion to articulate in writing what he already came to believe through his pastoral experiences in New York. Rauschenbusch's anticipation in heading to Europe was heightened by the joy of traveling with his sister, Emma. The two reunited after Emma had spent several years as a missionary teacher in India. Having studied at Wellesley College upon her return, she too found herself at a transitional point in her life.

Before heading to Germany, the two planned to travel through England. Eight years earlier, Rauschenbusch had largely bypassed extended travel in that country. Now he put his reservations about English society (and the Church of England) aside in an effort to learn more about Anglican socialism and other forms of British social Christianity. While in England, Rauschenbusch visited Liverpool, Birmingham, and London. He was especially impressed by the "municipal socialism" of Birmingham, a city in which all gas and water systems were municipally controlled and in which the schools provided free meals for children.[36] In London, he was fascinated by the work of the Salvation Army and admired greatly General William Booth's recent book, *In Darkest England*, as well as the Toynbee Hall settlement house. Not surprisingly, however, Rauschenbusch was left cold by the sacramental formality of the Church of England, and while he always claimed a great debt to Anglican socialists like Robertson and Maurice, it appears that Rauschenbusch did not attempt to contact any Christian socialist leaders in the Church of England. In many ways, the time in London had more of a dramatic impact on Emma than on her brother. Not only did she have a chance to reunite with her ecclesiastical supervisor, John Clough, whom she would marry within the next couple of years, but during her stay, she became fascinated with the work of Mary Wollstonecraft, the eighteenth-century British feminist. Emma was destined to return to missionary service in India. In the interim, however, she earned a doctorate at the University of Bern, becoming one of the first women in Europe or North America to receive a Ph.D.

In May, Emma and Walther made their way to Germany, where they first were reunited with Frida and her husband Georg Fetzer. This reunion boiled over in tension, brought on by the acrimonious relationship between Emma and her parents that had carried over since

36. Minus, 72.

her teen years in Rochester. Eventually Walther escaped the family turmoil and made his way to Berlin to consult medical physicians, but also to immerse himself in the library of the great German university, where his father studied and had received his intellectual grounding in the kingdom of God. Although left depressed by word that his hearing loss was likely permanent, he thrived in the intellectual atmosphere of the city. It was in the context of his intellectual pilgrimage that summer that he directly encountered the liberal theology of Albrecht Ritschl. The great German theologian had died two years earlier, but his stature as a theologian had already nurtured an intellectual movement that was sweeping Germany. In the same vein as Friedrich Schleiermacher and Johann Neander, Ritschl stressed the imperative that the importance of Christianity was experiential; however, he differed from his predecessors in the emphasis he placed on the doctrine of the kingdom of God. For Ritschl and his theological disciples, the kingdom of God was not merely an eschatological hope, an apocalyptic expectation that God would do away with the world. Rather, Ritschl emphasized that Jesus' imperative for the kingdom was social and grounded in the fabric of history.

Ritschl's influence spawned a distinctive school of German theological liberalism, reflected in the work of theologians such as Julius Kaftan, sociologist Albert Schäffle, and biblical scholars such as Bernard Weiss. While the work of these disparate scholars was characterized by different emphases, they were tied together by a common view that Christianity was a historical religion, and the way to understand the development of Christian theology since the time of the apostles was through historical study.

Rauschenbusch would be counted by later scholars as a Ritschlian disciple. There were, however, dimensions of Ritschl's thought and his German disciples that Rauschenbusch found wanting. In particular, he found in Ritschl a social conservatism that seemed antithetical to Jesus' teachings on the kingdom. Indeed, Rauschenbusch was dismayed that the intense nationalism of many of his conservative mentors at Gütersloh was echoed by the liberals as well! While in Berlin, Rauschenbusch was also disturbed by what he saw as the limits of German Christian socialism to stave off Germany's nationalist tide. Although he greatly admired and would later cite in his writings the work of the German Christian socialist pastor, Adolf Stöcker, he was distressed by Stöcker's anti-Semitism and pursued only one unsuccessful effort to contact him.[37]

Rauschenbusch never became a formal theologian in the model exemplified by nineteenth-century German liberals like Ritschl. However, what he gained from his time in Germany was a renewed appreciation for examining the connection between the early church and the kingdom of God. A burning question for him was simply: why did the church over time forgo its commitment to Jesus' gospel teachings on the kingdom of God? Over the next twenty years of his life, Rauschenbusch would forge an intellectual affinity with a German scholar who wrestled with the same question in his work: Adolf von Harnack. Harnack's work redefined the historical interpretation of Western Christianity for many theological liberals of Rauschenbusch's generation. Like Ritschl, Harnack emphasized the early church's reliance on the doctrine of the kingdom of God and the ongoing significance of that doctrine to the life of the church. Even more than Ritschl, Harnack stressed that what defined the theological significance of the church was not how it served as a repository for ancient doctrines, but how the church from generation to generation kept alive the timeless message of Jesus Christ. Rauschenbusch's embrace of German historical and theological scholarship was not without criticism. Over the years, he would bemoan the political conservatism and individualistic focus of much German theological scholarship, and when he prepared a reading list on social Christianity in the early 1900s, references to German scholars are scant.[38] At the same time, Rauschenbusch's later writing would display a strong debt to Ritschlian liberalism, especially evident in the way that his work over the next decade led him to the discipline of history as the primary means by which to recover the biblical and theological significance of early Christianity.

By far the major result of his travels was the writing of a massive manuscript that he likely completed while staying in Berlin during the summer of 1891. He gave the manuscript the awkward working title "Christianity Revolutionary,"[39] and in hundreds of handwritten pages

37. Minus, 78.

38. Rauschenbusch-penned bibliography, c. 1900, box 90.

39. Numerous scholars have cited this work under the title, "Revolutionary Christianity." However, Rauschenbusch used the title "Christianity Revolutionary," an indication that this was a work in progress. See materials in box 101.

he articulated his beliefs on how the contemporary church needed to reconnect itself with the revolutionary teachings of the kingdom of God. The theme of the manuscript was well summarized by the book's first sentence: "Christianity is in its nature revolutionary."[40] He explained that the significance of Jesus' ministry was in line with the prophetic mission of the Old Testament prophets, who had proclaimed a judgment on the social and political practices of ancient Israel. The first of seven sections outlined his proposition about the revolutionary aspect of Jesus' radicalism. The second, third, and fourth sections focused on an analysis of Jesus' social teachings, read in light of the Old Testament prophets. The final sections highlight how the revolutionary significance of Jesus' ideals was historically lost and comments on ways that the contemporary church might reclaim the revolutionary significance of the kingdom's power. The organization of the manuscript was loose. On many occasions, Rauschenbusch's style lapsed into the same editorial argumentation that characterized his writing in *For the Right,* with his biblical exegesis at some points secondary to his desire to offer commentary on the contemporary significance of particular biblical themes. Yet the manuscript contained an unfiltered, passionate writing style that characterized many of his later works.

Rauschenbusch began the work by sifting through a number of biblical texts from the Old Testament that highlighted the nature of Jesus' social ministry. Like other liberals of his generation, he cast the nature of Jesus' ministry in historical terms: Jesus represented the fulfillment of messianic prophesy, a radical redistribution of political and social power. "Jesus knew very well the difficulties of the work he had undertaken," Rauschenbusch noted. "He knew that those who have seats at the banquet where the old wine is served have little taste for the new. He knew that those who hold the places of power and privilege will seldom resign them without a struggle."[41] Significantly, Rauschenbusch's incorporation of German liberalism into his thinking led him to a growing clarity concerning the theological purpose of Jesus' mission. In effect, German liberalism gave him a theological framework for articulating the beliefs that he already had held for several years.

40. *Righteousness of the Kingdom,* 70.
41. Ibid., 75.

Whereas Old Testament prophesy emphasized the idea of fidelity to a specific Jewish nation, Jesus' conception of the kingdom united all nations into a spirit of oneness before God. According to Rauschenbusch, this enabled one to see that the nature of Jesus' mission was to inaugurate a kingdom based upon the teachings of prophetic love, realized through an individual's growth in the perfection of that love. Although he emphasized the way that Jesus' kingdom presented society with radical demands of social transformation, in good Ritschlian fashion the transforming power of the kingdom was to be gradual and not sudden. "The fact is that the experience of all these centuries has been a long commentary on one of the prominent doctrines of Jesus: the gradualness of the coming of the Kingdom." Although the prophets of the Old Testament and John the Baptist foretold of a sudden realization of the kingdom, "Christ emphasized the gradualness of it. It was a growth like the growth of a mustard plant. It was an organic process like the fermentation of yeast."[42]

Rauschenbusch's repeated use of the concept of organic development dovetailed into another concept that he drew from German liberal idealism — the nature of God's love was primarily directed toward the development of an individual's personality. Perhaps no theme dominated the rise of theological liberalism in America from 1890 to 1910 more than the idea that God shaped the development of human personality — leading one toward the realization of a higher moral life. In the context of earlier nineteenth-century revivalism, the primacy of personal conversion was the means that led ultimately to a regenerated society, bringing the church one step closer to realizing the kingdom of God. Rauschenbusch, picking up on an emerging tradition of Christian education pioneered by Bushnell and the idealism inspired by the German rationalism of Immanuel Kant, affirmed that Jesus' teachings pointed modern humanity in the direction of a just society that would emerge as individuals and groups embraced and embodied more Christlike qualities. Despite the later critique leveled against Rauschenbusch that he believed in a foreordained perfection of society (what Martin Luther King, Jr., called "the cult of inevitable progress"), Rauschenbusch was well aware in 1891 that self-interest would always serve to resist the forces working for the kingdom. "Selfishness is the

42. Ibid., 109.

primary force of human life, and selfishness is only to a very limited extent a unitive force."[43] Yet the teachings of Jesus, Rauschenbusch believed, gave modern Christians the basis to construct a higher form of social life that enabled humans to overcome self-interest. It was this hope that gave the church its contemporary mandate to work toward the promotion of the kingdom.

Rauschenbusch was short on specific social remedies in the manuscript, although he did make reference to the virtues of the single tax as a means to curb the abuses of unearned wealth and the need for contemporary Christians to embrace the social sciences as interpretive tools. The manuscript also revealed many of the religious and cultural biases he would espouse in his later writing, especially his largely negative views of the Catholic Church. He asserted an argument he never abandoned that the great sin of Catholicism was the way the church substituted the imperative to perpetuate its own ecclesiastical existence, at the expense of losing touch with the liberating idea of the kingdom. Rauschenbusch also gave expression to his late Victorian view that middle-class women in America were guilty of a cultural frivolity that laid waste the nation's material resources. "The obligation to break the force of ambition lies especially on the women," Rauschenbusch asserted. He argued that as men aspired to wealth, women would be tempted to renounce their responsibilities as wives and mothers. "It will be a great day for humanity when Christian young women refuse to bestow their love on young men who are so hostile to the Kingdom of God as to desire to 'rise in life,' instead of desiring to raise life."[44]

"Christianity Revolutionary" gave Rauschenbusch his first opportunity to articulate many of his hard-won social and theological convictions, expressing ideas that would not see the light of day in print for several years. In addition to insisting that Christians needed to suffer for their beliefs in social justice, Rauschenbusch gave early expression to a principle likely drawn from his affinity with the Anabaptist heritage: the primary means to achieve social change was through nonviolence. Like many social gospel liberals who followed him, he emphasized Paul's words from Romans that physical aggression, even

43. Ibid., 142.
44. Ibid., 205.

if directed toward a just cause, would ultimately result in the perpetuation of a larger injustice. Recalling the American Civil War, Rauschenbusch lamented that the war's sacrifices did not end the bitter animosity between the North and South in the United States, witnessed by the continued sin of racism.

> Slavery has been overcome in our country by force. It had to be overcome somehow, and all honor is due to those who poured out life, happiness, property to overcome it. But who can survey the terrible cost of life to both sides, the resentful anger which is so slow to die out between North and South, and especially the present sad condition of those on whose behalf all the sacrifices were made, without wondering whether there was no other way?[45]

Rauschenbusch would not always be consistent in his views on the use of coercive force, reflected in his later jingoism during the Spanish-American War. However, he gave expression relatively early in his career to an ethic of nonviolence that would become central in American social Christianity in the years following World War I. In words that presaged the sentiment of Martin Luther King, Jr., Rauschenbusch wrote that retaliation to a physical blow would only perpetuate the spread of violence.

> The blow given and not returned stands in naked meanness and compels even the man who gave it to take the part of the innocent sufferer. The evil has been checked. It has been confined within the narrowest compass, and its repetition has been rendered unlikely all around. Evil has been overcome by good.[46]

Rauschenbusch returned to New York on Christmas Day, 1891. Buoyed by the enthusiastic welcome of his congregation, Rauschenbusch decided to stay at Second German, turning down a position to serve as an editor for a German Baptist periodical in Cleveland. One month later, Rauschenbusch sent off "Christianity Revolutionary" to Nathaniel Schmidt in Hamilton, New York. Rauschenbusch told

45. Ibid., 194.
46. Ibid., 184.

Schmidt that the manuscript was written as a "joint utterance," expressing the views of Rauschenbusch, Schmidt, and Leighton Williams. Earlier in the month, Rauschenbusch had shared the manuscript with Williams, who largely commented favorably on the thrust of the argument.[47] Schmidt's critique of the manuscript, however, was much more thorough and apparently less complimentary.

While he praised his friend for the way he appropriated the concept of the kingdom of God in his writing, Schmidt critiqued the manuscript's shortcomings, especially related to its uneven use of biblical exegesis. "Where you are on your accustomed ground, you speak excellently, beautifully and forcefully. Where you tread on new and uncertain ground there is not the same firmness of tread, and you lag frankly in places."[48] Schmidt believed that Rauschenbusch largely made appropriate use of the kingdom concept, yet pointed out numerous spots where his friend's biblical exegesis did not keep pace with his practical applications. For all of Rauschenbusch's practical application of German theological liberalism, the manuscript did not show the same dexterity in terms of German biblical scholarship. Specifically, Schmidt challenged Rauschenbusch to hone his scholarly skills in Old and New Testament history, as a necessary step in the revision of the manuscript. Whether Schmidt's harsh critique of the manuscript discouraged Rauschenbusch from picking up the project again is unknown. Over the next several years, Rauschenbusch would mine and refine several arguments from "Christianity Revolutionary," resulting in several published articles. Yet he largely ignored Schmidt's suggestions to familiarize himself more thoroughly with German biblical higher criticism. Instead, it would be another American Baptist liberal, Shailer Mathews, who gave Rauschenbusch the biblical rationale he needed to formulate his ideas later in the 1890s. As the months and years passed, Rauschenbusch made some effort at revising the manuscript, yet these efforts were soon aborted. Consequently, the manuscript would remain hidden from the public for over seventy years, after which this "lost" work would be published in 1968 under the revised title *The Righteousness of the Kingdom.*

47. WR to Nathaniel Schmidt, January 22, 1892, box 101.
48. Nathaniel Schmidt to WR, n.d., box 101.

Many other affairs occupied Rauschenbusch's time and energy in the year and a half after his return from Europe that kept him from devoting time to the manuscript. In the months after his return, nothing was as significant as the fact that he and Pauline Rother had fallen in love. Having broken her earlier engagement, Pauline had allowed a deepened relationship with Walther. In September 1892, the couple became engaged. "You know that I think a great deal of that brother of mine," Emma wrote that fall to her soon-to-be sister-in-law, "and the woman who takes his hand to bless his life, will have a warm place in my affections."[49]

For his part, Rauschenbusch was ecstatic about his impending marriage. In the months leading up to his marriage, he flooded Pauline with love poems. At age thirty, romance had come relatively late in his life compared to his other friends. But the poems he penned to Pauline, unlike the ones he wrote of imaginary lovers while a student at Gütersloh, reflected the actual emotion of a man deeply in love.

> I walk through the streets of the city
> In the press and throng of the day,
> But the crowded walks are lonely,
> While my dearest friend is away.
> No warm, round arms to touch now,
> No eyes to look into mine;
> So there's always a want and a yearning
> And a lack that I cannot define.
> . . . .
> I wake at night from my slumbers
> And a groping hand I stretch,
> To where my love must be lying
> All warm and dear to my touch.
> But I touch an empty pillow
> With a dreamy pang of pain,
> And with half-conscious hunger
> I fall asleep again.[50]

49. Emma Rauschenbusch to Pauline Rother, October 29, 1892, box 139.
50. WR to Pauline Rother, December 25, 1892, box 139.

Rauschenbusch showed a bit of bravado as he spoke of his upcoming wedding. "Friends, Romans, Countrymen! I went out west, came, saw, and was conquered," he joked in a letter to his RTS classmates just prior to his wedding.[51] However, he knew that Pauline was someone who shared his social vision and who deeply loved him. Walther and Pauline were married in Milwaukee on April 12, 1893. For more than two decades as the couple grew into middle age, their passion and friendship for one another remained constant in every facet of their relationship.

When the couple returned to New York City that spring, Rauschenbusch had already inaugurated a new stage of his public ministry. If he had failed in his first attempt to give a clear literary expression to his vision of the kingdom of God, he would find a way to live out his beliefs in his public ministry. He would create a practical model that would embody his newfound faith in the kingdom of God.

51. Rauschenbusch, letter to RTS class of 1886, box 153.

5 Rauschenbusch's Assisi

If the 1880s and early 1890s represented the beginnings of the social gospel movement in America, then the years between 1892 and 1897 represented the movement's first "golden age." In addition to the popularity of leaders like Washington Gladden and Josiah Strong, the emphasis on "Christian socialism" epitomized by W. D. P. Bliss continued into the 1890s with the brief and controversial career of the midwestern Congregational cleric, George Herron. Economic recession in the early years of the decade was followed by a full-scale economic depression in 1893, causing a fresh round of labor unrest. William Carwardine, a Methodist minister in Pullman, Illinois, wrote a scathing expose against the tactics used by the Pullman Company in an effort to break a railroad strike in 1894. More popular still was the publication of William Stead's 1894 book *If Christ Came to Chicago!* Examining the political and economic practices in Chicago during the early 1890s, Stead, a prominent British journalist, called upon the city's clergy to rise up and apply Jesus' teaching to heal the economic and social sins of that great American city.

The mid-1890s were the golden age for the "social gospel novel," and the genre was shaped by one book: Charles Sheldon's *In His Steps.* Published in 1897 and set in a fictitious midwestern city, the novel tells the story of a church where a small group of parishioners take up the challenge to walk in the footsteps of Jesus for one year, guiding their lives by one simple question: what would Jesus do? The book tells a hopeful story of Christianization in America that results through the moral actions of these parishioners. The popularity of this book, as well as lesser works of this genre, caught a spirit of public optimism that characterized this early phase of the Progressive Era.[1] Numerous writers and civic reformers campaigned for legislation to build public parks, to advocate for safer working conditions, to abolish child labor, and to implement stricter federal and municipal standards for the elimination of contaminated food and safe drinking water. Politicians increasingly emphasized Jesus' "golden rule" as part of their reform policies, and throughout the nation's cities, settlement houses were established. Many of these were tied to a religious denomination, or at the very least, carried an explicitly religious orientation to their work.[2] Finally, several urban Protestant churches, not connected with settlement houses, took up "institutional church" work, deploying the physical resources of their buildings to engage in a wide-ranging number of ministries to meet the practical needs of the poor. Many institutional church ministries were sustained by the efforts of women's home missionary societies. By the early 1890s, increasing numbers of young single women were making the decision to serve Christ by reaching out to poor immigrant communities through deaconess societies in American cities throughout the North and South. These women embodied the hands-on vision of Christian discipleship envisioned by reform idealists like Charles Sheldon and William Stead.

While the reform sentiments that surrounded the social gospel were growing, Protestant churches remained largely divided on matters of social Christianity. The 1890s witnessed growing schisms over the place of "New Theology" liberalism in the church, and although increasing numbers of prominent Protestant preachers emerged in the decade with discerned liberal sympathies, few of their number actu-

1. See Susan H. Lindley, "Women and the Social Gospel Novel," in *Church History* 54 (March 1985): 56-73.

2. See Eleanor J. Stebner, *The Women of Hull House: A Study in Spirituality, Vocation, and Friendship* (Albany: State University of New York Press, 1997).

ally embraced a social gospel agenda. The 1890s also witnessed a continuing growth in popularity of premillennialism, where a new generation of American revivalists like J. Wilbur Chapman, Reuben Torrey, and an ex–baseball player named Billy Sunday were emerging from Dwight Moody's shadow to become the major spokesmen for the tradition of American evangelicalism.

Amidst all the religious and cultural shifts of the decade, Walther Rauschenbusch was entering perhaps the most important phase in the development of his social outlook. For the first time, Rauschenbusch achieved a degree of public stature as a new voice for social Christianity. Yet by 1897, he found himself again at a crossroads in his life — a place where a practical realization of his vision of the kingdom of God was blissfully sweet, but frustratingly elusive.

A NEW BROTHERHOOD

In May 1892, Rauschenbusch traveled to Philadelphia, where he delivered a keynote address before the Baptist Congress at its tenth anniversary session. A revision of the address was published under the title "A Conquering Idea" in the Baptist *Examiner* that summer. The speech was a succinct summary of his intellectual sojourn of the previous year and laid down ideas that served as the basis for his later writings. Picking up on Ritschlian arguments, Rauschenbusch explained that the ideal of the kingdom of God represented the core impetus for the early church and the church's loss of this ideal had led it to embrace a narrow understanding of salvation. While Rauschenbusch was clear that he did not reject a belief in personal salvation, he added that the Pauline doctrine of "the sin of the race in the first Adam floats upon the mill-pond of our systematic theology like the bowsprit of a sunken ocean vessel."[3] Taking an argument he espoused in "Christianity Revolutionary," he argued that the individual Christian obsession of getting into heaven at the expense of the kingdom had "pushed Christianity from an offensive to a defensive attitude," and "substituted asceticism for a revolutionary movement."[4] For

3. WR, "A Conquering Idea," *The Examiner* (July 31, 1892), reprinted in Hudson, 72.

4. Ibid., 73.

Rauschenbusch, the recovery of the kingdom doctrine for the modern church was as significant as the Protestant reformation's rediscovery of the Pauline doctrine of justification by faith. Just as the reformers of the sixteenth century went back in time to rediscover the Pauline tradition, so Christians of this era had done the same with the synoptic tradition of Jesus. Yet Rauschenbusch made it clear that the church's "rediscovery" of the kingdom doctrine was not only revolutionary but also a necessary practical step for the contemporary church. In themes he would emphasize in writings and speeches throughout the next decade, Rauschenbusch argued that the church's adherence to the kingdom served as a corrective to two extremes: political socialism and religious millennialism. While the socialists, Rauschenbusch explained, often advocated a reform agenda in accordance with the precepts of the kingdom, their message was devoid of the power of God. Similarly, contemporary millennialists held up the other end of the kingdom. Yet their placing of the kingdom beyond the reform of society "casts a halo about their aims, and puts a religious enthusiasm into their propaganda."[5] Rauschenbusch concluded that the matter of educating Christians about the imperative of working for the kingdom needed to be at the forefront of every working minister in the country. "It calls for investigation in every pastor's study, and for discussion wherever Christian men may meet."[6]

Rauschenbusch found that his views on the kingdom were being embraced by greater numbers of northern Baptist colleagues. Among those who gravitated to the social agenda of Rauschenbusch, Williams, and Schmidt was William Faunce, pastor of Fifth Avenue Baptist Church, New York, who would later become president of Brown University in Providence, and Samuel Zane Batten, a Philadelphia Baptist minister. Batten in particular was quick to embrace the theological message and much of the spiritual zeal that characterized the friendship and fellowship between Rauschenbusch, Schmidt, and Williams. At the conclusion of the Baptist Congress meeting, Batten agreed to meet with his new colleagues in New York that summer. On July 9, 1892, Batten, Williams, Schmidt, and two other Baptist ministers met in Rauschenbusch's apartment to construct a broader fellowship among northern Baptists for the discussion of the church and social questions. In addition to holding reg-

5. Ibid., 74.
6. Ibid., 74.

ular meetings, the group planned to publish a variety of materials that would disseminate their message to a wider audience. The name for the group, suggested by Batten, was "the Brotherhood of the Kingdom."[7]

The group adopted a statement of purpose at its initial gathering, committing itself to "the practical realization" of the kingdom of God in the world. The members adopted eight principles for membership in the Brotherhood including a willingness to promote the kingdom "through pulpit, platform and press," to communicate the teachings of the kingdom to "the common people, and to infuse the religious spirit into the efforts for social amelioration."[8] An executive committee was also established, with Batten as executive secretary, to work toward the dissemination of the group's philosophy through printed media.

Although Rauschenbusch's name would be synonymous with the Brotherhood's founding, in actuality the driving organizational force in the group initially was Batten. Batten's conversion to social Christianity had come through his crusades for temperance reform, and his zeal at times would alienate him from both his congregation and his ministerial colleagues.[9] In October 1892, Batten wrote Rauschenbusch expressing his concern that the group not lose interest in the Brotherhood idea. "I have tried to carry out one of our rules, and in private conversation have made many inquiries as to what my brethren think of the kingdom of God. The time is ripe for action, and we can count on many men whom we do not know at present."[10] The second meeting of the Brotherhood was subsequently called and held in Philadelphia at Batten's church in December.

If Batten was responsible for the Brotherhood's organizational impetus, then Leighton Williams supplied a physical context for the group to flourish. After the December meeting, the group did not convene again until the following August, when a group of ten Baptist ministers and one layman, Leighton Williams's brother, Mornay, gathered at the Williams family summer home north of New York City at Marlborough-on-the-Hudson. That summer conference represented the first in what would be almost two decades of consecutive summer

7. Minus, 85.

8. White and Hopkins, 73.

9. See Mitchell Bronk, "An Adventure in the Kingdom of God," *Crozer Quarterly* (January 1937), 23-24.

10. Samuel Batten to WR, October 29, 1892, box 93.

gatherings at the Williams home. In this bucolic setting, far removed from the noise and squalor of New York, Rauschenbusch and his colleagues gathered for several days away from their responsibilities. In a rural setting not unlike the atmosphere engendered by Moody's Northfield gatherings, papers were presented and critiqued and recent books and articles were discussed, but most especially the group relished the fellowship of the gathering.

The founding of the Brotherhood of the Kingdom has been seen by some scholars as a decisive development in the larger history of the social gospel movement in America. But the establishment of the Brotherhood was more a reflection of how the spirit of social Christianity, centered upon a liberal theology of the kingdom of God, was capturing the imagination of many Protestant leaders. Josiah Strong had pointed the way for many Protestants in *Our Country* when he proclaimed his hope that churches would bring all of the nation's social institutions under the reign of the kingdom. Washington Gladden with greater regularity picked up on this theme, and in 1894 he told the graduating class at Oberlin College,

> Every department of human life, — the families, the schools, amusements, art, business, politics, industry; national policies, international relations, — will be governed by the Christian law and controlled by Christian influences. When we are bidden to seek first the kingdom of God, we are bidden to set our hearts on this great consummation; to keep this always before us as the object of our endeavors; to be satisfied with nothing less than this. The complete Christianization of all life is what we pray for and work for, when we work and pray for the coming of the kingdom of heaven.[11]

Rauschenbusch and his Brotherhood colleagues shared the cultural suppositions of older men like Strong and Gladden related to their efforts at realizing the kingdom of God in America. Through the circulation of a series of pamphlets called "Brotherhood Notes," many of which were reprinted in the Baptist press and in other periodicals, the Brotherhood outlined its agenda for church and society.

11. Washington Gladden, *The Church and the Kingdom* (New York: Fleming H. Revell, 1894), 8.

In his early "notes" on behalf of the organization, Rauschenbusch gave a summation of the kingdom doctrine similar to that of Gladden. According to Rauschenbusch, the kingdom "means a growing perfection in the collective life of humanity, in our laws, in the customs of society, in the institutions for education, and for the administration of mercy; in our public opinion, our literary and artistic ideals, in the pervasiveness of the sense of duty, and in our readiness to give our life as a ransom for others."[12] Rauschenbusch accentuated the fact that the church, at its best, embodied the precepts of the kingdom, but the kingdom was never identical to the church. Despite his ongoing fascination with the utopianism of authors like Edward Bellamy and of Fabian socialism, he argued that the kingdom of God offered the contemporary church an ideal of a just society, not the realization of an earthly paradise. "We must recognize the truth that we have here no abiding city," he warned his readers. "Life at its best is transitory and unsatisfactory. The perfection of our personality is not attained on earth."[13] During the 1890s, the emerging social Christian concept of the kingdom of God would lead some Protestant liberals, like the Congregational minister George Herron, to express an optimistic certainty in the perfectibility of humanity to create a heaven on earth. Yet part of the evolutionary appeal that Rauschenbusch attached to the kingdom ideal was his belief that the concept of the kingdom of God was one of the few doctrines that could keep humanity from ascending into a downward spiral of sin. In an article published in late 1892, Rauschenbusch conceded that the fervor that accompanied the emergence of the social sciences in the 1880s had given him a brief faith that perhaps the condition of humanity would improve by virtue of greater knowledge and evolution. Reflecting his newfound fondness for German historiography, he asserted that while theories of evolution might explain the development for the rest of creation, "a new element enters in when it reaches the ethical nature of man. Ethically man sags downward by nature. . . . Moral gravitation is downward. It is accelerated in us by years of sin and by the swirling rush of centuries of wrong which pushes us from behind."[14]

12. WR, "The Kingdom of God," Brotherhood Leaflet reprinted in Hudson, 79.

13. Ibid., 78.

14. "Concepts of Missions," *The Watchman* (December 1892), quoted in

Rauschenbusch accepted the evolutionary suppositions of the kingdom of God doctrine as held by Gladden and Strong. Yet even early in his formulation of the doctrine of the kingdom, Rauschenbusch believed that the doctrine's progress in America would always be impeded by the reality of human sin. Rauschenbusch believed that over time the ethical precepts of the kingdom would find a way to interpenetrate the institutional fabric of society — yet such a reality was in the distant future.

At a moment when this liberal conceptualization of the kingdom of God was gaining increasing voice in American Protestantism, Rauschenbusch had little use for the kingdom doctrine as developed by George Herron during his fleeting popularity in the mid-1890s. On the surface, Herron and Rauschenbusch shared many similarities. They were the same age, and their intellectual pilgrimage to discover the truths of the kingdom doctrine led them through similar intellectual resources, including Richard Ely, Frederick Maurice, and Giuseppe Mazzini. Herron shared a view toward redemptive suffering similar to that of Rauschenbusch, arguing in an 1890 sermon that the cross "was not our release from, but our obligation to, sacrifice."[15] Unlike Rauschenbusch, Herron was a self-educated man who after barely succeeding in being ordained into the Congregational ministry and a brief pastoral stint, became professor of Applied Christianity at Iowa College in Grinnell, Iowa. Through the support of a wealthy benefactor, Herron secured an endowed chair and his lectures on "Christian Sociology" filled lecture halls on campus and later on the national lecture circuit. As the 1890s progressed, Iowa College would become the center of the so-called "Kingdom Movement," represented by social Christian scholars that included Herron, the college's president George Gates, and, briefly, the economist John R. Commons.[16] Yet the most magnetic and controversial member of the "Kingdom Movement" was Herron. With a rhetorical tone not unlike a revivalist,

---

Thomas W. Simpson, "The Prophetic Realism of Walter Rauschenbusch," in *Perspectives on the Social Gospel,* ed. Christopher H. Evans (Lewiston: Edwin Mellen Press, 1999), 132.

15. Peter J. Frederick, *Knights of the Golden Rule: The Intellectual as Christian Social Reformer in the 1890s* (Lexington: University of Kentucky Press, 1976), 163.

16. See Bradley W. Bateman, "Born Again in 1904: John R. Commons and the Social Gospel," in *Perspectives on the Social Gospel,* 221-38.

Herron blended together sources as disparate as Richard Ely and Francis of Assisi. Through his sermons, lectures, and ultimately books like *The New Redemption, The Christian Society,* and *The Christian State,* Herron called for nothing less than a society in which all social institutions would be controlled by the principles of the Golden Rule.

Unlike Rauschenbusch's ideal society, however, Herron's was one in which the state took a more aggressive role in the regulation of private property. Although Herron had initially found support for his work from men like Josiah Strong, inevitably these church leaders disassociated themselves from what was perceived as Herron's hostility not only to the church, but to most segments of American middle-class life. While attempting to be temperate in tone, W. D. P. Bliss probably gave an accurate assessment when he noted that Herron "has a noble scorn of schemes and plans and arrangements. . . . For institutions of any kind, he seems to have small respect."[17] George Herron likely would have dismissed the middle-class decorum of Brotherhood gatherings in the mid-1890s. On their part, the Brotherhood wanted no connection with what one member called Herron's "ultra-radicalism."[18]

In succeeding years after the first summer conference, numerous proponents of social Christianity made their way to Marlborough-on-the-Hudson, including W. D. P. Bliss and Josiah Strong. Yet the Brotherhood never became a large movement in the Baptist churches or in other Protestant communions. It remained a small organization that existed mostly for the intellectual and social edification of its members. At times Samuel Batten grew impatient with the group's limited influence and called for concrete social action. But the primary gift of the Brotherhood to its members was that it gave them the opportunity to hone their ideas before a sympathetic audience.

What emerged through the summer gatherings at the Williams home was a measured form of social idealism that had as its goal the dissemination of its message to a large middle-class following. Individual members of the Brotherhood had different specialties that members came to rely on in these meetings. Nathaniel Schmidt was called upon on matters related to the interpretation of Scripture; Mornay Williams, the layman of the group, critiqued papers that displayed "excess in

17. Frederick, 161.
18. Bronk, 25.

thinking and speech"; and a recent convert to theological liberalism, William Newton Clarke, served as the expert on matters of theology.[19]

Clarke, in some respects, was an anomaly in the group when it gathered for the first time at the Williams summer home. A generation older than his colleagues, Clarke had spent a lengthy career in the Baptist ministry when he was called to the chair of theology at Colgate University, where he became a colleague of Schmidt. Unlike his generational contemporaries, Washington Gladden and Josiah Strong, Clarke was largely unknown outside of his denominational circles. With the publication of his 1898 book *An Outline of Christian Theology,* he was heralded as one of the major expositors of American theological liberalism. Rauschenbusch gained from Clarke not only a theological guide, but also a close friend who in the years ahead would serve as a major source of encouragement for the younger man.

At the same time, Brotherhood gatherings largely centered upon Rauschenbusch, who was recognized as the group's primary leader. The way that his personality dominated the discussions made one member joke that the Brotherhood should have been called "Rauschenbusch's Assisi."[20] The Brotherhood idea would duplicate itself into the creation of independent chapters in a number of cities in the northeastern United States, yet the heart and soul of the Brotherhood was always the summer meeting at the Williams home. Like many aspects of Rauschenbusch's career in New York, however, his ties to the Brotherhood, while deeply rooted, would not be permanent. Increasingly, as years passed, members complained to Rauschenbusch that the routine of gathering at the Williams estate was wearing thin. "I am getting a little impatient of talk," one member complained. "We have all said all that we know, and it hardly seems to be worthwhile to come together to mark time as we do. . . . I enjoy the companionship of the meetings very much, but even that is not the natural companionship which we get in the midst of our ordinary lives, but there is a feeling of being dumped down together aimlessly."[21]

With the passing of years, the Brotherhood became a cheering section for Rauschenbusch's later public success as opposed to a

19. Ibid., 25.
20. Ibid., 23.
21. E. H. Crosby to WR, August 8, 1898, box 93.

transformative movement of social Christianity. The group did have modest success in some measures of activism, including a role in persuading the New York City Park Board to install sandpiles in city parks. Yet the greatest asset of the Brotherhood for Rauschenbusch was the tremendous intellectual stimulation that came from the fellowship, or as he put it, "the striking of mind upon mind." As Rauschenbusch gained greater fame and ultimately turned his attention to other pursuits, the Brotherhood collapsed, with its members moving out into other emerging arenas of social ministry. Nevertheless, in its first five years of existence, the Brotherhood gave Rauschenbusch a space for intellectual solace and renewal. It was also through his association with the Brotherhood that he came to accept, with greater regularity, the use of an English first name, Walter.[22]

A NEW LIFE

The demands on Rauschenbusch's ministry made it difficult for the Brotherhood to be anything more than a useful support network. Upon his return from Europe, he wrote editorials and Sunday school lessons for *The Christian Examiner* and *Christian Inquirer* and the German youth periodical *Der Jugend Herold.* Of greater importance was the need to reacquaint himself with his congregation and resume his pastoral responsibilities. Yet Rauschenbusch's newfound faith in the kingdom of God was emerging in his parish ministry in a variety of new ways.

Rauschenbusch had made great strides with his congregation, as a caring pastor and as an evangelist who built up the church's membership, its ministry program, and most especially led the church to construct a new building. At the same time, the church had its problems. Although Rauschenbusch did not abandon the pietistic emphasis in his preaching after his 1891 sabbatical, he did strive to integrate more sermons on social questions into his preaching, often encountering resistance from his congregation. Some congregational members worried that Rauschenbusch reflected too much enthusiasm for the views of

22. Rauschenbusch did not fully embrace the English spelling of his first name until 1902, after he became a professor of church history at Rochester Theological Seminary. He preferred the German form of his name within his family.

"modern" English-speaking churches, abandoning the church's German pietist heritage.

Several members were thus less than enthralled when Rauschenbusch initiated proposals for a series of new "institutional church" measures spearheaded by Leighton Williams in conjunction with neighboring Amity Baptist Church. Amity had taken up the sponsorship of a Baptist deaconess association, modeled after the inner-city mission work that employed young women in many large cities to reach out to the urban poor in the 1880s and 1890s. Although Rauschenbusch found support for this form of social ministry within his church, the proposal did not meet with uniform acceptance and echoed a larger suspicion within German-Baptist circles of anything associated with "the social gospel."

Rauschenbusch always sought to balance his pastoral concern for his church with his strong social convictions. Yet he found it difficult to make headway in his own church community and even less among the larger constituency of German Baptists in America. Prior to his sabbatical in 1891, he had engaged in a protracted literary feud with a prominent German pastor named E. Anschütz. In several issues of *Der Sendbote,* Rauschenbusch and his elder colleague exchanged views on the merits of theological liberalism and social Christianity. While Rauschenbusch confessed that his theological views were more radical than those of his colleague, he appealed to Anschütz on the basis that his interpretation of Christianity was merely a renewed version of an older Christianity, not a radical new creation. "I do not believe in overthrow but in development: 'First the grass, then the ears, and then the kernels in the ears.'"[23] Yet Rauschenbusch's pleas convinced few German Baptist constituents, and the son of August Rauschenbusch found himself increasingly struggling with the question of how he could reach his church and the German Baptist constituency in the northern Baptist churches with his message of social Christianity.

In the spring of 1893, Rauschenbusch gained a partner in his enterprises in the person of his wife, Pauline. The couple moved into the small apartment on the top floor of the new church building, and quickly Pauline confronted the expectations placed upon her as a minister's wife. "I can very well imagine your time being taken up very

23. Jaehn, 31.

much," Frida wrote to her new sister-in-law that summer. "With so many societies in your own church and so many churches in the neighborhood, where you have to go occasionally this cannot be otherwise."[24] Indeed Pauline took on the roles associated in that era with the "vocation" of minister's wife, hosting a variety of ladies' society gatherings in the church, assisting her husband with a number of social functions in the community, as well as managing the duties of cook and housekeeper. Speaking of her own role in her husband's ministry, she wrote him, "you must pray for your little girl dear one that she may always help you and never keep you back from your duty. That is my earnest desire to be a real helpmeet to you."[25] Pauline and her husband engaged in a deeply personal and loving correspondence where both made frequent references to their "sweet love" and the bond of friendship that they held for each other.[26] What characterized their relationship in their early years of marriage was an overt euphoria of being married, expressed by Pauline when she wrote to her husband a few months after their wedding, "what a heaven this earth would be if everyone had a husband like mine."[27]

Less than a year after their move to New York in March 1894, Pauline gave birth to their first child, Winifred, named after Walter's older brother Winfried who had died as an infant. Rauschenbusch wrote whimsically in a journal of his oldest child's birth that "she was a little confused in her ideas yet, for she didn't recognize her own father and didn't seem to think he was anything much."[28] In a little over a year, Rauschenbusch had gone from a long-accustomed existence as a single man to a family of three, living in a two-bedroom apartment adjacent to the choir loft overlooking the church's sanctuary.

For all of his happiness as a husband and new father, Rauschenbusch was expressing clear signs of frustration with his ministry at Second German. The nation's financial depression of 1893 had a direct economic effect on his parishioners, impacting financial giving. "The hard times have rested like a heavy pressure on our people and there has been no extra strength to spare for anything," he wrote to a friend. More dis-

24. Frida Fetzer to Pauline, August 18, 1893, box 135.
25. Pauline to WR, August 18, 1894, box 83.
26. See various correspondences in box 83 and Minus, 94-95.
27. Pauline to WR, September 23, 1893, box 83.
28. WR diary book, box 143.

tressing was the fact that his efforts as an evangelist, which had successfully brought in new members years earlier, no longer appeared to be effective. The number of new baptisms was down and he candidly observed in the spring of 1894, "I have often felt much borne down by this and feel that my ministry lacks in prayer and spiritual retirement."[29]

This was not the first time Rauschenbusch expressed dissatisfaction with his ministry. In a humorous poem entitled "Our Missionary Scapegoat," published in the *Christian Examiner* in 1892, Rauschenbusch made plain that the cost to the servant of Christ was a life of many responsibilities and few material rewards. Beneath the poem's humor, one can't help wondering if the poem bears an autobiographical resemblance to its author.

He joins in the marriage frolics;
He sits by the couch of pain;
He cheers the discouraged sinner
And sets him going again. . . .

One day the good face clouded,
For they cut his salary down;
They couldn't pay six hundred;
They were building a church up town. . . .

Good Christians all, behold him,
For his salary comes from us;
Thus we're serving the world by proxy
And going to heaven by bus. . . .

Will the Lord in the day of judgement
Call this little game too slim?
Will an angel arrest us for stealing
And turn over our sheaves to him?[30]

As a result of the nation's economic depression in 1893 and 1894, Rauschenbusch received repeated visits from beggars, asking for

29. WR to Will Munger, May 24, 1894, box 50.
30. Copy of poem in box 139 and reprinted in Sharpe, 100-101.

money, food, and even shoes. He did what he could to help the poor and often made arrangements for them to work off the costs for material items through volunteering their labors at the church.

By the summer of 1894, Rauschenbusch and Second German were pressing forward in support of a number of joint institutional church undertakings with Amity Baptist. In addition to co-sponsoring the deaconess mission, Second German supported a number of related undertakings spearheaded by Amity, including a "Heartease Home" for impoverished young women and a "coffee room" where young women could receive a hot meal. Williams's church also sponsored a "theological seminary" to train laity for missionary outreach into the city.[31] Rauschenbusch lent assistance to Williams in the supervision of these enterprises, and also recommended young women for membership in the deaconess home. For its part, Second German established a day care center for the children of working mothers.[32]

Despite the modest success of these enterprises, Rauschenbusch encountered tension in his church. In July 1895, a parishioner noted to Rauschenbusch that the church was at the "brink of the precipice" and on the verge of a major conflict.[33] "With the 2d German Baptist Church . . . my experience has been disappointing in 3 specific directions," the same disgruntled parishioner announced. "1st: The failure to branch out not heeding, in my opinion, repeated and well defined calls so to do. 2nd: What appears to me to be laxness in taking hold of needed reforms in providing for the poor in and out of the church. 3rd: In the adoption of an unbiblical deaconesse [*sic*] system."[34] The parishioner announced his imminent departure from Second German not without a spirit of regret, given his personal fondness for his pastor. "I love you too well, personally, . . . and as you are, or are becoming to be of an ascetic turn of mind and I belong to the 'common herd' it is a foregone conclusion that we cannot come to terms."[35] How widely rooted this sentiment of dissent was in the church is not clear. What is clear is that Rauschenbusch faced numerous potential divisions in his church. Some of these pitted "traditional German" members against "modern English" ones, but others revolved

31. Hudson, 18.
32. Minus, 98.
33. M. Albrecht to WR, July 6, 1895, box 135.
34. Ibid., June 27, 1895, box 135.
35. Ibid., July 6, 1895, box 135.

around tensions over the sponsorship of the deaconess home or the fact that the church was going too far, or not far enough in its social outreach.

Rauschenbusch's relationship to his congregation remained warm and affectionate. However, a resolution presented to Rauschenbusch on the tenth anniversary of his pastorate gave a subtle hint of an underlying tension beneath the praise for his work. "We have in him a perfectly fearless preacher, one caring nothing about criticism of any kind, but who always stands up, and in a manly, fearless way teaches and adheres strictly to Christ's teaching."[36]

TOWARD A NEW VOCATION

Rauschenbusch had accomplished much in his ten years in New York, highlighted by modest growth and a new building for his congregation. But by the summer of 1896, he was tired and somewhat uncertain of the next step in his ministry. His fatigue was no doubt exacerbated by the birth that spring of a second child, a son Hilmar, born on the day of his ten-year class reunion at Rochester Theological Seminary, and named after two relatives, including his great-grandfather, "both pious ministers and stout hearts."[37] In order to give himself and Pauline a break from the routine of their New York City existence, the entire family ventured to Williams's summer home to attend the annual Brotherhood gathering and to take an extended two-month summer break. In a letter to a friend, Rauschenbusch confessed that the thoughts for his future ministry rested in ways he could promote the fullness of the kingdom idea. "Daresay we of the Brotherhood are off the line, but I am very sure that the old evangelical conception is too small." Calling the kingdom "the supreme good and the supreme duty" and "the sum of all ethical and spiritual forces," he struggled with ways to reach a larger audience with the truth of this concept. "The common conception of it sanctifies some portions of life, but leave the great bulk of all callings, the farmers and mechanics, without any religious idea to enable and spiritualize their calling. I am looking for something that will do that."[38] Although

36. Minus, 99.
37. WR to Will Munger, July 11, 1896, box 50.
38. Ibid.

labeling himself a Christian socialist, Rauschenbusch held economic understandings that were still largely shaped by the ideas of Henry George and Richard Ely. He wavered between which presidential candidate to support in 1896, admitting that he did not understand the intricacies of Democratic presidential candidate William Jennings Bryant's "free silver" pledge. "I don't know nothin' about finances. Suppose it's a divine call to study up."[39]

Despite Rauschenbusch's self-deprecation, by the mid-1890s he was making an increasing name for himself in print. In addition to the second volume of the German hymnal with Ira Sankey, Rauschenbusch also published in 1895 a short study on the life of Jesus written in German for the laity. The topics of Rauschenbusch's writing in this period spanned wide interests including articles on the kingdom of God, the problems of wealth in modern society, and the relationship of the church to social problems. He also devoted energy to addressing numerous theological tensions of the decade, including the growing phenomenon of speaking in tongues, practiced by certain Holiness groups, and the rising popularity of premillennialism. In 1897, Rauschenbusch noted that he saw no problem with the speaking of tongues in the church, so long as these practices followed the Pauline injunction that these gifts edify the entire church. The witness of the early church proved that those who spoke in tongues "possessed no mere hearsay religion, but were conscious of a direct contact with God." At the same time, he worried that an overemphasis on this gift in the present might drive the church "dangerously near the verge of mental aberration."[40]

Of greater concern to Rauschenbusch was how the contemporary church should view the question of "millenarianism." In two highly sympathetic articles published in *The Examiner* in September and October 1896, Rauschenbusch conceded that those who followed a premillennialist theology were not entirely unjustified in their beliefs. He praised the millennial spirit of early Christianity for infusing the church with a revolutionary spirit, reflected in how Jesus' teaching

39. Ibid.

40. WR, "Speaking in Tongues — What Was It?" *The Watchman* (September 30, 1897), reprinted in the Walter Rauschenbusch "Scrapbook," copies in the American Baptist–Samuel Colgate Historical Library and the Ambrose Swasey Library.

turned the social order "bottom side up." For Rauschenbusch, millennialism in the early church was connected not only to an eschatological promise of a life beyond death but also to the early Christian hope that the social conditions of earth would approximate those of heaven. Although he did not associate himself with the tradition, Rauschenbusch gave expression to a postmillennialist vision that Christians needed to improve social conditions prior to the second coming of Christ.

Yet he acknowledged with the premillennialists that the social conditions in the world were not necessarily getting better. "The evil of the world today is appalling in amount," he wrote. "The way in which the devil gets a hold of the products of civilization, for instance, of the public press and of democratic institutions and uses them after his own heart is enough to make a Thanksgiving orator pause in his fingers."[41] Yet Rauschenbusch asserted that premillennialism fostered an uncritical, ahistorical view of the Scriptures. "The passages of Scripture are to them not portions of a living organization of thought," he argued. "They are rather adamantine pieces of dead matter, bits of glass distributed in boxes, which are to be arranged in a mosaic by the cunning workman in prophecies who has found the key, as if it was all a gigantic puzzle devised by the Almighty."[42] For Rauschenbusch the worst offense of premillennialism was the way it used Scripture to allow an indifference, if not outright pessimism, concerning the Christian's view of social reform. In drawing an analogy to the monastic tradition in the church he observed, "Millenarianism shares the despair of monasticism without braving its self-denials. It cultivates the attitude of separation while mingling with the world, and the consequence is frequently a life in two sections, the one expecting the Lord, the other conformed to the laws of the world."[43] In a somewhat wry tone, he contrasted the premillennialist anticipation of "the rapture" with their proclivity to store up material treasures on earth. "Faith in salvation by catastrophe cuts the nerve of action, but only in the unselfish pursuits of life. . . . I have yet to see proof that those who believe in the imminence of Christ's coming are indifferent to the security of

41. WR, "Our Attitude Toward Millenarianism," *The Examiner* (September 24 and October 1, 1896), quoted in Hudson, 91.

42. Ibid., 89.

43. Ibid., 92.

real estate titles, the length of leases, the education of their children, and other things that involve a long look ahead."[44] He concluded by posing a question: "Which will do more to make our lives spiritual and to release us from the tyranny of the world, the thought that we may at any moment enter into the presence of the Lord, or the thought that every moment we are in the presence of the Lord?"[45]

He cast premillennialism as an extreme expression of a larger Christian truth, in the same manner that political socialism, from the opposite extreme, was devoid of the power of God. For Rauschenbusch, the hope for the church lay between the two polarities. His views on premillennialism engendered a range of responses from readers. A Baptist pastor in Spokane wrote Rauschenbusch that he was ambivalent toward both pre- and postmillennialist outlooks for their extreme views. "Those who speak of the world getting better probably mean that Christianity is growing better, is salutary in its influence and is spreading but they can not mean that the 'world' is getting better. It is about as mean and selfish as ever."[46]

This letter highlights the skepticism Rauschenbusch had encountered in his social ministry, ever since his early days in New York City. Yet he was determined to define a position for the contemporary church that escaped the otherworldly orientation of premillennialism on the one hand and the church's acceptance of a status quo economic determinism on the other. His view of the church's ministry was fleshed out in two articles published in the *American Journal of Sociology* in 1896 and 1897.

The *American Journal of Sociology* and the *American Journal of Theology* were sister journals established in the mid-1890s by the John Rockefeller–financed University of Chicago. Founded in 1892, the university's vision of higher education was committed to a two-prong enterprise of cultivating Christian faith in a modern world and serving as a model of a new American research university. The university and its divinity school attracted a vital nucleus of scholars that made each school a center for the development of liberal thought. These men, including George B. Foster, Gerald Birney Smith, Shirley Jackson Case, and Shailer Mathews, would all play a major role in shaping the future

44. Ibid., 94.
45. Ibid.
46. O. W. Van Osdel to WR, May 24, 1898, box 93.

direction of American theological liberalism during the first third of the twentieth century.

Mathews was part of the first faculty wave recruited to the university soon after its founding. A native New Englander, he had served as a professor of sociology at Bates College in Maine, and when Albion Small, Mathews's former mentor on the Bates faculty, suggested Mathews for a chair in New Testament studies at Chicago, Mathews accepted — even though he had no graduate training in biblical studies or extensive teaching background in the field. He became a tireless promoter of German liberalism and higher criticism, and the launching of these two journals helped cement the university's reputation as a major American research center, reflecting what became known as "Chicago School" theological liberalism. Rauschenbusch developed a close friendship with Mathews in subsequent years and the two shared many similarities in thought, even though significant differences in their theologies and their intended audiences rose to the surface with the passing of years. Rauschenbusch had actually contemplated the possibility of pursuing a doctorate and accepting a teaching fellowship at the university, back in 1892. However, he rejected the opportunity, in part because he felt that the pursuit of a doctorate might deflect him from the style of writing he wanted to pursue. It is indeed interesting to speculate how the history of American liberal Protestantism might have been affected, had Rauschenbusch pursued a teaching post at the University of Chicago!

His first essay to appear in the *American Journal of Sociology* was entitled "The Ideals of Social Reformers." The essay reflected many ideas that had matured in Rauschenbusch's thought since his return from Europe and summarized many of the arguments he would espouse in upcoming years. Although acknowledging that most church members were ignorant or indifferent to social questions, he sought to clarify misconceptions about those who believed as he did. Speaking on behalf of the Brotherhood, he affirmed, "We believe in the spiritual life, in the fact of sin and corruption, in the need and possibility of salvation, in holiness and eternal life. We have no desire to see evangelical Christianity bled to death."[47] After expounding on the necessity of

47. WR, "The Ideals of Social Reformers," *American Journal of Sociology* (September 1896): 202.

working for social reform in the face of contemporary injustices, Rauschenbusch got to the crux of the matter — the church and the modern social movement needed one another. He praised the church for its contributions to modern life, at the same time that he praised modern socialists like Karl Marx for making humanity aware of the economic exploitation of workers. What Christianity offered the modern social movement that political socialism did not was an organic association that replaced selfish motives with unselfish ones. "True Christianity emphasizes to the utmost the value of the individual and has been the real motive power back of the efforts to secure personal liberty. But it contains more than individualism; it also contains the principle of association, and implants the trustworthiness, love and unselfishness which cement men together and make association a workable idea."[48] Consequently, political socialism was effective only to the point that it embodied these Christian ideals. Left to its own materialistic tendencies, socialism ran the risk of usurping individual freedom, violating the sanctity of the family, and creating an unhealthy spirit of nationalism. Rauschenbusch advocated a modest form of industrial nationalization, calling for restrictions on "natural monopolies," corporations that he believed had a direct impact upon the larger public welfare (such as railroads and electric and gas utilities). Yet he was not calling for a command economy controlled solely by the government. Democracy flourished only where there was individualism, and so measures of state regulation needed to be gradually implemented.

Rauschenbusch's ideal society was an updated version of the one espoused by Josiah Strong in *Our Country.* "Steady progress, measure by measure, is best, feeling our way from step to step with sure-footed Anglo-Saxon caution, keeping our feet on the ground, and not going off in a French balloon of abstract principles and logical schemes."[49] In the essay, Rauschenbusch gave shape to an ideal society that would characterize his later writing, one where government had enough power to regulate necessary public enterprises, while maintaining enough freedom to nurture the best attributes of American public and domestic life. Rauschenbusch hinted in the article at his ambivalence

48. Ibid., 210.
49. Ibid., 217.

toward working women when he castigated those reformers who would "loosen the rigor of the family bond."[50] For Rauschenbusch, part of the church's purpose in embracing the ideal of the kingdom of God was to affirm a society in which the family served as the source from which civic virtue flowed.

In 1891, Rauschenbusch's first attempt at an extended statement on social Christianity had led him to write a bulky, organizationally awkward, yet passionate statement on the revolutionary imperative of the church's future. Five years after he wrote "Christianity Revolutionary," Rauschenbusch presented similar ideas, yet they were now more refined in their appeal to the conscience of the American late nineteenth-century middle class. The kingdom of God for Rauschenbusch still represented a revolutionary hope for the church. But that hope was dependent on strengthening many preexisting social institutions, like the American family, that provided space in the home "whither a man could withdraw from the press of the world to the restful society of a beloved woman and his own children."[51]

The following June, Rauschenbusch published a follow-up essay in the *American Journal of Sociology* entitled "The Stake of the Church in the Social Movement."[52] Rauschenbusch reiterated his longstanding argument in support of a single tax remedy as a corrective to the imbalances of wealth in American society. He warned of the dangers of how wealth concentrated in the hands of the rich would have an adverse effect on the mission of the church, and acknowledged that the church symbolized the economic gap in America between the rich and the poor. "If we come to have a well-defined wealthy class and a permanently poor class, we shall also have rich churches and poor churches, with a gulf fixed between them," he argued. "No amount of gush about rich and poor meeting together in the church, no amount even of real Christian sacrifice will be sufficient to overcome the silent social forces which will stratify people in the churches according to their wealth."[53]

Rauschenbusch believed that revenue sharing on the part of the

50. Ibid., 213.

51. Ibid., 214.

52. Walter Rauschenbusch, "The Stake of the Church in the Social Movement," *American Journal of Sociology* 3 (July 1897): 18-30.

53. Ibid., 22.

rich would create a more balanced and ordered social and religious life within local congregations. In particular, he asserted that a redistribution of wealth would move poor women away from employment, giving them time to devote to building Christian homes and churches.

> How can a young woman put any brightness and sustained charm into her Sunday-school work if she has been standing for eleven hours a day behind a counter, perhaps without a chair to sit down in even during the intervals of her work? How can a man travel up and down tenement stairs and stand the physical and mental wear of house-to-house visiting when he has been working all the week in an ill-ventilated shop amid the clang of machinery? They do this extra labor; they rejoice in doing it; but often they break down under it.[54]

What is most revealing about Rauschenbusch's argument, however, was his ambivalence toward the "institutional church" model that he and Williams attempted to implement. "The institutional church is a necessary evil," he explained. At an earlier moment in history, the social needs of a community could be addressed through families and the extended community of a neighborhood. In modern times, Rauschenbusch argued, the church needed to compensate for the ways these traditional institutions were breaking down in the face of modern capitalism. "Make social life healthy and you can simplify church work. Let poverty and helplessness increase, and the work of the churches will increase too."[55] He warned, however, that the institutional church model required "immense demands on the energy, care, and organizing ability of the leaders" within such congregations.[56] Rauschenbusch's description of the institutional church as "a necessary evil" perhaps reflected his own ambivalence toward deaconess women whose pursuits were not geared toward finding husbands and building Christian homes.

What is clear is that Rauschenbusch's anxiety in the article was

54. Ibid., 24-25.
55. Ibid., 26-27.
56. Ibid., 25.

connected to a sentiment that was on the minds of most Protestant leaders of that era — a fear that the church was losing its power to speak to society as *the* definitive moral voice in the country. "Anything that impairs the morale of the church also impairs its reputation for moral superiority," he asserted.[57] What was needed, according to Rauschenbusch, was a church made up of members whose professional values were in step with the ethical values espoused by their churches. In other words, what the modern church needed was men who put Jesus' ethics ahead of their own needs. "Jesus demands that we shall not lay up treasures on earth," yet he conceded that this teaching was easier for those who are "sure of an opportunity to earn a living through every coming year."[58] The conclusion of the article revealed not only Rauschenbusch's social passion, but perhaps his own disillusionment over his inability to make his own congregation a beacon of the kingdom of God in America, while conceding that the social conditions in New York City made it difficult to give many a compelling vision of God's glory. "Her children in the city suck no sweetness from the bosom of mother earth, for her bosom is covered with asphalt and flagstones."[59]

What Rauschenbusch's state of mind was like toward his future in New York City when he wrote this article is unknown. However, by the time "The Stake of the Church" article appeared in the July 1897 edition of the *Journal of Sociology,* Rauschenbusch had already left New York. Augustus Strong had again made overtures to Rauschenbusch about the possibility of joining the German department at Rochester Theological Seminary in the summer of 1896.[60] It was not until May 1897, however, when a faculty member of the German department died suddenly, that the way was cleared for Strong to make another offer to Rauschenbusch to come to the seminary. Even as Rauschenbusch and Pauline prepared to take their leave of New York City, several seminary trustees expressed their reservations over Rauschenbusch's liberalism and his defense of socialism. Strong was able to pacify the trustees' concerns, however, citing how

57. Ibid., 27.

58. Ibid., 28.

59. Ibid., 30.

60. See various correspondences between Rauschenbusch and Strong in the 1890 file, box 23.

Rauschenbusch's published views on socialism reflected both its strengths and weaknesses.[61]

The departure from New York was accompanied by sadness and relief. On one hand, his years in New York had been marked by the success of nurturing a small congregation to a new level of growth, and parting from many of his parishioners and his colleagues in the city was difficult. Yet both he and Pauline were ready to leave New York City. In addition to the difficulties of doing pastoral work as a near-deaf minister, there was a growing anxiety, voiced frequently by Pauline, of raising a family amidst the squalor of Manhattan.[62] The position in Rochester offered Rauschenbusch greater financial rewards, and perhaps accepting the vocation of seminary professor might enable him to devote more time to his writing on social questions.

Rauschenbusch was also entering an uncertain future. As he noted years later, the fact that his appointment to Rochester Seminary was almost blocked reflected that his social enthusiasm needed to be tempered by a certain prudence of opinion in his new appointment. "The Church held down the social interest in me," he complained, "and when it was a question about giving me position or preferment, the fact that I was interested in the workingman was actually against — not for me."[63] Rauschenbusch was not just commenting on his own personal circumstances. In 1896, Nathaniel Schmidt was dismissed from his faculty position at Hamilton Seminary, due to his liberal theology. Although he found a position as a professor of Semitic languages at Cornell University, Schmidt's dismissal reflected a climate in the 1890s in which many Protestant seminaries vigorously attempted to root out "new theology" liberals.

For a number of years, Rauschenbusch had felt the climate of these theological constrictions in his own congregation. Although his pastoral and preaching ministry at Second German largely focused on providing comfort and spiritual uplift to his congregation, the inability to consistently integrate social Christian sermons into his ministry

61. Minus, 100.

62. Pauline expressed this sentiment many times to her husband in the early years of their marriage. See, for example, letter Pauline to Walther, September 12, 1894, box 83.

63. Minus, 101; additional information on Rauschenbusch's appointment can be found in box 93.

clearly disturbed him. For all of his social awakening after his 1891 sabbatical, Rauschenbusch's sermons on social questions frequently got him into trouble with his congregation. In February 1897 he preached an angry sermon, attacking the frivolous display of wealth at a recent social event hosted by a wealthy New Yorker. Rauschenbusch reminded his congregation of the chasm that existed in the city between the rich and poor, arguing against the sins of those who gained their wealth and status at the expense of the poor. "Justice is the real solution," he argued. "What justice requires and how it is to be applied is for us to think and work out. And I know of no more important task for this generation. I wish there was more disposition to work it out among us here."[64] When Rauschenbusch was criticized for the sermon from several parishioners, he remained undaunted in his position. His response to one parishioner reflected a somewhat righteous indignation that hinted at his state of mind at the conclusion of his ministry in New York.

> You tell me . . . what I ought to preach against: "dishonesty, impurity, evil-mindedness, envy, hatred, malice." I do preach against these and have tried to be faithful in dealing with myself and my hearers. But you forget a few real evils in your list: the vanity of women and the covetousness and oppression of men. The prophets of the Old Testament saw the danger of their people more in the latter than in anything else, and the discussion of these evils occupy [*sic*] more space in the teachings of Jesus than any other sin, except perhaps hypocrisy. Perhaps if you will incorporate these evils in your list and consider the baneful effect that they are having on our nation to-day, you will be less satisfied if the wealthy classes are merely satisfactory in the common virtues of family life.[65]

In July 1897, Rauschenbusch concluded his ministry in New York and reentered the middle-class Rochester culture that had nurtured him in his early life and formative education. The experience of the New York years, however, would never leave him, and whatever ani-

64. Rossol, "Walter Rauschenbusch as Preacher," 283-84.
65. WR to "Madame," February 16, 1897, box 23.

mosity may have existed between himself and his congregation soon gave way to enduring feelings of warmth and friendship. When the time came eight years later to begin work on the manuscript that ultimately made him renowned as the major American exponent of "the social gospel," he wrote in the introduction a simple but heartfelt expression of how this new book was written "to discharge a debt" to his former congregation. "I shared their life as well as I then knew, and used up the early strength of my life in their service. In recent years my work has been turned into other channels, but I have never ceased to feel that I owe help to the plain people who were my friends."[66]

66. WR, *Christianity and the Social Crisis,* xxxviii.

6 The Pleasures of Youth

Rochester, New York, in 1897 was a city in the midst of dramatic economic and population growth. Although no longer the American "boomtown" that August Rauschenbusch moved his family to in 1858, nor the urban metropolis of New York left behind by his son, Rochester was still a city on the leading edge of industry and urbanization in late nineteenth-century America. In 1884, a young bank clerk named George Eastman developed an inexpensive process for developing camera film that led to the founding of the Eastman Kodak Company. By the 1890s, Kodak's easy-to-use cameras had revolutionized the photography industry, enabling middle-class Americans to own a camera for the first time. In addition to Kodak, Rochester hosted a number of major industries in eye wear, manufacturing, and garments. From under 90,000 residents in 1880, the city grew to a population of 133,896 by 1890, 162,608 by 1900, and 218,129 by 1910, a population increase of almost 140 percent in thirty years.[1] In a time period when America's urban centers were filling up with European immigrants, Rochester was a popular destination. Although still possessing

1. Census data, *Thirteenth Census of the United States, 1910,* Volume III (Washington, D.C.: General Printing Office, 1913).

a large German population from earlier in the century, the city's residents now included significant Jewish, Catholic, and Eastern Orthodox immigrants from Russia, Poland, Italy, and the Balkans. From Rauschenbusch's perspective, and from the perspective of most American Protestant leaders of the time, this influx of non-Protestant immigrants led to the rise of unprecedented moral vice. Rochester clergymen were particularly alarmed by the large number of saloons that had emerged, especially prevalent in the immigrant working-class sections of the city. By the mid-1890s, Rochester's city directory listed 560 saloons in the city — one for every 250 residents.[2]

In the years that Walter Rauschenbusch taught at Rochester Theological Seminary and had his major impact as a leader of the social gospel, it was this urban context that shaped his vocation as a teacher, as a clergy leader, and, ultimately, as a propagator of what became known as "the social gospel." Rauschenbusch's engagement with the social context of his native city would emerge gradually over the course of several years. His first priority was to build upon the legacy of the German department, whose enrollment reached an all-time high just prior to his arrival. In his first five years teaching at Rochester Theological Seminary, Rauschenbusch devoted himself to numerous tasks related to the mission of the German department. Always in the back of his mind, however, was the larger issue of the kingdom of God and how the contemporary church could facilitate its coming.

GERMAN DEPARTMENT MINISTRY

Despite his move into a full-time teaching position, Rauschenbusch's first half-decade as a seminary professor provided him little time for original scholarly work. For one thing, his teaching load was enormous. Although he came to the seminary as a professor of New Testament, in actuality he taught practically every subject in the curriculum. He was responsible not only for teaching courses in the theological disciplines but also for courses in American history, civics, and even the natural sciences to his German immigrant students (in addition to

2. Blake McKelvey and Ruth Rosenberg-Naparsteck, *Rochester: A Panoramic History* (Sun Valley: American Historical Press, 2001), 87.

teaching an occasional course in the English department). Rauschenbusch's classroom dexterity, especially his mastery of American history, led him in 1902 to publish a small handbook in German on "Civil Government in the United States."

August Rauschenbusch's leadership had firmly established the German department, both academically and financially. Yet individual faculty in the department still carried a heavy burden to raise money. Consequently, in the years he spent in the German department, Rauschenbusch traveled constantly, speaking to alums and German churches from New York to North Dakota in an effort to raise the department's endowment.[3] Rauschenbusch also spoke regularly to various English-speaking Baptist constituencies concerning the importance of the German department's mission.

Beyond Rauschenbusch's work of fund-raising and teaching, he became devoted to another project in his early years at Rochester Seminary: assisting his father in the writing of his memoirs. By the mid-1890s, the elder Rauschenbusch was settled in retirement, living near his daughter Frida and establishing a tacit reconciliation with his wife, Caroline. In 1898, thanks largely to financial assistance from the Rockefellers, Rauschenbusch traveled to Germany to spend that summer with his father. The time spent with the old patriarch was apparently rewarding and it also gave him an opportunity to reconnect with his sisters, Frida and Emma, the latter on furlough from her missionary duties in India. After his return to Rochester, Rauschenbusch remarked how gratifying his visit was and, as it turned out, it was the last time he would see his father. In December 1899, August died at the age of eighty-three. Rauschenbusch picked up the responsibility of completing his father's memoirs, which were published in German in 1901. This largely hagiographical work was designed to cement August Rauschenbusch's place as one of the major patriarchs of nineteenth-century German Baptist pietism. Although the work was mostly unknown in English-speaking church circles, Rauschenbusch promoted the book's circulation for many years after its publication to a variety of Baptist constituencies in America and Germany. It was a final debt to a man whom the younger Rauschenbusch revered, yet from

3. Various correspondences between Walter and Pauline Rauschenbusch detail the extent of Rauschenbusch's travels during this period. See box 83 as an example.

whom he felt alienated. The book gave no indication of any acrimonious family relationships and for the reminder of his life, Rauschenbusch struggled to conceal his own painful feelings toward his parents. Until the end of her life in 1913, Caroline Rauschenbusch continued to live near her eldest daughter in Germany. While he would have occasion to visit his mother again prior to her death, Rauschenbusch strove for a psychological severance from the childhood pain caused by both of his parents. With his own children, he was determined that he would be a different parent from what he had experienced growing up. Nevertheless, like many middle-class Americans of that generation, Rauschenbusch stressed to his children that their family needed to conceal any familial dissension. It was a lesson he learned well from his mother and father.

FAMILY VALUES

In 1899, Rauschenbusch delivered a commencement address that he would use frequently over the next ten years entitled "The Pleasures of Youth." Despite the levity of the title, the address suggested a deep anxiety that Rauschenbusch felt toward the moral character of the nation's youth, especially American womanhood. The address described the ideal moral society envisioned by many Protestant leaders at he end of the nineteenth century, including numerous warnings about the inherent dangers of "drinking, smoking, licentiousness, late hours," and overeating sweets as things that deter youth.[4] Yet the tone of the address also highlighted his disdain toward the sins of frivolous wealth that he underscored in his controversial sermon at Second German Baptist in February 1897, specifically, his concern that American women were increasingly losing touch with their obligation of working toward the kingdom of God. From the earliest days of his ministry, he shared the taken-for-granted Victorian supposition accepted by the majority of middle-class men, and many women, that the primary role for women was in the home. In this address, he gave classic expression to the "separate spheres" argument of social equality, in that men and women each had domain over their own sphere of social life. Whereas

4. WR, "The Pleasures of Youth," unpublished address, box 17.

men performed the larger "public" roles of earning a salary and tending to affairs of the larger world, women had responsibility for the nurture and care of children. "Certainly women can take joy in their work," he explained in his address. "It beams from the face of a housewife when she ushers guests into a home which she has created in its neatness and thrift, or sets good food before them which she has made, or watches the children whose vigor and beauty is the result of her constant and caring love."[5]

Scholarship on Walter Rauschenbusch's life has amply demonstrated his conservative views on gender equality.[6] Although he would later articulate strong support for women's suffrage, he clearly was enamored of the nineteenth-century belief that women, by nature, possessed superior gifts for nurture that would contribute to a better society. Like many late nineteenth-century American middle-class men and women, Rauschenbusch idealized women's virtues, which symbolized all that was aesthetically pure in life. "With the growing education of women I look forward to a great increase of beauty in our lives, and consequently an increase in the amount of enjoyment we get out of them [women]. . . . Women themselves will live more simply and naturally, and consequently more healthfully and beautifully."[7] Rauschenbusch's praise for the virtues of American womanhood was tempered by his disdain for many upper-class women. As he had expressed as early as his 1888 "Beneath the Glitter" article, Rauschenbusch identified the materialistic zeal of upper-class women with a spirit that would drain the economic and moral resources of the nation. Although he did not go as far as some of his contemporaries in his idealization of women, his message was nevertheless clear: the task of realizing the kingdom of God in America was the primary task of married women who insured the well-being of the nation through their roles as wives and mothers.

5. Ibid.

6. See especially Janet Fishburn, *The Fatherhood of God and the Victorian Family: The Social Gospel in America* (Philadelphia: Fortress Press, 1981); Fishburn, "Walter Rauschenbusch and 'The Woman Movement': A Gender Analysis," in *Gender and the Social Gospel*, ed. Wendy J. Deichmann Edwards and Carolyn DeSwarte Gifford (Urbana: University of Illinois Press, 2003), 71-86.

7. "The Pleasures of Youth."

> For women whose life-work lies largely in the home, it is comparatively easy to shed the glory of God over their work by regarding it as a service to God's humanity. To create a good home, to keep it clean, beautiful and restful, to penetrate its life with the spirit of love, kindness and purity, to make it a place where the aged will be honored, where the youth will be trained, and where the presence of the great Father of all families will pervade all things — this is the task of most women, and there are few things in life more directly useful to the Kingdom of God.[8]

Rauschenbusch's vision of the kingdom of God that centered upon his ideal of American womanhood increasingly found expression in a largely private dimension of his writing. During his early years at RTS, Rauschenbusch endeavored to write works of fiction, an enterprise that produced numerous short stories and plays — remaining unpublished. Rauschenbusch's literary flair had found outlets during his New York City years in pieces like "Beneath the Glitter," and in some modern-day parables that he wrote in *For the Right.* After he moved to Rochester, Rauschenbusch submitted a variety of short stories to numerous publications, including for several years annual entries in a contest sponsored by the Sorosis women's shoe company in Lynn, Massachusetts. Even after he became famous, he labored to have his fiction published, often writing under a pseudonym. Rauschenbusch's stories are revealing, both for their semi-autobiographical themes and for the way they accentuate his own perspectives on themes such as gender and personal virtue.

In one story, entitled "A Fourth-Class Fight," he tells of the main character's experience of riding in the fourth-class section on a train in Germany (that character resembled Rauschenbusch during his years as a student at Gütersloh in several respects). Through defending the honor of a young woman from a gang of toughs, and then surviving a physical altercation with this gang, the main character is able to win the affections and love of the young woman.[9] In another story that he submitted for the Sorosis competition entitled "His Heart in Her Footsteps," Rauschenbusch writes a highly sentimental and (unintention-

8. Ibid.

9. Walter Rauschenbusch, "A Fourth-Class Fight," box 41.

ally) humorous account of how two male vacationers in Switzerland end up following the footprints made by two women hikers in the snow, and how the main character falls in love with one of the women: by virtue of her footprints. "The vigor of her face, her radiant health, the quiet self-possession of her bearing, were exactly as he had read them from her foot-prints, and her beauty was greater than he had dreamed." Yet much to the character's chagrin, he finds that this beautiful woman was wearing shoes that were ill-suited for alpine hiking. The character's faith is redeemed, however, when it is revealed that the two women switched shoes on their hike, thus the "stronger" of the women gave her shoes to the "weaker" one. At the end of the story, as the man and the woman, Robert and Stella, confess their love for one another, their dialogue reveals much about the worldview of Rauschenbusch and his era of Progressive Era masculinity.

> "Oh, then you didn't fall in love with me at all, sir; you fell in love with my shoes," she pouted. "Very well; I'll make you a present of a pair and that is all you will want."
>
> "You little tease," he whispered. "It isn't all I want. And I didn't fall in love with your shoes, but with you through your shoes. I loved the girl that had sense enough to get such shoes and who used them as you did."

The sentiments expressed in Rauschenbusch's fiction reveal his longstanding tension with regard to sexuality. While he had admonished Pauline in 1898 that their male children's "sexual purity" be preserved "from boyhood up,"[10] his fiction enabled Rauschenbusch to express overtly a theme that lay beneath the surface of many of his theological writings — the inevitable and irresistible sexual tension that emerged between young men and women. Perhaps reflecting on his own perceptions of himself as a younger man, Rauschenbusch's male heroes were upright, intelligent, but not physically overbearing heroes, while his heroines were persons of high intelligence and class standing (often of a higher class standing than the young men in the story), but not adverse to the advances of these men.[11] Rauschenbusch made it a

10. Walter Rauschenbusch, copy of will dated May 17, 1898, box 143.

11. Walter Rauschenbusch, "A Fourth-Class Fight" and "His Heart in Her Footsteps," box 41.

point in his stories to note the special qualities and virtues of American women, in ways that reflected upon their unique sexual appeal. In "a Fourth-Class Fight," the main character reflects upon the virtues of American women compared to those of Germany. "It takes the background of a foreign country to make one realize the charm of American girls. They hold their heads high, look you straight in the eye, and dare to call their souls their own. . . . The German Fraüleins are very good and sensible, but an American girl is like a thoroughbred filly in that paddock."[12]

These various assertions, gleaned from Rauschenbusch's fiction, reflect upon one of the paradoxes on women that emerged in his "Pleasures of Youth" address. For Rauschenbusch, a woman's ability to shun the material and embrace the simple (including a willingness to engage in physical exertion) was part of her sexual appeal. "The beauty of American women has increased wonderfully in recent years, since they have begun to dress more sensibly and to exercise more," he noted approvingly. "There is nothing sweeter and more beautiful to the eyes of men than the beauty of women, and why should we let that beauty be spoiled for us without a protest?"[13] Rauschenbusch's praise for women of intelligence and beauty was inseparable in his mind from the ability of women to resist the temptations of material wealth.

Rauschenbusch's own family served as a context for the working out of his idealized view of women, and in some way his image of the ideal American woman began and ended with Pauline. Since their marriage in 1893, the couple's bonding and dependency upon each other grew stronger. With his work often forcing him to spend days, and often weeks, away from home, Walther and Pauline's correspondence continued to reflect the yearning for closeness and physical intimacy that characterized their earlier relationship. In their first seven years in Rochester, three more children were born: Paul in 1898, Karl in 1900, and Elizabeth in 1904. Elizabeth's birth, when Pauline was almost 40, was the culmination of a difficult pregnancy that almost cost the mother her life. Daughter Winifred remarked years later that one of the only times she ever saw her father cry was when it appeared Pauline might not survive the birth. "I did not know my father could cry. . . . He

12. "Fourth-Class Fight."
13. "Pleasures of Youth."

didn't care what happened to the child, he only cared about my mother."[14] Winifred's statement was not made as a callous observation, but to reinforce her belief, one shared by her siblings, that Walther and Pauline were completely devoted to one another. "My brothers and sister and I used to discuss this matter of how much our mother was in love with father. We decided that if a ship was going down on the ocean, and Mother had to choose between saving her five children and her husband, she wouldn't hesitate. We knew we wouldn't come first, and we admired her for it."[15]

Although the two parents were devoted to their children, the increased size of the Rauschenbusch home put added burdens on the family, emotionally and financially. Like many white Progressive Era reformers of his generation, Rauschenbusch displayed a fixation to embrace an upper-middle-class lifestyle, befitting someone of his education and vocation. This desire to settle into the professional world of Rochester's upper-middle-class society brought him many rewards in terms of public recognition during his years on the seminary faculty. But it also added to numerous worries about his family's financial and social well-being that never left him.

The Rauschenbusches had settled in a middle-class neighborhood located not far from Rochester Theological Seminary on the east side of the city. In addition to the Rauschenbusch family, the household also included a woman named Caroline Schaefer. "Tante" Schaefer, as she became known by the family, was the widow of one of Rauschenbusch's parishioners in New York. Originally taken on as a housekeeper and nanny after the birth of Winifred, Schaefer moved with the family to Rochester. Her presence, no doubt, alleviated some of the parenting stress on Pauline. At the same time, the burdens of her husband's frequent absences contributed to an emerging melancholy and depression within Pauline that grew more acute with the passing of years.

Outwardly, Pauline was seen by her husband and children as the ideal wife and mother. Like many ministers' wives of that generation, Pauline also played a critical role in the public success of her husband's career. According to Winifred, her mother possessed a distinc-

14. Autobiographical statement by Winifred R. Rorty, c. 1966, box 167.

15. Winifred [Rauschenbusch] Rorty, testimony written about Pauline Rother Rauschenbusch, n.d., box 143.

tive charisma that captivated her husband's male colleagues. These "public" skills were invaluable to her husband's success, for while Rauschenbusch often dreaded social interactions due to his deafness, Pauline not only served as her husband's interpreter but also could engage in conversations in ways that allowed her to promote her husband's views (and her own). For all the ways that she followed social convention, however, Pauline Rauschenbusch showed an ability to flaunt convention and custom. Winifred recounted one occasion when her mother, without hesitation or embarrassment, attended a party accompanied not by her husband, but by a male family friend. Although the Rauschenbusch children considered this type of social behavior on the part of a married woman "risque,"[16] there is no evidence that Walther objected to his wife's social outing. Winifred also noted that among her husband's associates drawn to Pauline was John D. Rockefeller, Jr. While her husband engaged Rockefeller on matters of theology and the social applications of Christianity, Pauline discussed with John and his wife, Laura, family matters and mutual friendships. Winifred was not exaggerating when she wrote that Pauline was "a better publicity man than [P. T.] Barnum. What she did to publicize Father even Barnum couldn't have done better."[17] The continued Rockefeller patronage of the Rauschenbusches that had begun in New York City continued in Rochester, as the Rockefellers sent an annual gift of $200 to the Rauschenbusches for many years at Christmas time — gifts that were always generously acknowledged by Pauline. Yet the financial burdens of the family never seemed to abate and with the passing of years, Rauschenbusch's financial worries brought out a side of his personality that was almost morose.

An early indication of this crisis sentiment emerged in mid-1898. His frenetic schedule of teaching, speaking, and travel ultimately had an ill effect on his health, and Rauschenbusch made the decision to revise the will he had made after his marriage to Pauline. This document not only reveals the anxiety he felt toward Pauline's financial wellbeing, but clearly indicates Rauschenbusch's desire that his family perpetuate and defend the "separate spheres" values of Victorian society. He noted to Pauline his hope that Hilmar ("and any other boys")

16. Ibid.
17. Ibid.

be exposed to numerous forms of athletics, asking her to encourage their son(s) to engage in gymnastics, swimming, and games of "ball." Consistent with late Victorian ideas of masculinity, Rauschenbusch saw physical labor and sport as a means of developing the virtues of the American male. Significantly, Rauschenbusch told Pauline not to pressure any sons to enter the ministry, rather "tell them early and late that every profession must be not only a means of earning a livelihood and getting ahead, but of serving humanity; their contribution to the service of God and to the Kingdom."

Rauschenbusch's hopes for Winifred ("and her sister or sisters") were equally clear, as he expressed to Pauline his desire that they learn the "trade" of being wives and mothers. "Let them learn to cook well and rationally; to make their own dresses and trim their own hats; and to get manual skill in every way." Although he wanted to see his daughters gain exposure to the disciplines of a classical education, that education was to be confined to their roles as wives and mothers, concluding, "perhaps a dozen years from now women will have ceased to chase wandering lights, but if not, counteract those fallacious tendencies all you can in our girls." Rauschenbusch's tone in his 1898 will was not unlike his father's — expressing a conviction that his family needed to represent the highest traits of virtue, piety, and intellect. Although encouraging Pauline to remarry if he should die, he also warned her to be careful of any future spouse selection, for her sake and for that of the children's, admonishing, "do not let the high intellectual and moral tone of the family life which we have tried to maintain, be merged in anything common or base."[18]

In the years ahead, Rauschenbusch wrote eloquently on numerous matters of theology and the greater public good. However, his belief that the family served as the nucleus for the coming kingdom remained strong throughout his life. Unlike his own ambiguous relationship with his parents, Rauschenbusch's family would be the paradigm of the modern American family: a place free of strife and abounding in love. As the years unfolded, however, he found that he could not escape the ambiguity of his own upbringing, as his family would serve as a source for some of his greatest joys and severest disappointments.

18. Copy of will dated May 17, 1898, box 143.

TURN-OF-THE-CENTURY PUBLIC MINISTRY

Although Rauschenbusch's teaching and travel schedule made it difficult for him to speak and write extensively on matters of Christianity and the social question, he kept up as best he could his wider work in organizations like the Brotherhood of the Kingdom, the Baptist Congress, and wider connections with German Baptist leaders. One of Rauschenbusch's first public successes in the city of Rochester occurred when a Thanksgiving Day sermon he preached in 1898 was reprinted in one of the city's newspapers. His sermon, "The Present and the Future," reflected on the recently concluded Spanish-American War in a tone reminiscent of other Protestant leaders of America's past who equated America's greatness with the providence of God. "There is in the heart of our people a deep sense of destiny, of a mission laid upon us by the Ruler of history."[19] Seeing God's hand at work in the defeat of Spain, Rauschenbusch saw no problem with the American annexation of Puerto Rico and the Philippines — these acts were connected to the hand of God in history, a God who was leading America toward a more glorious future in the world of nations. "[God] has made clear his will by the irrepressible force of events. . . . As a nation we must learn to walk by faith and not by sight. And if we have needed the help and light of God in the past, how much more will we need him in the future."[20] Like most American Protestant leaders of his generation, Rauschenbusch was guilty of a jingoism that easily invoked the theme of providence to explain the ways that America was at the center of God's plan for the redemption of the world.

In the same vein, he reflected both chastisement and chauvinism when he wrote and spoke publicly on his views of Germany. Rauschenbusch's views toward Germany at the end of the nineteenth century reveal mixed motives, condemning the nation's militaristic heritage on the one hand while exalting Germany's cultural heritage on the other. Although by the late 1890s he was clearly aligned theologically with the tradition of Ritschlian liberalism, he also disdained the lack of a democratic tradition in Germany, which had an adverse affect on that nation's religious climate. "German religion has been taught to confine it-

19. Rauschenbusch, "The Present and the Future," reprinted in Hudson, 134.
20. Ibid., 135.

self to the inner life, the family, and the personal calling," he explained. "When religion affects political action in Germany, it is by ecclesiastical considerations rather than by an ethical spirit."[21] Yet, as he would argue after the outbreak of World War I, Rauschenbusch rationalized Germany's colonial expansion as an understandable desire to compete with the colonial expansion of France and Great Britain. He drew upon the analogy of Jacob and Esau in the book of Genesis, seeing England as a nation already blessed with great wealth and power, whereas Germany struggled to gain equal international political status with its "Teutonic" neighbor. Similar to Josiah Strong's faith in the superiority of Anglo-American culture, Rauschenbusch emphasized that England, Germany, and the United States represented the highest attributes of Western culture. Yet he feared that worldwide English colonial expansion might ultimately lead to a series of European alliances that might have disastrous consequences upon the West. "The very vastness of England's power will drive her opponents into coalition," he asserted; the result he believed might one day lead to an all-out European war.[22]

Rauschenbusch's war rhetoric and views of Western imperialism were less strident and more chastened than many of his peers. Nevertheless, his writings reveal an overt cultural chauvinism, typical of white American secular and religious leaders of the late nineteenth century. He largely accepted Josiah Strong's argument from *Our Country* that some form of Anglo-Saxon civilization would supplant "inferior" non-Western cultures. Rauschenbusch affirmed that one of the challenges facing America in the twentieth century would be living in a world of increasing religious and cultural diversity. In an address given in Rochester at the dawn of the twentieth century, he argued, "as the national life once emerged from the tribal life, so now the international life of humanity is looming into view like the peaks of a continent that is still below the horizon." He believed that the great civilizations of the world were "those of mixed blood," and that the twentieth century would see an "inbreeding" of Eastern and Western civilizations.[23]

21. WR, "England and Germany," *The Watchman* (January 1900), quoted in Handy, 303.

22. Ibid., 307.

23. Undated manuscript, circa 1900, box 20.

In asserting his hope that Western cultural traditions might assimilate non-Western cultures, Rauschenbusch came precariously close to equating cultural virtue with biological superiority. In a 1902 commencement address at Rochester Theological Seminary, he asserted his belief that the Teutonic race rose to prominence in the world because of "providential purposes." They were "a princely stock, these fair skinned men, an imperial race, as they stand at the forge of time and hammer out history."[24] Reacting to the immigration pattern in Rochester, Rauschenbusch frequently lamented the fact that English and German blood were being mixed together with "alien strains of blood — the French . . . the Spanish, the Slav."[25] In the context of a century that witnessed the Holocaust, spawned by the secular millennial rhetoric of German fascism, it can be difficult to forgive Rauschenbusch's own version of "ethnic purity." However, the Progressive Era in America was a time when such ideas were far from unique among various secular and religious leaders of the movement. While showing a degree of interest in the ideas of eugenics, as a form of "social engineering" (including the use of vasectomies to prevent criminals and the mentally impaired from having children), Rauschenbusch never threw his full support behind such measures.[26]

Like Josiah Strong and other Protestant leaders, Rauschenbusch feared the effect of immigration upon the nation's social institutions, especially its families and churches. Nevertheless, he was optimistic that the massive societal changes of the late nineteenth century might lead to unprecedented possibilities for the nation's churches in the twentieth century. For Rauschenbusch, the new century would be marked by two interchangeable realities: the advance of Western democracy and the advance of the kingdom of God. In his Rochester address on the twentieth century, Rauschenbusch outlined four points for a just society. Point number one for Rauschenbusch centered on the family. Drawing upon a biological analogy, Rauschenbusch feared the breakdown of the nuclear family as the primary "social organism" in America: "As long as the cells [families] are healthy, any local hurt of the body can quickly be re-

24. Quoted in John R. Aiken, "Walter Rauschenbusch and Education for Reform," in *Church History* 36 (December 1967): 460.

25. Ibid.

26. See, for example, J. N. Hurty to WR, February 7, 1910, box 26.

stored; if the cells break down, the body is doomed." Rauschenbusch warned that increasing divorce rates in "all civilized nations" was a dangerous symptom that suggested the disintegration of the family. More to the point, however, Rauschenbusch put the onus for preserving the family upon women. "We need a new consecrating ideal for the family life to meet the new era. That duty rests mainly with our women." Not only were women expected to marry and have children, but the fulfillment of a woman's destiny in the advance of the kingdom was met in the raising up of Christian children. "The greatest service of women to humanity will not lie in doing men's work . . . , but in doing the work that women alone can do, as mothers of the race, but now with a larger intelligence and nobler purpose than of old. And to those women who are taking up the old burden with a new spirit I call all true men to bow in fealty and reverence. They are doing the work of the Kingdom of God, whatever the rest of us may be doing."[27]

Rauschenbusch's final three points — raising the moral standards of the professional classes, advocacy for the rights of the laboring classes, and "a loftier standard of righteousness in political life" — were impossible to achieve without a foundation in the family. For Rauschenbusch private morality, related to the values of the home, was inseparable from public morality.

> It is clear that the functions of the organized community will inevitably increase in the future. Our health, our pleasure, our safety, our education will depend more and more on the purity and efficiency of our public life. Then we must raise its moral standard. We should be far on the way toward a better future, if in the past we had felt free to entrust power to our government. Those who use public power for private ends, are not merely tapping the public purse for a few dollars; they are tapping the veins of our patriotic pride and hopefulness, and weakening us in the race for our civic ideals.[28]

Rauschenbusch's self-identity as a Christian socialist that he carried since his New York City ministry would grow throughout the

27. Undated manuscript, circa 1900, box 20.
28. Ibid.

new century. However, his vision of social salvation largely accepted the earlier vision of men like Washington Gladden and Josiah Strong. While Rauschenbusch articulated a portrait of social salvation that strove for political and economic reforms that went beyond the other two men, he shared with them a common faith: a belief that Christianity's purpose was to raise up morally virtuous people, who would "Christianize" all public facets of American society. As a New York City pastor, Rauschenbusch labored to convince powerful men like John Rockefeller of their obligation to reach out to the nation's poor. That appeal, however, was always tempered by Rauschenbusch's belief that such a transformative faith could not be imposed by force. It needed to be imparted in a spirit of Christian charity and love.

Still, by 1902 many American Protestants considered the social reform measures advocated by Rauschenbusch and other proponents of social Christianity as naive, or nonsensical. One pastor wrote Rauschenbusch in 1901 commenting that although he appreciated many aspects of Rauschenbusch's position on social questions, he felt that such a perspective was essentially antithetical to the role of a working pastor. "The demands of every pastorate on the conscientious minister, who takes Christ as his example in work, are such as to leave only exceptional instances where social problems could enter seriously in his real work. . . . What with regular preaching, pastoral work, personal effort to convert men, and general administration, few pastors find time even to 'dabble' in current theological literature. A man ought not to 'dabble' in social problems, unless for recreation. The eternal problem for the minister is to find time and strength for the peculiar duties that belong even to him and to nobody else."[29] Yet Rauschenbusch must have been rewarded when he received an occasional letter from a pastor who responded favorably to an address on social issues. After reading a copy of an address that Rauschenbusch gave to a group of Rochester Theological Seminary alumni, one pastor reflected, "You have such a lucid way of putting things and your words are so strong and so true that there is a ring of a prophet's voice in every utterance."[30]

Rauschenbusch's view of social change, however, continued to

29. William Lovett to WR, March 2, 1901, box 24.
30. Everett Burr to WR, May 16, 1902, box 24.

be moderate. In an 1898 address to the Baptist Congress, where he shared the dais with another Baptist leader of social Christianity, Shailer Mathews, he argued that industrial reform needed a balance between government regulation and self-initiative on the part of workers. "Remember that every great strike that fails, strengthens the impression that self-help is futile, and that salvation comes only by State help socialism. If you wish to stave off socialism, stiffen the public opinion which backs up the labor movement."[31] In 1901, Rauschenbusch participated in a series of lectures through the Labor Lyceum movement in Buffalo, New York, where he spoke on the need for Americans to distinguish between "dogmatic socialism and practical socialism." His address, reprinted in Rochester newspapers, emphasized the dangers inherent within the resolute dogmatism of political socialism and its faith in a catastrophic social-political revolution. Rauschenbusch conceded the great contribution of Karl Marx to modern economic theory, but castigated Marx and his followers for their unshaken fidelity to their economic determinism that dismissed other reform options. As he had expressed in his earlier "Ideals of Social Reformers" article, Rauschenbusch equated political socialism with the sectarianism of premillennial Christianity in that both movements, while coming from different viewpoints, clung to an apocalyptic view of history that saw social catastrophe as inevitable.

Rauschenbusch had embraced the identity of "Christian socialist" by the early 1890s, seeing in many socialist principles the ethical spirit of Jesus in the modern world. He was a strong advocate for state regulation and, in some instances, state control of certain monopolistic interests. Yet in calling for a model of "practical socialism," Rauschenbusch emphasized measures that needed to be implemented gradually over time. He hated Marx's view that human history functioned as a clock that wound to an inevitable conclusion, marked first by class violence and then by the enshrinement of a classless society. What America needed was a society guided by the precepts of democracy. Such a society over time could eliminate many of the pressing social evils that Marx believed could only be solved through violence and rebellion. He concluded hopefully, "In America the current of socialist thought

31. "State-Help Versus Self-Help, or Paternalism in Government," Baptist Congress address, 1898, quoted in Handy, 299.

and sentiment does not run in the channel of the socialist parties, but is leavening the ideas of the people and will transform our social organization in the direction of socialism quietly and gradually."[32]

A NEW IDENTITY

In spite of his devotion to the heritage of German pietism and his commitment to the ministry and mission of German Baptists at Rochester Theological Seminary, by 1902 it was evident that he felt ambivalent about his work in the department. As he later expressed to Augustus Strong, he felt that his experience in the department made him a "pedagogic hack," someone who could skim the surface of many disciplines but who could not dig deeply into a distinctive discipline.[33] Publicly the seminary extolled the virtues of the department, and although its enrollment was still high, the department was in a secondary position compared to the English department. The anti-German sentiment unleashed in America during World War I would hasten the demise of the German department. It is however likely that even without the war the department would have found it difficult to maintain its mission. Increasingly, German congregations moved away from German to English-language services, and gradually the distinctive role of German churches as ethnic enclaves gave way to greater assimilation as the twentieth century progressed.[34]

Rauschenbusch's commitment to the ministry of the German department made it difficult for him to engage in the sustained reflection on social issues that he had done while in New York in the 1890s. There were occasions for him to speak on social matters. But these occasions were always secondary to his teaching and fund-raising responsibilities in the German department. Rauschenbusch was also at a dead end in his efforts to raise the social consciences of larger German

32. "Dogmatic and Practical Socialism," *Rochester Democrat and Chronicle* (February 25, 1901); quoted in Handy, 322.

33. WR to Augustus Strong, April 11, 1904, box 24.

34. By the 1930s, the conservative pietism of the German department grew increasingly at odds with the liberalism of the English seminary. The German department became an independent seminary in the 1940s and in 1949 relocated to Sioux Falls, South Dakota, as North American Baptist Theological Seminary.

Baptist constituencies in the United States. Although he continued to write reviews and articles in German Baptist periodicals and continued to extol the distinctive contributions and virtues of Germany to American society, the pietism of German-American Baptists was increasingly premillennial and in conflict with his postmillennial vision of the kingdom. The son of August Rauschenbusch remained a respected figure among German Baptists in the United States. Yet many of them believed that this man had abandoned the faith of his father.

Rauschenbusch's life took a sudden turn late in the summer of 1902, when Professor Benjamin True in the English department, one of the men responsible for instilling Rauschenbusch with a love of church history back in his student days in the 1880s, died suddenly. In early September, just prior to the beginning of the academic year, Rauschenbusch assumed True's chair in the English department. Although viewed by Augustus Strong as a competent church historian, Rauschenbusch later conceded to the seminary's president that he considered himself ill-prepared to teach certain fields, especially medieval and modern church history.[35] Yet Rauschenbusch was strongly attracted to the church history position, not only because of the prospect of teaching in the English department but also because of his affinity to the discipline of historical studies. "My ambition is to be a real historian, who could make the past live, because he has lived in it. If our denomination has any such man know [*sic*], I don't know it."[36]

Rauschenbusch's appointment was greeted by praise from many of his colleagues. His friend, William Faunce, now president of Brown University, affirmed, "I am sure that now you will have the opportunity for all the leisure and study that is necessary for your life work. God's hand is in it all, I am sure."[37] Many of his former students in the German department reacted with ambivalence to the appointment, yet acknowledged that the appointment was likely in Rauschenbusch's best interest and that of the seminary. "I think it was wise on your part to accept the position; so much of your time was taken up with work of secondary importance, . . . and your influence for good will be much

35. Rauschenbusch to Strong, April 11, 1904, box 24; additional papers related to the church history appointment are located in box 39.

36. Ibid.

37. Letter William Faunce to WR, September 26, 1902, box 24.

larger in the English Seminary, and while our German work suffers, the general cause will be the gainer."[38] Another former student summed his feelings succinctly by affirming, "Your connection with the German department did not only raise the standard of that institution, but also gave it a standing such as it never had before."[39]

Walter Rauschenbusch's move to the English department at Rochester Theological Seminary brought closure to a component of his life that had begun when he accepted the pastorate of Second German Baptist Church in 1886. His departure from the German department did not immediately give him more time to devote to his writings on social Christianity. But the ability to teach full time in the field of church history provided him with an outlet that complemented and enhanced his earlier work on social Christianity. The move to the English department opened a door for him to pursue the intellectual avenues that ultimately proved germane to his later legacy in the social gospel movement. Rauschenbusch's social concern was spawned by the conditions of his parishioners in New York. However, his zeal to propagate a "social gospel" was always in competition with his desire to uplift the ministries of German immigrant pastors and laity. While Rauschenbusch never turned his back on his ancestral homeland, nor completely abandoned the faith heritage so loved by August Rauschenbusch, the German audiences nurtured by this pietist heritage would no longer be a primary focus for his work. In addition to embracing an English spelling for his first name, from 1902 to 1907 Rauschenbusch explored how the church's historical legacy provided a means for discerning its mission in the present. While not trained as a professional historian, Rauschenbusch would use history as a means to help his students discern signs of the kingdom in their midst.

38. Samuel Haemel to WR, October 6, 1902, box 24.
39. Frank Kaiser to WR, October 4, 1902, box 24.

7 The New Apostolate

Rauschenbusch's appointment to the church history chair at the age of 40 was a major professional accomplishment. His concern, however, about being a "pedagogical hack" in terms of his mastery over the discipline of church history would plague him in the initial years he taught in the English department. Yet Rauschenbusch quickly developed a clear dexterity as a history professor, both in his style as a teacher and in his methodology as a historian, even though he published little original research in his field. At the same time, Rauschenbusch's social activism, while still secondary to his teaching, took on a heightened level of intensity in terms of his involvement in the Rochester community. The roles of Rauschenbusch as a church historian and as an activist minister culminated during the summers of 1905 and 1906, when he decided to pick up the long abandoned task of writing an extended manuscript on the topic of the church and the social question.

THE VOCATION OF TEACHER AND CHURCH HISTORIAN

In the evolution of American theological education in the nineteenth century, church history emerged relatively late as a viable discipline.

Largely through the efforts of the Swiss-American historian Philip Schaff, church history gained acceptance as a distinctive theological discipline in many North American theological seminaries by the beginning of the twentieth century. Rauschenbusch, despite his reservations about his qualifications, was well suited to the intellectual temper that characterized the emergence of church history as a field of theological inquiry. Rauschenbusch's career coincided with an era in American theological education in which seminaries debated the extent that curriculums needed to "modernize" in the face of societal change. Not only were many seminaries incorporating German trends in biblical scholarship and liberal theology but also they were raising questions related to the place of sociological and other social scientific disciplines in theological education. The result often led to controversy, and between 1890 and 1910 numerous seminaries dealt with a host of heresy debates, often pitting seminaries against more conservative church judicatories, leading in some cases to the firing of high-profile seminary professors.[1] Later generations of Americans identified Rauschenbusch as a theologian, and many of his contemporaries identified him (as well as other well-known social gospel clerics) as a "Christian sociologist." After 1902, however, Rauschenbusch viewed himself professionally as a church historian, and it was this identity that gave shape to his views on theology and social reform.

Consistent with the way that his social thought matured during the 1890s, the study of church history had one primary goal for Rauschenbusch: to seek signs of the kingdom of God in history. As Henry Bowden points out, Rauschenbusch's views toward his discipline were directly tied to the theological legacy of late nineteenth-century German liberalism, building upon a succession of German idealists like Friedrich Schleiermacher, Albrecht Ritschl, and Adolf von Harnack.[2] For Rauschenbusch, the most important aspect of the church's existence was not centered upon debating matters of ecclesiastical doctrine or dogma. Rather, history was a means to discern how churches as social organisms embodied, or failed to embody, the teachings of Jesus

1. The most famous case in this regard involved the heresy trials of Charles Briggs at Union Seminary in New York. See Gary Dorrien, *The Making of American Liberal Theology,* Volume I (Louisville: Westminster John Knox Press, 2001).

2. Henry Warner Bowden, *Church History in the Age of Science,* 171.

concerning the centrality of the kingdom of God. Rauschenbusch became identified by many contemporaries and later commentators as a disciple of Ritschl. Yet he was clear about the limits of Ritschl's theology, both for understanding church history and for building a basis for contemporary Christian social action. "Ritschl has done more than any one else to put the idea [the kingdom of God] to the front in German theology," he wrote in 1917, "but he does not get beyond a few great general ideas. He was born too early to get sociological ideas."[3]

In this regard, Rauschenbusch largely modeled his view of church history after the towering work of Adolf von Harnack. By the early twentieth century, Harnack was the preeminent German historian, whose work at the University of Berlin had a critical influence upon a generation of American liberal Protestant leaders like Rauschenbusch. Following in the tradition of historical study crafted by Ritschl, Harnack devoted himself to the task of recovering for modern times the social and theological significance of Jesus' teachings. His seven-volume magnum opus *The History of Dogma* (originally published in the 1890s) and his two-volume *Mission and Expansion of Christianity* (originally published in the early 1900s) were works frequently cited by Rauschenbusch in his lectures and writings on the early church. Rauschenbusch embraced Harnack's admonition that the task of the good church historian was to distinguish between what was the "kernel" and "husk" in Jesus' teachings. Harnack emphasized that if the modern historian dug deep enough into the cultural and social world of the first century, one would recover the essence of Jesus' message. In a fashion similar to Harnack, Rauschenbusch challenged his students to discover the theological "kernels" within the teachings of Jesus that would have revolutionary consequences for the present-day church. Inevitably, these "kernels" pointed students toward understanding the social significance of Jesus' teachings concerning the kingdom of God. In 1911, the affinity between the two historians was marked when Rauschenbusch was one of two American church historians invited to sign an appeal that observed Harnack's sixtieth birthday.[4]

3. Rauschenbusch, *A Theology for the Social Gospel* (New York: Macmillan, 1917), 139.

4. Bowden, 170. The other American to sign this appeal was A. C. McGiffert at Union Theological Seminary, New York.

Despite his fondness for German scholars like Harnack, in many ways Rauschenbusch found the tradition of German theological liberalism to be too individualistic in its interpretation of Jesus' teachings. Consequently, he looked with greater regularity to a developing tradition of American biblical and theological scholarship that drew on many German sources, but greatly expanded the social significance of Jesus' teachings. After 1902, several of Rauschenbusch's writings made frequent reference to two books: Shailer Mathews's *The Social Teaching of Jesus,* published in 1897, and Harvard ethicist Francis Greenwood Peabody's *Jesus Christ and the Social Question,* published in 1900. Both books stand as classics in the liberal Protestant movement to uncover the historical Jesus. While both denied that Jesus could be understood as a contemporary twentieth-century social reformer, they did assert in varying degrees that the original mission of Jesus was inherently social and tied to the specific societal contours of the first-century Middle East. Mathews and Peabody revealed the extent to which many late nineteenth-century liberals viewed modern historical scholarship as a means to disclose the secrets of the social-political world in which Jesus lived and ministered.[5] Both Mathews and Peabody conceded that Jesus' ministry carried an apocalyptic tone, yet their interpretation of the historical Jesus centered upon the question of how his teachings could be reappropriated by future generations. Picking up on these themes, Rauschenbusch spoke of the study of history in scientific terms. "History is the biological language of humanity," he noted, and it was through such study that one could discern how churches and societies over time were living up to the standards set down by Jesus in the first century. As he argued frequently in his classes, "the spirit of Jesus is the ultimate canon by which every historical personality, institution, or movement must be judged, and our personal absorption of his mind and spirit is the ultimate qualification for a really useful study of the history of the Church."[6] Like many liberals of his generation, Rauschenbusch viewed history and theology as a two-sided coin, with each half dependent on the other. "The future of

5. See William McGuire King, "The Biblical Base of the Social Gospel," in *The Bible and Social Reform,* ed. Ernest R. Sandeen (Philadelphia: Fortress Press, 1982), 59-78.

6. Quoted from Bowden, 175-76.

Christian theology lies in the comprehension of Christianity in history. The future of Christianity itself lies in getting the spirit of Jesus Christ incarnated in history."[7]

Increasingly by the second decade of the twentieth century, liberal scholars like Mathews ultimately were won over to more of an apocalyptic view of Jesus' ministry. Rauschenbusch, however, always resisted the apocalyptic interpretation as a dangerous slippery slope. Taking his cues from Ritschl and Harnack, Rauschenbusch argued that historical processes never completely disappeared from one generation to the next. Rather, it was up to the student of history to be vigilant to the ways historical contexts were continuously reinterpreted by each new generation. As he wrote in a 1907 article, "Human life is continuous, and a subsequent period of history is always the most valuable interpreter of an earlier period."[8]

Rauschenbusch's interest in historical inquiry was not primarily geared toward abstract philosophical or theological insight. Although he valued the tradition of liberal German historical-theological inquiry, Rauschenbusch's primary interest in the study of church history was practical. For Rauschenbusch, history was nothing less than a way for Christian ministers to reinterpret the timeless truths of the Bible *and* a means for men and women to become advocates for the kingdom of God. As Henry Bowden summarizes, Rauschenbusch's classroom pedagogy used historical antecedents as a way to move his students toward a heightened social activism. "His lectures had the general effect of alerting students to social injustice and of urging them to act in the name of religion and humanity. . . . The tone of prophetic urgency about working for the future was one of Rauschenbusch's lasting contributions to the study and writing of American church history."[9]

Rauschenbusch covered a broad scope of topics in his history classes, ranging from early church to modern church history. What is significant about his teaching and writing, however, was the high emphasis that he placed upon the nascent discipline of American church

7. WR, "The Influence of Historical Studies on Theology," *The American Journal of Theology* XI (January 1907), p. 127.

8. Ibid., 114.

9. Bowden, 178-79.

history. Rauschenbusch's emphasis on American church history tended to focus on two interrelated ideas, first, how churches and historical figures worked toward, or impeded, the realization of the kingdom of God, and, second, how the nation's churches embodied a principle largely absent from European Christianity: political democracy. Rauschenbusch's fondness for American democracy was deeply ingrained in his love of history and in his faith in the kingdom of God. Church history at its best represented the passing down of the highest cultural, intellectual, and social advances from one generation to the next, and historically, one of the highest virtues was religious liberty. Rauschenbusch saw this spirit of liberty at work in St. Paul, calling him "the first great Protestant,"[10] and also in his fondness for the sixteenth-century continental Anabaptists. In a 1905 article in the *American Journal of Theology,* Rauschenbusch gave his approval to the ways the Anabaptists bequeathed to the church virtues of individual freedom and personal religious experience, while standing against the vanities of "illusive ritual" and "the impressiveness of ecclesiastical vestments and utensils."[11] Rauschenbusch taught his students that the sacrifices and martyrdom of these continental Anabaptists set the stage for the democratic Protestantism that would emerge in America.

Rauschenbusch resisted an interpretation of church history that saw the progressive realization of the kingdom of God as inevitable. Rather signs of the kingdom, not the kingdom itself, occurred periodically throughout history, and if there was one nation that embodied the possibilities of actualizing the promises of the kingdom of God, then it was the United States. In a frequently delivered address entitled "The True American Church," Rauschenbusch cited with approval how the evangelical traditions of American Protestantism, spearheaded primarily by Baptists and Methodists, gave rise to a shared ethos of personal liberty and democratic equality, despite their ecclesiastical differences. "The most decisive fact for the essential unity of these great bodies is that they have all thoroughly assimilated the principle of democracy," he affirmed. Rauschenbusch looked to the

10. WR, "The Freedom of Spiritual Religion," WR Scrapbook, Volume 2, ABSC Library.

11. WR, "Critical Note: The Zurich Anabaptists and Thomas Müntzer," *The American Journal of Theology* (January 1905): 106.

abolition of slavery as one historical instance in which the nation's churches used their moral weight to affect a revolutionary societal change. These evangelical traditions were the great catalysts historically for the redemptive social forces that he hoped the nation's churches could bring to bear upon twentieth-century American life.

> Their vast numbers, their wide dissemination, and their quiet assimilation together prove that these Churches are the fullest expression we have of native American religious life. They are a product of our national history. In turn they have formed the moral and spiritual life of our nation. Our literature, our national aspirations and convictions, the moral ideas which are axiomatic with the average American bear the impress of that religious genius which characterizes these Churches collectively and distinguishes them from other types.[12]

Not surprisingly, these "other types" that Rauschenbusch referred to were the churches with high liturgical and sacramental traditions. Rauschenbusch greatly admired the social activism and ecumenical spirit of "broad church" Anglicanism. That admiration was tempered by his disdain for the liturgical and sacramental practices that dominated the tradition. For Rauschenbusch, high church sacramentalism was but a fragment of a discarded history that would fade from the scene like all outdated ritualism. Such ritualism, he argued, pushed faith communions like the American Episcopal and Lutheran churches away from the larger spirit of cooperation that had characterized the nation's evangelical heritage. "The more we mingle on a basis of equality and good will and practical co-operation, the better will the assimilating forces of the common spirit of Christ be able to do their work, silently weeding out what is non-christian or obsolete."[13]

Rauschenbusch saved his major diatribes for the Roman Catholic Church. Although Rauschenbusch held out hope that high sacramental traditions like the Episcopalians and Lutherans might be won over to the cause of Americanization, his view of Catholicism was over-

12. WR, "The True American Church," unpublished manuscript, box 40.
13. Ibid.

whelmingly dim and dismissive. "In spite of the fine Americanism of many of its members and leaders, this Church is an isolated and foreign body in the midst of our national life," he asserted bluntly. In 1904, his entry on "Protestantism" for *The Encyclopedia Americana* initially raised the concern from the volumes' editors that his position harbored too strong an anti-Catholic bias.[14] While respectful of Catholic colleagues, his views on Catholicism were far from repentant. "As a Protestant I regard certain institutions and tendencies in Roman Catholicism as harmful, just as Catholics regard Protestantism as heretical and evil," he noted in a letter in a Rochester newspaper in late 1904.[15] Despite the deep affection he had for individual Catholics like Edward Hanna, Rauschenbusch clearly evidenced the deep-seated American Protestant suspicion of all things Catholic. In every respect, his views represented a continuing chapter of the largely ambivalent, if not hostile, response of nineteenth-century American Protestants toward their Catholic counterparts.

Rauschenbusch held the highest esteem for his own Baptist heritage. Because of their democratic polity, he believed that the Baptists came the closest of all contemporary movements to capturing the spirit of the early church. Rauschenbusch took great pride in the way that the Baptist historical legacy contributed to the virtues of religious liberty. Although he taught in a seminary that arose out of a Reformed Protestant heritage closely allied with the Calvinist theological legacy of New England Puritanism, Rauschenbusch (like his father) was prone to equate the history of American Baptists with the sixteenth-century Anabaptists. He was especially fond of the work of the Anabaptist historian Richard Heath. An English Baptist, Heath wrote *The Captive City of God* in 1904, which welded an Anabaptist ideal of the church to the goal of creating a democratic socialist society. Rauschenbusch shared Heath's enthusiasm for the goal of creating a church that "does not exist simply to be a fold where the sheep may securely feed, but to be a City in which a divine society may develop."[16]

14. See various correspondences, 1904 file, box 24.

15. Letter to *Rochester Union & Advertiser,* December 27, 1904, box 24.

16. Richard Heath, *The Captive City of God: The Churches Seen in the Light of the Democratic Ideal* (London: Arthur C. Fifield, 1904), 174.

Rauschenbusch returned repeatedly in his history classes to the theme that a truly prophetic Christianity meant opposing societal forces of power and privilege. As he argued in his classes, it was this distinctive contribution of the Baptists that contributed to the development of democracy in the United States, especially the unique American phenomenon of the separation of church and state. Yet Rauschenbusch was also aware that he came out of a faith tradition that frequently favored religious individualism over the need to transform society. He noted with disdain the way that many contemporary Baptists insulated themselves from the major societal problems of the day.

> Now that religious liberty is conceded by all and most of the great churches, abandoning their ancient ecclesiastical pride, have adjusted themselves to the practice of equality, the Baptists may safely modify their militant individualism and enter into that community religion which seems to be the present destiny of American religious life. It is one of the minor tragedies of history that this individualism, which was essentially a fighting attitude, now handicaps the Baptists to some extent in adjusting themselves to the social needs of the present day.[17]

Rauschenbusch, quite appropriately, is not mentioned in the lexicon of great names associated with the writing of American religious history. He wrote no great works of historical scholarship that redefined the parameters of the historical discipline, and the few articles that he published dealing with church history represented works on historical methodology, as opposed to original research. Yet in his own way, Rauschenbusch did contribute toward the twentieth-century articulation of historical study as a critical discipline to the task of theological inquiry. Analogous to how biblical scholarship of that era used history as a means to discern new interpretations of the Bible, Rauschenbusch used history as his doorway to investigate larger theological and social movements within the Christian church. As he wrote in a 1907 article:

17. WR, "Contributions of the Baptists to Civil and Religious Liberty," manuscript copy in box 19.

> History is to the race what memory is to the individual. It can understand its present and forecast its future only in the measure in which it really comprehends its past. . . . The fundamental fact in the Christian revelation was that the Word became flesh. Therefore Truth became History. Christianity was first a single life, then a collective life, then a stream of historical influences, and always a healing and saving power.[18]

Rauschenbusch emphasized repeatedly that the spirit of Jesus not only inspired transformative social movements but also accentuated how individuals needed to embody in their lives the distinctive personality of Jesus. That aspect of Rauschenbusch's methodology was certainly evident in the impact that he had upon his students. On the surface, Rauschenbusch often displayed the same formal demeanor that had characterized August Rauschenbusch. Yet he also had the gift of using humor in his classes, in ways that often surprised, and instructed, his students. When one student, overconfident in his intellectual acumen, received a paper back from Rauschenbusch, he was chastened to find but a single comment written by his professor: "cockle-doodle-doo."[19] As a former student recalled, "These occasional flashes of humor made for humanity and honesty of treatment; they laid bare many a holy sham; they invested with fellow-feeling many a situation remote from our experience."[20]

Accounts of his humor reflect upon the constant humility that Rauschenbusch displayed in his personal interaction with students, friends, and colleagues. "Rauschie," as his students nicknamed him, developed a reputation as a kind and generous man, whose sharp criticisms were softened by a warm and inviting personality. Rauschenbusch's classes were almost entirely lecture-driven, in part a reflection of the prevailing academic pedagogy of the era and in part a result of his deafness, which made dialogical classroom exchanges with his students nearly impossible. As a consequence, Rauschenbusch came to rely on a number of student secretaries who not only served him as

18. "Influence of Historical Studies on Theology," 127.

19. "Edwin Dahlberg in Conversation: Memories of Walter Rauschenbusch," Transcribed by John E. Skoglund, in *Foundations* 18 (1975): 209.

20. "Rauschenbusch Number," *Rochester Theological Seminary Bulletin* (November 1918): 34.

teaching assistants, but often served as interpreters in various public forums. Even with the difficulties of communication brought on by his hearing loss, Rauschenbusch kept an open door at the seminary and frequently opened his home for students to come for a meal and, on occasion, would join students on canoeing excursions on the nearby Erie Canal. Rauschenbusch also did not let his deafness interfere with his love of music. The family possessed a piano and it didn't take much persuasion on the part of students and guests to get Rauschenbusch to play a few songs, even as he professed his sorrow for those who had to listen to his playing.[21]

Rauschenbusch's popularity at the seminary was reinforced by the piety he displayed in his classes and in seminary chapel services. On numerous occasions, he would set aside class time for outside speakers to give Christian testimonies. Edwin Dahlberg, who served as one of Rauschenbusch's student secretaries, recalled one incident when Rauschenbusch, at his own expense, brought to one of his classes a man named "Spike" from neighboring Syracuse (ninety miles east of Rochester) to give his testimony on his transformation from professional robber and safe cracker to practicing Christian (thanks to his conversion at a Billy Sunday revival).[22] This incident indicates that despite his reservations about the premillennialism of preachers like Sunday, he still admired the way in which these preachers led seekers to receive Christ.

In his public interactions at the seminary, Rauschenbusch developed a reputation as being a sedate but profound speaker. Recalled Dahlberg, "He spoke very quietly; he was not an orator at all. He was not a public speaker in any grandiloquent sense at all, not spectacular; but he spoke with a real human feeling." Students especially looked forward to the occasions when Rauschenbusch would lead worship in seminary chapel services, especially absorbed by many of his pastoral prayers and his "beautiful chapel talks."[23]

In his early years on the English faculty, Rauschenbusch attempted to make himself available as a resource to local Baptist congregations. Despite the later public success of his ministry, Rau-

21. See, for example, WR to Winifred Rauschenbusch, October 4, 1908, box 143.

22. Dahlberg, 211.

23. Ibid., 212.

schenbusch always maintained a degree of activity within various Baptist, and non-Baptist, churches in Rochester, and even spoke later as a guest in an area Reform Jewish synagogue. The roles that Rauschenbusch played at the seminary and in the community were not without tensions. When Rauschenbusch joined the English faculty in 1902, he was one of only two liberals on the faculty, along with Walter Betteridge, professor of Old Testament. Yet Rauschenbusch was part of the first generation of liberal faculty that the increasingly theologically irenic Strong brought to the seminary from 1902 until his retirement in 1912. In 1903, another liberal, J. W. A. Stewart, was named the seminary's first academic dean, and in 1906 Cornelius Woelfkin became professor of homiletics.[24] Although by 1907 the seminary was split between the liberals and conservatives, the school's conversion to theological liberalism was well underway as the continuing retirements of old-guard stalwarts, including the venerable Strong in 1912, saw these men replaced by liberal faculty, including George Cross in theology, Justin Wroe Nixon in Old Testament, and Rauschenbusch's own protégé in church history, Conrad Moehlman.

Rauschenbusch's relationship with Augustus Strong remained conflicted. On the one hand, he greatly admired this elder statesmen of American Protestantism and showed him great respect as a colleague. Yet Strong never forgot that Rauschenbusch, once upon a time, was a former student, and their relationship since Rauschenbusch's graduation from RTS had always invoked a subtle tension that often emerged in correspondence. Prior to his appointment to the seminary, Rauschenbusch, on Strong's invitation, frequently spoke and lectured at the seminary. While these events evoked laudatory comments from Strong, he could not help but express his concern over the young man's apostasy. "I am glad to find you proclaiming *so much* truth, and doing it so vigorously," Strong wrote in 1892. "I only want you to be open to truth on the orthodox side as well as on the other side."[25]

While Rauschenbusch hinted at some of the theological tensions that existed with Strong and more conservative faculty in his first decade at Rochester, a far more pressing matter troubled him: faculty sala-

24. See LeRoy Moore, Jr., "The Rise of American Religious Liberalism at the Rochester Theological Seminary, 1872-1928."

25. Augustus Strong to WR, April 1, 1892, box 23.

ries. When Rauschenbusch joined the seminary in 1897, his income jumped considerably from the annual salaries he made in New York. However, he objected to the $3,000 ceiling that the seminary's trustees placed on salaries, asserting that such egalitarianism did not take into account that some faculty had outside sources of income, and that others, like himself, needed the money to support their families. "Most of the prof who were in the faculty five years ago had private income," he noted in a memo to Strong written around 1909. "Those who have no additional income and do have children, all have to struggle to get along. . . . I have given all my time to my work, but we have to live very plainly."[26] For many years, Rauschenbusch withstood Strong's paternalism in the face of repeated faculty requests for pay raises. Publicly, Rauschenbusch accepted this situation as a fait accompli. Privately, he came to resent the fact that he increasingly needed to find ways to supplement his salary with income generated from outside speaking appearances — opportunities that would come to him in abundance once his fame grew. Yet as Pauline noted bitterly in a letter many years later, she believed the seminary never fully valued Rauschenbusch's contributions to the school, reflected, in part, through what she believed was an inadequate salary. "Just think what it would have meant to Walter if he had a decent salary — or if the trustees realizing his worth had made up a fund . . . and made life easier for him."[27]

Rauschenbusch's married life had always been marked by anxiety over money, and that anxiety grew as his children moved into adolescence. With the family settled into a home that they purchased in 1900, Rauschenbusch had stepped into the middle-class prosperity that his father's family had enjoyed. Despite the concern to Pauline in his 1898 will that his daughters learn how to be proper late Victorian women, Rauschenbusch expected that they would aspire to the same educational standards as his sons. He spent his free hours drilling his children on school lessons, and frequently became cross with their teachers for being too lax on matters of discipline and academic rigor. The shadow of his father emerged when it came to his views on education. Rauschenbusch staunchly believed in the educational discipline and method he learned from his father, and he did not take kindly to

26. WR to Strong, c. 1909, box 50. See also additional correspondence in box 25.
27. Pauline Rauschenbusch to Edmund Lyon, March 28, 1920, box 112.

situations when the pedagogies of his children's teachers clashed with his own well-ordered views. As he complained to Winifred's teacher in 1904, "She tells me this evening that you objected to the things I had shown her and said that they were too hard for a child. . . . I am sure you will agree with the general purpose of my suggestions and I should be happy if you would co-operate with us in making her writing look less Persian and more English. I am sorry to say that in other points too her methods are unsatisfactory."[28] Rauschenbusch's life as an adult had moved him far beyond the cultural and theological world of his father. Yet his fidelity to certain aspects of the cultural world of August Rauschenbusch would be slow to subside and would often bring to the surface the most traditional side of his personality.

THE KINGDOM OF GOD IN ROCHESTER

Rauschenbusch's first five years in Rochester afforded him a degree of visibility in the local community, and in subsequent years the city became a staging area for many of his beliefs. In 1902, his growing stature in the community, coupled with his service to the seminary, earned him an honorary Doctor of Divinity degree from his alma mater, the University of Rochester. However, Rauschenbusch's first five years in the English department saw a heightening of his role as a civic leader that produced mixed results.

By the early twentieth century, Rochester was a city that fostered a number of liberal preachers who shared many aspects of Rauschenbusch's reform outlook. Numerous congregations in that city experimented with the institutional church model that he and Leighton Williams had utilized in New York a decade earlier. At a time when socialist agitation was on the rise in America, Rochester had its share of political socialists, who largely looked with disdain upon the city's churches. Many of the city's clergy were sympathetic to the cause of political socialism, and the ground appeared ripe for the city's clergy to join together in common cause. However, Rauschenbusch learned that at times ecclesiastical and practical differences were still strong forces to overcome. In the fall of 1903, he finally succeeded in organiz-

28. WR to "Miss Corey," December 6, 1904, box 24.

ing a Rochester chapter of the Brotherhood of the Kingdom. Rauschenbusch had attempted for several years to interest Rochester-area clergy in the Brotherhood endeavor, and the initial meeting of the Brotherhood was held in the parish house of an Episcopal priest named Algernon Crapsey.[29] Crapsey represented one of the most enigmatic religious leaders of his generation. The strongly activist minister of St. Andrews Episcopal Church in the city, Crapsey not only carried strong socialist sympathies but also was a staunch theological modernist in his views. In a series of lectures in 1904, Crapsey condemned a host of what he saw as obsolete church doctrines, including belief in the virgin birth, that led to him being tried for heresy by his Episcopal diocese in 1906.[30] Crapsey ultimately left parish ministry for a career as a writer and activist.

Crapsey's decision not to affiliate with the Brotherhood was a pattern followed by many clergy in the city. While they were sympathetic to the demands of working-class immigrants, there was no clear consensus as to the best means to reach out to that group. Rauschenbusch envisioned the Rochester Brotherhood as a group that would replicate the best attributes of the New York model. He wanted a group grounded in the spirituality of his fellowship with colleagues like Leighton Williams and Nathaniel Schmidt, and a group devoted to the serious study of social issues. "We should seek to give still greater solidity and educational value to our meetings for study, perhaps by studying several important books in common and discussing them along definite lines," he suggested.[31] Yet he conceded that his colleagues needed to be tentative in their efforts at organizing, acknowledging the gaps in perspective that existed. "There is at present no body of real vitality in our city. . . . All that we do to create oneness of judgment on current questions among us would then make it easier to act together promptly and with practical unanimity."[32] Despite Rauschenbusch's attempts to bolster the Brotherhood concept locally, the Rochester chapter of the Brotherhood of the Kingdom never suc-

29. WR, "The Future of the Brotherhood," unpublished document, May 1904, box 90.

30. Blake McKelvey, "Walter Rauschenbusch's Rochester," in *Rochester History* 14 (October 1952): 14-15.

31. WR, "The Future of the Brotherhood."

32. Ibid.

ceeded in capturing the spirit of enthusiasm that galvanized the New York group ten years earlier.

Although results with the Brotherhood were disappointing, Rauschenbusch did forge critical friendships with prominent clerical and professional interests in the city that cemented his status as a middle-class reformer. From the business community, Rauschenbusch drew constant support from Joseph Alling and Edmund Lyon. When Rauschenbusch spoke of the need for the church to advocate for the cause of a gradualist reform vision, Alling epitomized the type of Christian lay reformer that social gospelers like Rauschenbusch envisioned who would labor for the kingdom. The head of a prominent Rochester paper company, Alling was the president of the local YMCA and conducted an annual men's Bible class at the Central Presbyterian Church in the city that attracted thousands, reportedly the largest such gathering in the nation.[33] Alling was also a major civic force within the "good government" movement that campaigned for bipartisan support against political corruption and on behalf of a number of reform initiatives. Edmond Lyon was a Rochester entrepreneur, whose wealth was channeled into a host of philanthropic initiatives including Rochester's first school for the deaf. In subsequent years, Lyon also was a member of the seminary's board of trustees and one of Rauschenbusch's staunchest supporters on the board. Among his friends in the clergy, Rauschenbusch was closest to Paul Moore Strayer, pastor of the city's historic Third Presbyterian Church (the very church where Charles Finney decades earlier had staged his earliest revivals in the city). In later years, the friendship between Strayer and Rauschenbusch would initiate one of that city's most innovative efforts at kingdom building.

Rauschenbusch's stature in the community was fully acknowledged when he was appointed in 1904 as the head of a YMCA-sponsored committee to investigate the city's social conditions. This was not his first effort at communitywide activism. In 1902, he waged a successful campaign against Rochester Gas and Electric that led that company to lower its utility rates. The following year, he delivered a speech in support of Democratic mayoral candidate James Johnston,

33. Minus, 120, and McKelvey and Rosenberg-Naparsteck, 96.

the only occasion in Rauschenbusch's career where he gave a speech on behalf of a political candidate.[34]

The YMCA commission was given the task of preparing a report on social conditions in the city, and Rauschenbusch saw the commission as an opportunity to unite the city's churches behind a common social vision. He worked to prepare a questionnaire that was sent out to the city's clergy and engaged civic leaders like Alling on specific reform measures that might be undertaken. Of particular concern was how Rochester would deal with the major influx of immigrants that had been pouring into the city for several years. Rauschenbusch received many sympathetic responses to his solicitations, yet he also had his skeptics. One recent English immigrant to the city, while generally applauding Rauschenbusch's motives, remained skeptical that the YMCA commission would effect lasting change in the city. "But after you find out all these things and prove that these evils really do exist, you will only know what hundreds of other people (common people) know, what all the politicians and all the government of the city know. And personally or by committee you can do absolutely nothing by way of reform."[35] From the writer's perspective, Rochester's politics, like that of most cities, was horribly corrupt and no amount of golden-rule Christianity could root out the city's vices. The man concluded with a diatribe that in all likelihood struck Rauschenbusch as a painful truth. "And as a rule the ministry . . . just moves in a little circle of their own and do not understand the wants, wishes nor aims of the great army of intelligent men whom their actions and their preaching have failed to bring into the church."[36]

Rauschenbusch was pained by such accusations and recognized the truth behind them. The YMCA commission issued its final report in May 1904 and its recommendations represented both the best and the worst aspects of Progressive Era reform efforts. The report contained a number of recommendations that called upon the city's political, civic, and religious leaders to apply their moral and political force to alleviate the problems of the inner city, epitomized by urban overcrowding and an overabundance of saloons. As he had done in New

34. Minus, 122.

35. Arthur E. Davey to WR, February 16, 1904, box 24.

36. Ibid.

York, Rauschenbusch pushed hard for the construction of playgrounds and other recreational facilities for the city's poor immigrant communities. He also recommended that the city institute free Sunday band concerts as a means of providing wholesome entertainment alternatives to the city's saloons. Both the playground and the concert measures created a degree of opposition from some leaders, but these reform efforts were supported by the majority of civic leaders, who joined forces with Rauschenbusch. While Rauschenbusch was not the  only Rochesterian to lead the city to expand its existing playgrounds, he did play a critical role in building public sentiment to make the city one of the major centers for the "playground movement" in the United States.[37]

At the same time, the concern expressed to him earlier by the task-force skeptic, that the nation's middle-class churches were out of touch with the workers, reflected a critical weakness of social gospel and Progressive Era activism. For most of his public ministry, Rauschenbusch displayed a tremendous empathy for working-class people. However, his goals as a reformer, like many other secular and religious leaders of that time, were predicated on making the religious and cultural values of the white Protestant middle class available to the masses. No recommendation of the YMCA commission proved more controversial, and more insightful into Rauschenbusch's social vision, than the commission's recommendations on marriage and family. Expressing an argument he would use in succeeding years, Rauschenbusch argued that the problem of moral vice in Rochester was caused not only by problems of immigration, tenement housing, substandard wages, and poor recreational and educational opportunities for the poor. It was also the result of the fact that immigrants were delaying marriage out of economic necessity. Consequently, the commission recommended raising  wages as a measure to promote marriage. In words most certainly written by Rauschenbusch, the report affirmed, "Next to a man's relation to God, his relation to the opposite sex is perhaps the most determining fact of his life. The home life of the people is certainly the most important factor in their happiness and goodness." Citing recent census data, the report bemoaned the fact that economic conditions in Rochester pushed not only young men into the labor force but also young women

37. McKelvey and Rosenberg-Naparsteck, 106, 108.

as well. If this pattern continued, the report warned, the consequences upon the city could be catastrophic:

> when a large percentage of men remain chronically unmarried for years . . . , it is a symptom of trouble and it breeds vice. Unmarried men imply unmarried women, women who for years, presumably during their best and most efficient years, are cut off from the home-life for which God has destined them, and are compelled to seek their support in other callings in which they find no happiness and in which they frequently compete with the men who might be their husbands and make it still harder for them to support a wife. This is a vicious cycle.[38]

More alarming still, however, was the fact that those who did marry early and produced offspring represented the least Americanized immigrant groups, in particular immigrants from non-Protestant eastern Europe. He warned Rochesterians that "the class that marries early will have a great preponderance of offspring."

> The alarming number of childless or almost childless marriages among the so-called better classes is partly due to the late age of marriage. This leaves it to the foreigners to replenish the population of America. . . . The physical and intellectual fibre of the people is improved by residence in this country; our women are better educated than the women abroad; these qualities might be transmitted by heredity and home training; but this tremendous power by which the present might lift the future is frustrated by the widespread reluctance to marry and to rear children.[39]

As noted in the previous chapter, Rauschenbusch's views in regard to race and ethnicity were typical of his time. In a similar vein as Josiah Strong, Rauschenbusch was advocating an American society predicated on specific cultural standards, as opposed to advancing arguments for the biological supremacy of Anglo-Saxon (or German) Americans. Yet his comments underscore the way that he, and other

38. YMCA report, box 96.
39. Ibid.

social gospel liberals, viewed social progress through a distinctive late nineteenth-century lens. For Rauschenbusch, the theological task of building the kingdom of God was also synonymous with the advancement of specific cultural values and suppositions of white middle-class Americans.

Rauschenbusch in the upcoming years continued to be involved in numerous efforts to rid Rochester of the city's illegal saloons, repeatedly advocated for the city to use municipal resources to build recreational facilities, and argued as well to improve the city's public transportation system. He and his reform colleagues in the community were modestly successful in many of these areas. However, they did not anticipate that the biggest substitute for the saloon and other vices would not be the city's parks or the free band concerts, but the growing number of motion-picture houses that opened in the city prior to 1910.[40] These movie houses soon became one of the city's major entertainment resources among the working class, surpassing in popularity Protestant-sponsored initiatives of reform.

THE NEW EVANGELISM

Rauschenbusch's responsibilities in the English department significantly reduced the travel schedule that went with his role as fundraiser in the German department. However, his teaching responsibilities at the seminary still left little time for extended speaking and writing on social questions. He spoke regularly to Baptist regional associations and local churches in the Northeast and the Midwest, on topics ranging from contemporary morality, the role of Christianity in the modern world, and the church and "the social question." In early 1904, Rauschenbusch submitted an article on the relationship of evangelism to contemporary Christianity to *Outlook* magazine. Although the editors appeared intrigued by the piece, they turned it down. Rauschenbusch then submitted the article to the *Independent*, another important popular periodical of that era, which accepted the piece and made plans to publish it that spring.

With the exception of his later books, none of Rauschenbusch's

40. McKelvey and Rosenberg-Naparsteck, 108.

writings reached as large an audience as his article "The New Evangelism," which appeared in the *Independent* in May 1904. Rauschenbusch's article is significant not only for how he spelled out many of his ideas on "the social gospel" but also how he related it to the larger historical tradition of Protestant evangelicalism. The article makes clear that Rauschenbusch viewed evangelism as the historical lifeblood of the church, and that his "new evangelism" was not simply discarding the old for the new, but grafting the new onto that which was indispensable from the old. This new evangelism "will have to retain all that was true and good in the old synthesis, but advance the human conception of salvation," he explained. "It will have to give an adequate definition of how a Christian man should live under modern conditions, and then summon men to live so."[41]

Rauschenbusch believed that the church historically advanced two understandings of evangelism: the first "proclaims new truth, as Jesus did to his nation, or Paul to the Gentiles, or as a missionary does to the heathen." The second, modern version of evangelism "summons men to live and act according to the truth which the Church has previously instilled into their minds and which they have long accepted as true."[42] The purpose of the first type of evangelism, Rauschenbusch argued, was primarily centered upon the self; the latter, in contrast, focused upon the Christian's ethical imperative to serve one's neighbor.

It is easy to see in Rauschenbusch's critique a certain hostility to a tradition of individualistic salvation. However, the article captures the sense of ambiguity that Rauschenbusch and other social gospelers felt about the changes within modern industrial society. He believed that the early years of the twentieth century revealed unprecedented social upheaval, and the only way for the church to live up to its mandate to spread the gospel would be for the church to discover effective means to spread its teachings. For Rauschenbusch, Christian conversion was not simply a matter of being "saved" by God as individuals. Conversion was a matter of placing the entire society, both the rich and poor, under the judgment of God in the face of America's failure to live out the moral virtues of Christian teaching. "The powerless-

41. "The New Evangelism," *Independent* (May 12, 1904), 6, pamplet in box 40.
42. Ibid., 3.

ness of the old evangelism is only the most striking and painful demonstration of the general state of the churches," he lamented. The church's impotence had nothing to do with lack of hard work or vibrant devotional spirits on the part of Christians. "It lies in the fact that modern life has gone through immense changes and the Church has not kept pace with it in developing the latent moral and spiritual resources of the Gospel which are needed by the new life."[43] Rauschenbusch's "new evangelism" would be marked by a regenerated social behavior on the part of humans, especially by a spirit of repentance on the part of the rich toward the poor. "A compelling evangel for the working class will be wrought out only by men who love that class, share its life, understand the ideals for which it is groping, penetrate those ideals with the religious spirit of Christianity, and then proclaim a message in which the working people will find their highest self."[44] As his involvement on the Rochester city YMCA task force reflected, it was often difficult for Rauschenbusch to distinguish his sincere desire to be in "solidarity with the oppressed" on the one hand from his paternalism toward the working class on the other. At the same time, his "New Evangelism" article represented an excellent convergence of the theme of social crisis coupled with the optimism that the present was a unique moment for change. For too long, he asserted, the church's message had been shaped by the power of wealth, as opposed to the power of the gospel. The time was at hand when the church needed to free itself from that bondage, with a message of hope to those who were oppressed. This blending of the contrasting themes of crisis and hope would characterize much of his writing in the years ahead. As he concluded in his article:

> I have full faith in the future of the Christian Church. A new season of power will come when we have put our sin from us. Our bitter need will drive us to repentance. The prophetic spirit will awaken among us. The tongue of fire will descend on twentieth century men and give them great faith, joy and boldness, and then we shall hear the new evangel, and it will be the Old Gospel.[45]

43. "New Evangelism," 5.
44. Ibid., 6.
45. Ibid.

The less-than-subtle reference to William Arthur's *Tongue of Fire* in the article's final sentence reveals how fervently Rauschenbusch believed that the church had entered a distinct era of history. At the center of transformation in the church, he believed, was the laity, and in the year after "The New Evangelism" appeared, he cited with strong approval a series of religious revivals that broke out in Wales. Noting the ways in which the Welsh revivals expressed a deep continuity with a deep-seated tradition of European and American revivalism, Rauschenbusch affirmed how the biblical gift for speaking in tongues was analogous to the religious enthusiasm of the Welsh people. "The singing in the Moody and Sankey revivals formerly, and still more in the Welsh revival today, occupies the same place as the 'speaking with tongues' in the primitive church," he observed. "It is a movement of the people and has evoked their latent powers, thereby making the ministers less prominent and predominant. It has awakened the true religious consciousness of immediate relation to God, including a sense of spiritual enlightenment and compulsion in the utterance of faith."[46]

Rauschenbusch remained wary of excessive emotionalism in worship, reflecting his negativity toward the Holiness movement from his Ocean Grove experience in the summer of 1887. His contemporary sanction of the spirit of God in the present, however, suggested to him that God was at work transforming the contemporary church in an exciting new way. "The true way for us will be, I think, not to copy slavishly the phrases and manners of the Welsh revival, but to recognize the great avenues of approach to God which are rediscovered in every revival and to take our people along these paths to meet God."[47] (Rauschenbusch's assertion turned out to be prophetic, since he wrote this article less than a year before the Azuza Street revivals in Los Angeles, marking the birth of the spirit-filled movement called Pentecostalism.)

Walter Rauschenbusch clearly believed that personal conversion was an important step in one's relationship with God, but as he made clear in "The New Evangelism" and his article on the Welsh revivals, it

46. "The Welsh Revival and Primitive Christianity," *The Watchman* (June 15, 1905), quoted in Hudson, 110.

47. Ibid., 110.

was only a partial step. It remained to be seen whether the Welsh people would move in the necessary direction of making their Christianity an "ethical revival." Their religion "leaves the mine worker to toil for his bare wage. . . . It leaves the children to go to hard work as soon as the law permits. The exploitation of the people by rent and the wage-system will go on."[48] For all of his affirmation of a spirit-filled evangelism, Rauschenbusch was wary of the twin dangers of religious "perfectionism" on the one hand and "the vagaries about the second coming" on the other. Yet he was confident that with the passing of time these traits would become spiritual anomalies in the modern church.

Rauschenbusch genuinely sought a theological integration between a spirit-filled evangelicalism centered on individual renewal and a liberal theology that insisted on the ethical renewal of society. As a worldwide movement, he stood confident that the ethical imperative of primitive Christianity would ultimately supersede a Christianity based on the singular objective of getting individuals into heaven.

Rauschenbusch's "New Evangelism" article led to an interesting array of reactions, and garnered sympathy from unlikely sources. Russell Conwell, the popular minister associated with his message of wealth and prosperity, concurred with many of the article's points, conceding that Rauschenbusch was essentially right in pointing out the way that churches were often held captive by the motives of the rich. "It looks to the writer," Conwell surmised, "as if the confusion is to be greater, the darkness deeper and the fermentation more violent, before the 'future' church will begin to crystallize into definite form." However, William Rainsford, rector of St. George's Episcopal Church in New York, one of the nation's largest "institutional churches," protested what he felt was Rauschenbusch's undue pessimism about the church's ability to reach out to the nation's workingmen. "There is a new evangel. It is here today. It is leavening the Church, it is salting the world, and it cannot be trodden under the foot of men."[49] While many clergy responded sympathetically to Rauschenbusch's appeal for a new evangelism, several laity remained unconvinced at the wisdom of his appeals. "Boiling it all down, sympathy for our fellow men is the supreme motive," conceded one businessman. "The Professor how-

48. Ibid., 110-11.
49. See Handy, 323.

ever, wishes to apply this according to a special way, while I think that the best thing the church can do is to preach it on general lines."[50]

The perspective of this letter was echoed by many in America who advocated that churches largely needed to take a "hands off" posture toward matters of social-economic reform. Indeed, the social enthusiasm that captured the imagination of several church leaders during the 1890s had appeared on the wane by the early 1900s. Although no less a figure than Josiah Strong had asserted in 1902 that the nation's churches were on the verge of a social Christian "great awakening," the signs by 1905 were less than encouraging. Despite the continuing popularity of authors like Charles Sheldon and of liberal clergy like Washington Gladden, many of the original propagators of social Christianity in the 1880s and 1890s had disappeared from the public eye. By the early 1900s, George Herron's career was effectively over, after he acknowledged having an affair with his benefactor's daughter. He resigned his faculty chair at Iowa College and became more interested in promoting the cause of political socialism than that of social Christianity. While W. D. P. Bliss continued as an activist, he found himself increasingly under attack for his views, as did Richard Ely, whose popularity declined after 1900. Troubled by the lack of Protestant unity in America that he predicted back in the 1880s, Ely shifted his professional interests away from social Christianity in his later career, although he continued to advocate for a number of municipal reforms that reflected the arguments of his early career.[51] Even as American politicians and newspapers increasingly attacked the practices of business monopolies and condemned the working conditions of the nation's cities, the nation's churches appeared to have little to say. As one observer commented in 1904, "the churches, . . . if we may judge by what one hears in churches, or what one sees taking place in their great assemblies, do not seem to be very greatly disturbed by the situation."[52]

The Progressive Era was on the rise in America between 1902 and 1907. Symbolized by the leadership of President Theodore Roosevelt,

50. John Wiechers to F. W. C. Meyer, November 17, 1904, box 24.

51. Handy, 182.

52. Donald Gorrell, *The Age of Responsibility: The Social Gospel in the Progressive Era, 1900-1920* (Macon: Mercer University Press, 1988), 35.

numerous leaders pushed for a variety of reforms in industry, child labor, and the environment. However, the nation's churches appeared to resist an engagement with these larger reform movements. A statement from an annual conference of Chicago area Methodist church leaders in 1901 was typical of the church's conservatism. As representatives of the nation's largest Protestant denomination, in one of America's most industrialized and populated cities, the assembly affirmed that matters of economic inequality could largely be solved through Christian philanthropy. "While wealth brings with it great temptations to corruption, it nevertheless indicates the wisdom of our national leaders and the blessings of God upon our fields and commerce. It makes possible the greater comforts of the home, the increased privileges of all classes, the enlargement of educational and philanthropic enterprises, and the universal spread of the kingdom of God."[53]

Yet underneath the surface of this sentiment, the religious and social passions that had fueled the first wave of the social gospel in the 1890s were still evident within American society. Settlement houses continued to grow into the twentieth century, many of which reflected a strong religious orientation. The ranks of young women devoting their lives to the vocation of home missionaries in the nation's inner cities continued to grow, as did a variety of institutional churches in the nation's major cities. While reflecting a definite minority among American Protestant clergy, ministers such as Rauschenbusch's colleague Samuel Batten in the Brotherhood of the Kingdom, Harry Ward in Chicago, and Frank Mason North in New York were strong advocates for causes of Christian social reform. Another New York City minister, Charles Stelzle, became head of the Presbyterian Home Mission Society in 1903, launching his career as one of the most flamboyant leaders of the social gospel. That same year, Frank North wrote his famous hymn, "Where Cross the Crowded Ways of Life," a meditation upon the church's need to address the social misery of the inner city. The zeal that had galvanized social Christianity in the 1880s and 1890s, while perhaps dormant in the minds of many, was far from dead. In fact, a second, more permanent movement of liberal social Christianity was about to emerge.

53. *Minutes of the Rock River Annual Conference of the Methodist Episcopal Church* (Chicago, 1901), 71.

In the summer of 1905, Walter Rauschenbusch made the decision to revisit and refine many of his earlier writings on social Christianity into a book-length manuscript, drawing largely on his published and unpublished writings from the early and mid-1890s. The book that emerged from his effort would forever change the way in which many in the twentieth century viewed the relationship between religion, politics, and social reform.

Portrait of August Rauschenbusch, taken in the early years of his tenure
at Rochester Theological Seminary

Caroline Rauschenbusch, 1869

Rauschenbusch *(right)* with his sisters
Emma *(left)* and Frida *(center)*, 1865

Rauschenbusch and his sister, Emma, in a portrait from 1879,
just prior to his departure for Germany where
he would study for the next four years

Rauschenbusch as a Rochester Theological Seminary student, 1884

Rauschenbusch in the early years of his
New York City ministry, around 1888

Pauline Rother prior to her marriage to Walter Rauschenbusch, 1892

Rauschenbusch in his early years on the
Rochester Theological Seminary faculty

Pauline and Walter Rauschenbusch with their five children prior to their departure for Europe in the spring of 1907 (the children *left to right,* Elizabeth, Paul, Winifred, Karl, Hilmar)

Rauschenbusch with Leighton Williams at a Brotherhood of the Kingdom gathering at the Williams' family home, 1909

Walter Rauschenbusch at his desk.
This picture was taken not long after his return to America in 1908 where he was met by national acclaim following the success of *Christianity and the Social Crisis.*

Walter and Hilmar Rauschenbusch on a family outing, circa 1914

Winifred Rauschenbusch in an Oberlin College school play, around 1914. Winifred served as one of her father's chief confidants in his later years, despite their considerable differences on matters of religion.

Walter Rauschenbusch, April 1918, three months prior to his death

Portrait of Augustus Strong from the 1880s. One of American Protestantism's major theologians of the late 19th century, Strong became concerned over Rauschenbusch's theological orthodoxy during the latter's years as a student at Rochester Theological Seminary.

George Coleman, Baptist layman who was the primary architect of the Open Forum movement, one of the major speaking outlets for Progressive Era intellectuals, like Rauschenbusch, to disseminate their ideas

Samuel Zane Batten, northern Baptist clergyman and influential co-founder and leader of the Brotherhood of the Kingdom (From *Nebraska Baptist Annual*, 1903)

Cornelius Woelfkin, pastor of the Fifth Avenue Baptist Church, New York City. A former faculty colleague of Rauschenbusch, Woelfkin became the central figure in the final public controversy of Walter Rauschenbusch's career.

8 A Psychological Moment

On September 17, 1906, Rauschenbusch sent a chapter draft for a book manuscript to the Macmillan Company. While modest about his own professional qualifications as a writer, he nevertheless spoke boldly about the subject of the proposed book. "I am sure that my book covers a great deal of ground which has not been touched in previous discussions in this country, and it approaches the subject by different methods. . . . The subject is bound to remain under discussion for years to come and just now a large number of ministers and others are opening their mind to social questions, who have been indifferent before, and are seeking an adjustment between their old views and the new."[1]

Rauschenbusch's assertion was indeed farsighted. However, the story of how he came to write the book that would ultimately be titled *Christianity and the Social Crisis* reflected the culmination of work that he began fifteen years earlier when he wrote the "Christianity Revolutionary" manuscript. Although Rauschenbusch abandoned the possibility of revising this earlier work, he mined themes in the manuscript for several articles that appeared in both denominational and in academic journals like the University of Chicago's *American Journal of So-*

1. WR to Macmillan Company, September 17, 1906, box 46.

ciology.[2] One such article, "The Stake of the Church in the Social Movement," written at the end of Rauschenbusch's New York City pastorate, served as an outline for one of the chapters in the new manuscript. The book's final chapter derived from an address that he had given in New York back in 1896.[3] Yet when Rauschenbusch sat down at a friend's summer cottage in Canandaigua, New York, in June of 1905 to begin the task of synthesizing his work on the church and the social question into a book-length manuscript, he was still somewhat ambivalent about writing a book on social Christianity. For one thing, Rauschenbusch was troubled by the fact that he had yet to produce a major work dealing with the subject of church history. While still interested in carrying forward his interest in writing on the Anabaptists, he also pondered the prospect of writing a more general study of the Christian church. Coincidentally, after he nearly finished work on the social Christianity manuscript, he turned down an invitation from a professor at the University of Chicago to write a book on the theme "Great Men of the Christian Church." The proposed manuscript, which would have been designed for church laity, reflected Rauschenbusch's desire to reach a larger audience, and the invitation from Chicago appealed to that instinct. "You know the history, you are interested in the people for whom the book is to be prepared, you write in a charming style, and from every point of view I have felt desirous that you should undertake the writing of the book."[4]

Although he did not acknowledge it as such, Walter Rauschenbusch's manuscript on social Christianity was largely a revisionist account of Western church history. As he sifted through old addresses and articles, the new manuscript flowed quickly from his pen and typewriter. He wrote two complete chapter drafts in the summer of 1905 and largely blocked out the outline for the rest of the book. When he picked up the project again during the following summer, despite some trepidation about its quality, he finished up the manuscript in six weeks.[5] Rauschenbusch did not have to wait long for a response from

2. See, for example, Rauschenbusch, "The Stake of the Church in the Social Movement," *The American Journal of Sociology* 3 (July 1897): 18-30.

3. See Handy, 331.

4. Ernest Burton to Rauschenbusch, July 19, 1906, box 25.

5. See Rauschenbusch, "The Genesis of 'Christianity and the Social Crisis,'" in *Rochester Theological Seminary Bulletin* (November 1918): 51-53.

Macmillan. In October they reviewed the entire manuscript and in November 1906 they accepted the manuscript for publication.

Rauschenbusch realized he had written a unique book that cast fresh light on the issue of the church's relationship to contemporary social problems. As he anticipated the book's publication in early 1907, he did not realize that he had written what many of his contemporaries, as well as future commentators, would see as the first definitive narrative of a Christian political social vision for twentieth-century society.

THE MEANING OF THE CONTEMPORARY SOCIAL CRISIS

The intellectual resources that Rauschenbusch assimilated into the book's arguments were familiar names in American social Christianity and in theological liberalism. In his notes compiled during the book's writing, he mentioned such Americans as Francis Peabody, Shailer Mathews, and Richard Ely, the German sociologist Karl Kautsky, as well as the historical theology of Albrecht Ritschl and Adolf von Harnack. The style of the manuscript, however, and the substance of the argument were distinctively Rauschenbusch.

The first four chapters in the book — half of the manuscript — represented a historical synopsis, where Rauschenbusch fleshed out the prophetic nature of religion in ancient Judaism and Christianity, explaining his reasons why historically the contemporary church had lost sight of the social significance of Christianity. In these chapters, Rauschenbusch sought to restate many of the arguments he had used in his lectures on church history at RTS. Picking up on the influential work of Shailer Mathews's *The Social Teaching of Jesus*, Rauschenbusch acknowledged that although Jesus was not a social reformer in the modern-day sense, he nevertheless revealed, both to his time and to the present era, the essence of the Christian message embodied in the kingdom of God. While Jesus geared his message to individuals, the nature and outcome of that message was profoundly social. Taking his cues from many of the themes that he espoused in the opening chapter of "Christianity Revolutionary," Rauschenbusch argued that Jesus "nourished within his soul the ideal of a common life so radically different from the present that it involved a reversal of values, a revolutionary displacement of existing relations."[6] As he had stated many times previously, the essence of Christianity, when it had the revolutionary power to proclaim the radical good news of Jesus' social hope for the kingdom of God, manifested itself when the church functioned as a democratic body. The early church manifested the full force of its power, according to Rauschenbusch, when it "brought with it a strong leaven of democracy and protest which unsettled men."[7]

Like his father before him, Rauschenbusch insisted that the ideal church was one free of state coercion, but also free of the ecclesiastical excess and nondemocratic ethos associated with the history of the Roman Catholic Church. Although he saw the disintegration of the spirit of Christian independence and democracy occurring early in church history, epitomized by St. Paul's admonishments for Christians to submit themselves to state authority, Rauschenbusch clearly placed the lion's share of the blame for the loss of the church's social message on the shoulders of the medieval Catholic church. The revolutionary implications of Jesus' message were lost amidst the rise of an institutional Christianity that obscured Jesus' message through the sacraments "and superstitious rites with which to placate and appease the Father of Jesus."[8] Picking up on a frequently argued point, Rauschenbusch believed that the essence of the Catholic church's sacramentalism not only propagated a harmful self-serving aestheticism but also focused the church's ministry upon the goal of perpetuating itself ecclesiastically, thereby obscuring the ethical imperatives taught by primitive Christianity. The Reformation set the context for the modern renewal of Christianity. Yet the social-economic changes of the nineteenth century placed the contemporary church in a unique position to recover the social meaning of the kingdom as taught by Jesus in the first century. Rauschenbusch believed that the millennialism of early Christianity, which served to undercut the social nature of the church's ministry, was largely dying out in modern society. He castigated the asceticism and apocalyptic themes inherent in the millennialism of St. Paul and the primitive church. As he had done in his 1896 articles on millennialism, however, he praised what he saw as the revolutionary

6. Rauschenbusch, *Christianity and the Social Crisis*, 90.

7. Ibid., 133.

8. Ibid., 94.

spirit inherent in early Christian millennialism, which planted the seeds for a radical redistribution of power in the ancient world. "The millennium was the early Christian Utopia," Rauschenbusch asserted. While conceding that the early Christians did not envision an economic restructuring of society, the millennial hope of the early church made them look toward a complete transformation of society. "They hoped for a change complete and thorough; for an overturning swift and catastrophic; for an absolute transition of power from those who now rule to those who now suffer and are oppressed. What else is revolution?"[9]

It was this "kernel" of truth — the social expression of this millennial hope — that Rauschenbusch believed had the possibility of rekindling within the modern church the true nature of its mission grounded in Jesus' teachings on the kingdom. Rauschenbusch looked hopefully for signs that the radicalism of this social message would be unleashed upon contemporary society. Consequently, the essence of modern Christianity would no longer be grounded in an ascetic gospel, preaching only an exclusive message of individual salvation. Rather the church would pursue the social hope of Jesus and the primitive church to embrace the world and to transform it with a radical new message of salvation.

When Rauschenbusch wrote the book in 1905 and 1906, he fervently believed that an age of Christian asceticism and superstition synonymous with the liturgy and sacramental system of the Catholic church would die out in Western Christendom. "Ceremonialism, which early clogged the ethical vigor of Christianity, was broken in the Reformation and is slowly dying out." Although elements of this tendency remained in Catholicism and in certain Protestant traditions, these were churches that failed to comprehend the significance of Jesus' teachings on the kingdom for the church in the modern world. Rauschenbusch remained confident that these historical forces at work in these "romantic reactions toward the past" would ultimately disappear in modern Christianity. "The prophet can prepare to enter his heritage, provided the prophet himself is still alive with his ancient message of an ethical and social service of God."[10]

9. Ibid., 108.
10. Ibid., 205.

Rauschenbusch's historical exposition set the context for his readers in the first half of the book. It was in the second half of the book, however, where he presented the main thrust of his argument, discussing how Jesus' message of the kingdom of God might be applied to the specific conditions of modern American society. Rauschenbusch characterized his arguments of social reform as "dangerous," for the ways he challenged the social conservatism within many of the nation's churches. Yet his outlook largely consisted of many ideas already propagated by other social reformers of that time synthesized into a distinctive theological message that came to define the heart and soul of the social gospel.

While Rauschenbusch clearly identified himself with an 1890s tradition of Christian socialism, he made it clear in the book that his socialism derived not from the materialism of Marx, but from the democratic ethos of Jesus. "Socialism is the ultimate and logical outcome of the labor movement,"[11] he asserted in the book's final chapter. While the capitalist system dehumanized the worker, and provided him no access to the wealth he produced, socialism symbolized an egalitarianism consistent with modern Protestantism. "Just as the Protestant principle of religious liberty and the democratic principle of political liberty rose to victory by an alliance with the middle class . . . , so the new Christian principle of brotherly association must ally itself with the working class if both are to conquer."[12] Although his views on state regulation went further than Gladden's tendency to rely on a "Golden Rule" faith in mutual cooperation between labor and management, Rauschenbusch insisted that the impetus for any type of political socialism needed to come from Christianity. "The idealistic movement alone would be a soul without a body; the economic class movement alone would be a body without a soul. It needs the high elation and faith that come through religion."[13]

Rauschenbusch sent out a plea for Americans to embrace the logic and wisdom of socialism. However, a discussion of the finer points of socialist theory occupied a relatively small part of the book. What gave the book its distinctive hue, compared to previous writings on American social Christianity, was the way that Rauschenbusch bal-

11. Ibid., 408.
12. Ibid., 409.
13. Ibid.

anced the dual themes of social crisis and constructive opportunity for Christian social action, similar to what he had done in his "New Evangelism" article a few years earlier. Using the language of a physician diagnosing a patient's illness, he laid out a discussion of themes contained in his earlier writings and speeches on social problems, focusing on the problems of labor, unregulated land speculation on the part of the rich, and the perpetuation of moral vice in America caused by economic inequalities. Despite the problems that characterized the growth of late nineteenth-century industrialism, Rauschenbusch believed that the West, and especially America, stood at an epoch of history that might lead either to "social regeneration" or social catastrophe. The catastrophe would be the result of the capitalist system that had the potential to exhaust the economic and moral resources of America. Yet amidst the potential for social disaster that hung over the nation, Rauschenbusch made it clear that he was "not a despiser" of his age. "There is no other age in which I should prefer to have lived."[14] It was his task in the final 200 pages of the book to make a case for Christian involvement in the social crisis. What emerged from his appeal was a radical theological message of prophetic transformation cloaked in a strong social conservatism.

Rauschenbusch's style lacked the overt jingoism and ethnocentrism of Josiah Strong, but many of Rauschenbusch's arguments would easily have fit into the paradigm of American exceptionalism advocated by Josiah Strong in *Our Country.* In chapter five, entitled "The Present Crisis," he identified three themes that were ripping apart the social fabric of America: the exploitation of labor, the crumbling of political democracy, and the decline of the moral climate of America. In his discussion on the plight of American workers, he argued the case of reform, relying on a distinctive separate spheres ideology and citing how the social crisis caused by American capitalism was eating away at the core institution in American society: the family. "A man's work is not only the price he pays for the right to fill his stomach," Rauschenbusch asserted, "it is the output of his creative energy and his main contribution to the common life of mankind. The pride which an artist or professional man takes in his work, the pleasure which a housewife takes in adorning her home, afford a satisfaction that ranks next to hu-

14. Ibid., 220.

man love in delightsomeness."[15] Rauschenbusch did not posit a full-scale assault upon the institutions and values of American life. Rather, his chief concern was to address how the changes in America, caused by industrial capitalism, could be countered by the moral force of Christianity. While he gave voice to the economic problems created by capitalism, he was equally concerned with how capitalism was eroding the moral fabric of the nation. Taking a page from his own experience in New York, he made a key insight that undergirded much of the book's outlook. For Rauschenbusch, capitalism's greatest sins transcended economic variables, but reflected how the system destroyed the moral fabric of both the oppressed *and* oppressing classes of Americans. He reflected upon his own experience of living in New York City during the economic depression of the mid-1890s:

> I saw good men go into disreputable lines of employment and respectable widows consent to live with men who would support them with their children. One could hear human virtue cracking and crumbling all around. Whenever work is scarce, petty crime is plentiful. But that is only the tangible expression of the decay in the morale of the working people on which statistics can seize. The corresponding decay in the morality of the possessing classes at such a time is another story. But industrial crises are not inevitable in nature; they are merely inevitable in capitalism.[16]

Rauschenbusch tapped into a rhetoric of the American family with deep roots in nineteenth-century America. His discussion of substandard nutritional conditions for the inner city poor made him not only reflect on the need to protect the poor from food-contaminating bacteria but also to suggest that housewives strive for wholesome standards of food preparation. "Canned goods are a sorry substitute for fresh food," he mused. "The ideal housewife can make a palatable and nourishing meal from almost anything. But the wives of the workingmen have been working girls, and they rarely have a chance to learn good housekeeping before they marry."[17]

15. Ibid., 234.
16. Ibid., 238.
17. Ibid., 241.

At the center of such assertions was his dire fear that industrial capitalism was destroying the heart of a democratic society: the family. Rauschenbusch viewed the family as analogous to living cells in a larger body — if the cells died out then so would the larger body. What especially concerned Rauschenbusch was the way that modern capitalism impeded the growth of the larger body, by delaying the marriages of young men and women. "The existence of a large class of involuntary celibates in society is a more threatening fact even than the increase of divorces," he argued.[18] Reflecting upon his own work on the Rochester YMCA commission a few years earlier, he worried that the increases in European immigration would not only exacerbate the economic problems of urban life but also cause an explosion in immigrant populations that native-born Americans could not match. As much as Rauschenbusch detested the social Darwinism of Herbert Spencer, he used an argument that turned Spencer's social philosophy on its head. "Education can only train the gifts with which a child is endowed at birth. The intellectual standard of humanity can be raised only by the propagation of the capable. Our social system causes an unnatural selection of the weak for breeding, and the result is the survival of the unfittest."[19] Rauschenbusch's social revolution would be galvanized by white middle-class families, who shouldered the responsibility for modeling the behavior expected of Christian families in America.

The task of prophetic Christianity was to advocate for the downtrodden in society. Yet the prophetic voice also needed to represent the traditional standards of social and moral decorum embodied by the ethos of late nineteenth-century Victorian Protestantism. Rauschenbusch's ideal social order was one in which workers would receive a livable wage, have access to public parks, and safe working conditions, and eat untainted and nutritious food. Yet it was also a nation where the strong (native-born Protestants) would look after the interests of the weak (immigrants) and where the Victorian family model represented the cornerstone of a stable, democratic society. For Rauschenbusch, preserving and maintaining the fabric of American society centered upon preserving the moral purity of the nation's women.

18. Ibid., 272.
19. Ibid., 275.

Rauschenbusch was outspoken in his castigation of the working conditions endured by working-class women. The social degradation that women experienced in the workplace removed them from their roles in marriage and as wives and mothers. In rehashing a long-standing argument, he chafed at what he saw as the frivolous wealth of upper-class women, whose excesses in fashion set a poor example for working-class women and girls. While he believed that most American women were predisposed to marriage and having children, the desire of poor women to aspire to wealth was both vain and idolatrous. These women "crave for the clothing, the trinkets, the pleasures that glitter about them," Rauschenbusch complained.[20] Although Rauschenbusch expressed his empathy for the plight of poor women, beneath his concern was his desire to defend one of the most sacred beliefs embedded in the worldview expressed by many women in late nineteenth-century Protestantism: Christian womanhood was essential for creating a Christian nation. "To any one who realizes the value of womanly purity, it is appalling to think that the standard of purity for their whole sex may drop and approximate the standard prevailing among men."[21]

His perspective on the American family, on immigration, and especially on the moral virtue of American womanhood reflected a "separate spheres" view of social equality that advocated that women and men were inherently equal, but fulfilled different roles in society. Although Rauschenbusch moved beyond many fellow late Victorians in his views of women's public voice, especially related to suffrage, he, like most Americans, was far removed from the voices of radical feminism of the late nineteenth and early twentieth centuries that attacked the suppositions of this ideology. In Christopher Lasch's famous study, Rauschenbusch's view of an ideal society was one grounded in a nation where men braved the consequences of public life and women offered men and their children "a haven in a heartless world."[22]

The ends of the "revolutionary society" that Rauschenbusch sought were often quite conservative. Still, his theological language embodied a distinctive liberal tradition that helps explain his appeal for a

20. Ibid., 278.

21. Ibid., 279.

22. Christopher Lasch, *Haven in a Heartless World: The Family Besieged* (New York: Basic Books, 1977).

later pantheon of twentieth-century Protestant theologians who often refuted, yet built upon, his theological foundations. In writing the manuscript, Rauschenbusch mined many contemporary liberal theological arguments related to the social teachings of Jesus and the kingdom of God, and one finds in the manuscript copious citations from individuals like Shailer Mathews and Adolf von Harnack. What separated Rauschenbusch from the German liberal school was the way he tied his historical and theological narrative to the rise of America in the nineteenth century as the great political and moral exemplar in the world. And what (easily) separated him from individuals like Mathews and Francis Peabody was the literary flow of his narrative. His was not a technical account of Jesus in the abstract, but a concrete translation of how Jesus' social teachings could lead to a just society in which God prepared a place for all people, regardless of economic wealth.

Rauschenbusch's legacy in twentieth-century theology rests partly in how he connected Christianity to the necessity for political engagement. Inherent within Christianity's mission was the imperative to work for democratic social change. "Approximate equality is the only enduring foundation of political democracy. The sense of equality is the only basis for Christian morality."[23]

More than any other social gospel leader up to that time, Walter Rauschenbusch wrote what amounted to a manifesto for the white Protestant middle class. Like Richard Ely before him, he advocated moderate economic reform measures, epitomized by his continued devotion to the single-tax solutions of Henry George. Rauschenbusch's style rivaled the rhetorical morality of Washington Gladden's published sermons and essays. But unlike these authors and a spate of other social Christians of the previous twenty years, Rauschenbusch's book gave a historical and theological rationale and blueprint of how *and* why the nation's churches needed to address the great social problems that emerged in the late nineteenth century. Unlike the tone of George Herron's work in the early 1890s that took a socialism-at-all-costs stance, Rauschenbusch appealed to the moral conscience and sensibilities of the American middle class. Ray Stannard Baker, one of the most popular writers of the Progressive Era, explained the book's impact in a 1909 article by commenting on how it balanced a thorough

23. *Christianity and the Social Crisis*, 247.

social analysis with a clearly irenic spirit. "Though he writes strongly of social conditions, though his convictions are deep, nowhere in his book will there be found a note of hatred; and he leaves the reader inspired with a new faith in the power of religion to meet and solve the most complex of the problems of the day."[24]

While Rauschenbusch and his critics never viewed it that way, *Christianity and the Social Crisis* was also a profoundly theological work that set the tone not only for the development of the social gospel in America but also for the subsequent development of American theological liberalism in the twentieth century. At a time when premillennialist sentiment was rising, Rauschenbusch, consciously or unconsciously, propagated a powerful reformulation of an early nineteenth-century postmillennial Protestantism, restating for early twentieth-century Americans the imperative for Christian social reform. Rauschenbusch would be criticized by many theological critics and supporters for placing too much emphasis on the prophetic dimensions of the Old and New Testaments, ignoring the eschatological and individual conversionary dimensions inherent within Christian history and especially evident in nineteenth-century Protestant evangelicalism. Yet Rauschenbusch insisted that the church had room for a theology that included the necessity of both personal and social conversion.

Although Rauschenbusch had little use for John Calvin or his theological successors, he tapped into a distinctively historical Calvinistic ethos in which the church existed not just as a separated, sectarian body, but as a leavening force responsible for raising the social and moral outlook of the larger community. "The men who have worked out the new social Christianity in their own thinking and living will constitute a new type of Christian," he asserted toward the climax of the book.[25] "After twenty or thirty years the young men who now embrace the new social faith will be in the controlling positions in society and will carry into practice some fractional part of the ideals of their youth."[26] Rauschenbusch highlighted a number of nineteenth-century influences that were the leaven for the later rise of social Christianity, citing movements as

24. Ray Stannard Baker, *The Spiritual Unrest* (New York: Frederick A. Stokes Company Publishers, 1910), 271.

25. *Christianity and the Social Crisis*, 352.

26. Ibid., 353.

wide-ranging as Brook Farm Transcendentalists and the evangelicalism of the YMCA and the Salvation Army. What the future of Christianity held for him was a church and a nation that valued social welfare at the same level as individual welfare. "It is the function of religion to teach the individual to value his soul more than his body, and his moral integrity more than his income. In the same way it is the function of religion to teach society to value human life more than property only in so far as it forms the material basis for the higher development of human life."[27]

The most significant aspect of the book's future legacy in Protestant theology, however, was the way that Rauschenbusch tied his theological vision of social justice to the theme of social crisis, presenting to readers a unique historical opportunity to act in the face of injustice. Here is where Rauschenbusch's indebtedness to a legion of German historians from Neander to Harnack was most evident. Nineteenth-century German historiography had a deep-seated tradition of wedding human experience with a belief, epitomized by Harnack, that moments in history gave individuals and groups the opportunity to realize a higher social hope. Later critics would criticize Rauschenbusch for what they viewed as his optimism in human social progress. Yet Rauschenbusch made it clear in the book, as he had done throughout his ministry, that he dismissed any notion that human social and moral progress was somehow divinely ordained. "History laughs at the optimistic illusion that 'nothing can stand in the way of human progress.' It would be safer to assert that progress is always for a time only, and then succumbs to the inevitable decay."[28]

Christianity and the Social Crisis was not Rauschenbusch's strongest statement on the merits of Christian socialism, nor was it his most incisive theological rationale for tying together Christianity and social reform. However, it was a book that combined these themes into a message that directly addressed the contemporary anxiety that faced many middle-class Americans in the early twentieth century. Although Rauschenbusch believed fervently in the ideal and the concrete realization of social progress, his view of human progress was based upon periodic advances, juxtaposed with times of defeat. "Nations do not die by wealth, but by injustice,"[29] he reasoned. For although a na-

27. Ibid., 372.
28. Ibid., 279.
29. Ibid., 284.

tion might outwardly manifest the fine furnishings of art, culture, and wealth, that nation might already be spiritually dead to the social wrongs being committed against the masses. Echoing themes from the prophets of the Hebrew Scriptures, he asserted that the primary hope for the regeneration of a nation was the rising up of moral forces made up of individuals willing to lay down their lives for a higher cause. "If there are statesmen, prophets, and apostles who set truth and justice above selfish advancement; if their call finds a response in the great body of the people; if a new tide of religious faith and moral enthusiasm creates new standards of duty and a new capacity for self-sacrifice; if the strong learn to direct their love of power to the uplifting of the people and see the highest self-assertion in self-sacrifice — then the intrenchments of vested wrong will melt away; the stifled energy of the people will leap forward; the atrophied members of the social body will be filled with a fresh flow of blood; and a regenerate nation will look with the eyes of youth across the fields of the future."[30]

In one respect, Rauschenbusch shared something in common with his premillennialist critics: a belief that history was connected to a web of human suffering and pain. However, while premillennialists viewed this suffering as a sign to be on the lookout for the end times, Rauschenbusch, and a generation of liberals that followed him, viewed human suffering as an ongoing social reality that had the potential to be redemptive. As one scholar noted, "What Rauschenbusch envisioned was a commonwealth of justice, mutual love, cooperation, and service that could only be purchased at the price of conflict, suffering, and sacrifice."[31] For Rauschenbusch, the supreme enemy of such a vision was a faith rooted solely in personal salvation, because it moved one selfishly away from the world, whereas a social faith called one to renounce one's self-interest by calling one to reach out to one's neighbor and, by extension, the world.

In this regard, Rauschenbusch's understanding of the kingdom of God reached a new level of importance in American theology. For even as historical opportunities might slip away from one generation to the next, the ideals of the kingdom, grounded in a faith in social jus-

30. Ibid., 285.

31. Douglas Ottati, Foreword to *Christianity and the Social Crisis* (rev. ed., 1991), xxvi-xxvii.

tice, would pass from generation to generation. In the book's final pages, Rauschenbusch admonished Christians that the social struggle on the road ahead would be a difficult one, but to nevertheless maintain an optimistic view of the future.

> In asking for faith in the possibility of a new social order, we ask for no Utopian delusion. We know well that there is no perfection for man in this life: there is only growth toward perfection. In personal religion we look with seasoned suspicion at any one who claims to be holy and perfect, yet we always tell men to become holy and to seek perfection. We make it a duty to seek what is unattainable. . . . At best there is always but an approximation to a perfect social order. The kingdom of God is always but coming.[32]

In the book's final paragraph, Rauschenbusch could not resist adding his hope that nineteen centuries of church history had finally put Christianity in the position to actualize the power of its liberating message to society.

> Last May a miracle happened. At the beginning of the week the fruit trees bore brown and greenish buds. At the end of the week they were robed in bridal garments of blossom. But for weeks and months the sap had been rising and distending the cells and maturing the tissues which were half ready in the fall before. The swift unfolding was the culmination of a long process. Perhaps these nineteen centuries of Christian influence have been a long preliminary stage of growth, and now the flower and fruit are almost here.[33]

Rauschenbusch believed that he had written a provocative book, going so far as to call it "a dangerous book," because of the possibility of the negative reaction it would induce from various quarters in the church. Indeed, part of Rauschenbusch's misgivings rested on how the book's liberalism would be received by his faculty colleagues and the trustees of Rochester Theological Seminary. At the very moment

32. Ibid., 420-21.
33. Ibid., 422.

that Macmillan published *Christianity and the Social Crisis* in April 1907, Rauschenbusch and his family embarked on a year-and-a-half-long sabbatical in Germany. The timing of the sabbatical with the book's publication was as much a coincidence as it was a desire for Rauschenbusch to escape any potential scrutiny caused by his book. He had been a faculty member at RTS for nearly ten years by the spring of 1907, with the primary focus of his work focused on his teaching and administrative duties at the seminary. The eighteen-month sabbatical not only gave Rauschenbusch an opportunity to engage in leisurely study and research, but just as important, gave his children an extended opportunity to be immersed in the German culture so critical to his own youth.

Rauschenbusch was also likely cognizant of the fact that while his social outlook was not universally embraced by many rank-and-file clergy, his theological liberalism was no longer the novelty it had been even fifteen years earlier. Although Rochester was still viewed as an orthodox seminary, liberalism was showing signs of making inroads, even within the writings of Augustus Strong. Strong still prided himself as a paragon of theological orthodoxy, yet his own theology increasingly made small concessions to liberalism in the 1890s and early 1900s.[34] William Newton Clarke even joked in a letter to Rauschenbusch in late 1906 that the venerably orthodox Strong was coming close in his views to some of Clarke's and Rauschenbusch's own evangelical liberal insights, noting somewhat wryly, "it is good to welcome so mighty a man into a healthy heresy."[35]

Rauschenbusch did have reason to be worried, however. Given the acrimony that surrounded his hiring in 1897, he braced himself for what he believed would be inevitable criticism. He could not help but worry that the seminary's board of trustees might force Strong to discipline, or worse yet, remove Rauschenbusch from his position. Some seminary trustees expressed dismay over the book, and the board's chair, a prominent Cincinnati businessman, wrote Strong demanding Rauschenbusch's resignation. Yet Strong staunchly refused such pres-

34. See Grant Wacker, *Augustus H. Strong and the Dilemma of Historical Consciousness* (Macon: Mercer University Press, 1985).

35. William Newton Clarke to WR, December 9, 1906, box 25.

sure, making it evident to the trustees that "if Rauschenbusch had to go to the cross, he too must go."[36]

At the same time that Strong staved off internal pressure to remove Rauschenbusch, the first reviews of *Christianity and the Social Crisis* began to appear. The British periodical *Manchester Guardian* lauded the book, and the reviewer's sentiments echoed those on both sides of the Atlantic. "The name of Professor Rauschenbusch . . . is unfamiliar to us, but this strong and stimulating book should secure him a place among the thinkers and writers who are really worth reading. . . . No one can read these pages and imagine that for their author these are only pious phrases suitable for the pulpit but not for the market-place. His book is too earnest and too disquieting for any such suppositions."[37] Similar rave reviews rolled in from a host of religious and secular periodicals. The *Cumberland Presbyterian*, a journal not associated in the past with the aims of social Christianity, lauded the book for uttering "a call to a distinct service, to a high consecration." The reviewer asserted that Rauschenbusch "succeeded in one of his main purposes, which is to prove that the hand of Jesus himself points us and all men to that better way, which shall 'transform the life on earth into the harmony of heaven.'"[38] Similar laudatory reviews appeared that year from a variety of religious and secular publications. The *Outlook* placed the book in "the foremost rank" of works dealing with religion and economic questions, and the reviewer for the Louisville *Review and Expositor* made the grand assessment, "outside of the Bible I have not read a stronger, saner, better book on social religion."[39]

Likewise, Rauschenbusch received praise from his friends in the Brotherhood and other colleagues in the cause of social Christianity. Josiah Strong called it "a luminous presentation of the Christian program" and "an equally striking exemplification of the Christian spirit. I wish it might be read by every professing Christian who occupies the individualistic point of view."[40] Similar accolades were expressed by men such as William Newton Clarke and William Faunce; Augustus Strong

36. LeRoy Moore, Jr., "Rise of American Religious Liberalism," 40.
37. *Manchester Guardian* (June 28, 1907), clipping in box 155.
38. *Cumberland Presbyterian* (May 23, 1907), clipping in box 155.
39. *RTS Bulletin*, "Rauschenbusch Number," 44.
40. Josiah Strong to WR, December 13, 1907, box 25.

predicted that the book would be as epoch-making as Henry George's *Progress and Poverty* (at the same time that he made the critical observation that Rauschenbusch tended to "systematically take the side of the underdog"),[41] while Francis Peabody used the book that spring in one of his courses on Christian ethics at Harvard Divinity School.[42]

Rauschenbusch also received scores of appreciative letters from business executives, university administrators and professors, a Chicago city police superintendent, and a variety of church leaders who saw in the book the genesis of a new Christian movement taking hold of the nation. A YMCA executive wrote Rauschenbusch in June his belief that "your book is altogether the greatest utterance along this line which America has produced."[43]

THE SOCIAL CRISIS AND PROTESTANT CLERGY

For all of the book's popularity, however, by far the biggest audience for the book was Protestant clergy and young seminarians, who were galvanized by the book's message. As much as Rauschenbusch addressed the book to a middle-class Christian audience, and despite his protests against the priestly tendencies in church history that muted the voice of laity and stifled Christian democracy, the task of building a new Christian "apostolate" in America fell on the nation's preachers. "A Christian preacher should have the prophetic insight which discerns and champions the right before others see it. . . . If the ministry would awaken among the wealthy a sense of social compunction and moral uneasiness, that alone might save our nation from a revolutionary explosion."[44] As had been the case in his own relationship with John Rockefeller during his New York years, Rauschenbusch's plea to the nation's men of power was not to alienate them from the gospel, nor to dismantle their wealth; it was to appeal to their consciences in the hope that these individuals would join in the cause of social evangelism.

41. Augustus Strong to WR, June 27, 1907, box 25.
42. Harvard seminarian to WR, May 1, 1907, box 25.
43. C. Nesbit to WR, June 3, 1907, box 25.
44. *Christianity and the Social Crisis,* 363, 368.

Throughout 1907, and for the rest of his life, Rauschenbusch received letters from large numbers of Baptist, Methodist, Congregational, Presbyterian, and Episcopalian clergymen who gave vivid testimonies on how the book changed their lives. A Congregational minister in North Adams, Massachusetts, wrote that he was recommending the book to his entire congregation. "It is altogether the finest work of the kind that I have read, and I hope for it a very wide reading, as I am persuaded it will do great good in arousing the church to the amazing need there is of a social gospel."[45] A Baptist minister in Hartford, Connecticut, concurred, noting that Rauschenbusch was "a great man to write such a book, and I hope it does make a stir, for truly, the pudding that is not stirred by such a spoon as this will not be worth the eating."[46] These responses were echoed in letters from ministers throughout all regions of the country who praised Rauschenbusch for the book's prophetic message. Many of these letters from clergy also shared a common theme — Rauschenbusch's "social gospel" gave them a reason for staying in the ministry. A letter written by a Rochester Theological Seminary alum in late 1908 was typical.

> To you I feel a great debt. The ministry never seemed so glorious a calling to me. The task that is set before us to realize in this world the kingdom of righteousness and brotherhood is big enough to stretch our minds to the utmost and to call forth all our devotion. . . . Had it not been for what you more than anyone else have enabled me to see, I doubt whether I should long have remained in the ministry. It seemed too much detached from life when seen from the old individualistic basis. Now, in the light of the social gospel, I can preach the gospel for the individual with a new earnestness and a new power. To you as the one who introduced me to these things, I am profoundly grateful.[47]

As letters were forwarded to Rauschenbusch in Germany throughout 1907, he was both delighted and shocked by the book's popularity. "It seems rather a pity that you cannot be in this country just now when it is

45. Theodore Busfield to WR, October 21, 1907, box 25.
46. Harold Pattison to WR, May 2, 1907, box 25.
47. Virgil Johnson to WR, December 11, 1908, box 25.

fresh from the press, for you would get many echos which may not all resound clear across the sea," a colleague wrote to Rauschenbusch that summer.[48] Increasingly, Rauschenbusch needed to devote greater time during his sabbatical to respond to the mail that was being forwarded to Germany. He was delighted by the praise the book was receiving, but found himself overwhelmed by the number of invitations that came his way to speak to a variety of church, civic, and academic gatherings.

THE POWER OF WORDS

The fall and winter of 1907 and 1908 was an especially pleasing time for Rauschenbusch. Settling his family in the historical city of Marburg, he delighted in exposing his children to the cultural heritage of his ancestral homeland and also giving them an opportunity to get to know many of his German relatives, especially their Aunt Frida. Unlike his own father, Rauschenbusch enjoyed spending time with his children and the time away from his responsibilities at the seminary was clearly rejuvenating for him. In January 1908, in a letter to his friend Edmund Lyon, Rauschenbusch expressed his delight at the time he was sharing with his family, and also gave a somewhat whimsical observation concerning his book's success. "Here I am in another country, and without further effort on my part these thoughts, which were part of me, are doing their work beyond any power of mine to follow, control, or estimate. It is like a child that detaches its life from ours and goes out to live its own life. But it has given me a deepened sense of responsibility."[49]

While the majority of reviews for the book were overwhelmingly positive, there were notable dissenters. Certain academicians believed Rauschenbusch's definition for socialism was too vague and newspapers like the *New York Post* conversely castigated the book for what it viewed as Rauschenbusch's anti-business posturing. Additionally, the book came under heavy scrutiny from church periodicals predisposed to premillennialism. Especially harsh was the review from the conservative Baptist periodical *Journal and Messenger* that dismissed the book

48. John Mason to WR, July 5, 1907, box 25.
49. WR to Edmond Lyon, January 10, 1908, box 108.

as nothing more than socialist propaganda. While such reviews were in the minority, they nevertheless served as a foretaste of the criticism Rauschenbusch would receive in subsequent years.

As Rauschenbusch neared the end of his sabbatical in the spring in 1908, he planned on an extended European holiday with Pauline. It was decided that Pauline and the children would stay in Germany an additional six months, after Rauschenbusch's return to America that summer. Although he viewed this decision as an opportunity to further his children's education in the intellectual and cultural legacy of Germany, the ensuing separation from his family would be painful for Walter, Pauline, and their children. It would also unintentionally begin a period of increased conflict with his two oldest children, Winifred and Hilmar, who upon their return to America in early 1909 entered a period of adolescence that signaled a subtle but discernible rebellion against their father.

In the meantime, while the children stayed with their Aunt Frida, Walter and Pauline left on their European tour in April 1908 with visits through major cities in Germany, Switzerland, and Italy. Rauschenbusch kept a journal of his impressions, especially related to the European religious context. In Basel, he worshiped in Ulrich Zwingli's former cathedral church and discussed the state of German theology with a group of friends. He criticized German theology for being "stale on the social side," suggesting that the absence of a genuine social Christianity in German theology related "to timidity and repression, and revenged itself by intellectual sterility in the lines abandoned."[50] He and Pauline spent most of their trip in Italy, culminating with a stay in Rome, where he witnessed a papal procession. While Rauschenbusch's journal reveals his deep appreciation for how the trip made history come alive for him, not surprisingly, the trip also gave him an opportunity to berate the superstitious proclivities of the Catholic church.[51]

The trip with Pauline turned out to be a calm respite in what would increasingly become a frenetic life for Walter Rauschenbusch. The two returned to their children in early June, and in August Rauschenbusch said good-bye to his family and sailed for America. Upon his arrival in New York, he immediately realized that the impact of his

50. WR private journal April 25, 1908, box 106.
51. Ibid.

book was greater than he had thought. With little time to recover from his sea voyage, he delivered a lecture at a New York hotel before 500 "distinguished people," an event that tantalized Rauschenbusch, but also unnerved him. When Rauschenbusch returned to Rochester in advance of the fall academic semester at the seminary, he was relieved to be home, but also cognizant of the fact that his life had changed. He was deluged with more letters that had not reached him in Germany and more speaking invitations than he could possibly handle.

Five years later, Rauschenbusch gave an account in a Rochester newspaper, attempting to explain the impact of *Christianity and the Social Crisis.* While the article displayed a characteristic modesty about his talents as a church leader, he did not shy away from his belief that he had written a unique book. "The social movement got hold of me, just as the social awakening was getting hold of the country. The book came out at a psychological moment, and was taken as an expression of what thousands were feeling."[52]

Rauschenbusch was not exaggerating the impact of this psychological moment. In December 1907, a group of socially active Methodist clergymen founded the Methodist Federation for Social Service, a caucus organization that saw its mission as bringing the message of social Christianity to "neglected social groups." The MFSS drafted a social creed that espoused many measures of social reform including a worker's minimum wage, "a day off in seven," support for labor unions, and a general appeal to the Golden Rule as the sure remedy for the nation's social and economic ills. The following spring, in 1908, the Methodist Episcopal Church, the largest branch of American Methodism, adopted this document at its General Conference as the church's official social creed, the first such creed sanctioned by an American Protestant denomination. In December 1908, Rauschenbusch was present in Philadelphia at the formation of the Federal Council of Churches in Christ, which incorporated in its charter a revised version of the Methodist social creed. A direct descendant of a variety of ecumenical organizations, such as the Evangelical Alliance, emerging from the middle of the nineteenth century, the Federal Council was an organization that pushed forward the American Protestant quest for church

52. WR, "The Genesis of 'Christianity and the Social Crisis,'" from *Rochester Theological Seminary Bulletin* (November 1918): 53.

unity combined with the zeal for social Christianity. Its founding represented an illustration of Rauschenbusch's "psychological moment" and signaled a decisive event in the emerging institutional turn of establishment Protestantism toward the liberalism that would in a few years become widely known as "the social gospel."

It is perhaps ironic that Rauschenbusch's *Christianity and the Social Crisis* eclipsed in popularity another book brought out by Macmillan in the spring of 1907 on the theme of "Christianity and the Social Crisis": *The Church and the Changing Order* by Shailer Mathews. In 1927, when Mathews published an article on the development of American social Christianity, he made reference to both his and Rauschenbusch's 1907 books. Mathews conceded, however, that Rauschenbusch's work possessed a distinctive spirit and style that his own work lacked. He acknowledged that Rauschenbusch's work "was more incisive in its criticism of the present economic order," and also noted that Rauschenbusch "possessed a style of singular brilliancy" that served as a "potent influence" upon the nation's clergy.[53]

Yet Mathews was telling only half of the story. The success of *Christianity and the Social Crisis* reflected the beginning of a new chapter in the history of American Protestantism. Selling an unprecedented 50,000 copies in multiple editions between 1907 and 1910, not only was the book one of the biggest selling nonfiction books of the social gospel era, but it opened the floodgates to a variety of interpretations of modern social Christianity. There had certainly been no shortage of social Christian literature in American Protestantism before 1907, attested by the brief success of George Herron and the long-term durability of Josiah Strong and Washington Gladden. Yet Rauschenbusch's success quickly turned the issue of "Christianity and the social question" into an important topic that increasingly demanded the attention of the nation's book publishers. The social gospel may very well have been a small elite movement in America at the end of 1908. At the same time, few would deny that men like Rauschenbusch carried a distinctive message that needed to be addressed by the church and by the nation. The social gospel as an institutional movement in the United States was just entering its major period of influence.

53. Shailer Mathews, "The Development of Social Christianity in America During the Past Twenty-Five Years," in *Journal of Religion* 7 (July 1927): 381.

9 The Social Awakening

One of the tributaries created by *Christianity and the Social Crisis* emerged soon after the book's publication in Boston. At the center of the current was a Baptist layman named George Coleman. Seven years younger than Rauschenbusch, Coleman was a leader of the Christian Endeavor movement, one of the largest Protestant youth organizations of the time, and the publisher of *Christian Endeavor* magazine. Long showing an interest in the teachings of social Christianity, Coleman was a member of the Brotherhood of the Kingdom who had come to know Rauschenbusch in the 1890s, when the two met at a Christian Endeavor rally. While Rauschenbusch was still in Germany, and largely unaware of his mounting fame, Coleman conceived of a plan to carry the spirit of *Christianity and the Social Crisis* to a larger audience. "We have plans laid already that look toward a dissemination of some of the truths which you teach,"[1] Coleman wrote to Rauschenbusch soon after reading the book in 1907. His idea was to create an intellectual movement that would carry the spirit of social Christianity

1. George Coleman to WR, May 11, 1907, box 25; see also Arthur S. Meyers, "'The Striking of Mind upon Mind': The Open Forum and the Social Gospel," in *Baptist History and Heritage* (Spring 2000): 23.

to the American middle class. The effort spearheaded by Coleman was symbolic of how many Americans were becoming increasingly aware that the pressing social problems of the day were, at their core, problems of religious faith.

THE OPEN FORUM MOVEMENT AND THE SOCIAL GOSPEL

Coleman's first response in the summer of 1907 was to organize the Sagamore Sociological Conference. Typical of many Progressive Era gatherings, these annual summer conferences were held in an idyllic resort location near Cape Cod, Massachusetts, and provided several days of leisure and discussion for their presenters and participants. This conference became an annual forum for many of the nation's top Progressive leaders to discuss an array of social-economic problems, with emphasis on the relationship of Christianity to these social problems.

On a more popular scale, however, Coleman envisioned a national forum movement that would bring the message of *Christianity and the Social Crisis* to the masses. What later was to be called the Open Forum Movement closely paralleled the intellectual model of the late nineteenth-century Lyceum and Chautauqua movements. However, Coleman's vision harkened back to a New England town meeting format, where audiences could not only have an opportunity to hear the great secular and religious intellectuals of the day, but engage them in a question and answer format. Centered at Ford Hall, Boston, a recently constructed auditorium named after Daniel Sharp Ford, a nineteenth-century Baptist layman and philanthropist, the first scheduled session in February 1908 attracted a mediocre turnout. However, in the years 1908 and 1909, attendance at Ford Hall meetings grew in popularity and scope. Like the Chautuaqua movement, the open forum movement attracted the most prominent secular and religious leaders of the era, and the unique lecture-discussion model of the forum enabled audiences to interact with individuals who read like a who's who of American Progressivism: Louis Brandeis, Charles Stelzle, Florence Kelley, Albion Small, Ray Stannard Baker, Stanton Coit, and Shailer Mathews. The Ford Hall meetings also included frequent appearances by prominent Jewish and Catholic advocates of social reform, including Rabbi Stephen Wise and Father John Ryan, and

African-American leaders like W. E. B. DuBois. Within a few short years, the open forum model was being duplicated in a number of cities, and by 1915, open forum meetings were held throughout the northeast and midwestern United States.

While many leaders of the Progressive Era drew huge audiences to open forum meetings, the heart and soul of the forum movement was Rauschenbusch. Coleman envisioned the forum movement as a way for modern Americans to reclaim the heritage and spirit of democracy, in which every American was a stakeholder. He shared Rauschenbusch's belief that the essence of Christianity was revealed in how it bequeathed a democratic ethos to modern society. The spirit behind the open forum movement was defined by how it propagated Rauschenbusch's assertion from *Christianity and the Social Crisis* that in America, "Democracy is a holy word." Although forum gatherings catered to an educated middle-class constituency, these meetings drew large audiences and served as a foundation for the dissemination of a number of public forum movements later in the twentieth century.

Rauschenbusch served as one of the featured draws at Ford Hall, making semi-annual appearances for several years. He also made countless addresses to open forum gatherings across the country through 1917. The appeal of Rauschenbusch as a public speaker is both surprising and ironic, given both his near total deafness and the fact that he frequently expressed dissatisfaction with his public oratory. At the same time, part of his appeal related to an irenic spirit that came from his personality. As Coleman himself reflected in 1915, "No speaker who comes to Ford Hall is more beloved than Professor Rauschenbusch. Jew and Christian alike feel the same warmth of affection toward him. He has kept in the closest touch with our enterprise almost from the very beginning, and his great name and influence were a tower of strength to us in our troublous days."[2]

Because of his hearing disability, he depended on assistance from another person who would be responsible for receiving, on paper, the audience's questions that Rauschenbusch could read. This responsibility was usually carried out by a number of student assistants from Rochester Theological Seminary, like Edwin Dahlberg or Dores Sharpe,

2. George W. Coleman, ed., *Democracy in the Making: Ford Hall and the Open Forum Movement* (Boston: Little Brown, and Company, 1915), 109.

who often traveled with their professor on his speaking trips, or on occasion by Pauline. Yet despite his reliance on these assistants, Rauschenbusch displayed a command over an audience that shocked those familiar with his hearing handicap. On one hand, he projected a very gentle demeanor with audiences that at times gave one the impression that he was not fully engaged with his environment. However, those who witnessed Rauschenbusch in a forum setting were amazed at his intellectual dexterity. Vida Scudder, professor of English literature at Wellesley College and one of the few women social gospel theologians of her era, reflected years later that Rauschenbusch demonstrated an unusual charisma with an audience. Despite his hearing loss and a high-pitched speaking voice, she noted that his response to questions was "sharp, illuminating and to the point." For Scudder, and others, Rauschenbusch had the ability to incisively challenge the intellectual worldview of his audience, "but the serenity of his manner made piquant contrast with the audacity of his thinking."[3]

More significantly, Rauschenbusch's lectures strove for a simplicity in language and also carried forth the sense of humor that he displayed with his family and students. As he noted to a friend years later, he attributed to his father, August, an ability to express ideas in simple and concrete terms, striving to avoid condescension or paternalism toward an audience. "I learned to put my message in simple words, and to adjust myself to the view-point of extremely conservative people." Like many late nineteenth-century liberals, Rauschenbusch valued the notion of intellectual inquiry and strove to respect the wide range of theological and political views present in his audience. At the same time, he was candid when he asserted that his objective as a speaker was to win an audience to his point of view, striving to find ways by which "conservative minds could be enlarged and freed." "Some of my liberal friends, who have heard me speak, have told me that I seemed to be able 'to put over more radical stuff, without exciting animosity.'"[4]

Rauschenbusch could be deeply wounded by criticism, yet as his fame grew he took criticisms from theological adversaries in stride. After *Christianity and the Social Crisis* received a negative review from a

3. Vida Scudder to Dores Sharpe, April 18, 1941, box 155.
4. WR to Prof. W. G. Ballantine, February 4, 1918, box 93.

conservative Baptist journal, Rauschenbusch went to great pains to explain his perspective to the paper's editor. "It is the task of our generation to discern a little more of that inherited social injustice and remove it," he noted in an irenic tone. "I may have erred in detail in trying to understand such latent wrongs and in trying to awaken men to them, just as you may have been partly wrong in evangelistic preaching about the sins of the individual. But neither you nor I will be willing to forgo our mission to bring men to repentance because we make mistakes in applying our message." He still believed that it was possible to reconcile the perspectives of individual and social salvation. "Misunderstandings are all in the day's work for anyone who really follows the Master and tries to teach those parts of his thought which are not yet common property. But if I could correct the misunderstanding a little, I should be glad, for I value the respect and confidence of you and your associates and friends."[5]

PEOPLE'S ROCHESTER

As Rauschenbusch's career was moving him further away from direct interaction with leaders of Protestant premillennialism, in subsequent years his exchanges with that movement's leaders would grow increasingly confrontational and less conciliatory. Rauschenbusch's life was propelled by the emerging currents of social liberalism that reflected the public optimism at the height of the Progressive Era on the eve of World War I. Within months of his return from Germany, the open forum idea gave Rauschenbusch impetus for another experiment in social democracy closer to home. With the financial backing of several prominent Rochester business leaders, Rauschenbusch and a group of Rochester area clergy launched the People's Sunday Evening in November 1908.

Largely the brainchild of Rauschenbusch's friend Paul Moore Strayer, pastor of the Third Presbyterian Church, the People's Sunday Evening was designed to offer an array of speakers on contemporary social questions. With leadership largely provided by Rauschenbusch, Strayer, and Episcopal clergyman James Bishop Thomas, the Sunday Evening experienced modest success in drawing audiences from the

5. WR to George Lasher, March 13, 1909, box 25.

city's blue collar and working-class sections. With meetings held in various city theaters and auditoriums, these Sunday night forums dealt with a number of topics dealing with the nation's social-economic ills, and how Christian socialism could provide the nation with an alternative to the market-driven forces guiding the nation. The Sunday meetings usually began with a classical music concert put on by area musicians and, in addition to speakers like Rauschenbusch and Strayer, the People's Sunday Evening occasionally featured national leaders of social Christianity and American Progressivism such as Jane Addams, Graham Taylor, and Washington Gladden.

Although the Sunday Evening adapted the open forum model of question and answer periods after each speaker, Rauschenbusch frequently expressed hope that the Sunday Evenings would serve as a means to expose working-class Rochesterians, who had been alienated from traditional Christianity, to the values of a higher cultural Christianity. With no small amount of pride, Rauschenbusch remarked to a colleague that the People's Sunday Evening had become one of the largest congregations in the city, succeeding to reach a constituency that had been all but ignored by the city's churches.[6]

The Sunday Evening and open forum models embodied a classic Progressive hope that the values of white middle-class America would act as leaven that might lead to the conversion of all recalcitrant theological and social forces at work in the nation. As Rauschenbusch had done in earlier phases of his ministry, he still modeled a style of Christian social reform that was largely contingent upon using the culture of middle-class America to appeal to the consciences of the masses. Consequently, he could not escape a paternalism toward the very groups whom he sought to offer succor. When criticized by a leading Baptist that his social reform scheme would naturally encourage laziness on the part of the working class, Rauschenbusch was quick to respond that he had no intent to condone the behavior of any person who refused to work for the benefits of a democratic society. If a man refused to earn a living wage, then he could expect little sympathy from Rauschenbusch: "I would have him undergo medical examination to see if there was any constitutional trouble, and if not, I would let him starve."[7]

6. Minus, 129-130.

7. WR to George Lasher, March 13, 1909, box 25.

Since his early days in New York City, Rauschenbusch struggled, and never quite succeeded, in stepping beyond the paternalistic and conservative worldview that often contradicted his radical vision of Christian social reform. The early twentieth century witnessed a time of varied approaches to social reform offered by an array of Progressive leaders in government, business, education, and popular culture. For all the ways that Rauschenbusch would gain the public's attention for his radical views on religion in the decade after the publication of *Christianity and the Social Crisis,* he was in some ways quite conservative compared to other American Progressives. This inherent social conservatism within Rauschenbusch's thinking, and that of many Progressive Era leaders, was highlighted by a new local initiative headed by Rauschenbusch in late 1908.

For years, Rochester's public schools were facing a crisis that was reflective of the larger strains in American public education during the early twentieth century. Due to the immigration explosion at the end of the nineteenth century, Rochester's schools found themselves flooded with diverse non–English speaking immigrant children, teacher shortages, and a passionate debate among the city's school board over how best to address the crisis through school curriculum. The school board in the early 1900s developed a policy of vocational education advocating greater flexibility in curriculum planning, and emphasized individual creativity over standardized achievement. In September 1908, Rauschenbusch found himself speaking out against these new educational views at a public school board meeting. In short order, he was appointed the chairperson of a task force commissioned to conduct an investigation into the city schools and report back to the school board with specific recommendations for reform.

It was Rauschenbusch's first foray into a local political issue since his chairmanship of the YMCA task force in 1904 and he embraced his work on the school board task force with crusading zeal. The "Rauschenbusch Commission," as it was dubbed by the local press, conducted a series of tasks, including interviews with city school teachers and questionnaires sent to parents to ascertain conditions in the city schools. As he quickly found out, the majority of letters he received from parents shared Rauschenbusch's concern for tightened standards. "There seems to be no moral or intellectual backbone, no pride in achievement, no high standard of scholarship to be striven for and won,"[8] one disgruntled parent complained to Rauschenbusch that fall. After two months, the commission made its report to the city school board at a public forum in November 1908. Although Rauschenbusch was very clear about the need to offer equal educational opportunities for all the city's children, he was outspoken that this model of education needed to be styled after the German model for a liberal arts education that he himself had experienced. When the Rauschenbusch Commission made its report, it noted that most of the problems facing the city's schools related both to the educational methods being employed and to an inherent intellectual laziness within the students. The tenor of the report bears the unmistakable penmanship and tone of the commission's chairman. "The children of today are readily interested, but they want all things made interesting for them," the report complained. "They are not willing to rivet their attention on a piece of work and see it through."[9] The most chauvinistic dimension in the report was its concern that the city schools had too many women teachers, noting the "corrosive effect" that women had on the intellectual development of the city's youth.[10]

Rauschenbusch's stance put him at odds with the progressive coalition on the city school board, including the first woman elected to the board, Helen Barrett Montgomery. Years later, Montgomery went on to fame as the first woman president of the Northern Baptist Convention and would later be praised for her leadership in steering the Northern Baptists through the waters of a potential liberal-conservative schism in the early 1920s. Yet her views on the city board were diametrically opposed to Rauschenbusch. Montgomery and others, who controlled the board, reflected a growing spirit of pragmatism that segmented educational requirements on the basis of ability and interest. Rauschenbusch, however, continued to insist that the best way to educate young minds was through embracing the same standards of intellectual rigor that he had received from his own father and through the system of the German Gymnasium. He called for more formal classroom drill and a return to uniform standards of classroom examination, making no dis-

8. Mrs. W. H. Miller to WR, October 5, 1908, box 50.

9. Quoted in John Aiken, "Walter Rauschenbusch and Education for Reform," *Church History* 36 (December 1967): 464.

10. Aiken, 464.

tinctions based upon student abilities. For Rauschenbusch, a quality education was not a matter of pragmatic social engineering, but represented the time-honored traditions of developing the capacities of rote and discipline in the young mind. "The fundamental distinction between civilized man and the savage, is that the civilized brain can concentrate attention and keep it up, while the wandering interest of the savage picks things up with a grunt of delight and swiftly wearies of them."[11]

In the short run, Rauschenbusch won the battle. In the aftermath of the November public forum, a committee of nine advisors, chaired by Rauschenbusch, was founded for the purpose to serve as an advisory panel to the city school board. However, the board made no major concessions to Rauschenbusch and within a few years, the advisory board ultimately dissolved.

The school board controversy highlighted a subtle, but significant, rift in Progressive Era thought that would grow more pronounced in later years. Religious leaders, like Rauschenbusch, believed that the task of Christianization was symbolic of how Americans from a variety of backgrounds and classes needed to accept shared standards in religion, education, and the arts. Secular progressives, however, epitomized by John Dewey, increasingly stressed that educational standards needed to be tailored to the specific and unique abilities of each student. Progressive public school education had won out in Rochester, but it was a model of Progressivism that Walter Rauschenbusch, among others, found wanting.

THE KINGDOM OF GOD AND THE RAUSCHENBUSCH FAMILY

As Rauschenbusch basked in his initial successes with the city school board, he suffered an intense loneliness at the separation from his family and was overjoyed to be reunited with them in the winter of 1909. Rauschenbusch's role as a father to his five children was filled with tremendous affection, but also echoed some of the sternness of his own father. As his son Paul later recalled, his father had a wonderful sense of humor that frequently displayed itself when Rauschenbusch was re-

11. Ibid., 464.

laxing at home or on family vacations. Yet Paul also sensed that his father's deafness created a social anxiety that caused him tremendous insecurity around his children.[12] Rauschenbusch's letters to his family in the fall of 1908 reflect his loneliness at the separation from his family, but also highlight the way that he attempted to educate his children in a manner consistent with his own well-ordered principles. Throughout that fall, Rauschenbusch wrote Winifred, who had recently turned fourteen, that she carried the added burden of being a role model for young womanhood. "You are all half-orphans now while I am away, and there will be lots of chance for you to love and help and be thoughtful for others. There is nothing else that we love so in a woman as such gracious helpfulness."[13] At a point in her life when Winifred was showing visible signs of teenage rebellion, Rauschenbusch castigated her repeatedly about the need to keep up her appearance, in accord with being a cultured young woman. "Our body is one of God's great gifts to us," he lectured Winifred just before Christmas in 1908. "If we are vain about it, we take it all for ourself selfishly. But it is possible to be proud of it, and to take joy in it, and yet regard it as part of our equipment for serving God and humanity."[14] Although in subsequent years he would continue to give similar lectures to his eldest daughter, a pattern was clearly emerging. With the exception of Pauline, Rauschenbusch increasingly took Winifred into his confidence in ways that he would not, or could not, with his other children.

Conscious of his own strained relationship with his parents, Rauschenbusch wanted to raise his children in ways that mixed together discipline and friendship. Over the next several years, the children would see the friendship side of their father mostly during summer vacations. In 1908, Rauschenbusch arranged to buy a tract of land on Lake Sturgeon in Ontario, Canada, and built a summer cottage. Beginning in 1909 and for the next several years, the Rauschenbusch family was able to spend a couple of months of rest and recreation at the cottage. Rauschenbusch relished these vacations, reserving time

12. Paul Raushenbush to Winifred R. Rorty, June 18, 1978, box 143. (All of Rauschenbusch's children adopted the spelling "Raushenbush" for their last name in the years following their father's death.)

13. WR to Winifred, September 8, 1908, box 143.

14. WR to Winifred, December 10, 1908, box 143.

each day to write yet also indulge his love of the outdoors, spending time hiking, fishing, and boating.

The necessity of spending extended chunks of time away in Canada became essential for Rauschenbusch, given the fact that he found himself increasingly separated from his family for the bulk of the year. Whereas prior to 1908 his demand as a speaker was defined either by his role as a fund-raiser for the seminary or his involvement within a variety of Northern Baptist fellowships, Rauschenbusch suddenly found himself in a situation where the demand for his services exceeded his availability.

The years between 1908 and 1912 witnessed the institutional ascendency of the social gospel in American Protestantism and Walter Rauschenbusch was at the center of that movement. In the aftermath of the founding of the Federal Council of Churches, Protestant denominations increasingly channeled their resources into the development of a number of caucuses and social service commissions, modeled after the Methodist Federation for Social Service. Unlike that of church leaders such as Frank Mason North, Harry Ward, Samuel Batten, Charles Stelzle, and Charles Macfarland, however, Rauschenbusch's relationship to the social gospel's rise was more inspirational than organizational. His great contribution to the rise of the social gospel was the role that he played as a theological propagator of the movement, as opposed to being an institutional mover and shaker. In the years before 1912, the social gospel manifested itself in many ways, highlighted by the ecumenical work of North, the institutional church ministry of Stelzle, the pulpiteer model of Washington Gladden, and the denominational caucus activism of Ward. Yet Rauschenbusch, more than any other figure, served as the ideological core for the movement.

Rauschenbusch accepted a wide range of speaking engagements. As his popularity as a speaker grew, however, he was largely unable to accept engagements in local churches, unless it was a conference sponsored by a particular organization, caucus, or denomination. In addition to Ford Hall and other open forums, Rauschenbusch spoke regularly at YMCA conferences and conventions, and was also a regular fixture at Coleman's summer Sagamore Conferences. Rauschenbusch also became a popular college speaker, giving numerous addresses and sermons on campuses throughout the United States.

Noteworthy in his speaking itinerary were the times that

Rauschenbusch spoke in a number of Reform synagogues, in Rochester and in other parts of the country. His views toward Jews, much like Catholics, carried a note of benevolent paternalism, certainly a carryover from his exposure to the Jewish immigrants he encountered during his New York City ministry. The fact that Rauschenbusch used the term "Christianization" as a generic metaphor of social reform reflected a common liberal bias that saw Jesus' ministry as something that could be grafted uncritically upon non-Christian groups. However, the way Rauschenbusch utilized the prophetic books of the Hebrew prophets, relating Jesus' significance directly to that tradition, touched a nerve with liberal Jewish traditions, and Rauschenbusch's writings were read and admired by many Americans Jews of that time. He struck up a friendship with the prominent Reform rabbi Stephen Wise, who dubbed him "one of our few saintly prophets and prophetic saints,"[15] and years after Rauschenbusch's death, many American Reform Jews saw Rauschenbusch as a positive model of what it meant to be a Christian.

At the same time, Rauschenbusch demonstrated a worldview that would become more commonplace in liberal Protestantism in succeeding generations: an acceptance of religious pluralism. He was appalled by the anti-Semitism of German social Christians like Adolf Stöcker, and vigorously defended the rights of Jews to worship unimpeded by secular or religious coercive forces. When later criticized by a conservative Christian periodical for not invoking the name of Christ in a prayer that marked a national day of prayer against tuberculosis, Rauschenbusch castigated the magazine's editor for his lack of sensitivity to Jewish Americans.

> What would you do, Mr. Editor, if you were asked to lead in prayer in a congregation composed of Christians and Jews on some popular civic occasion? Would you insist on using the ordinary Christian terms, or would you consider the feelings of the Jews whose prayers you were expected to lead? Perhaps you would feel bound to mention the name of Christ at all cost. But is not another man within his right if he chooses the other way, speaking to the Christ

15. Stephen Wise to Edgar Wiers, November 30, 1914, box 28; see also Minus, 175.

whom he trusts? I was leading a great congregation of all kinds of people when I wrote that prayer, and I do not believe Jesus Christ frowned on me.[16]

Rauschenbusch's irenic posture toward American Judaism did not carry over to his relationship with American Catholicism. At a time when Catholic-Protestant cooperation was at a virtual standstill, Rauschenbusch's staunch anti-Catholicism was far from unique. He did share a cordial relationship with the Catholic social reformer Father John Ryan, as both men were featured speakers at open forum gatherings. At the same time, Ryan's social vision, rooted in Catholic doctrinal teaching, was alien to Rauschenbusch's views. For Rauschenbusch and for many social gospel Protestants, the essence of Christian reform was rooted not in church tradition, but in the kingdom ideal, and the kingdom of God was not embodied by church hierarchies, but through democratic institutions in church and society.

Increasingly, the demands on his schedule forced him to juggle his responsibilities at the seminary. He often traveled in Pullman cars on weekends to speaking engagements and returned to Rochester just in time to teach his classes. Rauschenbusch's addresses were motivated by a desire to propagate his message, but he was also drawn by the financial incentives offered by these appearances. His itinerary from 1909 through the first half of 1911 reveals the frenetic pace of his life. The year 1909 was spent largely speaking to forum gatherings and church-related associations, as well as several denominational and ecumenical assemblies. After a series of addresses on the East Coast late in the year, including an address at Rabbi Stephen Wise's Free Synagogue in New York City, Rauschenbusch headed south to give a series of addresses in Nashville churches and at Fisk College. He then returned to the Northeast in January 1910 to speak to a variety of gatherings in New England. Following a brief respite in the late winter, Rauschenbusch was on the road again that spring, traveling to Berkeley, California, in April to give the Earl Lectures at the Pacific Theological Seminary. On his way back to the East Coast he preached a keynote sermon at the Northern Baptist Convention in Chicago. After

16. WR to the editor of the *Herald and Presbyter,* Cincinnati, October 12, 1916, box 30.

another brief respite in Rochester, in June he headed to New England for a series of addresses on behalf of the YMCA International Training School, held in Springfield, Massachusetts, before sailing to Europe for speaking appearances in England and Germany.

While in Europe, he spoke to audiences in Liverpool, Berlin, and Cologne. Rauschenbusch was received appreciatively by his British audience and while he would develop a supportive following in Great Britain, he continued his ambivalent view of English society and its churches, especially toward that country's Anglican religious establishment. While Rauschenbusch received a cordial welcome from many of his hosts in Germany, he was perceived more as an American curiosity, as opposed to a major intellectual figure. It is ironic that as much as Rauschenbusch claimed and embraced the late nineteenth-century intellectual tradition of liberal Protestantism born in Germany, his work would largely go unknown in that country during his lifetime.

In the fall, after a brief vacation respite in Canada, Rauschenbusch jumped back on the lecture circuit with various addresses that carried him through the Northeast and back to Nashville for the start of 1911. His spring was filled with a series of addresses culminating in his presenting the Merrick Lectures at Ohio Wesleyan University. Ohio Wesleyan possessed a deeply rooted reputation at the turn of the century for being a center for training pietistic Methodist missionaries. Yet its faculty and administration, epitomized by the zeal of its president, Herbert Welsh, one of the founders of the Methodist Federation for Social Service and soon to be elected a bishop, highlighted how the school had already produced graduates who were on the verge of becoming central leaders of the social gospel, including Bishop Francis McConnell and Ernest Fremont Tittle, who would become one of the prominent liberal preachers in America between the world wars. Rauschenbusch enjoyed his stay at Ohio Wesleyan, not only for the lectures but also for the opportunity to enjoy an extended visit with one of his heroes in nearby Columbus, Washington Gladden. As he had formed a friendship with Josiah Strong years earlier, Rauschenbusch had developed a bond with another elder statesman of Protestant social Christianity. In the upcoming years, Gladden and Rauschenbusch would exchange periodic correspondence.

In an annual report written to Augustus Strong in the spring of 1911, Rauschenbusch attempted to be modest about his growing popularity. Noting that he had given sixty-one addresses over the previous year (excluding his teaching at the seminary and People's Sunday Evening addresses), he expressed hope that his speaking schedule would advance the mission of the seminary and of social Christianity. "My sincere wish is to be let alone," he confided to Strong. "In all Christian humility I believe that the small amount that I have actually been able to contribute toward this vast demand has been of real use to the Christian life of our country, and I hope that it has also directly benefitted the reputation, influence, and spirit of our Seminary."[17]

Yet Rauschenbusch was quietly paying a price for his newfound status. He confided to his family in frequent letters that he was somewhat bemused to explain the reasons for his popularity, frequently giving humorous, self-deprecating accounts of his addresses. Yet behind the facade of his humor, there was the reemergence of a melancholy nature that he had not displayed for many years. In part, he lamented a lack of time to engage in scholarly work. After the publication of *Christianity and the Social Crisis,* he had planned to focus his future writing more directly on historical scholarship. But the demand for his services as a speaker and the continued popularity of the 1907 book made a sequel to the book inevitable. The impetus to write a follow-up to *Christianity and the Social Crisis* largely came from his acceptance of the Merrick Lectures, which carried a stipulation for a book. With contract in hand from Macmillan, Rauschenbusch planned to use the summer of 1911 to revise both the Merrick and the Earl Lectures from the previous spring into a coherent book manuscript. Yet the lure of revenue generated from his speaking put Rauschenbusch on the road for much of the summer, including another teaching and lecturing stint in California. To his friend, the young New York City social gospel minister John Haynes Holmes, he described his West Coast experience as "torrid and rather rough on me."[18] Such responses to his travels would become more typical in subsequent years.

There was another source for Rauschenbusch's mood that was brought on by his travels. He desperately missed his wife and children, expressing his guilt for his prolonged absences from home. He soon grew tired of what was becoming a routine of traveling from

17. Minus, 174.

18. WR to John Haynes Holmes, August 3, 1911, box 26.

train station to train station. And even though he frequently spoke in churches and auditoriums filled with hundreds, if not thousands, of listeners, his deafness exacerbated a sense of loneliness. In early 1911, during a speaking engagement in New York City, he expressed in a letter home his thankfulness that the family was no longer living in the overcrowded tenements of that city. As he reflected on his years there, he expressed a melancholy side that would grow more pronounced in the coming years. "I'd rather be home and play with the children," he confided. "Forgive me if I am sometimes impatient or severe. I always suffer for it myself afterward. I can't tell [you] how much I love you all."[19] Whenever Rauschenbusch saw other children who resembled his own, it made him even more homesick. Yet when he was at home, Rauschenbusch repeatedly found himself struggling with the gap that existed between himself and the awakening adolescent world that his oldest children were entering. In addition to the tension he felt with Winifred, Rauschenbusch labored in his relationship with his oldest son, Hilmar. Hilmar remained an enigma to his father. While frequently expressing his love and affection in letters, Rauschenbusch bemoaned the fact that his son seemed somewhat detached from the rest of the family. As Hilmar entered adolescence, Rauschenbusch increasingly addressed him as a younger friend, attempting to offer himself to his son as a kindly mentor. Not long after he arrived in England in the summer of 1910, he confided to Hilmar his hopes for their future relationship. "I hope we shall understand each other better all the time and be real chums. We have only a few years more together, perhaps. Then you will be going away for education and work, and the close companionship of these years may be over. . . . You are my oldest boy, and I have always loved you dearly."[20]

An emerging tension within the family centered on the fact that it was becoming increasingly clear to Rauschenbusch that his children did not share his Christian faith. As the children matured, he relished the fact that they embraced his social passion. But the distinctive evangelical faith that undergirded that passion was missing from all of his children. In part, his children's rejection of the church likely stemmed from their own ambivalence toward the German pietism that was so

19. WR to family, January 7, 1911, box 108.
20. WR to Hilmar, July 19, 1910, box 108.

important to Walter and Pauline. The fact that their family attended a German Baptist congregation in Rochester might very well have been an issue for the increasingly Americanized generation of younger Rauschenbusches. Furthermore, the importance of a personal conversion experience, the cornerstone of the evangelicalism of Rauschenbusch's youth, was now giving way to an emerging liberal outlook that saw conversion as a matter of process and development. Education, not emotionalism, was the key watchword for the future of those who would steer Protestant America into the twentieth century. Yet Rauschenbusch lamented that the conversion experience, so important in his own faith development, was absent from his children.

SPIRITUALITY AND THE SOCIAL GOSPEL

The relationship between personal and social salvation in the social gospel movement has been elusive for historians. As a whole, leaders in the social gospel in its formative years from 1908 to 1912 were persons who did not discount the importance of a personal conversion experience. At the same time, the way that social gospelers spoke of personal conversion in relationship to social transformation was not systematically spelled out by most of these leaders. In late 1910, Rauschenbusch published a short book that came to symbolize the spiritual ethos of the social gospel. The book, *Prayers of the Social Awakening,* was a collection of fifty-eight prayers (all but two written by Rauschenbusch) for use in a variety of public and private occasions. The book's evolution began in 1909 when J. S. Phillips, the editor of the *American Magazine,* a popular periodical of the time, invited Rauschenbusch to submit material on the life of Jesus for the magazine. Instead, Rauschenbusch utilized his deep love for prayer and submitted several that he had written over the years to the magazine. Beginning in late 1909 and extending through the next year, the periodical ran several of these prayers, which received a great deal of public enthusiasm. Rauschenbusch adapted these prayers, and others published in the periodical the *Survey,* in book form and also included a contemporary exposition on the meaning of the Lord's Prayer.

More than any of his other writings, *Prayers of the Social Awakening* reflected the devotional side of his faith and symbolized for later generations the distinctive evangelical-liberalism of the social gospel. Rauschenbusch expressed his hope that the book might serve as a model for liturgical and devotional works that would explore the social message of Christianity for modern Americans. "The ordinary church hymnal rarely contains more than two or three hymns in which the triumphant chords of the social hope are struck," he noted in the book's preface. "Our liturgies and devotional manuals offer very little that is fit to enrich and purify the social thoughts and feeling."[21] His exposition on the Lord's Prayer, consistent with his earlier theology, placed that prayer's significance in the context of the human struggle to build the kingdom of God. "No form of religion has ever interpreted this prayer aright which did not have a loving understanding for the plain daily relations of men, and a living faith in their possible spiritual nobility," Rauschenbusch observed. "And no man has outgrown the crude selfishness of religious immaturity who has not followed Jesus in setting this desire for the social salvation of mankind ahead of all personal desires."[22] In ways that echoed his arguments in *Christianity and the Social Crisis,* Rauschenbusch surmised that the Lord's Prayer captured the ethos of social Christianity. "It assumes the social solidarity of men as a matter of course. It recognizes the social basis of all moral and religious life even in the most intimate personal relations to God."[23]

The prayers in the book followed out the premise of relating the ideal of "social solidarity" to the individual, and were organized in sections that included daily prayers, prayers of praise and thanksgiving, prayers for social groups and classes, prayers of wrath (including prayers against war, alcoholism, and impurity), and prayers for the progress of humanity. Many of the prayers highlight the depth of Rauschenbusch's personal faith. One of the prayers, a table grace entitled "In Time of Trouble," captured a great deal of how Rauschenbusch turned to God for personal solace and support.

> O Lord, thou knowest that we are sore stricken and heavy of heart. We beseech thee to uphold us by thy comfort. Thou wert the God

21. Rauschenbusch, *Prayers of the Social Awakening* (Boston: Pilgrim Press, 1910), 10.

22. Ibid., 18-19.

23. Ibid., 23.

> of our fathers, and in all these years thine arm has never failed us, for our strength has ever been as our days. May this food come to us as an assurance of thy love and care and a promise of thy sustenance and relief.[24]

The prayers also display Rauschenbusch's literary and poetic eloquence, as evidenced by this morning prayer :

> O God, we who are bound together in the tender ties of love, pray thee for a day of unclouded love. . . . Forgive us if we have often been keen to see the human failings, and slow to feel the preciousness of those who are still the dearest comfort of our life. May there be no sharp words that wound and scar, and no rift that may grow into estrangement. . . . May our eyes not be so holden by selfishness that we know thine angels only when they spread their wings to return to thee.[25]

True to the book's title, the majority of prayers reflect upon specific dimensions of social salvation, as evidenced by the prayer "For Men in Business."

> Grant them farsighted patriotism to subordinate their profits to the public weal, and a steadfast determination to transform the disorder of the present into the nobler and freer harmony of the future. May thy Spirit, O God, which is ceaselessly pleading within us, prevail at last to bring our business life under Christ's law of service, so that all who share in the processes of factory and trade may grow up into that high consciousness of a divine calling which blesses those who are the free servants of God and the people and who consciously devote their strength to the common good.[26]

Although Rauschenbusch warned his readers against the sins of class bias, many of the prayers hint at his male Victorian worldview. His distaste for frivolous wealth was displayed in his prayer for young

24. Ibid., 42.
25. Ibid., 30.
26. Ibid., 64.

couples, "For All True Lovers," when he prayed that "no tyranny of fashion and no glamour of cheaper joys filch from them the wholesome peace and inward satisfaction which only loyal love can give."[27] And in his prayer "For Women Who Toil," he expressed his ambivalence toward women in the workplace, clearly seeing working women as an aberration from the proper role of women in the social order.

> Save them from the strain of unremitting toil that would unfit them for the holy duties of home and motherhood which the future may lay upon them. . . . If it must be so that our women toil like men, help us still to reverence in them the mothers of the future. But make us determined to shield them from unequal burdens, that the women of our nation be not drained of strength and hope for the enrichment of a few, lest our homes grow poor in the wifely sweetness and motherly love which have been the saving strength and glory of our country.[28]

By the same token many of the book's prayers reflect the way that Rauschenbusch's thought had evolved since his move to Rochester in 1897, epitomized by his prayer "Against War." In contrast to his jingoism during the Spanish-American War, Rauschenbusch reflected a chastened attitude toward military aggression, appealing to his audience to put the cause of American patriotism on a higher moral ground.

> Grant to the rulers of nations faith in the possibility of peace through justice, and grant to the common people a new and stern enthusiasm for the cause of peace. Bless our soldiers and sailors for their swift obedience and their willingness to answer to the call of duty, but inspire them none the less with a hatred of war, and may they never for love of private glory or advancement provoke its coming. May our young men still rejoice to die for their country with the valor of their fathers, but teach our age nobler methods of matching our strength and more effective ways of giving our life for the flag.[29]

27. Ibid., 94-95.
28. Ibid., 55-56.
29. Ibid., 109-10.

Prayers of the Social Awakening offers a significant window into both the spirituality of Walter Rauschenbusch and how that spirituality reflected the optimistic spirit of American progressivism. The prayers sought to distill a reform-oriented spirit into every dimension of American middle-class life, including prayers for immigrants, children, doctors and nurses, judges, lawyers, writers and newspaper men, and ministers. Yet the book also captured something of Rauschenbusch's humility and his own personal dependence on God, expressed eloquently in the book's final prayer, entitled "The Author's Prayer."

> O Thou who art the light of my soul, I thank Thee for the incomparable joy of listening to thy voice within, and I know that no word of thine shall return void, however brokenly uttered. If aught in this book was said through lack of knowledge, or through weakness of faith in Thee or love for men, I pray Thee to overrule my sin and turn aside its force before it harm thy cause. Pardon the frailty of thy servant, and look upon him only as he sinks his life in Jesus, his Master and Saviour. Amen.

The public response to *Prayers of the Social Awakening* was overwhelmingly positive. Friends and social gospel colleagues like Helen Barrett Montgomery, Josiah Strong, and Charles Sheldon praised the book and, as was the case with *Christianity and the Social Crisis,* Rauschenbusch was deluged by appreciative letters from ministers across the country. "It is the only collection that I have seen any prayer which I would gladly use in public worship," wrote an Episcopal priest in Massachusetts.[30]

Yet the book also met with its critics. Some reviewers complained of the book's socialistic spirit, while some conservative Christian journals complained that none of the prayers made any reference to Christ. Rauschenbusch was deeply wounded and offended by the latter accusation and in subsequent years defended the book against it. Writing to the Baptist journal the *Western Recorder,* he defended both the book and his spirituality. "My religious and intellectual life have both been built up on Jesus Christ to a degree which I think is not common. He

30. Malcolm Taylor to WR, January 4, 1911, box 106.

has been the determining force in all the main leadings and undertakings of my life."[31]

Many who read the book saw in it a spirit of mysticism, reflective of the spirituality of the eighteenth-century Quaker mystic, John Woolman. However, Rauschenbusch resisted this interpretation of his spirituality. He acknowledged to his family and friends that spirituality for him was based more on action than personal contemplation. "I have never realized the restful side of religious life, as some do," he confessed once to Pauline. "For me it is conflict, work."[32] Rauschenbusch held to notions of a life beyond death; however, he did not view the afterlife in ways that reflected popular evangelical notions of heaven. William Faunce reflected sentiments likely shared by Rauschenbusch, and other liberals of his generation, when Faunce commented on the death of his father in a 1911 letter to Rauschenbusch. "Strange to say, I have no special longing to see my Father as an *individual* in another world. . . . Am I inhuman? Or is this the temper of our generation? Profoundly I believe in the conservation of my Father's brave strong life in the life of God. . . . But to meet again as individuals, separate, struggling, limited — is that what we really desire?"[33]

Historian William McGuire King noted that a primary characteristic for many social gospel leaders like Rauschenbusch was that social struggle was a central component of being religious. Contrary to the later caricature that the social gospel epitomized a doctrine of naive or inevitable social progress, movement leaders like Rauschenbusch saw social progress as episodic. "Moments of victory emerged only out of a web of suffering and tragedy."[34] Rauschenbusch hints at this cycle in his prayer "On the Harm We Have Done" through offering the petition "Change us by the power of thy saving grace from sources of evil into forces for good, that with all our strength we may fight the wrongs we have aided, and aid the right we have clogged."[35]

31. WR to the *Western Recorder,* September 30, 1916, box 30.

32. Walter Rauschenbusch (no date), clipping saved by Pauline, box 120.

33. William Faunce to WR, February 5, 1911, box 25.

34. William McGuire King, "An enthusiasm for humanity: the social emphasis in religion and its accommodation in Protestant theology," in *Religion and 20th-Century American Intellectual Life,* ed. Michael J. Lacey (Cambridge: Cambridge University Press, 1989), 68.

35. *Prayers,* 127.

Rauschenbusch expressed and embodied the optimism of the day, but his optimism in the Christian social movement was rooted in a faith that strides toward the kingdom would emerge within a context of human struggle. At the end of 1911, however, he found himself looking at a national landscape that suggested to him that the present day embodied a historical moment that was ripe for success. It was a time when the social order could indeed be transformed by the power of this new gospel.

10 The Struggles of Kingdom Building

Rauschenbusch began 1912 determined to slow the pace of his schedule. Since he had returned from his 1908 sabbatical in Germany, he spent practically every week on the road, dividing his time between teaching at the seminary and lecturing throughout the United States. Even as he made the decision to decline several attractive speaking engagements during the first half of the year, including an invitation to teach two courses at Columbia University, he recognized the financial loss to his family. Besides the fact that Winifred would be going away to college that fall, Pauline and Walter made the decision to purchase a new home on Rochester's fashionable east side. The home, owned by the widow of Rochester Theological Seminary faculty member Harold Pattison, not only was located a few blocks from the seminary but also was in one of the city's wealthiest neighborhoods, located directly behind the mansion of photography mogul George Eastman. With plans to move into the house in March and with the home in need of extensive renovation,[1] Rauschenbusch needed money generated through his public speaking. He was, however, under con-

1. See various correspondences in box 26.

tractual obligations with Macmillan to publish a follow-up book to *Christianity and the Social Crisis*, and he was determined to write.

He hoped to expand his Earl Lectures delivered at the Pacific Theological Seminary in 1910 and his Merrick Lectures at Ohio Wesleyan University from the previous spring into a volume that would complement the themes in *Christianity and the Social Crisis*. Even with his resolve to complete the volume, he was disturbed by the book's slow pace. "The book is moving along slowly, much more slowly than I had hoped," he confided to a Congregational minister in Madison, Wisconsin. "Some sections I have written three or four times. But I do feel that it is getting better and clearer all the time."[2] Despite his optimistic assessment, Rauschenbusch found it difficult to devote sustained effort on the book. For about a year, he received pleas from a variety of Protestant church leaders to throw his efforts behind the Men and Religion Forward Movement. Conceived in 1910 as a grand evangelical Protestant crusade sponsored by numerous denominations and ecumenical organizations, the movement's purpose was to win over to Christ the nation's men and youth through an extensive array of educational materials, proposed social service initiatives, and missional projects. The movement was launched in the spring of 1911 with rallies in cities throughout the United States. At the core of the movement's social evangelism was the goal "to increase the permanent contribution of the Church to the best life of the Continent, socially, commercially and physically, and to emphasize the modern message of the Church in social service and usefulness." The movement's chief organizational catalyst was the well-known Presbyterian minister, Charles Stelzle, and it drew financial support from an array of American business leaders representing diverse theological persuasions, including John D. Rockefeller, Jr., John Wanamaker, J. P. Morgan, and Cyrus McCormick.[3]

Rauschenbusch readily accepted many of the ideological suppositions of the movement, especially related to the need for American society to create an environment that would aid the social and moral

2. Walter Rauschenbusch to Richard Henry Edwards, January 27, 1912, box 26.

3. Donald K. Gorrell, *The Age of Social Responsibility: The Social Gospel in the Progressive Era, 1900-1920* (Macon, GA: Mercer University Press, 1988), 165-79.

development of young boys. As he noted to his friend and onetime Rochester school board ally Charles DePuy later that year, the American boy "is one of a great group, swept along by the social life of his own boy-tribe, who are all being made or unmade by the permanent influences with which the past and the present surround them, victims of our sins, and in turn transmitters of social good or social evil to the next stratum of boys that look up to them." Reflecting the arguments that would appear in his upcoming book, Rauschenbusch saw in the Men and Religion Forward Movement the opportunity to challenge the social and economic forces that exacerbate "the inevitable perils of boyhood, breaking down the home which is the true shelter of the child, thrusting him out into the street, robbing him of his old and wholesome sports and the contact with nature, almost forcing him into the gang, and impressing him early into the exhausting monotony of machine labor."[4] For Rauschenbusch, the Men and Religion Forward Movement struck to the heart of his belief that building the kingdom of God in America revolved around a solid family structure.

Although he wholeheartedly supported the Men and Religion Forward Movement's agenda, Rauschenbusch had reservations about the movement's organization and planning. He warned one of the organizers that the movement needed to attract prominent Christian speakers who manifested an irenic spirit, capable of educating the public in various dimensions of the social question, and avoid the appearance of social radicalism. "We are still at a stage where thought is fermenting, and the speakers will do good work if they simply awaken the Christian public to the gravity of the situation, get their minds to lie open to social ideas, and indicate in what general direction we must move."[5] Even though he was reluctant to pull himself away from his writing, he agreed to speak in Chicago at a number of planned concluding rallies for the Men and Religion Forward Movement in April.

He was also receiving pleas from Charles Macfarland, president of the Federal Council of Churches, to take a more active role in the Federal Council's ministries. Although the FCC's founding in 1908 had been a watershed in the development of American Protestant

4. WR to Charles DePuy, November 29, 1912, box 26.
5. WR to C. A. Nesbit, July 14, 1911, box 26.

ecumenism, the organization in its early history was stymied by a limited budget and a recalcitrant membership. Rauschenbusch was a member of the Council's Commission on Social Service. However, he played a secondary role on the committee, a fact about which Macfarland politely, but firmly, reminded Rauschenbusch. The previous fall, Macfarland had tried to get Rauschenbusch to take a leadership role for an FCC project that would publish educational material designed to promote the spread of the social gospel among ministers and laity. Although somewhat receptive to the idea, Rauschenbusch believed that the way to bring the social gospel to laity required more than didactic materials. "We need hymns that will voice the new social enthusiasm. As you know the old fashioned hymnals are almost bare of any such material. . . . But if we had some small collection . . . which could [contain] the most beautiful and dependable hymns of that character . . . I think this is really of great deal more importance than other more scientific undertakings that we might contemplate."[6] As indicated by his *Prayers of the Social Awakening* and his earlier hymnal collaboration with Ira Sankey, Rauschenbusch believed that a major part of the social gospel needed to be expressed devotionally through worship and hymn singing. Although he resisted greater involvement in the work of the Federal Council, he did accept the invitation to give the keynote address at the FCC's second quadrennial meeting that December.

In part, Rauschenbusch's ambivalence toward accepting greater participation in the Men and Religion Forward Movement and the Federal Council of Churches related to his writing and his responsibilities at Rochester Theological Seminary. But more significantly, it highlights how his deafness made protracted meetings arduous and frustrating events for him. When he declined an offer to serve on a Men and Religion Forward planning committee in 1911, he candidly admitted that committee work was usually intolerable for him due to his deafness. "I shall not be able to get as distinct and direct an impression of the action of the work done . . . as those who can attend the sessions with full hearing power."[7] As Rauschenbusch was painfully aware of how his poor hearing adversely affected his relationship to his family,

6. WR to Charles Macfarland, October 27, 1911, box 26.

7. WR to James Cannon, December 7, 1911, box 26.

so it increasingly affected his ability to interact with his peers in the cause of advancing the social gospel in America.

A DIVIDED PROTESTANTISM?

Rauschenbusch was also disturbed by a controversy with the pastor of the First Baptist Church in New York City, Isaac Haldeman. One of America's more prominent premillennialist ministers, Haldeman published a 1911 pamphlet critiquing *Christianity and the Social Crisis.* The pamphlet attacked Rauschenbusch in terms of his biblical exegesis (his failure to read the Scriptures through an apocalyptic lens) and in the fact that Rauschenbusch elevated the false paradigm of church history over biblical studies. "Professor Rauschenbusch comes into the New Testament with the conviction that the New Testament itself is responsible for the failure and vagaries of the early Church — responsible, because of its plain apocalyptic statements and catastrophic promises concerning the kingdom. . . . Professor Rauschenbusch uses Church history as a lever to pry the New Testament out of its place of final authority in the definition and interpretation of true Christianity, and standing on the ground furnished by Church history, makes that history the basis from which the New Testament shall henceforth be 'sanely interpreted.'"[8] In place of Pauline texts and the apocalyptic Scriptures of the New Testament, Haldeman charged that Rauschenbusch had merely substituted "modified German rationalism, . . . twentieth century humanitarianism, and the doctrine of a Christ and a Church unknown to Paul."[9] Haldeman concluded that Rauschenbusch was clearly outside of the boundaries of biblical Christianity. "The earnestness of the book, its manifest sympathy with the toilers by the way, its subtle denial of inspiration, its discount of New Testament integrity, and the unmiraculous Christ in whose name it comes, make it a dangerous bit of reading to unformed faith, and to minds swayed by sentiment rather than a 'thus saith the Lord.'"[10]

8. I. M. Haldeman, *Professor Rauschenbusch's "Christianity and the Social Crisis"* (New York: Charles C. Cook, 1911), 40.

9. Ibid., 42.

10. Ibid.

Rauschenbusch's friends encouraged him to dismiss Haldeman's diatribes. Mornay Williams wrote that Haldeman was a good man with a lamentable view of Christianity. "As far as I can see, he is about in the stage of development that Peter was before he denied his Lord."[11] A Baptist colleague in Ohio added, "You could not wish any higher compliment than that of being lined up as an opponent of the Pre-Millenarian vagaries."[12] Yet Rauschenbusch increasingly had to acknowledge the widening gap that existed in America between those who viewed the coming kingdom of God as the dawning of a social awakening and those who saw the kingdom as an impending apocalypse. When he began his New York City ministry in 1886, it was still possible for Protestant leaders to put aside theological differences and embrace a common mission to make America conform to the values of a Christian civilization. By the early 1910s, however, the irenic Protestant spirit of cooperation characterized by Dwight Moody was coming unraveled. Conservative and liberal Protestants still found common ground on certain social questions, especially evident in the wide support garnered for a temperance amendment to the United States Constitution. The publication in that decade, however, of *The Fundamentals,* a series of pamphlets written by an eclectic assortment of orthodox Calvinist theologians and premillennialist evangelicals, reminded liberals like Rauschenbusch that the goal of building the kingdom through social reform would not be shared by all. In 1912, the use of the term "fundamentalist" as a theological designation was still a decade away. At the same time, *The Fundamentals,* with their promotion of biblical literalism, their attack against biblical higher criticism, and their premillennial overtones, were clear evidence of an emerging fault line in the Protestant establishment that erupted in the 1920s.

Yet as 1912 progressed, hopeful signs appeared that the social gospel was gaining acceptance within American Protestantism. In addition to the fact that the major leaders of the Federal Council of Churches were men sympathetic to the social gospel, most of the major Protestant denominations in the North had adopted social creeds, establishing a number of commissions designed to promote practical

11. Mornay Williams to WR, November 23, 1911, box 26.
12. Leon Latimer to WR, January 16, 1912, box 26.

"social service" initiatives on both a denominational and a grassroots level. Nevertheless, Rauschenbusch received numerous reminders from colleagues that church leaders in America had a long way to go to convert the masses to the cause of the social gospel. His old comrade Samuel Batten wrote from Philadelphia in his new position as head of the Northern Baptist Social Service Commission that he and like-minded colleagues faced an uphill battle in their struggle to propagate the social gospel agenda to contemporary America. "I feel isolated out here and get lonesome often for the fellowship of other days," he lamented to Rauschenbusch as he recalled the role that the two men played in establishing the Brotherhood of the Kingdom back in the 1890s. "I am convinced that the time is here when we must get together a number of men who are in protest and consider our duty under the circumstances. Is the church going to misread the signs of the times today as of old?"[13]

Others within Protestant Christendom, however, believed that the social gospel had gone too far. George Fisher, the editor of the periodical the *Gospel Message*, took an approving view of Haldeman and other conservatives who defended the old faith from the encroachment of the new. Fisher accused Rauschenbusch of having no business passing off his teachings as Christian, questioning the wisdom of his presence on the faculty of a theological seminary that had defended Protestant orthodoxy. "I do not see how you can with peace of mind continue in a position in an Institution, which is supposed to stand for evangelical faith, and hold the views that you promulgate in your book" [*Christianity and the Social Crisis*]. While acknowledging that he bore Rauschenbusch no personal animosity, Fisher noted when it came to his teachings, "I am at swords' points with all my heart."[14]

In spite of the stinging attacks of critics like Haldeman and Fisher, Rauschenbusch continued to take comfort from the numerous letters he received weekly from ministers throughout the country and abroad who praised him for *Christianity and the Social Crisis* and *Prayers of the Social Awakening*. A seminarian in Great Britain wrote Rauschenbusch after reading *Christianity and the Social Crisis* for the third time that the work was critical in shaping his theology of minis-

13. Samuel Batten to WR [1912], box 26.
14. George Fisher to WR, April 17, 1912, box 26.

try. "I leave college with a deeper feeling than ever of the need for a social gospel, or rather a gospel for the individual that shall translate itself into social work. And here it is that your book has proved its value to me. . . . It has been, and will be, a source of inspiration to me in my work."[15] Rauschenbusch's spirits were no doubt buoyed by such praise, as they were by the hundreds of letters he received yearly from his former students. Rauschenbusch took pains to respond to all of his correspondents, often trying to help these young men deal with questions ranging from the practical implementation of Christian socialism to offering them assistance in solving parish crises. Throughout these correspondences, he emphasized a persistent theme — that the so-called social gospel was nothing more than a rediscovery of ancient Christianity.

TOWARD A CHRISTIANIZED SOCIETY

The early months of 1912 provided little opportunity to engage in the writing he craved. Only weeks before the family's move, Pauline suffered a serious illness that required her to spend several weeks convalescing at a health spa in nearby Dansville, New York. Pauline's illness was partly related to physical exhaustion. However, her letters home suggest that she was also fighting depression and that her problems were exacerbated by mounting domestic tensions. She expressed to her husband her anxieties over the family's impending move and her feelings of inadequacy as a wife, mother, and housekeeper. "The fact of the matter is that I never take anything lightly — I think it is one of my limitations that I take everything so seriously." Noting the ways she had always tried to carry on an optimistic facade in the company of family and friends, she confessed her deepest insecurities surrounding her usefulness to her husband. "Sometimes you think I am interested only in your personality — not your work . . . but I am often oppressed by the details and worries of the family and fail to ask you about it or you are not in the mood to talk and I am diffident or the opportunity of talking about it goes by."[16] As Pauline made clear in a letter to her son,

15. "George" to WR, October 26, 1912, box 26.
16. Pauline Rauschenbusch to WR, no date, box 123.

Paul, she was determined upon her return home to make their new household at 4 Portsmouth Terrace a model of a loving Christian family.

> I think one of the things that always wears on me and on father [much] more than on me — is the almost constant quarrelling and bickering between you children — making each other cry and saying harsh unkind things — you would not do it to a stranger but among yourselves you think it allright [*sic*] — it wears me out. We must all help father — he has no easy task in life. But if everything goes well at home it helps him very much indeed.[17]

Pauline's letter to Paul reflected her determination in the future to do all she could to assist her husband's ministry. "You have a rare father — I want to devote myself more to him when I come home and let other things go. . . . Always pray for me — without God we are nothing — it is only God who in the last instant can help."[18] For his part, Walter tried to reassure Pauline that all was well on the domestic front and that he and the children were making excellent progress preparing for the move. "What I want now is that you get well and sleep well. I wish when you lie down at night you would repeat to yourself a number of times, 'Walther wants me to sleep quietly . . . , and I shall do it.'"[19]

When Pauline returned to Rochester, just prior to the family's move, she remained exhausted and physical ailments continued to plague her for much of the year. Numerous domestic responsibilities consequently fell upon her husband. By spring, after the family had settled into their new home, he too was on the verge of illness and physical exhaustion. James Jackson, the resident physician at the Dansville clinic who cared for Pauline, wrote Rauschenbusch that March warning him that he needed rest, observing that " procrastination is not your ruling passion, but you are too avid for work, no man can do everything at once."[20] Nevertheless, not long after the family

17. Pauline Rauschenbusch to Paul Rauschenbusch, February 17, 1912, box 120.

18. Ibid.

19. WR to Pauline Rauschenbusch, February 15, 1912, box 53.

20. James Jackson to WR, March 9, 1912, box 26.

move to Portsmouth Terrace, Rauschenbusch made preparations to go to Chicago to address the Men and Religion Forward Movement rallies. His attitude for this venture was improved by the acquisition of a new hearing device, one that not only allowed him to hear conversations several feet away, but also one that lacked "the high strident tones of the other instruments."[21]

Rauschenbusch's experience in Chicago was filled with ambivalence. The enthusiastic climax hoped for by the Men and Religion Forward organizers was muted by the news of the *Titanic* sinking. Rauschenbusch gave several addresses in Chicago, and had the opportunity for meetings with two Progressive Era colleagues, Graham Taylor and Jane Addams. Although Rauschenbusch would later speak glowingly of the Men and Religion Forward Movement as "the most comprehensive evangelistic movement ever undertaken in this country," he confided to a friend that he felt the organization for his Chicago appearances was weak and he was dismayed about the lack of media coverage attached to the rallies.[22]

At the end of the spring academic semester, Rauschenbusch looked forward to completing *Christianizing the Social Order* during the family's annual summer vacation in Ontario. He did interrupt his schedule briefly in June to give an address to the Baptist Congress in Cleveland, but for the first time since the summers he spent in Canandaigua working on *Christianity and the Social Crisis* in 1905 and 1906, he was unencumbered with extensive speaking obligations. Nevertheless, Rauschenbusch still faced a difficult task in finishing the manuscript. He wanted to write a detailed narrative that would show Americans specific aspects of "the social question" in the nation and provide a practical analysis of how churches could live out that social vision. Instead he found himself immersed in a project that mushroomed into a manuscript of several hundred pages. During the summer, Rauschenbusch asked the editor of the *American Magazine*, J. S. Phillips, if the magazine would be interested in publishing selected chapters of the new book, in an arrangement similar to the publication two years earlier of the prayers that later became *Prayers of the Social*

21. WR to Edmund Lyon, April 15, 1912, box 26.

22. Walter Rauschenbusch, *Christianizing the Social Order,* 19; WR to Lyon, April 15, 1912, box 26.

Awakening. Phillips was initially excited about the prospect. However, Rauschenbusch's fastidious criticisms of his work and Phillips's reservation whether the chapters on their own would be suitable for the magazine's popular readership made both men agree not to publish any of the material. Phillips assured Rauschenbusch that he would love him to write something for the magazine "with a little less rigor than in this book,"[23] but Phillips also confided to Rauschenbusch's editor at Macmillan that he thought the project in a "very curious state."[24] Rauschenbusch did strike an agreement with the editor of Pilgrim Press to publish, in book form, a short tract on Christian social work that was designed for laity.

Soon after his return from Canada in September, Rauschenbusch sent the long anticipated follow-up to *Christianity and the Social Crisis* off to Macmillan. He noted in the book's foreword his belief that the earlier book represented his last word on contemporary social problems. But in response to the signs he saw of the social awakening in America, he wanted to flesh out in greater detail the themes he laid out in his earlier work. "I have urged a moral regeneration of social institutions, a christianizing of public morality," he explained. "The problem of christianizing the social order welds all the tasks of practical Christianity with the highest objects of statesmanship. That the actual results of our present social order are in acute contradiction to the Christian conceptions of justice and brotherhood is realized by every man who thinks at all."[25]

Christianizing the Social Order was as much a progress report on the state of American social Christianity since 1907 as it was a sequel to *Christianity and the Social Crisis*. Despite any personal concerns he may have had about the pace of Christian social reform in America, the book's 476 pages resonate with hope that America's churches were moving the entire nation closer to the kingdom of God. The book was divided into six parts. The first two sections examined Protestant initiatives that Rauschenbusch felt signaled the contemporary social awakening of the churches. Reiterating arguments from *Christianity and the Social Crisis* related to how early Christianity abandoned the

23. J. S. Phillips to WR, September 25, 1912, box 26.
24. J. S. Phillips to George Brett, September 12, 1912, box 26.
25. *Christianizing the Social Order*, viii.

"social hope" central to the Old Testament prophets and to Jesus' ministry, he gave a positive assessment of recent social ministries adopted by various Protestant denominations to Christianize America. Like most social gospel leaders, Rauschenbusch did not use the term "Christianize" in a theocratic sense. His use of the term reflected Rauschenbusch's desire to make contemporary cultural institutions conform to the teachings of Christ.

> We call this "christianizing" the social order because these moral principles find their highest expression in the teachings, the life, and the spirit of Jesus Christ. . . . To the great majority of our nation, both inside and outside of the churches, he has become the incarnate moral law and his name is synonymous with the ideal of human goodness. To us who regard him as the unique revelation of God, the unfolding of the divine life under human forms, he is the ultimate standard of moral and spiritual life, the perfect expression of the will of God for humanity, the categorical imperative with a human heart.[26]

The thrust of the book's argument, contained in the final four sections, consisted of an exposition on ways American social institutions could be Christianized, focusing on matters of government, economics, education, religion, and the family. The book expounded on familiar economic themes, including detailed discussions on the sins of the profit motive, the merits of government regulation (especially with regard to "natural monopolies" such as electric and gas utilities and railroads), the abuses of unfair land speculation practices, and the rights of working-class Americans to receive a just wage and to unionize. Rauschenbusch looked hopefully to an emerging national reform ethos, centered upon legislative action by the federal government. However, the book also indicates that his model of a Christianized society was rooted in the need for local communities to share common values related to labor, educational values and standards, and healthy Christian recreation. His arguments pertaining to American education echoed many of the same themes he advocated as the president of the Rochester City School task force in 1908. Castigating private schools as

26. Ibid., 125.

the domain of the rich and powerful, Rauschenbusch believed that America's tax-supported public schools represented one of America's brightest hopes for the future. Observing that public education in America had already passed through "a regenerating process," he looked to a future in the twentieth century where public schools would lead Americans in Christianizing the industrial forces of American capitalism.

> That enthusiasm for education, which is one of the finest characteristics of our country and has gone far to redeem us from the charge of gross mammonism, was kindled and fed by the churches and ministers, by the denominational academies and colleges, and by the men and women who were bred in both. These forces have infused that missionary spirit into our educational system which reaches out a summoning hand to the needy and aspiring.[27]

Rauschenbusch's assessment is ironic, given his earlier criticism of the Rochester public schools.

As he argued in *Christianity and the Social Crisis,* Rauschenbusch reiterated his worry that the capitalist system would brutalize the moral foundation of the American family, especially preventing women from fulfilling their roles as wives and mothers. He noted his support of women's suffrage, arguing that suffrage "will abolish one of the last remnants of patriarchal autocracy" in America.[28] At the same time, Rauschenbusch was deeply concerned that the American wage system was driving women into the workplace, depriving them of the opportunity to have children and displacing male workers. Reiterating points he had expressed in *Christianity and the Social Crisis,* Rauschenbusch warned that when "the wife is away at work, the home is bereft of the home maker and loses its meaning. . . . The higher spiritual satisfactions of the home are washed away like the soil from a denuded mountain side."[29] Rauschenbusch fervently believed in the equality of men and women, and his high esteem for suffrage pioneer Susan B. Anthony and his friendships with women reformers like

27. Ibid., 147.
28. Ibid., 131.
29. Ibid., 264.

Helen Barrett Montgomery, Jane Addams, and Vida Scudder indicate the respect he held for these women as public leaders. Yet he continued to define the primary social role of women to be that of wives and mothers.

Christianizing the Social Order expressed Rauschenbusch's confidence that American society was making great strides toward Christianization. From his perspective, the nation's churches, schools, families, and its system of government were all being infused by the spirit of prophetic Christianity and displaying signs of this "social regeneration." The one segment resisting this movement toward Christianization was the economic order. Many of Rauschenbusch's proposals for regulating the economic private sector continued to rely on the ideas of late nineteenth-century reformers such as Henry George and Richard Ely. At the same time, he acknowledged that any economic reform measures needed to avoid the class violence inherent in movements of radical socialism. At points in the book, Rauschenbusch seems to support the argument made by later generations that he promoted a view of inevitable historical progress. "To-day the area of popular intelligence has widened; the means of common action have improved; progress has become fairly continuous. Religious dogmatism and superstition, which used to lubricate the axis of progress with rubber cement, has lost some of its strength." Although acknowledging that self-interest remained in the political realm, "democracy has put the levers where the people can reach them whenever they need them badly."[30] Rauschenbusch acknowledged that self-centered economic interests remained powerful in American corporations, conceding that transforming the American private sector would take nothing less than the moral force of the nation. "Business is the unsaved part of the social order. . . . The saved portions of the social order must stand together in the consciousness of moral and religious superiority and go after the lost Brother."[31]

Rauschenbusch recognized the significant economic barriers that separated classes of rich and poor Americans in the early twentieth century. Applying the historical Protestant concept of a "means of grace" as a metaphor to speak of the right for workers to obtain eco-

30. Ibid., 411.
31. Ibid., 411.

nomic power, he asserted, "a condition in which one fourth of the race holds all the opportunities of livelihood in its arbitrary control, and the other three fourths are without property, . . . and without an assured means of even working for a living, is neither American nor Christian. Property is a means of grace, and a good job is another."[32] Not only did Rauschenbusch believe that government had the responsibility to make private businesses provide better pay and safer conditions for the nation's working class, but these companies had the responsibility to distribute a share of their profits to improve the social welfare of the nation's poor. Rauschenbusch's appeal for government regulation of the private sector was rooted in his belief that the nation's major corporations were directly tied to the greater public welfare. "A private business that employs thousands of people, uses the natural resources of the nation, enjoys exemptions and privileges at law, and is essential to the welfare of great communities is not a private business. It is public, and the sooner we abandon the fiction that it is private, the better for our good sense."[33]

Christianizing the Social Order would be criticized by later theologians and ethicists who chided the book's optimistic assessment regarding the extent to which America and its institutions had been Christianized. Rauschenbusch clearly saw the nation's churches at the vanguard of a movement that would transform American society into a democratic oasis of freedom and justice. Paraphrasing the famous nineteenth-century German historian Leopold von Ranke, he asserted that "'the only real progress of mankind is contained in Christianity'; but that is true only when Christianity is allowed to become 'the internal, organizing force of society.'"[34] Yet Rauschenbusch spoke eloquently in the book about the dangers inherent for Christians who saw social action as a substitute for an authentic Christian faith. "We do not want to substitute social activities for religion. If the Church comes to lean on social preachings and doings as a crutch because its religion has become paralytic, may the Lord have mercy on us all!"[35] Asserting that any Christian theological vision for social reform needed to be

32. Ibid., 350.
33. Ibid., 427.
34. Ibid., 458.
35. Ibid., 464.

rooted in its biblical and historical foundation in the kingdom of God, he warned readers of the dangers represented by too much faith in personal salvation *and* the opposite extreme of placing too much confidence upon human ability to perfect the world. "To concentrate our efforts on personal salvation, as orthodoxy has done, or on soul culture, as liberalism has done, comes close to refined selfishness. . . . A religion which realizes in God the bond that binds all men together can create the men who will knit the social order together as an organized brotherhood."[36] Rauschenbusch concluded with the caution that working toward such a vision required great sacrifice on the part of those willing to strive for the achievement of a just society. As he warned his readers toward the end of the book, "The resistence of the upper classes has again and again blocked and frustrated hopeful upward movements, kept useful classes of the people in poverty and degradation, and punished the lovers of humanity with martyrdom of body or soul. The cross of Christ stands for the permanent historical fact that the men who have embodied the saving power of God have always been ill treated by those who profited by sin."[37]

FAMILY TRANSITIONS

Rauschenbusch's own cautious hope about America's future was chastened by events in his own family. Increasingly, he was coming to grips with the fact that his own family life was a far cry from the ideal of the American family that he praised in his writings. Rauschenbusch struggled constantly with feelings of guilt concerning his own shortcomings as a husband and parent. In spite of the fact that he deeply loved his children, his demeanor with them could change quickly from being a playful, affectionate, and humorous companion to being a stern judge. Rauschenbusch was proud that he was offering his five children the best of a German-American cultural heritage. He insisted that his children use both English and German in their family correspondence and he frequently chastised them when they used poor grammar in their letters. In effect, the same educational standards he wanted

36. Ibid., 464-65.
37. Ibid., 470.

brought to the Rochester city schools four years earlier were standards he expected of his own children.

This paradox in Rauschenbusch's parental role created a discernible rift with his oldest children, Winifred and Hilmar. Although his relationship with his two oldest children was filled with many happy memories, especially during their summer vacations in Canada, it became more difficult for Rauschenbusch to communicate with them as both moved through their teens, especially after the family's return from Germany in 1909. Hilmar, who in the fall of 1912 entered his junior year in high school, was an excellent student and a member of East High School's debating team. Yet Rauschenbusch worried about his oldest son's reserved and, at times, taciturn personality, fearing that it signaled a father-son breach.

Equally stressful was his relationship to Winifred, a relationship marked by deep intimacy but also tremendous conflict. This relationship to his oldest child embodied many of his conflicting views toward women. On one hand, he expected academic excellence from Winifred, holding her to the same high standards to which he held his sons. Yet his Victorian proclivities frequently emerged in his letters to her, as he expressed his hope that his eldest daughter would become a model of American womanhood. Increasingly, Winifred made it clear that she did not share her father's vision. As a teenager, she grew increasingly rebellious and both Walter and Pauline were often at wit's end in terms of how to control her behavior. Yet Walter showed remarkable tenderness toward his daughter, frequently confiding his great love for her, in spite of the generational and gender divide that increasingly separated the two. In one poignant letter written not long after Winifred turned 16, he noted sympathetically, "Children misread their parents, often cruelly. They have not yet the experiences of work and suffering that would give them understanding by sympathy. I am sure they never gauge how much we love them. . . . On the other hand we fail to understand you children. Partly because we have lost your point of view, your emotions, dreams, and passions . . . it takes a lot of love to comprehend entirely."

But Rauschenbusch also recognized that the relationship crisis that emerged between Winifred and himself had as much to do with his deafness as it did any difference in generational perspective. "A hundred little things that would give me a peek into your soul when it is open by chance, escape me because I can not hear." Often the only way he could get close to his children and reveal the full extent of his feelings was in his letters. "You will never have a friend who will love you as steadfastly as we do. And no lover or child will ever love you as unselfishly."[38]

Winifred's departure to Oberlin College in the fall of 1912 exacerbated the divide between Rauschenbusch and his oldest child. He became angry when Winifred was slow to answer letters and when she did write, the elder Rauschenbusch frequently provided his daughter with much unwelcome parental advice. Yet the father yearned to be close to his daughter and her silence brought out his own insecurities as a parent. "I think of you oftener than any of my children," he confided to her that November. "My heart is always crying out for my daughter and I can't find her. I seem to have lost her years ago."[39] Rauschenbusch's letters expressed an inner agony that his children were rejecting him. At times, his letters took on a pleading tone. "You have been too silent and have made it impossible for me to understand you. I have probably spoken too much. But it was always a reaching out after you, an effort to call you and get an answer, a struggle of thwarted love."[40]

Moreover, Winifred's absence from Rochester exacerbated Walter's strained relationship with Hilmar, who grew more sullen in the absence of his older sibling and close friend. Rauschenbusch in a melancholy tone confessed to Winifred that November how his relationship to Hilmar mirrored his relationship to all of his children. "He has been a burden on my mind for weeks, but I always supposed it was some school trouble, or that I had hurt his feelings and I had become so used to being shut out from the confidence of my children, that I stood helpless, hoping that it would pass over."[41] Rauschenbusch's insecurities are revealed in a letter to Hilmar, where he attempted to combine the roles of disciplinarian and friend.

> You can not imagine how much your comradeship means to me. I am always a lonely man. Winifred to my great grief stands aloof

38. WR to Winifred Rauschenbusch, July 19, 1910, box 143.
39. WR to Winifred Rauschenbusch, November 15, 1912, box 180.
40. WR to Winifred Rauschenbusch, no date, circa 1912, box 180.
41. WR to Winifred Rauschenbusch, November 15, 1912, box 180.

> and I despair of entering into comradeship with her. Your friendship and effort to meet me on equal terms, — as a man, — have been an unexpressible comfort to me. I can not yet abandon the attitude of government toward you, for you are still a boy in many ways, and need bracing and command at times. Probably I take that attitude when it is not really needed because it has become habitual, and because it is the shortest and easiest for a tired man. But I do not want to repel you. I want your manhood to grow to independence in time.[42]

Yet as Rauschenbusch affirmed his hopes for his children's future, he lived constantly with a fatalistic sense of failure as a parent. His conclusion in his letter to Hilmar reflected an almost morose tone. "I often feel like drawing out of all interference in the family since I can do it only badly, and since it seems to lose me the confidence of my children. But I know there would be other bad effects and it would leave Mother without a backing. She feels the burden of it all so deeply that when I said to her recently that you might all be better off without me, she replied that she was so discouraged that she would want to die if she did not have me to lean on."[43] Rauschenbusch may have exaggerated the depth of his frustrations. But his musings indicate that life in the Rauschenbusch household was more complicated than that in the ideal family he espoused in his writings.

THE SUCCESSES OF KINGDOM BUILDING

Rauschenbusch was likely pleased by the early reviews of *Christianizing the Social Order.* Only a few weeks after publication, Augustus Strong wrote Rauschenbusch on Thanksgiving Day noting that he thought the book would be a classic and was reading sections of the book aloud to his wife. "We are greatly pleased with its incisive style and its Christian spirit."[44] Reviewers from a variety of secular and religious publications praised the work. The Springfield, Massachusetts,

42. WR to Hilmar (no date), box 54.
43. Ibid.
44. Augustus Strong to WR, November 28, 1912, box 26.

Republican called it "one of the most important sociological books of the year,"[45] while the *Methodist Review* observed that the book was "a silver trumpet sounding an advance to the hosts of Israel, saying with no uncertain sound, 'Go Forward.'" The same reviewer concluded, "No Christian business man can afford to pass up this book, and no preacher will think of doing anything of the kind. The author's fame is a guarantee against that."[46] Various colleagues in the cause of the social gospel also praised the book in letters to its author. Francis Peabody, the prominent Christian ethicist, gave a warm assessment of the book as did Washington Gladden. In December, a self-avowed Christian socialist wrote that the book would have greater impact than *Christianity and the Social Crisis.* "I predict that this book will of itself be one of the 'channel buoys' that will aid in showing the way from this era to the better one that's to come. It is sure to have wide influence with the great middle class; and, I hope the appeal to men of wealth will be rewarded."[47]

Christianizing the Social Order sold well. But it did not cause the public stir that *Christianity and the Social Crisis* did. Some of Rauschenbusch's friends saw this reaction as evidence that many of the new book's suppositions, which would have struck most as radical five years earlier, had now been accepted by many rank-and-file Protestants. Nevertheless, the book attracted its share of critics, not just among conservatives, but from individuals with socialist leanings who felt that Christianity and socialism were anathema to one another. One critic wrote that Rauschenbusch's perspective on the ability of the church to influence the social contours of America was myopic. "The claims of religion have been discredited so often in our higher education, how can it hope to teach a system of economics that is opposed to this theory? . . . At present time, who do you make your appeal to? If religion has lost prestige in education, how can the social movement acquire prestige from religion?"[48] Others were more blunt, arguing that the church could never play a constructive role in building a better social order. "Why could you not wait until you had another

45. Springfield, Mass., *Republican* (December 30, 1912), clipping in box 94.

46. *Methodist Review* (May-June 1913), clipping in box 94.

47. Robert McJunkin to WR, December 18, 1912, box 26.

48. "Carl" to WR, no date, box 26.

message, instead of coming out again with a rehash, padded out with so much that isn't so," asserted one particularly hostile critic. "When this 'Church' gets off the back of the workers — it will be time enough to consider whether the 'Church' be even allowed to follow the procession, much less lead it, as you would have us believe."[49] Rauschenbusch's response showed that he could be acerbic, in a dignified and humorous manner. "Your judgement . . . that the new book is a mere rehash of the old is entirely incorrect. I have reasons to know this, because I had to do the hard work of writing it. . . . I should also like to add that the influence of men like yourself would be much greater if you would handle language a little more carefully. Many men think that they have to be brutal in order to be energetic."[50]

This exchange indicates that many political socialists continued to view Rauschenbusch's "Christian socialism" with dubious eyes. He expressed to Francis Peabody that although Christianity and socialism were estranged in the public's mind, socialist leaders were missing signs of the social regeneration taking place within the church and society. "I am not going to tell the Socialists that I expect them to remain atheists. I shall tell them that they are now religious in spite of themselves and that an increased approach to religion is inevitable as they emerge from the age of polemics and dogmatism."[51]

The optimism expressed to Peabody was evident in Rauschenbusch's short tract *Unto Me*, published that October. Accentuating his conviction that modern "social work" in the church had its origins in the example of the Hebrew prophets and the ministry of Jesus, the book carries a strongly devotional theme, showing how Rauschenbusch sought to connect personal religious experience to a larger social context. It also gave him an opportunity to reflect on a component of his theology central to other evangelical liberals of his generation: one could not understand the cross as a theological symbol without somehow bearing Christ's own pain. "For ages the cross of Christ has stood at the center of Christian theology. But many good men who are loud in their insistence on the cross as the only means of salvation have apparently never had any experience of the

49. Henry Stuart to WR, December 23, 1912, box 26.
50. WR to Henry Stuart, January 10, 1913, box 26.
51. WR to Francis Peabody, December 14, 1912, box 26.

pain of the cross."[52] Rauschenbusch bemoaned those who saw religion as a means of gaining social status, who on the surface were charitable and good men. "But their goodness was never so good that it waked up the devil. They never antagonized profitable sin; so they never got hurt."[53] Rauschenbusch surmised that those who engaged in authentic Christian social work that delved into the social miseries plaguing America represented "the only form of Christian work that involves risk of persecution. Thereby it opens to us a living experience of the cross of Christ and a fellow-feeling with all his followers of the Church Militant, which has moved down the centuries in a thin red line, but to which the Church Dormant owes all it enjoys of the higher life."[54]

Rauschenbusch's argument came to typify a tendency of several social gospel leaders who cast divine judgment upon the wealthy power brokers of American capitalism. Nevertheless, he emphasized that God's love was the central fabric in all social relations. "To love men, then, is an avenue to the living experience of God."[55] The work of social reform, vital to the church's mission, depended on those who embodied Christlike love in their service to humanity. "Jesus was always uncovering the spiritual meaning in the common actions of life," he explained. "To him the giving of a cup of cold water was a sacrament of humanity."[56]

Although his writings placed the upper class and wealthy under judgment, in the face of social-economic inequalities, Rauschenbusch was extremely diplomatic in his dealings with the prosperous. As he sought to do with his friend and benefactor, John D. Rockefeller, he hoped to stir the consciences of the wealthy, believing that the benevolence of the rich was vital in the social regeneration of society. An incident that demonstrates his irenic posture occurred earlier that year, in the aftermath of a winter address that Rauschenbusch gave to a Rochester civic organization. Afraid that an attorney friend of his was offended by his remarks against big business, Rauschenbusch wrote this person a letter of apology. "My sole aim in a speech . . . is always to

52. Walter Rauschenbusch, *Unto Me* (Boston: Pilgrim Press, 1912), 28.
53. Ibid.
54. Ibid., 28-29.
55. Ibid., 20.
56. Ibid., 12.

strike straight for the idea in question and to brush everything aside to get at it." In the same breath, however, he pondered if he "sometimes hit harder" than necessary in driving home his points. "I want your unclouded friendship, and would much rather have kept silent or fallen down on the job thrust on me than to have you go away with even a mosquito-bite to itch you."[57] The attorney's response to Rauschenbusch's apology was simple and direct: "You are a great, big hearted fellow."[58]

These paradoxes in Rauschenbusch's writing and personality earned him modest criticism from a few church leaders, especially from those who, unlike Rauschenbusch, joined the American Socialist Party. Vida Scudder wrote expressing her concern that Rauschenbusch, while espousing the virtues of socialism, was not a party member. For Scudder, it was important for people like Rauschenbusch to join the Socialist Party, in part "to vindicate the honor of Christianity." "I covet you for the party. My being in it doesn't count except to myself. Yours would. It would draw many, & we could get a political socialism of a better type."[59]

Rauschenbusch, however, remained clear about his intention not to join the party. In an exchange of letters with a Socialist Party member in 1914, Rauschenbusch noted that his decision not to join centered on his fear that such an action might cost him a large segment of his audience. While acknowledging that he enjoyed being called "comrade" by Socialist Party members, he expressed his reservations that the Socialist Party had the ability to become the dominant political party in America. "I think it is still an open question whether the Socialist Party will ever so commend itself to the body of the American people that it will become the majority party. It may be that its platform will gradually be carried into effect by such movements as the Progressive Party because the latter will appeal more to the average mind, including the religious and moral temperament."[60]

It is probable that as Rauschenbusch was writing these words, he

57. WR to Walter Hubbell, March 2, 1912, box 26.

58. Letter Walter Hubbell to WR, March 7, 1912, box 26.

59. Quoted in Jacob H. Dorn, "The Social Gospel and Socialism: A Comparison of the Thought of Francis Greenwood Peabody, Washington Gladden, and Walter Rauschenbusch," in *Church History* 62 (March 1993): 99.

60. WR to L. B. Avery, June 12, 1914, box 28.

was thinking of the outcome of the 1912 presidential election. Rauschenbusch's correspondence indicates that he may have had a preference for the Socialist Party candidate, Eugene Debs, in that election. However, it is likely that he, like other American progressives, shared as much enthusiasm for Teddy Roosevelt's third-party presidential candidacy as he did for Debs. As many scholars have pointed out, most progressives in that election could look with consolation and hope to the election of Progressive Democrat and Presbyterian layman Woodrow Wilson. The fact that all the "major party" candidates in that election shared common reform ideals in all likelihood only reaffirmed Rauschenbusch's conviction that American political institutions were moving in the direction of Christianizing American society.[61] The year 1912 represented the apex of an era when many Protestant leaders were willing to subordinate specific beliefs and opinions in favor of an irenic reform spirit that believed that churches were on the verge of realizing the social hope of redeeming America. Nowhere were these hopes embodied more fervently than in the Federal Council of Churches.

In December 1912, Rauschenbusch returned to Chicago to give his address before the quadrennial meeting of the Federal Council of Churches. The address not only reflected a summation of Rauschenbusch's theology up to that point but also captured the dreams shared by other social gospel leaders of the time. He began his address by affirming that the greatest force working for the betterment of society was the nation's churches, with the Protestant ecumenical movement signifying a larger spirit of social cooperation at work in America. He noted that the Federal Council was "a child of destiny," adding, "All live religious movements are always closely connected with the great movements of the national soul; hence, live religion is never something apart from the general life that may be housed in a separate little enclosure."[62]

Rauschenbusch affirmed his belief that the social crises of modern culture presented the nation with unique opportunities unknown to previous generations. "One great tendency of the present age is that

61. See, for example, Eldon Eisenach, *The Lost Promise of Progressivism* (Lawrence: University Press of Kansas, 1994), 239-43.

62. Reprint of address in *Christian Work* (January 23, 1913), box 94.

toward solidarity, toward the integration of humanity. . . . So humanity is gradually being bound together, and that great tendency, which is due to the practical energy of the far-sighted men, the men in touch with the realities of modern life, has found its necessary component in the domain of religion."[63] According to Rauschenbusch, the greatest imperative facing the church was showing Americans how the ecumenical movement challenged rampant individualism in American Christianity. He reiterated his long-standing belief that when he spoke of social salvation he did not mean "a displacement of the old experience of religion, but rather an intensification and an expansion of it." What he was advocating for was not simply social service, but social regeneration:

> But we want more than social service; I am not satisfied with the term. A man might render social service who was at the same time defrauding people; he may be exacting from little children fourteen hours' work in the canneries; he might be raising the price of anthracite coal and using that advance in social service. That is not enough. We want not only social service, but social repentance; we want social shame; we want social conversion; we want social regeneration.[64]

Rauschenbusch saw this regeneration as the only authentic model for Christian conversion. Reasserting a theme he had used in many of his writings, sermons, and speeches, he asserted that being a Christian necessitated subjecting one's self to the full truth of the Bible — a message that by necessity afflicted pain on the socially prosperous. "We are not told in the Bible that the living Word of God is a pin that will scratch thru the skin, but a two-edged sword which cuts down into the marrow, and when it cuts down into the marrow it will have to split our bones in order to get there. Those of us who have been thru a genuine religious experience know what that sort of bone splitting ordeal is."[65]

What his keynote address made clear was that Christian unity was not a matter of doctrine, but a matter of faithful service that gener-

63. Ibid.
64. Ibid.
65. Ibid.

ates acts of love. "We are a wasteful nation," he lamented. Not only was America guilty of industrial and economic waste related to environmental pollution and infant mortality, "but the greatest waste of all has been the waste of religious enthusiasm." Although he expressed a common conviction that matters of doctrine were subordinate to matters of service, he ignored the fact that amidst an assembly that embodied Protestant hopes of church unity, doctrinal issues were already driving wedges among the organizational forces of Protestant Christendom. Instead Rauschenbusch asserted optimistically that the Federal Council "has eliminated that waste and brought us together into an organic unity in order that we might be brothers in Christ." Rauschenbusch the church historian predicted that the sectarian spirit that he associated with conservative Protestant groups would ultimately disappear because of the ecumenical movement's insistence that service to one's neighbor would foster greater social solidarity. As he summarized, the gains made by Protestants over the last twenty-five years represented a spirit that would break down the walls of religious sectarianism in America. "As long as we preach individual salvation only, we strengthen the sectarian spirit. On the other hand, when we work for the redemption of society, that is necessarily social; that is not competitive, but co-operative Christianity, and, therefore, creates unity."[66]

In the years ahead, Rauschenbusch's life reflected a renewed quest to publically promote the larger reform vision he espoused in his Federal Council address. For a year and a half, Rauschenbusch labored in certainty that the actualization of his social vision was at hand. Events after August 1914, however, would cause Rauschenbusch to reassess whether America was, or could ever be, a Christianized society.

66. Ibid.

11 Social Redemption

In the eighteen months following his address to the Federal Council of Churches in December 1912, Walter Rauschenbusch and the social gospel entered their apex in the United States. He observed to a colleague that since *Christianity and the Social Crisis* was published, "there has been a foolish but wide demand for me as a speaker and lecturer."[1] Although he had long contracted with a speaker's bureau in Boston to assist him in his bookings, he found himself since 1908 declining hundreds of speaking invitations annually. As he explained, "I judge mainly by two factors; whether the invitation stands for an unusual opportunity to impress ideas on some important body of people; and whether I can do the work with slight outlay of time and with good financial income."[2]

A review of Rauschenbusch's itinerary from 1913 to 1914 reveals a diverse array of audiences, ranging from preaching at prestigious universities to conducting Bible studies with men's and women's groups in local churches. After a series of Rochester addresses in January 1913, which included a highly publicized debate with socialist

1. WR to Horace Cole, October 31, 1913, box 27.
2. Ibid.

leader John O'Rorke at a People's Sunday Evening, Rauschenbusch hit the road. That winter his travels took him to cities such as Brooklyn, New York; Springfield, Massachusetts; Newton, Massachusetts; Pittsburgh; and Grand Rapids, Michigan. In the spring he spoke in Hartford; Buffalo; Providence; Cincinnati; Grinnell, Iowa; and Troy, New York. Before heading to his summer home in Ontario, Rauschenbusch offered a YMCA summer course at Lake Geneva, Wisconsin, and that fall he gave a series of addresses in Kansas City and Chicago, including serving as a guest preacher at the University of Chicago. In the winter of 1914, Rauschenbusch traveled through the Northeast, and in February he gave the Gates Lectures at Iowa College in Grinnell, Iowa. He returned to the Midwest in April for speaking engagements in St. Paul and later that month kicked off the forum season at Ford Hall in Boston, where he also preached at Harvard University.

In the years prior to World War I, the social gospel movement in America was building institutional momentum and Walter Rauschenbusch was its undisputed spokesperson. In the months following the publication of *Christianizing the Social Order,* he promoted its central message that the economic order, the final unregenerate social force in American society, could be Christianized, if the nation's churches were up to the task. Amidst Rauschenbusch's optimism, however, doubts lingered. Age-old dilemmas in his social thought, especially related to the issue of gender equality and racism, still plagued and perplexed him. Closer to home, he continued to struggle in his relationship with his oldest children, who Rauschenbusch sorrowfully realized had abandoned the Christian faith so dear to him. As perplexing and painful as these problems were, they paled in comparison with world events that occurred in August 1914 — events that served as a final catalyst in the developing social thought of Walter Rauschenbusch.

GENDER AND RACE IN A CHRISTIANIZED SOCIETY

As Rauschenbusch candidly confessed to colleagues, the chaotic pace of his schedule was determined in part by a desire to spread his message, but also by the need for money. With Winifred in college, and Hilmar preparing to graduate from high school in 1914 and head off to Amherst College, Rauschenbusch increasingly depended upon the added income generated by his public appearances. There were also other family responsibilities that plagued him, financially and emotionally. After the death of his sister Frida's husband, Georg Fetzer, in 1909, Rauschenbusch took on the responsibility of caring for Frida and her children in Germany, both soliciting funds for them from Baptist missionary societies and sending them money from his own income.

An increased source of family tension, however, centered upon Rauschenbusch's relationship with his sister, Emma. Her years in India had exposed her to a variety of Hindu sects and increasingly she became enamored with theosophy, a movement of the late nineteenth century that combined elements of Hinduism and Western spiritualism. In the early 1900s, Rauschenbusch read with alarm his sister's letters in which she described in detail her newfound beliefs in her contacts with the spirit world — including her belief that she was the reincarnation of her deceased brother, Winfried. Beneath these assertions, Emma made it clear that the faith of her parents, the same faith that had fueled her zeal to become a missionary, was no longer valid in her life. "Mentally I have already broken with the forms of the past: I cannot be a Baptist," she wrote to her brother in 1906. "I can't [answer] to the ABMU [The American Baptist Missionary Union]. Their propaganda-making is wrong, opposed to true spiritual teaching."[3] With her husband's health in decline, Emma returned to America in 1909, and after John Clough's death the following year, Emma settled in Rochester and rented an apartment not far from Walter and Pauline. However, she found it difficult to reacclimate herself to life in America. The once close bond between the siblings gave way to an increasingly acrimonious relationship, in which Emma largely retreated into an inner world that she never could escape. Where she once shared a close bond with her brother, the two now engaged in constant family warfare, where Walter was forced to justify and defend his sister's behavior to other family members. Rauschenbusch confided to Frida that Emma's behavior brought back painful memories of their mother's personality. "Her long isolation in India, her domestic unhappiness which ate into her soul, . . . her present loneliness and inactivity all create an abnormal state of mind in which the foot-fall of a fly is like the

3. Emma Clough to WR, November 14, 1906, box 36.

tread of an elephant."[4] Rauschenbusch's analogy in this letter was very evident in the acrimonious relationship that arose between Pauline and Emma. After an incident in which Emma castigated Pauline for her cooking, Walter angrily reprimanded his sister. "No one has ever treated our home as you have done, and no one would get a second chance without a very searching apology. You have created a painful and difficult situation, and I do not see what I can do. You have created it and you will have to undo it."[5]

At the same time, Rauschenbusch assisted his sister in completing her late husband's memoirs, published by Macmillan in 1914 under the title *Social Christianity in the Orient: the Story of a Man, a Mission, and a Movement.* He was clearly pleased with her sister's efforts of recovering John Clough's voice and wrote to one reviewer that Clough's career reflected how an orthodox theology could reorient itself to embrace the social and cultural realities of Eastern society, while still Christianizing the social order.[6] Yet Emma Rauschenbusch never succeeded in readapting herself to the Victorian Western society she had left behind in the 1880s to become a missionary. The remaining decades of her life were lived largely as an outcast from the evangelical Protestant culture and the Victorian values that were of such great importance to her brother.[7]

However, by 1913, Rauschenbusch revealed that there were chinks in the armor of his largely ordered view of Victorian society, especially as he struggled to make sense of the issues of racial and gender equality in the United States. In the fall of 1913, Rauschenbusch published one of his few pieces dealing solely with the topic of gender, an article in the *Biblical World* entitled "Some Moral Aspects of the 'Woman Movement.'" Rauschenbusch had certainly addressed the

4. WR to Frida Fetzer, September 12, 1913, box 36.

5. WR to Emma R. Clough, March 26, 1915, box 36.

6. See WR to Howard Bridgman, October 12, 1914; see also WR review of Clough's book in box 36.

7. Emma Rauschenbusch Clough remained in Rochester many years after her brother's death, dying in 1938. Her sister Frida died four years earlier in 1934 still living in Germany. For an overview of Emma Rauschenbusch's career as a missionary, see Paul William Harris, "The Social Dimensions of Foreign Missions: Emma Rauschenbusch Clough and Social Gospel Ideology," in *Gender and the Social Gospel*, 87-100.

question of women's rights in previous writings, most recently in *Christianizing the Social Order.* Yet his *Biblical World* article reflected his ambivalence about the changing role of women in America, even as he argued that a change in women's roles was inevitable. "Women have arrived — in industry, in education, in politics. They pervade all domains of life, not passively as adjuncts, but with a sense of equal rights and a feeling of new-found destiny. . . . This thing through which we are passing is a social revolution."[8] Ever the historian, Rauschenbusch lauded the role women played in the history of American religion, citing women's leadership to advance causes like temperance reform. "In our American Protestant churches women, who have been mute and passive in the church for ages, have found a voice and have freely uttered their religious ideas and sentiments, molding the vital and working religion of the country."[9] Citing the growing number of women in industry, engaged in political activism, and enrolled as students in colleges and universities, Rauschenbusch acknowledged that the movement toward social equality that was taking place was not just inevitable, but just. "Plainly women are here as our equals in religion, in the intellectual life, in industry, and in the life of our commonwealths. When a thing is both right and inevitable we might as well accept it and go ahead."[10]

Rauschenbusch drew upon many of the article's chief arguments in numerous addresses that he delivered from 1913 through 1915. While he supported the idea of social equality, he clearly had major concerns over the methods employed by women to achieve that equality. In previous years, he looked favorably on "ecclesiastical suffragettes" who sought to open up the nation's Protestant denominations to the lay participation of women on church boards and assemblies. When he spoke to a southern Methodist gathering in 1910, he chided the group for the fact that the Methodist Episcopal Church, South, was one of the few Protestant churches that did not allow women "to vote on church matters."[11] Yet Rauschenbusch believed that women's equality, like many other reform matters, was evolutionary rather than

8. "Some Moral Aspects of the 'Woman Movement,'" in *The Biblical World* 42 (October 1913): 195.

9. Ibid., 196.

10. Ibid., 196.

11. WR to family, March 1, 1910, box 37.

revolutionary in its implementation in American society. Taking a page used by many middle-class Protestant women of the nineteenth century, Rauschenbusch believed that the "feminine" values that women inherently possessed, ultimately manifested through the power of the vote, represented a key component that would create a democratized, Christianized social order.

At the same time, he had little tolerance for what he viewed as the militant feminism of certain suffrage groups that resorted to more extreme forms of social protest. Reflecting a highly paternalistic tone, he chastised more radical suffrage leaders for resorting to force, commenting, "Women rarely commit brutal murders; they prefer poison or get their men to use the violence."[12] Rauschenbusch's article reiterated a longstanding concern: a belief that women's newfound freedom would lead them into wanton behavior that would make them renounce their responsibilities toward Christianizing society. In particular, he castigated upper-class women for the time and money wasted on "accentuating the charms of women, young and old, with a framework of clinging stuffs, of jewels, of elaborate hair, of furniture, of lights, of houses." He went so far as to suggest that "throughout history the women of the upper classes have dropped into a parasitic and idle life faster than their men."[13] Rauschenbusch took this Victorian sentiment to an extreme in an address at Ford Hall in the spring of 1914 when he observed that women's perceived virtue over men engendered toward them, at times, an unwarranted sympathy.

> A man may beat his wife and she may nag him, but she gets all the simpathy [*sic*]. There you have one of the fundamental inequalities of men and women, that men, when they are mad, become unlovable, and women, in the same case, awaken our pathetic pity. Women make up a very small part of the penitentiary offenses. But isn't it partly due to the fact that men commit many offenses to which they are inspired by women?[14]

12. "Some Moral Aspects," 198.

13. Ibid., 198.

14. "Is the Woman Movement Going to Save Society?" *Ford Hall Folks* (April 26, 1914), 1, box 18.

Rauschenbusch's view toward social equality was always marked by his tendency toward gender stereotyping, quite common among American middle-class males of that time. No doubt, however, some of the ambivalence he expressed concerning women's social equality reflected many of his own struggles to understand the generational perspective of his own eldest daughter. In the conclusion to his Ford Hall address he hinted to his audience his own insecurity toward losing touch with his daughter and her own emerging social world. "Children do not appreciate their fathers," he lamented. "And yet many fathers love their children as much as the mothers do. Women are compelled by Nature to love children, because they bear and nurse them, but men, I think, deserve credit for loving them. We have over-idealized the mother."[15]

Rauschenbusch's assertion is surprising given his own previous exaltations of motherhood. However, his arguments in support of women's rights reflect the way that he was attempting to make sense of the social changes occurring in early twentieth-century America. "I believe in the woman's movement and have always supported it," he affirmed at the end of his *Biblical World* article. Yet privately he struggled to make sense of gender roles, especially as they related to Winifred's growth into adulthood. Although he took great pride in much of her work at Oberlin, Rauschenbusch still found much in his daughter's habits that puzzled and unnerved him. He celebrated his daughter's intellectual curiosity and took great pride in her accomplishments as a student leader, especially when she was elected president of Oberlin's student socialist union. Yet he chastised her when she failed to live up to his own character standards, both intellectually and as a cultured young woman. Rauschenbusch grew fretful when Winifred didn't write him (and when she did write, it was primarily to ask for money), and often he could not hide his disappointment in his eldest child. In response to Winifred's musings in 1915 over her academic and personal woes, Rauschenbusch showed his own father's steely demeanor. "Perhaps by this time you will sympathize a little with the soreness I felt when the daughter whom God and I had fitted out with brains enough to do honor work flunked her freshman work. . . . This is one of the last remnants, I hope, of the unregenerate

15. Ibid., 4.

Winifred, of whom black fingernails, unsanitary habits, late hours, bad spelling . . . were other symptoms."[16] Yet Rauschenbusch's fondness for Winifred never abated, and in subsequent years he frequently took her into his confidence in ways that he seldom did with his other children, or, at times, even Pauline.

Rauschenbusch's qualified endorsement of women's rights also reflected his views toward racial justice. In one of his rare statements on American racism, an article that was reprinted in Baptist and southern Methodist periodicals, he judged that the plight of the nation's African-Americans was one that largely could be solved through Christianizing the social order. Like many northern Progressive Era leaders, Rauschenbusch largely saw race as a problem of the rural south that could be solved through economic means. Writing at a time preceding the great migrations of African-Americans to urban centers in the north, he called for the abolition of the sharecropping system in the south, decrying how this system kept African-Americans in a state of economic serfdom. In a similar way that Christians addressed the social problems caused by European immigration, so Rauschenbusch believed that the church could enhance the social and economic standing of poor blacks.

> When Christian missionaries equip the Eskimos with reindeer herds; when they teach Negroes of the Black Belt scientific farming; when they implant democratic ideals in the hearts of young men in Turkish or Chinese empires and supply the idealistic forces for vast political upheavals, is that, or is it not, a social function of first-class value? I say that this is not merely social service but social salvation.[17]

Rauschenbusch and other white social gospelers have been criticized for their lack of attention to issues of racial justice, and to a point this critique is justified.[18] Some historians see the social gospel's origins through the home missionary movement after the Civil War, in

16. WR to Winifred, July 16, 1915, box 180.

17. Rauschenbusch, "The Belated Races and the Social Problems," article clipping, box 40.

18. See Ralph Luker, *The Social Gospel in Black and White* (Chapel Hill: University of North Carolina Press, 1991), and Ronald White, *Liberty and Justice for All* (rev. ed.; Louisville: Westminster John Knox Press, 2002).

which a number of northern denominations sponsored the founding of black schools and colleges in the south. Although Rauschenbusch frequently lectured at black colleges and vocational schools, he shared much of white Progressive Era America's paternalistic view toward African-Americans. He embraced the view of many liberals of his generation who believed that in the eyes of God, social equality was inherent within all persons. Yet he shared the social gospel's larger tendency to absorb African-Americans into other "unregenerate" ethnic, non-Protestant groups that required Christianization. Like other immigrant groups who flooded American cities in the late nineteenth and early twentieth centuries, African-Americans would be transformed by the wisdom and example of the white middle class. He found the poverty of the rural south hard to comprehend and his infrequent contact with African-Americans often brought out the racism that lay under the surface of most white Americans at that time (in his correspondence to his family, for example, he occasionally used the expression "pickaninnies" to describe the rural black children he encountered in his travels).[19]

In part, Rauschenbusch's paternalism and racism was due to a lack of firsthand exposure to the plight of African-Americans. Rochester's African-American population during his lifetime did not exceed one thousand and his experiences as a white urban northerner repeatedly caused him to see racial reform as largely a matter of cultural assimilation. At the same time, he tended to see ministry toward African-Americans as a heavy burden of responsibility that few in white America would, or would want to, undertake. When Winifred in her senior year in college contemplated applying for a teaching position in an African-American school, her father was less than enthusiastic. "If you felt called by God to devote your life toward the black race, I might say, 'God bless you, my child,' and should be proud of you. But if a temporary step is a stairway, it seems to me very unadvisable."[20]

For a white progressive of his era, Walter Rauschenbusch's views on racism were neither exceptional nor intentionally malevolent — they were tragically typical. Despite the different racial ideologies embraced by white social gospel leaders, most of these leaders saw race

19. See, for example, WR to Elizabeth Rauschenbusch, June 14, 1916, box 114.
20. WR to Winifred Rauschenbusch, February 25, 1916, box 144.

as a problem that could be solved through the paternalistic benevolence of white middle-class Protestantism. Rauschenbusch and other social gospelers emphasized a vision of racial equality that reflected their belief in the dignity and worth of human personality. They were, however, unable to deal with the systematic dimensions of racism that, in W. E. B. Dubois's words, created two Americas. For Walter Rauschenbusch and the majority of white social gospel leaders, their optimism in the future hope of an economic transformation blinded them, along with most of white America, to understand how historically racism was defined by factors that transcended economic ones.

DARE WE BE CHRISTIANS?

Social gospelers like Walter Rauschenbusch had reason to be optimistic in 1913 and the first half of 1914. The gains in the Protestant ecumenical movement made him hopeful that Americans were increasingly willing to hear and receive his message, and as he crisscrossed the country on speaking tours, he continued to draw large crowds and media attention. His addresses at open forums, lecture halls, churches, and universities were widely reprinted in area newspapers, and the *Independent* magazine in 1913 named Rauschenbusch one of the nation's most prominent religious leaders, along with Lyman Abbott, Washington Gladden, and Billy Sunday.

Rauschenbusch also emerged as a candidate to succeed Augustus Strong as president of Rochester Theological Seminary after the latter's retirement in 1912. Rauschenbusch's liberalism, however, was still a major concern for some of the seminary's trustees. Yet by Strong's retirement, Rochester Theological Seminary was for all intents and purposes a liberal seminary. For the aged Strong, retirement was bittersweet. The Baptist patriarch was responsible for molding together the current liberal faculty in the final years of his tenure as president, revealing how his own theology reflected a nuanced liberal turn. However in his twilight years, Strong had second thoughts about his flirtation with liberal theology and he sought opportunities to reassert his faith in an orthodox Protestant theology.[21]

21. For a discussion of Strong's encounter with theological liberalism in his

Between 1912 and 1915, during an interim administration, Rauschenbusch served on the presidential search committee to appoint a successor to Strong. He recommended two candidates for consideration. The first was Rauschenbusch's old friend, Brown University president William Faunce, and the second was a young homiletics teacher at Union Theological Seminary in New York, Harry Emerson Fosdick.[22] In the end, the school chose the head of the search committee, Clarence Barbour, as its new president. Barbour embodied the ethos of an emerging generation of evangelical-liberal church leaders. As the pastor of Rochester's Lake Avenue Baptist Church, his congregation included Rauschenbusch's friend Helen Barrett Montgomery and other progressive city reformers. Barbour also gained distinction as the individual responsible for setting Katharine Lee Bates's poem "America the Beautiful" to the now familiar melody by Samuel Ward. Rauschenbusch biographer Paul Minus is likely accurate in noting that Rauschenbusch's value to the seminary was enhanced more by his presence in the classroom than in the president's office.[23]

The high confidence that Rauschenbusch must have been feeling, both personally and for the state of a Christianized America, was evident when he delivered the Gates Lectures at Grinnell College (formerly Iowa College) in February 1914. Named after the school's reform-minded president, George Gates, the series afforded Rauschenbusch the opportunity to speak on the theme of social redemption in the same setting where George Herron briefly became the most celebrated and controversial proponent of social Christianity twenty years earlier. Rauschenbusch's addresses at Grinnell emphasized the distinctive dimensions of twentieth-century life that were calling Americans to embrace a new understanding of Christianity. "We all feel that our nation during the last five or ten years has entered into a formative era in its history. . . . Every friend of humanity is stirred by a sense of immense and immediate opportunities before us," he surmised in one lecture. Unlike *Christianity and the Social Crisis,* which warned of the dangers inherent in modern American economic life, Rauschenbusch now

---

own theology, see Grant Wacker, *Augustus Strong and the Dilemma of Historical Consciousness* (Macon: Mercer University Press, 1985).

22. WR to Clarence Barbour, June 12, 1914, box 28.

23. Minus, 143.

spoke increasingly of the spirit of prophetic religion as a functional reality in American life. "Our social order works only because through its paganism flow rivulets of love and goodwill, of honor and duty, of comradeship and solidarity which issue from the living springs of religion in the hearts of us all."[24] Yet Rauschenbusch the church historian, in the spirit of his German liberal theological mentors, warned of recalcitrant social forces that would resist the Christianization of the social order. As he told his Grinnell College audience, "We all realize the immense opportunities for action in the present state of the public mind. But historical opportunities rarely last long. The red iron blackens even as it lies on the anvil. Therefore strike now."[25]

Yet Rauschenbusch's optimism of a new day was tempered both by the continued misgivings from socialist colleagues and from ongoing sniping from premillennialist leaders. In early 1914, the prominent premillennialist William Riley accused Rauschenbusch of heresy, renewing many of the allegations made against him in previous years by Isaac Haldeman that Rauschenbusch denied the divinity of Christ. He answered his accuser, "It so happens, dear Dr. Riley, that on this point I am entirely orthodox, and that if you deny the growth of the body and mind of Jesus, you are denying the true humanity of our Lord and are yourself the heretic." Unlike past confrontations with premillennialists, however, where Rauschenbusch often went to great lengths to defend his theology, he made it clear that he had no intention of being drawn into a public debate over doctrine, noting that he found Riley's confrontational style anathema to the spirit of true Christianity. "When you charge me with 'denying the Lord that brought me' you hurt me just as if you charged me with being false to my wife or cruel to my children. . . . I have written you as a Christian man to a Christian man, and I should be glad if this letter served as a warning, not only in my case, but in general against the methods often used by your school of thought."[26] Like many social gospelers, Rauschenbusch grew increasingly wary of premillennialism. The irenic spirit he held toward Christian unity when he wrote on the subject in the 1890s was replaced by a growing disdain

24. Manuscript of opening to Gates Lecture, box 22.

25. Ibid.

26. WR to William Riley, March 24, 1914, box 28.

toward premillennialism as he came to see the movement as one of the great obstacles for the contemporary church to overcome.

Yet Rauschenbusch in his addresses avoided direct engagement with premillennialist leaders and instead focused on emphasizing his hope that the church was on its way to Christianizing American life. In the summer of 1914, he arranged to have an advertisement run in several American newspapers that announced, quite confidently, that affairs were in order for American churches, defending American Protestantism from the charge that churches were impotent in their ability to affect social change. Noting that "elevating the morality of a nation is like raising a sky-scraper with jackscrews," Rauschenbusch nevertheless looked with satisfaction on the church's role in America, leading the nation on matters such as temperance reform. In his appeal, Rauschenbusch noted four principles to guide the church's actions in the modern world: (1) friendship for American workingmen, (2) denominational cooperation based upon "Christian equality and mutual respect," (3) a "sincere and scientific comprehension of the social causes for sin and misery," and (4) "An undying determination to get the will of God realized in the organized life of every community and to see the life of Christ reappear in every man and woman."[27]

His consistent appeal to this social vision of Christianity did not mean that Rauschenbusch negated the importance of an individual's faith, but that discussion of an individual's spirituality was inconsequential, unless it was spoken of as part of the larger society. This theme was expressed in a tract, published in book form in late 1914 under the title *Dare We Be Christians?* Like *Unto Me* two years earlier, *Dare We Be Christians?* was the victim of a limited print run and attracted few sales upon its publication. However, later generations would seize upon this work, along with *Prayers of the Social Awakening*, as the best illustrations of Rauschenbusch's blending of personal spirituality and social responsibility. Likely written during the spring or summer of 1914, the work is unique, for it was one of Rauschenbusch's few attempts to address Paul's famous text of 1 Corinthians 13. The book is more meditation than exegesis, and his assessment argues that the nature of Christian love resembled a series of concentric circles that extended out from the

27. Clipping from the *Baltimore Sun*, "Will the Church Disappear?" (September 19, 1914), box 42.

individual to the family and then the larger social order. For Rauschenbusch, love was meaningless unless it was manifested within a larger community. "Our understanding of life depends on our comprehension of the universal powers of love. Our capacity to build society depends on our power of calling out love. Our faith in God and Christ is measured by our faith in the value and workableness of love."[28] Rauschenbusch interpreted the Pauline passages to suggest that true love negated self-interest and initiated the movement toward social reform. "Every step of social progress demands an increase in love," he affirmed.[29] The tract ends with the assertion that the nature of love was never finite or self-containing with one specific community or group, but extended throughout the social fabric of creation. In words that captured the ethos of Rauschenbusch's vision of social equality he proclaimed, "Christianity stands for the doctrine that we must love one another — all men, without distinction of 'religion, race, color or previous condition of servitude.' . . . It stands for the solidarity of the race in its weakness and strength, its defeats and conquests, its sin and salvation."[30] For Rauschenbusch, the essence of Christian love was the way that it galvanized persons to recognize the possibilities of using divine love to transform society. As he noted in the book's final paragraph, "Every man can profit by the historical influences of Christianity and be a passive pensioner on its vested funds. But it clearly needs active personal agents who will incarnate its vitalities, propagate its principles, liberate its undeveloped forces, purify its doctrine and extend the sway of its faith in love over new realms of social life."[31]

The book met with the strong approval of Rauschenbusch's friends and colleagues. Vida Scudder called the book "a fount of wisdom," and Josiah Strong noted that Rauschenbusch had "spread and served a table at which the English-speaking church has been spiritually fed."[32] *Dare We Be Christians?* reflects also a distinctive faith statement of the social gospel impulse in America by mid-1914. The book gives a noteworthy paraphrase of 1 Corinthians 13 that summarized

28. *Dare We Be Christians?* (reprint, Cleveland: Pilgrim Press, 1993), 26.

29. Ibid., 26.

30. Ibid., 46.

31. Ibid., 47

32. Vida Scudder to WR, December 14, 1914, box 28, and Josiah Strong to WR, January 4, 1915, box 29.

much of the social gospel's view of a just social order — a society predicated on a vision that was not yet realized, but was still conceivable in some not-too-distant future.

> The values created by love never fail; but whether there are class privileges, they shall fail; whether there are millions gathered, they shall be scattered; and whether there are vested rights, they shall be abolished. For in the past strong men lorded it in ruthlessness and strove for their own power and pride, but when the perfect social order comes, the strong shall serve the common good. . . . For now we see in the fog of selfishness, darkly, but then with social vision; now we see our fragmentary ends, but then we shall see the destinies of the race of God sees them [*sic*]. But now abideth honor, justice, and love, these three; and the greatest of these is love.[33]

For all the ways that Rauschenbusch could express his vitriol toward the interests of American wealth and power, his vision of a just society, like many social gospelers of his generation, returned to the idea that the social truths of Christianity would transform the hearts of the oppressors to embrace a common good. As Rauschenbusch observed, love was the source that made understanding possible between different groups of people, serving as "the greatest educator" and "the most permanent stimulus of the intellectual life."[34] Although Rauschenbusch expressed some interest in the ideas of "social engineering," where experts in the natural and social scientific fields would increasingly provide the guidance and expertise in which America could be "Christianized," he was not part of this wing of the social gospel movement.[35] His focus on the social redemption of America was rooted in his belief that he was first and foremost a Christian evangelical who spoke to the conscience of the church and the nation.

The opening pages of *Dare We Be Christians?* reveal something of Rauschenbusch's state of mind in the early part of 1914, making reference to the joy and rejuvenation that came to him during the family's extended

33. Ibid., 37.

34. Ibid., 38.

35. See William McGuire King, "The Emergence of Social Gospel Radicalism" (Ph.D. dissertation, Harvard University, 1978).

summer vacation at their beloved summer cottage in Ontario. As much as he expressed the conviction that Christian faith was inseparable from social struggle, his faith made him contemplate the physical and spiritual home he came to rely on when the family was together in the Ontario wilderness. "I know a place, . . . where the Gull River tilts around the rocks and sweeps in a curling crescent of foam around the wooded basin below the rapids. That place is mine because I swam in it with my boys; the river carried us down the rapids and around the whirlpool, shouting and laughing."[36] In the spring of 1914, Rauschenbusch's speaking engagements pointed to the reward of a summer of recreation and writing. After several engagements in the Midwest and then back to the East Coast, where he spoke at the annual Sagamore Conference, Rauschenbusch joined the rest of the family in Canada. In June, he wrote a friend a letter that revealed both his fatigue and his excitement for the future. "Pauline and I are getting older, but we still have our full working capacity; only we tire more easily and are perhaps a little more irritable on that account." He reflected on his children's accomplishments, noting that he was confident that each would find a suitable vocation to match his or her talent. "They are an unusually promising lot of children, and God and their mother . . . deserve much gratitude for having developed them so well." Rauschenbusch reflected on his professional accomplishments, noting with pride that *Christianity and the Social Crisis* was being translated in several different European countries. However, he mused over the fact that a translation of this now world-famous book had not appeared in German. "I am beginning to suspect that the book is too radical for the Germans and that they are afraid of burning their fingers," he joked. Yet he looked forward to an upcoming trip to Germany, where he had not visited since his European tour in 1910.[37]

In the meantime, Rauschenbusch turned his summer agenda toward hammering out the Gates lectures from that winter into a book that was under contract with Macmillan. In August, the work on revising these lectures was abruptly halted. As he later wrote to a colleague, "the war at that time killed any productive capacity and I have never been able to get at it since."[38]

36. *Dare?* 1-2.
37. WR to Minna Gebel, June 17, 1914, box 28.
38. WR to John Phillips, April 24, 1917, box 31.

THE END OF HAPPINESS

Rauschenbusch, like the majority of American Progressives, struggled to make sense of the war between the European alliance of Great Britain, France, and Russia and the Central Powers of Germany, Austria-Hungary, and the Ottoman Empire in August 1914. His reactions toward the war in the remaining months of 1914 reflect a mixture of responses that attest to his own difficulties of coming to terms with what was becoming termed "The Great War." On one hand, students and colleagues at Rochester Theological Seminary noticed immediately a change in Rauschenbusch's demeanor when he returned to campus that fall. In the classroom, he still showed vestiges of his humor, but the jokes were fewer and his behavior reflected a more melancholy quality. When Rauschenbusch lectured, he wore a small black bow on his lapel, as a way of protesting the war. One day in a class on the Reformation, he reflected much of his personal pain when he commented on the war by lamenting, "We thought we had begun to make some social progress, and then this happened."[39] Rauschenbusch echoed that sentiment when he told New York City social gospel minister John Haynes Holmes that the war represented the death of the social movement in the churches.[40]

Rauschenbusch immediately realized that the war had far reaching consequences for the ability of churches to lead the world forward in the task of social redemption. He had long viewed war as the great enemy to the church's social mission, and although he was not a pacifist, his views had moved away from the jingoism he carried into the Spanish-American War sixteen years earlier. However, Rauschenbusch also did not necessarily see the war as derailing, or destroying, the church's social mission. In the fall of 1914, he gave numerous addresses where he told audiences that the war had the potential to awaken Christians to the true nature of its mission to promote peace. "It has taken all the time since the Civil War to make the leaders of the Church realize that our capitalistic system will eat up the nation if it is allowed to obey its own greed. The churches have always been for peace in theory. Perhaps this great war will consolidate their sentiment

39. Memories of Willis Webb, RTS class of 1915, box 145.

40. *Transcript-Boston,* October 20, 1914, clipping, box 94.

to the point of action."[41] However, Rauschenbusch was struggling to make sense of the unprecedented scope of the war's carnage in lives and property destruction. His optimism was not only shaken by the accounts of the war's destruction but also by how the war placed him in the position of having to come to terms in a new way with his German ancestry.

Rauschenbusch's initial critique of the war centered upon arguments he had used years earlier related to the economic and militaristic posturing of Great Britain and Germany to establish European dominance. In a letter to a colleague that October, he wrote that the war was a consequence of this European imperialism. "Germany is in the situation of the able and newly rich man; England is an old duke with lots of land; the new man has insufferable manners; the old man has them too but they sit well on his corpulence."[42] This idea was amplified in an essay published in the *Congregationalist* that fall, entitled "Be Fair to Germany." The article was widely reprinted and excerpted in newspapers and periodicals throughout the country and contributed negatively to a reputation that he was "a pro-German divine." The article largely recast the portrayal of Germany that he used in an earlier article on England and Germany published in 1899. However, what had once struck Americans as an informed portrait of the political situation in Germany was now interpreted differently in North America.

In the article, Rauschenbusch tried to be an impartial judge, calling upon Americans to stay neutral in the conflict. "We are the only great Christian power that is detached and really neutral," he reasoned. "We represent the largest and most effective unit of public opinion. The other nations have a high opinion of our political and moral intelligence."[43] Rauschenbusch then launched into a larger defense of German motives for their aggressive military actions. He argued that the German invasion of Belgium did not reflect the true cultural makeup of the nation. Echoing his long-standing sentiments, he wrote, "In almost every element of the higher life Germany leads the world. In creative science and philosophy every scholar knows that

41. Clipping from the *Dispatch-Pittsburgh,* December 13, 1914, box 94.

42. WR to "Professor Burton," October 9, 1914, box 28.

43. *Rochester Evening Times* clipping, November 13, 1914, box 94. A typed copy of this manuscript is in box 19; various clippings of the article are in box 94.

this is true. . . . In intellectual spirituality the Germans compare with the English and Americans as the Greeks compared with the Romans."[44] While acknowledging the factual basis of German atrocities committed against civilian populations, Rauschenbusch attributed this fact to the nature of war, not an inherent barbarism of the Germans. "The Allies have not burned German towns nor harmed German women because they have not set foot on German soil. . . . If they marched on Berlin, we shall see what we shall see. This simple difference seems to me to demand a stay in judgement from every fair-minded man." Rauschenbusch reiterated his long-standing point concerning Germany's need to defend its interests, in the face of jealousy from England. "What looks like aggressive militarism on the part of Germany is in large part the bitter need of self-defense. Every fair-minded man should make due allowance for this fundamental fact." Rauschenbusch noted his belief that the war represented a collision of competing European interests, making it clear that England was equally culpable for bringing about the war. As he concluded his article, "The future will place the blame for the war where it belongs and in the meantime it is not only silly but absolutely wrong for people of a neutral country like the United States to hand down long-range guesses as statements of fact in an attempt to prove that Germany, or England, or Russia started and is to blame for the war."[45]

Reaction, however, to Rauschenbusch's article was less than sanguine in both North America and in Great Britain. James Stalker, a liberal minister, author, and theology professor in Aberdeen, Scotland, castigated Rauschenbusch for turning a blind eye to German atrocities against Belgium civilians, noting that the allies were at war "because of the violation of Belgian territory, and we shall shrink from no sacrifice of blood or treasure that may be required to drive the enemy out of the country which they have harried so cruelly and are now occupying."[46] Stalker dismissed Rauschenbusch's argument concerning German cultural superiority as ludicrous, noting that Germany's military appetite was fueled by the godless vision of Nietzsche. Reaction toward Rauschenbusch was especially hard in Canada, which as part of

44. Clipping from *Literary Digest,* November 7, 1914, box 94.
45. *Rochester Evening Times,* November 13, 1914, clipping, box 94.
46. Clipping, December 25, 1914, box 94.

the British commonwealth had entered the war on the side of the United Kingdom. A Canadian cleric decried Rauschenbusch's stance, asserting that it was difficult for him "to imagine anything less 'open-minded' or more unfair to England" than Rauschenbusch's argument. In discussing the anger generated in Canada toward the article, the minister concluded, "We do not in the least expect or desire that America should be solely pro-British, but as the German side appears it is only right that the opposite view should also be seen."[47]

Yet Rauschenbusch seemed unmoved by these critiques. As he had made clear on many occasions, he hated the aristocratic and autocratic elements in German culture that he always associated with that country's militarism. He also made no qualms about his distaste for German Christianity, seeing in his own pietistic heritage an inherent conservatism that diminished Christianity's ethical imperative. Yet in the North American cultural Zeitgeist of 1914, Rauschenbusch's criticisms of Germany went unnoticed by the public and his desire to defend Germany from negative public opinion was taken by many as a sign of an unequivocal support for Germany.

Additionally, Rauschenbusch worried constantly about the safety of his sister, Frida, and other members of his extended German family. While he did not share his sister's justification of German military action, he repeatedly lobbied Baptist denominational officials and government representatives for information on his sister's and nieces' physical and financial safety. Professionally and personally, Rauschenbusch was finding it difficult to remain neutral. The first public censure of Rauschenbusch came in November 1914 when an invitation to address a Methodist conference in Saskatchewan, Canada, was rescinded. More painful still was the fact that the Rauschenbusch family began to receive anonymous threatening letters from Canadians warning the family to stay away from their summer home.

Despite the anxiety caused by the cancellation of the Saskatchewan speaking engagement and the family's decision to bypass their vacation at their summer home in 1915, Rauschenbusch's personal popularity showed few signs of waning. In January 1915, he gave the Enoch Pond Lectures at Bangor Seminary in Maine and stuck to his usual frenetic schedule of public speaking that took him up and down

47. Article clipping by Rev. W. H. Griffith Thomas, December 23, 1914, box 94.

the East Coast in the winter and spring. In May, he headed to California to give a series of lectures, culminating in his teaching that summer at the Pacific Theological Seminary in Berkeley. Due largely to his desire to protect his family from the uneasiness over the public mood and partly out of a sense of trying to discern his next move, Rauschenbusch said practically nothing more on the war after his "Be Fair to Germany!" article. Much of his speaking at that time returned to the themes that he had expounded upon in the years preceding the war. In addresses such as "The Economic Basis for Democracy" and "The Forces behind the Social Movement," he still expressed confidence that America's churches could serve as the yeast that would lead to social-economic reform in America. He still drew standing-room audiences in the cities where he lectured. Yet no matter where he lectured or taught, he could not escape the shadow of the war and by the spring of 1915, his depression over the war was cutting into his optimism.

His melancholy state was evident during the summer of 1915, as Rauschenbusch's West Coast lecturing culminated when he reached Berkeley, California, to teach at the Pacific Theological Seminary. The sinking of the British passenger ship *Lusitania* by a German U-boat in May 1915 caused a decisive American reaction against Germany and a heightened suspicion of German Americans. It also brought about an increase in munitions shipments from America to Great Britain. In this context of growing anti-German hostility, Rauschenbusch made a decision to speak out against American military involvement in the war. Rauschenbusch was shocked and outraged by the sinking of the *Lusitania,* yet he viewed the sinking as an illustration of how America was increasingly viewed by Germany as a munitions supplier to the Allies. With the aid of Charles Aked, a Congregational minister in San Francisco and a recent émigré from England, he drafted a letter entitled "Private Profit and the Nation's Honor." Although the document echoed Rauschenbusch's previous plea for the United States to stay neutral, it castigated the role that American corporations were playing in supplying arm shipments to the Allies. "This war trade is not for patriotism but for profit. . . . Capitalism has often sacrificed the higher values of humanity to make big profits." The letter singled out several American corporations that were manufacturing munitions, arguing that these enterprises undercut any positive role that America could play as a neutral nation. The authors largely blamed England for creating the economic circumstances that brought on the war, and argued that England's economic needs were now cutting innocent German civilians off from receiving humanitarian aid. "However our theories may run, the fact is that we are today part of the economic and military system of Great Britain and her allies. . . . Our partiality is all the more painful because we have allowed Great Britain for many months now to close the free highway of the ocean against our neutral vessels loaded with grain and cotton for Germany."[48]

Rauschenbusch and Aked wrote the letter as an appeal to a "Christian sentiment" among Americans. They hoped that the letter would cause readers to understand the moral issues at stake in the Great War, planning to release the statement to the press that summer. However, even as the two men wrote the document, Rauschenbusch's mood grew increasingly despondent over the war and his absence from his family. During his West Coast sojourn, he was approached about the possibility of accepting a teaching position at Pacific Theological Seminary. Although showing some enthusiasm for the move, he cooled on the idea when Pauline reminded him that his salary would be less than it was in Rochester.[49] With a third Rauschenbusch child, Paul, approaching college age, neither Pauline nor Walter wanted to confront the geographical or financial boundaries entailed by a move to California.

During his time in California in the summer of 1915, Rauschenbusch was desperately lonely for his family. He craved every letter he received from his family, and especially was pained by the fact that he received little word from Winifred, who had finished her junior year at Oberlin College. He gave a bland assessment of his teaching performance at Pacific Theological Seminary, despite the fact that his class was well attended. His mind was likely distracted by the fact that he began his Berkeley lectures right at the moment when the Aked-Rauschenbusch statement was published. As he wrote to Pauline, "I concluded that I had no right to be silent. It would have been cowardly."[50]

48. Charles Aked and Walter Rauschenbusch, "Private Profit and the Nation's Honor"; various clippings of this article are in box 94.

49. See, for example, Pauline to WR, June 20, 1915, box 37.

50. WR to Pauline, April 4, 1915, box 29.

The Aked-Rauschenbusch letter appeared in numerous newspapers throughout the nation, meeting almost immediate negative fallout. One of the first critics was Algernon Crapsey. The controversial Episcopal priest, who had briefly flirted with joining the Rochester chapter of the Brotherhood of the Kingdom in 1904, condemned the Aked-Rauschenbusch initiative in an editorial that appeared in a Rochester newspaper on July 19. Rauschenbusch responded to Crapsey upon his return to Rochester in August, in a published editorial that defended his letter and clarified his stance on Germany. While he strongly condemned the German violation of Belgian neutrality and expressed his distaste for the "German military class," he did not accept Crapsey's view that the Allies were morally superior to the Central Powers. Rauschenbusch reiterated his belief that the war trade was responsible for escalating the war, and rejected Crapsey's argument that the conditions for world peace and international order could only be obtained by the destruction of Germany. Displaying a rare sarcastic tone, he accused Crapsey of being hopelessly naive if he believed that the destruction of Germany would somehow lead to the creation of a peaceful world. "You assume that a partisan league of that sort would wield a beneficent sway of peace over all the world. All these assumptions are impossible. You offer a utopian scheme as a justification for emasculating and hog-tying one of the great parts of humanity. . . . You ask me if I know of any other way to establish peace than your scheme. I know of no better way to banish both peace and liberty."[51] Rauschenbusch defended his stance in other newspaper editorials, yet his responses seemed to acknowledge that he was fighting an uphill battle against American public opinion. In a letter to the *Chicago Standard,* he admitted that most Americans were no longer interested in moral arguments against the war. "Very many have now swung away from that because they believe the Germans, if victorious, will destroy freedom and civilization and that we are justified in being unneutral."[52]

Increasingly, Rauschenbusch's colleagues in the social gospel movement shared the sentiment that building the kingdom of God in America was predicated on the military defeat of Germany. While sig-

51. Clipping from *Rochester Herald,* August 23, 1915, box 94.
52. WR to the Rev. Clifton Gray, editor, *Standard,* August 23, 1915, box 29.

nificant numbers of Americans favored that America stay out of the war, public support for the Allied war effort was high. As theologically divided as American Protestantism was becoming, a growing consensus was developing that the German "Hun" was an enemy to the cause of winning the world for Christ. This emerging Protestant consensus did not diminish Rauschenbusch's popularity as the chief American exponent of the social gospel. But it did leave him in a situation where his voice left him in the minority. As American interests moved the nation closer to war, Rauschenbusch's theology was undergoing a subtle, but important transition. As he expressed in the conclusion of his response to Crapsey, "I am glad I shall not live forever. I still trust that good will be the final goal . . . , and that the wisdom of the Eternal does not end where my little understanding ravels out."[53] The statement was a reflection of his own melancholy state, but also indicated his own uncertainty on the direction in which America seemed to be headed.

53. Clipping from *Rochester Herald,* August 23, 1915, box 94.

12 A Few Brave Souls

Even though he attempted to avoid the subject of the war as he toured the Northeast for speaking engagements during the fall of 1915, Rauschenbusch spent much of the time digesting the negative reaction brought about by his letter with Aked. A Congregational pastor in Minneapolis berated Rauschenbusch for his association with the "erratic" Aked. "Such an astounding and insolent request takes away one's breath and were it not that your entire course since the outbreak of the War marks you first of all a German and only incidently an American citizen, one might be justified in thinking you slightly beside yourself." The pastor concluded with a note of sarcasm that, no doubt, wounded Rauschenbusch to the quick. "I shall use this copy of your protest to good purpose — an example of the manner in which the German propaganda is being pushed by men supposed to be American citizens. . . . Were a man to come to my home and make such a proposition as you dare to make, I should show him the door."[1] There were a few letters that applauded the Rauschenbusch-Aked letter; most, however, echoed the sentiments of the Minneapolis pastor. "Are you now willing to denounce, . . . the invasion of Belgium, or the

1. Ernest Day to WR, August 18, 1915, box 29.

shelling of Hartlepool, or the sinking of the *Lusitania*, or the Zeppelin raids of defenceless cities? When you send out a letter denouncing these then we may listen to you on the question of our clean hands."[2]

He was especially hurt by the loss of friendships among members of the Rochester community, especially Joseph Alling. Once one of his staunchest supporters in the promotion of social reform in that city, Alling broke harshly with Rauschenbusch over the matter of the war. "I expect it is entirely useless to continue the correspondence, for frankly I think you are blind to the crime Germany is committing against the world." Alling was incredulous that Rauschenbusch, a man devoted to upholding the rights of the oppressed, could now turn a blind eye to the brutality of German militarism. "You have decried the business efficiency that ignored human powers, and that rode rough shod over the rights of the weak . . . ; but now you are defending Herr Juggernaut, or at least you are denouncing those who would seek to arm his victims against ruthless attack."[3]

While rejections of his positions, especially from persons like Alling, wounded Rauschenbusch, there were many social gospel leaders who stood by him. John Haynes Holmes wrote Rauschenbusch concerning his bafflement over the public's anti-German response. "A year ago I felt that the European war would bring a revulsion of feeling in this country which would bring about a mighty renaissance of faith. But alas, just the opposite has taken place!"[4] Yet Rauschenbusch conceded that there was no more he could do at the time to change American opinion on the war, acknowledging that his and Aked's appeal was "exhausted and it is not likely that we shall take any further steps in the matter."[5]

Rauschenbusch's retreat from speaking out against the war, while not attributable to a lack of prophetic nerve, was nevertheless an indication that he was both baffled and frustrated by the inability of Americans to "listen to reason" on the subject. Yet clearly Rauschenbusch was grappling with the emergence of geopolitical realities that completely caught him off guard (as it did most American leaders of

2. H. P. Scratchley to WR, August 26, 1915, box 29.
3. Joseph Alling to WR, September 16, 1915, box 29.
4. John Haynes Holmes to WR, September 24, 1915, box 29.
5. WR to Mrs. Samuel Untermeyer, September 27, 1915, box 29.

his generation). As he reflected later on, "all these questions of the war were comparatively novel to me when the war broke out and I have had to educate myself on them, which was not easy for a man in my circumstances." Rauschenbusch somewhat wryly noted to one critic that his policy toward silence was partly a manner of self-reflection that those who supported the allied war effort would be wise to adopt. "If you will consider how readily I might have talked, and how much you for instance have probably talked, I think you ought to see that some self-restraint has been at work. Diffidence about my competence was one motive."[6] Staying silent on the war, however, soon proved not to be possible.

THE SOCIAL PRINCIPLES OF JESUS FOR A NEW AGE

Amidst these ongoing criticisms over the war, and the pain they caused Rauschenbusch, the demand for his services as a speaker didn't let up. Despite the cancellation of his appearances in Saskatchewan in the summer of 1915, Rauschenbusch still spent lots of time in Pullman cars, making a Ford Hall appearance in Boston that October, as well as several other addresses in New England. The early part of 1916 would be no different, with several forum appearances scheduled in New England, followed by more speaking engagements in the Midwest. Rauschenbusch looked forward to the 1915 Christmas holiday as an occasion to relax with his family and to cherish the homecomings of both Winifred and Hilmar from college.

The Christmas holiday, which should have been a time of solace for Rauschenbusch, served only as a forgettable coda to an arduous year. Walter and Pauline were delighted to have both Winifred and Hilmar home; however, the joy of having their two oldest children in Rochester turned to a tense and conflicted occasion, brought on by an incident precipitated by Winifred. During a Christmas party, in which Walter and Pauline invited several family friends, Winifred "in a spirit of fun" brandished a revolver before the guests. Purchasing the gun with Christmas money she had received from her parents, Winifred attributed this incident as a symbol of her independence, and her desire

6. WR "to a friend," March 7, 1917, box 31.

to embrace the "novel" and "unconventional" in life. As she explained to her father after returning to college, "If you ask me why I don't drop unconventionality altogether — I'll have to be disappointing and say, I can't yet."[7]

But neither Walter nor Pauline saw anything remotely funny about the incident, as they quickly confiscated the gun and sold it. Winifred, however, remained unrepentant about her behavior, and as she approached graduation from Oberlin, she repeatedly admonished her father to let her live her life. "I'm an explorer and I'm going to follow my bent without compromise and with all the common sense I can muster. But I'm my own captain, of necessity, can't you see that?" In words that were a direct assault on her father's own understanding of the role of women in society, Winifred expressed her desire to break free of the ordered Victorian household of her youth. "I'm not one of your demure young lady admirers, who humbly hope they can do their little share in the world. I'm not a lady; I'm merely chaotic youth, formless, full blooded, strong and soaring. . . . And so it may hurt you to have a daughter who is a feminist. I'm one by process of growth."[8]

Winifred's praise of such women as Charlotte Perkins Gilman, Emma Goldman, Isadora Duncan, and Olive Schreiner directly challenged the "separate spheres" beliefs of her father. As a means to understand his daughter's experiential work, Rauschenbusch read the writings of many of these pioneering early twentieth-century feminists. However, he believed that these women promoted a model of equality that appealed to the basest elements of human nature, mainly a sexual promiscuity that would ultimately destroy the social fabric of the American family. Reacting with disdain to a book by the English feminist Olive Schreiner, Rauschenbusch argued that women who

7. Winifred to WR, February 11, 1916, box 144; see also discussion of the relationship between the father and daughter in Casey Nelson Blake, "Private Life and Public Commitment: From Walter Rauschenbusch to Richard Rorty," in *A Pragmatist's Progress? Richard Rorty and American Intellectual History,* ed. John Pettegrew (Lanham, MD: Rowman & Littlefield, 2000), 85-101, and Christopher H. Evans, "Gender and the Kingdom of God: The Family Values of Walter Rauschenbusch," in *The Social Gospel Today,* ed. Evans (Louisville: Westminster John Knox Press, 2001), 53-66.

8. Winifred to WR, no date, box 144.

sought friendships only with other men were doomed to lives of "sadness and melancholy."[9] Increasingly, however, Winifred flaunted her independence before her father, making it a point to tell him in her letters that she was spending much of her time with male as well as female friends. Rauschenbusch repeatedly voiced his fears that Winifred would end up being preyed upon as a sexual object by these men. "I am not . . . trying to impose my authority on you in this, but feel rather like an older friend trying to make a young and impetuous friend see the wider bearings which she is inclined to overlook." Fearful that his daughter would end up in a loveless relationship, where she would be exploited as a sexual object, Rauschenbusch repeatedly warned Winifred of how her behavior might impact negatively her family. "Our family is bound up in a small solidarity which means a lot to us all. Each of us banks on the common resources considerably, and any of us can inflict severe losses on the rest. . . . You have made a splendid beginning in your work, and I see great possibilities open for you. But the greater the treasure in your hands, the more carefully must you walk."[10]

In his own way, Rauschenbusch was reflecting an important theme in his theology of the kingdom, related to how each member of the American middle-class family was under obligation to practice the highest standards of personal morality. Put simply, he was terrified that Winifred's reckless behavior might cause damage to the honorable reputation of their family. "For years the main consideration for me . . . that I must not injure you children and must not diminish the moral capitalization which is now contained in my reputation and influence. The Almighty may have great things reserved for you. Don't frustrate the future."[11]

Yet Winifred made it evidently clear to her father that as much as she loved him, she was following a destiny different from his. After her graduation from college in June 1916, she took a position as a field secretary for the Ohio Woman's Suffrage Association. While Rauschenbusch approved his daughter's path to a point, he worried insistently that in her work traveling throughout the state of Ohio she would fall

9. WR to Winifred, December 8, 1913, box 180.
10. WR to Winifred, November 4, 1916, box 144.
11. Ibid.

prey to the sexual advances of men. In a scolding letter written that fall, Winifred fired back at her father, telling him bluntly that her life was hers to live without interference. "I prefer to be frank; it is my nature. I am diplomatic enough however to tell people only as much of the truth as they can assimilate. . . . Now, I'll always be just as frank with you, as your attitude will permit." In a tone that was ironically a reflection of her father's own letters to her over the years, Winifred lectured him on how she viewed the current state of American youth.

> Of course youth never has all the data and consequently makes blunders. But youth cannot be controlled by fear, adventure, daring and confidence are its familiars, so that the fears of maturity and the experiences of maturity are no good school for youth. It must read life for itself, not from the page of another's book. All that parents can do is to build a sure foundation and give children so much training in independent action that they can rely on their steering powers when it comes to a crisis — and then trust that foundation and those steering powers.

Rauschenbusch must have been taken aback by the letter's concluding sentence. "Well, Belovedest, I am very much your daughter in many ways: strong, independent, ardent, interested in human affairs, with a streak of humour and another of sanity and another of daring, with a smiling countenance to the world and a deep seriousness inside, so give me your blessing and continue to love me."[12]

Rauschenbusch's struggle to understand the worldview of his children worked itself out professionally in the time he spent in late 1915 and early 1916 writing a book to be used as a course of study on religion for college students. The book, entitled *The Social Principles of Jesus,* was published late in the spring of 1916 and proved to be a popular work, with sales of almost 15,000 copies in its first three months.[13] Rauschenbusch noted to Ray Stannard Baker his hope that the book would reach a popular audience, showing how Jesus' life might address the problems of modern society.[14] Wellesley College professor

12. Winifred to WR, October 24, 1916, box 144.
13. WR to John Phillips, April 24, 1917, box 31.
14. WR to Ray Stannard Baker, October 10, 1916, box 30.

Katherine Lee Bates, the author of the poem "America the Beautiful," concurred, telling Rauschenbusch that the book's influence "will radiate out through thousands of young lives, and help in solving this great problem of our time and of all time."[15]

The book was partly a rehash of arguments presented in his previous works, with sections on "the social convictions of Jesus," "the recalcitrant social forces," and "the conquest by conflict," in which he outlined steps that young people could take to stand up to social injustice. With a style more didactic than inspirational, the book nevertheless gave him a chance to reiterate his beliefs on ways contemporary Christians could work for the kingdom, even as the war challenged one's faith that Christianity could build social solidarity among the nations. "The Great War of 1914 has been the most extensive demonstration of the collapse of love which any of us wants to see. As soon as one nation no longer recognizes its social unity with another nation, all morality collapses, and a deluge of hate, cruelty, and lies follows." He confessed in the book that the events of the Great War were a reflection on factors that church leaders, like him, did not foresee only a few years earlier. "The problem of international peace is the problem of expanding the area of love and social unity. It is the sin of Christendom that so few took this problem seriously until we were chastised for our moral stupidity and inertia. The young men and women of today will have to take this problem on their intellect and conscience for their lifetime, and propose to see it through."[16]

Rauschenbusch made clear that the onus for working toward the kingdom of God centered upon the nation's youth, who could apply Christianity to confront the great social problems of the age. In a chapter entitled "A New Age and New Standards," Rauschenbusch sought to illustrate that an advance closer to the kingdom of God meant an advance in personal ethical standards. ". . . every advance toward the Kingdom of God, that is, toward the true social order, involves a raising of the ethical standards accepted by society. This is a principle of social progress which every leading intellect ought to know by heart."[17] As he attempted to teach his own children, Rauschenbusch appealed to youth to accept personal restraint "and the mastery of the spirit over physical de-

15. Letter Katharine Lee Bates to WR, September 21, 1916, box 30.
16. *The Social Principles of Jesus* (New York: Association Press, 1916), 26.
17. Ibid., 90.

sires." He affirmed that part of the significance of Jesus' social teaching was that it validated the role of women as equals beside men. "Today Christianity is plainly prolonging the line of respect and spiritual valuation to the point of equality between men and women — and beyond."[18] He continued to make the point that the religions of Jesus and Paul were antithetical to each another, relying on the same Christology of the historical Jesus that he first articulated in "Christianity Revolutionary" years earlier. "Jesus was the culmination of the Hebrew prophet breed; Paul was the fore-runner of Greek theology." Because Paul expected no earthly kingdom, his theology was "no use for any effort to improve this world. He lived in another atmosphere than Jesus."[19]

Rauschenbusch made this point clear in the second to last chapter of the book, entitled "The Cross as a Social Principle," where he accentuated one of the key themes of his later theology: "Social Redemption Is Wrought by Vicarious Suffering."[20] He pronounced to his young audience that the demands of the gospel required that youthful consciences be stirred by the injustices of the present. "Pain is a merciful and redemptive institution of nature when pain acts as an alarm-bell to direct intelligent attention to the cause of the pain," he explained. Rauschenbusch believed that human sensitivity to the sufferings of the oppressed — child laborers, tenement dwellers, and working-class poor — ought to stir people to ensure that the suffering of the marginalized would be redemptive.

> The death of the innocent, through oppression, child labor, dirt diseases, or airless tenements, ought to arrest the attention of the community and put the social cause of their death in the limelight. In that case they have died a vicarious death which helps to redeem the rest from a social evil, and anyone who utilizes their suffering for that end, shows his reverence for their death. We owe that duty in even higher measure to the prophets, who are not passive and unconscious victims, but who set themselves intelligently in opposition to evil.[21]

18. Ibid., 91.
19. WR to J. E. Franklin, March 3, 1916, box 30.
20. *Social Principles of Jesus*, 167.
21. Ibid., 180.

Rauschenbusch's discussion of the cross accentuated one of the classic theological precepts of the social gospel: a belief that following Christ necessitated that one suffer for the sake of the kingdom. When Rauschenbusch wrote "Christianity Revolutionary" in the early 1890s, he had underscored that theme in the manuscript. Like Charles Sheldon's characters who repeatedly raised the question "What would Jesus do?" the consequence of following Christ might very well lead one to suffer the fate of a lonely prophet. Over the years, Rauschenbusch's own emphasis on the church's confident posture to work toward the kingdom superseded the theme of Christlike suffering. By 1916, however, Rauschenbusch's theology returned to this earlier emphasis, so critical to his formation as a young pastor in New York, asserting that the sacrifices of a current generation of American youth might lead to a just society. "The moral soundness of a nation can be measured by the swiftness and accuracy with which it understands its prophetic voices, or personalities, or events. . . . The more the Kingdom of God is present, the less will prophets be allowed to suffer. When it is fully come, the cross will disappear."[22]

Yet Rauschenbusch made it clear, as he had repeatedly in his earlier writings, that history would not witness the culmination of the kingdom. As he expressed his devotion to the kingdom ideal, he warned his readers that signs of the kingdom were often fleeting and hard to recognize. Alluding to the devastation of the war, he concluded while the kingdom is never realized in history, "the memories which are still sweet and dear when the fire begins to die in the ashes, are the memories of days when we lived fully in the Kingdom of Heaven, toiling for it, suffering for it, and feeling the stirring of the godlike and eternal life within us. The most humiliating and crushing realization is that we have betrayed our heavenly Fatherland and sold out for thirty pieces of silver. . . . We think we see its banner in the distance, when it is only the bloody flag of the old order."[23]

The Social Principles of Jesus signaled Rauschenbusch's shift away from a theology that emphasized the primary goal of Christianizing America. Instead, he picked up on a current in liberal theology that had emerged at the turn of the century that spoke of how the teachings

22. Ibid., 180.
23. Ibid., 197.

of Jesus instilled within modern humanity the highest attributes of Jesus' personality, making personal and social regeneration the imperative of Christian faith. Rauschenbusch had long been attracted by this theology of personalism, a diffuse movement of liberal idealism associated with an array of early twentieth-century American theologians. At the center of the movement was Borden Parker Bowne, a professor of philosophy at Boston University. Reflecting many of the influences of German theological liberalism, Bowne and other personalist theologians emphasized that the nature of moral growth and development came through understanding how God's being embodied the attributes of human personality.

By 1916, personalist theology was having an increased impact on the nature of the social gospel in America. While Bowne showed little interest in contemporary reform questions, by the time of his death in 1910, numerous Protestant leaders had already begun exploring how Bowne's idealism related to contemporary society. Not only did personalist theologians like the influential Methodist bishop Francis McConnell seize upon Bowne's teachings on God's theological immanence, his followers also insisted that the task of building a just society rested upon the ability of the church to nurture personal and moral growth within each individual. George A. Coe, a classmate of Rauschenbusch's at the University of Rochester, had become one of the social gospel's main theorists in the field of Christian education. As a professor at Northwestern and Columbia universities, and later as an active leader in the Methodist Federation for Social Service, Coe incorporated Horace Bushnell's theories on Christian education into an emerging turn-of-the-century liberal theological worldview accentuated by personalism. By the early years of the new century, Christian educators like Coe were calling upon Protestant churches to turn away from theological traditions that emphasized human depravity and the necessity of one having a "saving" conversion experience in order to join a church. Instead, they argued, the church needed to nurture the goodness within small children, and through the "modern" tools of Christian education help young people grow into awareness of a Christlike faith.

The Social Principles of Jesus made frequent reference to the personalist writings of one of Rauschenbusch's closest professional colleagues, Oberlin College president Henry Churchill King. "The principle of reverence for personality is the ruling principle in ethics, and in religion," asserted Rauschenbusch quoting King. "It constitutes, therefore, the truest and highest test of either an individual or a civilization; it has been . . . the guiding and determining principle in all human progress; and in its religious interpretation, it is, indeed, the one faith that keeps meaning and value for life."[24]

Between 1905 and 1935, personalism emerged as one of the dominant theological traditions in liberal Protestantism, and *The Social Principles of Jesus* reflected how Rauschenbusch was becoming increasingly influenced by certain themes of this movement. Not only did personalism support Rauschenbusch's evolutionary view of social progress, but its underpinnings in late nineteenth-century German liberalism gave the tradition a strongly optimistic view concerning the ability of humanity to overcome the social forces opposing the kingdom of God. Using the term "social gospel" for one of the first times in his writings, Rauschenbusch concluded with the assertion that the nation's youth carried a primary responsibility for the spread of this new form of Christianity — a Christianity that needed to become part of the social fabric of every community in the nation.

> Think what it would signify to a local community if all sincere Christian people in it should interpret their obligation in the social terms which we have been using; if they should seek not only their own salvation, but the reign of God in their own town; if they should cultivate the habit of seeing a divine sacredness in every personality, should assist in creating the economic foundations for fraternal solidarity, and if, as Christians, they should champion the weak in their own community.

Rauschenbusch's summons to the nation's youth was predicated largely upon the innovations of theological liberalism of the late nineteenth and early twentieth centuries. Yet he preached from a distinctive tradition of American Protestant postmillennialism, asserting to his audience that the time was at hand for the nation to build upon the ashes of an evangelical legacy that Rauschenbusch was increasingly distancing himself from. "We need a power of renewal in our American communities that will carry us across the coming social transition,

24. Ibid., 14.

and social Christianity can supply it by directing the plastic force of the old faith of our fathers to the new social tasks."[25]

While the book contained references to the war, it also reflected Rauschenbusch's self-imposed public retreat from overt criticism of the war, focusing primarily on matters of economic reform. Nevertheless, he continued to address his concerns on the European conflict in numerous letters to friends and political leaders. He told a friend in the spring of 1916 that he was certain that any public statement on his part would be misinterpreted by the public as uncritically pro-German. "I had the naive impression that people were influenced by argument even in the midst of war. I have modified my opinion on that."[26] At the same time, Rauschenbusch was becoming increasingly dismayed by the leadership of Woodrow Wilson. Originally seeing Wilson as a man capable of leading American under a progressive banner of reform, by 1915 he had become convinced that Wilson's motives related to the war were leading Americans toward economic entanglement with England, making Germany the scapegoat to justify the righteousness of the Allied cause. Writing to a congressman in February 1916, Rauschenbusch expressed alarm over Wilson's questioning of German American patriotism, especially in the aftermath of the sinking of the *Lusitania,* calling many of the President's accusations "irresponsible aspersions of millions of faithful citizens."[27] In another letter to a congressional representative that spring, he attempted to once more clarify his views on Germany, while expressing his displeasure over the motives of President Wilson. Looking with dismay at Wilson's use of American troops in Mexico in pursuit of the Mexican revolutionary Pancho Villa, Rauschenbusch remained convinced that America was being used as a pawn by the Allies to manipulate the nation to enter the war. He continued to argue that entering war in pursuit of "vindictive vengeance" would result in the unnecessary slaughter of many innocent American lives. Yet in an eerily prophetic manner, Rauschenbusch spelled out that the entry of the United States in the war would mean the disintegration of civil liberties for those of German ancestry. "The great mass of the loyal Germans will be in-

25. Ibid., 196.
26. WR to John Petrie, May 29, 1916, box 30.
27. WR to H. G. Danforth, February 26, 1916, box 155.

volved in this hatred and humiliation — as they already have been by the indiscriminate invective in high places. . . . Have not the millions of people of German blood a right to be protected in advance against loss of income, loss of social standing, loss of racial honor?"[28]

Even as Rauschenbusch pleaded his love for America, he took the position that a person's faith came before one's love of country. In a letter to a Rochester newspaper in April 1916, he affirmed that "a man's religion is the inner citadel of his personality, and if any man or any State undertakes to invade that or break it down, there should be a good reason for it. . . . It used to be the Church that invaded men's conscience and tried to domineer over his religious conviction. To-day the Church has become tolerant, but the State and the Money-Power persecute their heretics."[29] Rauschenbusch in his public speaking was careful to avoid a direct discussion of the war. Yet he made it clear that his political preferences were increasingly with Socialist party leaders, like Eugene Debs, who were unapologetic in their opposition to the war. "I find myself getting more radical on the militaristic question all the time, and more disgusted with the terrible slump in our national morality."[30]

A DISTURBING DIRECTION

Despite all the controversy surrounding Rauschenbusch's stance on the war, his speaking schedule for 1916 remained full. He began the year with Open Forum, YMCA appearances, as well as assorted lectures in the Northeast and Midwest. No sooner had Rauschenbusch celebrated Winifred's college graduation at Oberlin (where he was also given an honorary doctorate) than he was back on the road. Rauschenbusch had agreed to go on a Chautauqua tour in late June and the first half of July. Despite the fact that by 1916 the Chautauqua model had become one of the primary means by which the social gospel was disseminated in the United States, Rauschenbusch's summer tour was the first time he had actually participated in a Chautauqua series. The trip, which took Rauschenbusch through many southern states, was an ex-

28. WR to Thomas Dunn, April 25, 1916, box 30.
29. WR in *Rochester Herald,* April 27, 1916, box 30.
30. WR to William Cochran, August 8, 1916, box 30.

hausting and frustrating experience, marked by hearing-aid difficulties, hot weather, poor food, and many nights spent in cheap hotels. Occasionally, Rauschenbusch wrote favorable impressions of his speeches, but generally he felt inadequate in his addresses. ". . . in the main I don't think I am a howling success at this business," he conceded in a letter to his family.[31] As opposed to the ordered decorum of Open Forum gatherings, whose structure suited better his personal tastes and his deafness, Rauschenbusch felt that his Chautauqua experience was characterized more by an atmosphere of noisy entertainment as opposed to serious thinking. "I suppose they want helloquence and jokes."[32] He also looked with a degree of judgment and disdain upon the moral behavior of a young acting company that he toured with. "I don't like to see girls admit all kinds of liberties in a RR car with strangers to grin and smirk."[33]

The primary reason that Rauschenbusch accepted the Chautauqua engagement was that he needed money for his family. The task of financing his children's college education proved daunting, and despite the financial assistance he received from the Rockefellers and repeated offers of assistance from friends like Edmund Lyon, Rauschenbusch continually was on the lookout for ways to add to his family's revenue. As much as Rauschenbusch was genuinely committed to public speaking, at this point of his life, most speaking invitations were rehashes of what he had become accustomed to since 1908. Yet a surprising opportunity crossed his desk at the end of 1915 that he couldn't refuse: an invitation to deliver the prestigious Nathaniel Taylor Lectures at Yale University.

Rauschenbusch was surprised by the opportunity to give the Taylor lectures, named in honor of the great New England Calvinist theologian and revivalist of the early nineteenth century, whose recent lecturers included such eminent Harvard theologians as George Moore and William E. Hocking. Yet he was somewhat bemused that he was selected for this honor. "These lectures are in the field of systematic theology about which I know almost nothing," he admitted to John Phillips. Yet he was intrigued by the idea of giving a series of

31. WR to family, July 5, 1916, box 114.

32. Ibid.

33. WR to family, June 17, 1916.

lectures that would show how "the old doctrines of theology would have to be prolonged and expanded in order to take in the ideas which are actually being preached by those who believe in the social gospel."[34] In truth, however, Rauschenbusch was still finding it difficult to commit to a writing project. The book that was supposed to emerge from his Grinnell College lectureships in 1914, while still being announced by Macmillan, never materialized. Yet he committed himself to the Taylor Lectures and devoted a sabbatical leave in the fall of 1916 to the development of the four lectures that were to be delivered in April 1917. Even amidst the sabbatical, Rauschenbusch accepted several speaking engagements that fall including an address to the Intercollegiate Socialist Society in late September, and a series of addresses to colleges and clergy associations in the Midwest in November.

By the end of 1916, Rauschenbusch's state of mind continued to reflect a deep-seated melancholy, if not outright depression, a condition that was exacerbated by his financial difficulties. Both Walter and Pauline were quick to point a finger at the board of trustees of Rochester Theological Seminary for what they considered to be a low salary for such an esteemed faculty member. Rauschenbusch's relationship to Rochester Theological Seminary had always existed in the context of a "lover's quarrel." On the one hand, he was grateful for the ways the administration had repeatedly supported his work, and his fondness for men like Augustus Strong never wavered. Yet he always considered himself, perhaps melodramatically, to be just a step above poverty. This tension exploded in August 1916, when Rauschenbusch took out an insurance policy, precipitated by the accidental death of the family dog. Clearly Rauschenbusch was thinking the worst — that he might be the target of violence due to the unpopularity of his views and he lamented to Pauline that his salary did not allow him to take out a larger policy.[35]

In spite of Rauschenbusch's personal lamentations, 1916 represented a banner year for the social gospel in America. Protestant denominations, even in the more religiously traditional South, had passed a variety of social resolutions or creeds, and the Federal Coun-

34. WR to John Phillips, April 24, 1917, box 31.

35. Pauline Rauschenbusch to Edmund Lyon, March 28, 1920, box 112.

cil dramatically expanded its emphasis upon social Christianity. Increasingly, this movement synonymous with the legacy of Josiah Strong, Washington Gladden, and now Walter Rauschenbusch had come to dominate the institutional fabric of American Protestantism.

Yet Rauschenbusch took little solace from these successes. Only a few years earlier, Ray Stannard Baker had cited Rochester and Walter Rauschenbusch as embodying what was best about the new Christianity. Now not only was Rauschenbusch's integrity being challenged by former reform allies in that city, but many of the causes that he had worked hard to establish in Rochester were collapsing. In addition to his falling out with religious leaders like Algernon Crapsey and business leaders like Joseph Alling, 1916 saw the end of one of Rauschenbusch's favorite endeavors: the People's Sunday Evening. With financial contributions to this cause falling off due to the war, attendance for the meetings dwindled, and with the program's leaders unable to raise money to attract national speakers, the People's Sunday Evening ultimately fell victim to a lack of funding and the advent of a new phenomenon: Sunday motion pictures.[36]

A symbolic event in American Protestantism had also occurred earlier that spring when Josiah Strong, whose writings shaped much of the evangelical thrust of social Christianity in the late nineteenth century, succumbed to illness at the age of 68. One of the last letters Strong wrote, from his hospital bed in New York, was to Rauschenbusch. "I have always felt drawn to you and I wish that in the future circumstances might draw us into closer relations; but wherever we are we are at work on the same great temple, in which I have the greatest joy."[37]

As Rauschenbusch absorbed these personal and professional losses, the intensity of his feelings toward the war only increased. He told the Chicago social gospel preacher Jenkin Lloyd Jones that he continued to believe that Germany was being unfairly victimized by the war, seeing the conflict more about economic profits, rather than the preservation of democracy. "If anyone had foretold in 1913 that, in case of a great world war, our function would be to grow rich on a trade in arms, no doubt, it would have been treated as slanderous. I be-

36. See WR to Edmund Lyon, December 10, 1915, box 29.

37. Josiah Strong to WR, April 17, 1916, box 30.

lieve in one way or another God will exact retribution for what we have done."[38]

At the same time, Rauschenbusch was becoming increasingly attracted to a new peace organization, the Fellowship of Reconciliation. The FOR in its infancy was a movement made up of a small cadre of religious and secular socialists who denounced American intervention in the war and called for peaceful international participation on the part of the United States. Its leaders, A. J. Muste and a young disillusioned Presbyterian minister, Norman Thomas, crafted an organizational movement that in the 1920s and 1930s became one of the chief conduits for American social radicalism, especially the organization's embrace of pacifism. This newfound support of the FOR gave Rauschenbusch a renewed buoyancy in articulating his views against United States involvement in the war, although he largely remained muted in public. Although he denounced the unjust treatment of German Americans in an address to a German Baptist conference on Labor Day 1916, most of his public addresses that fall dealt with topics focusing on the virtues of Christian socialism and, in anticipation of his upcoming Taylor Lectures, the necessity of how the social gospel needed to replace the old religious faith. Yet as 1916 gave way to the new year, and as war with Germany grew more imminent, Rauschenbusch was prodded by several of his friends to clarify his stance on the war. In a lengthy response to this issue to his old friend, William Faunce, Rauschenbusch took pains to analyze his position on the war, admitting that part of his stand was motivated by his love of his ancestral homeland. "I could have purchased the right to an enthusiastic hearing if I had publicly denounced Germany. I should then have had a place on the front page. But my sense of honor recoiled from putting my knife into the land of my fathers, where my father and mother are buried. . . . I should not consider it morally decent to make a peroration out of my father's grave." Although Rauschenbusch denied Faunce's assertion that he was "loyal to the powers controlling Germany," he conceded that the nature of German militarism made that nation an easy scapegoat for many Americans.

Rauschenbusch's letter to Faunce revealed that he not only felt constricted to speak by American ignorance of European politics but

38. WR to Jenkin Lloyd Jones, November 11, 1916, box 30.

also that it would be inconsistent with his core beliefs to change his stance on the war. "I am touched by your grief about me, and by your feeling that something has been lost to the cause of right by my silence and the knowledge of the public that I do not take the orthodox side," he concluded in his letter. "I am still a Socialist, and see the real causes of war in the exploiting classes and nations. I am still a Christian, and in the midst of the war have written an exposition of the Social Principles of Jesus, in which few Christians believe. I am more than ever a pacifist."[39]

Less than two weeks after Rauschenbusch wrote this letter, and believing that war between the United States and the Central Powers was now a fait accompli, he broke his silence with an address against the war at a Rochester peace rally, sponsored in part by the Socialist Party. Rauschenbusch's keynote address, before a packed audience in the city's Avon Theater on the evening of February 25, 1917, received an enthusiastic response from the largely socialist and pacifist audience. "I say it takes a higher brand of patriotism to stand against the war clamor than to bellow with the crowd," he asserted in his speech. Affirming the convictions of the socialists that economic wealth and militarism were coconspirators in creating the climate that made war inevitable, he called upon his audience to stand up for peace, in the face of a national climate that believed that such talk was a dishonor to the legacy of America. Rauschenbusch retorted,

> It is dishonor for the richest country in the world to let mobs of poor women cry for bread for their children. It is dishonor to let the price of living be pushed up till all wage earners and salary earners are being jammed against the wall. It is dishonor to let the policies of the country be directed by people who want to make 50% on investments and to forget the mass of people who want nothing but a plain living for themselves and for the young children whom God has given them to feed.

Rauschenbusch steadfastly believed that the best solution for America was to stay neutral. "There is no honor for us in going in to this war," he concluded. "If the allies win, they will want all the honor

39. WR to William Faunce, Febuary 11, 1917, box 32.

for themselves. If the Central Powers win, we shall be on a fool's errand, and may have to pay dear for it. The real path to honor lies in being the sincere friend of all the nations, and helping them all out of this devil's trap in which they are caught. That is the honor which I covet for my country."[40]

Walter Rauschenbusch's position on the war by the spring of 1917 is difficult to summarize given the paradoxes in his stance. On the one hand, Rauschenbusch's stance toward Germany highlighted his tendency to disregard the reasons why American public opinion was so hostile toward Germany. He had a tendency to regard American pubic opinion as unenlightened on matters of European politics and he genuinely feared that any statement he made that appeared to be pro-German would be misinterpreted by the public. At the same time, Rauschenbusch never equivocated in his assertion that his primary allegiance lay with the United States, even if he disagreed with the policies of its government. "I neither now feel any preference for Germany, nor have I ever felt it," he wrote to a friend in early March 1917. "On the contrary, I have always expressed strongly my preference for America. I have no other country, and never want to have."[41] Nor, despite Rauschenbusch's own assertion that he was a pacifist, is it likely that his commitment to pacifism was absolute. Winifred believed the correct characterization of her father's position was antimilitarist rather than pacifist, and evidence corroborates her assertion. For Rauschenbusch pacifism was as much an ideal of Jesus as it was an absolute unequivocal prescription for national policy. While candid about his jingoism at the time of the Spanish-American War, he acknowledged that his beliefs on nonviolence came from the same attitudes he had cultivated from Jesus' teachings since 1887.[42] Yet the national temper in the spring of 1917 was that the war was a necessary evil that would ensure the triumph of America's democratic heritage on a worldwide scale. Rauschenbusch and other social gospel liberals soon found themselves confronted with the challenge of addressing how Christianity could be relevant amidst these changing realities.

40. Walter Rauschenbusch address and newspaper clipping, box 50.

41. WR "to a friend," March 7, 1917, box 31. For Winifred's views on her father's stance on the war, see various correspondence between Winifred and Dores Sharpe in box 155.

42. Ibid.

A NEW WORLD

On April 7, 1917, the United States declared war on the Central Powers. When President Wilson asked Congress for a declaration of war, he uttered the famous assertion, "The world must be made safe for democracy." The tone of Wilson's rhetoric was brilliant in appealing to a popular progressive sentiment in America. Unlike Rauschenbusch and others who saw war as a defeat of the principles of American democracy, Wilson appealed to the consciences of Americans to embrace the war as a crusade to root out the militaristic forces that would destroy the progressive virtues and values of democratic living so sacred to Americans. For all that was at stake in America, Rauschenbusch took the declaration of war as a foregone conclusion, but noted to a friend, "I feel deeply moved and sorrowful about the direction in which we are heading. We are laying a great yoke and weight on the generations who will have to pay our debts."[43]

Although the majority of American church leaders vigorously supported the war, a significant number shared Rauschenbusch's fears that the war might be a harbinger of Western militarism, as opposed to making the world safe for democracy. Washington Gladden, the elder statesman of the social gospel and one of the movement's major supporters of the war, nevertheless shared much empathy for Rauschenbusch's anti-war stance. Encouraging him to hold fast to his convictions, Gladden encouraged Rauschenbusch not to be afraid "of the gusts of ignorance and prejudice and passion."[44]

In the aftermath of the American declaration of war, Rauschenbusch's popular appeal remained strong. Demand for Rauschenbusch's services as a speaker for the Open Forum, Chautauqua, and especially American universities remained high. He still spoke frequently to ministerial associations throughout the country and, as had been a habit since 1907, turned down numerous invitations to write articles and books.

Less than a week after the American declaration of war, Rauschenbusch delivered his Taylor Lectures at Yale. The theme of his lectures is instructive of his state of mind, as they dealt with the question:

43. WR to Helena Dudley, April 10, 1917, box 31.

44. Gladden to WR, November 13, 1917, box 155.

what is to be the theological legacy of the social gospel? At the end of his lectures, Rauschenbusch's spirits were buoyed by a contract from Macmillan to publish the lectures and he looked forward to the summer to revise them in book form. Additionally, Rauschenbusch accepted an overture from Oberlin College president, and social gospeler, Henry Churchill King to teach at the college that fall. The desire to teach at Oberlin may in part have been motivated by a desire to be near Winifred (who at the time was working for the Ohio Woman Suffrage Association), or it may have reflected his desire to seek another teaching position. However, there was clearly a financial incentive that Rauschenbusch couldn't pass over.

Yet financial pressures were still not abated in Rauschenbusch's mind. As America entered the war, he finalized the sale of the family's beloved summer home in Ontario. More distressing for him was whether Hilmar would enlist in the armed forces. Rauschenbusch's already strained relationship with Hilmar continued to plague him. After a visit to Amherst, he acknowledged that Hilmar was free to make his own choices as an adult, but he confessed his long-standing fear that he was being shut out of his son's confidences. ". . . my love for you craves understanding, and partial knowledge breeds misunderstanding. If only I understood you children. . . . You must help us to make the transition from parenthood to friendship."[45]

In the meantime, Rauschenbusch's tug-of-war relationship with his eldest daughter continued. In a response to her father's concerns over her safety, Winifred repeatedly teased him over his worries, yet reaffirmed her love for her father. "I cannot think of you as anything but preposterously young. I guess you're a serious bear sometimes, but, I've never seen much of it. . . . I can just see you reading this at the breakfast table and I hope you'll grin some over my inability to grow up. . . . Be good to yourself and your little red beard."[46] Any chance that Walter had of seeing his daughter on a regular basis that fall ended, however, when Winifred was accepted into the University of Chicago's prestigious graduate school program in sociology, to study with the famed sociologist Robert Park. Twenty years earlier, Rauschenbusch had written to Pauline his hopes that his daughters pre-

45. WR to Hilmar, May 1, 1917, box 50.
46. Winifred to WR, March 8, 1917, box 144.

pare for vocations as wives and mothers. Now his oldest daughter was a pioneer for her generation, becoming part of a wave of women in the early twentieth century to pursue graduate studies at the preeminent American research university.

As Rauschenbusch struggled to process his daughter's independence, he showed signs of expanding his understanding of gender. In June 1917, Rauschenbusch gave the commencement address at Simmons College, a women's liberal arts college in Boston. Although he made allusions to some of his traditional Victorian understandings of gender (including his fear that the war would cause a shortage of young men for the purposes of marriage), his address clearly indicated that social changes brought on by the war modified some of his earlier views on the role of women. "Outside of the home, this world in the past was a man's world; our art and literature, our methods of organization, and our creative intellectual life and science, were man's domain. . . . But today many women are quite capable of doing what men have done, and 'then some.'"[47] While Rauschenbusch still bemoaned the frivolity of many "high-heeled" American women, he acknowledged that women were assuming a new public role in the country, one they were unlikely to renounce once the war ended. "The permanent results of the war are nearly all still a matter of conjecture. But this seems one of the most assured, that women will never again vacate the place into which they stepped while the men were fighting."[48]

It is evident in several sections of this address that Rauschenbusch's thought was being influenced by his own struggles to understand the worldview of his children. As much as he may have clashed with the directions they chose for their lives, his commencement address made it clear that he looked upon their generation with more envy than condemnation. "Youth alone is in possession here. The young used to reverence the old. Today the old reverence the young. They have beauty, buoyancy, dash, daring, self-confidence, arrogance — all the qualities we wish we had."[49] Yet Rauschenbusch confessed, in an unmistakable biographical commentary, of his own ambivalence

47. Rauschenbusch, "The Issues of Life," *Simmons Quarterly* 7 (July 1917): 5.

48. Ibid., 6.

49. Ibid., 1.

about his role as a father to his own daughters. "Fathers may well inquire where they come in," he reflected. "Nature has given them none of the fierce pangs and joys which she gives to woman, none of the intimate brooding over the baby. To serve their children they usually have to leave their children, and they see them only when they are most tired, and the children either asleep or busy." In addressing an audience of young women not unlike his eldest daughter, he revealed something of his own regrets as a father, yet also his hope that his future relationship with Winifred might be marked by friendship and greater understanding between the two. "Fathers will miss a lot unless you help them. A daughter's love is a great thing to a mature man, the most wonderful renewal of youth and sex."[50]

Rauschenbusch's understanding of gender was still predicated on the Victorian suppositions of his youth, but by 1917 his views reflected a subtle but significant shift in his theology. Echoing arguments made in *The Social Principles of Jesus,* Rauschenbusch spoke less of the need to "Christianize" society and more of the need to foster the growth and development of human personality as a means of building the kingdom. As he explained in his Simmons College address, the ability to build a just society required the cultivation of individual virtues of intelligence, freedom, and moral virtue. "Personality is developed by good work; good work can be done only by intelligent and free personalities."[51] Even as many social gospel leaders viewed the world war as an idealistic crusade to save the world, increasingly its leaders spoke less of the need to Christianize America, and more of how Christian teaching might serve as the basis to build a new type of society in a postwar world. As Rauschenbusch affirmed in the conclusion of his address, "Our personality, our work, our love we must give to our nation. We must save our soul and the national soul by keeping supreme those higher purposes which we have proudly affirmed, but which will surely be swamped and submerged unless we hold them tenaciously."[52]

Whatever the future held in the postwar years, Rauschenbusch was confident that the generation of youth, represented by his own

50. Ibid., 8.
51. Ibid., 6.
52. Ibid., 9.

children, would be up to the challenge. As he noted in his commencement address at Simmons College, there were grounds for hope in the future, even amidst the uncertain chaos of the present. "You and I will come out of this time of stress either weaker or stronger than we should have been in ordinary times. There will be many wrecked existences, but there will be some brave souls who will work out the eternal truths under the pressure of life, and cooperate with God in the salvation of the nations."[53] It was in this weary, but hopeful spirit, that Rauschenbusch looked ahead toward the uncertain future facing America and the social gospel in a time of world war and its aftermath.

53. Ibid., 9.

13 The Little Gate to God

For much of the summer and fall of 1917, Rauschenbusch worked on revising his Taylor Lectures for publication. With his failure to complete the proposed "Social Redemption" manuscript for Macmillan, Rauschenbusch worked diligently to complete the manuscript entitled "A Theology for the Social Gospel" in a timely fashion, in part to move on to other projects, in part to stay in the good graces of his publisher, Macmillan Press. Even as he worked on the manuscript, he mused over the idea of finally writing a book on church history. "It is one of my permanent desires to write at least one book on Church History before I die," he noted to an editor of Association Press. "The social movement has hitherto consumed my output of books. I want to do for Church History what has been done for the Bible by a great number of writers in recent years, — to give it a social interpretation, to see it from the Kingdom point of view, to view the life and work of the Church not as an end in itself, but to judge it by what it has done for mankind."[1]

Yet Rauschenbusch had come to accept and embrace the role that he played in the minds of many as *the* spokesperson for social Chris-

1. WR to Frederick Harris, June 23, 1917, box 31.

tianity. When the distinguished Episcopal bishop Charles Williams dedicated a book to Rauschenbusch, he received the honor in a spirit of humility and bemusement. "It is a great privilege to know that a man like you has been able to get good out of my work. But I am not nearly as much of 'a man of God' as I hoped to be when I entered the ministry. Carrying five children on his back, and being handicapped for years by physical loneliness, compels a man to climb the Hill of Difficulty with short steps. I can only trust that God will understand."[2] By 1917, Rauschenbusch had reluctantly accepted his identification with the term "social gospel." He believed that the phrase was somewhat misleading, because the teachings of Jesus on the kingdom represented *the* gospel that required no modifying adjective. Nevertheless, for the first time in his writing he used this term without qualification, seeking to articulate how this emergent theological tradition might give guidance to a church and a nation that looked beyond the carnage of the world war.

ENVISIONING A POSTWAR CHRISTENDOM

Rauschenbusch's two major earlier books on the Christian "social movement," *Christianity and the Social Crisis* and *Christianizing the Social Order,* were works predicated upon his interpretation of church history. The Taylor manuscript, however, was in some respects his first attempt to write an explicit book on theology, with an effort to develop the manuscript topically around major tenets of Christian theology and doctrine, including sin, the fall, the nature of evil, personal salvation, the church, the kingdom, the conception of God, the Holy Spirit, the sacraments, eschatology, and the atonement. As Rauschenbusch noted in the book's opening sentences, "We have a social gospel. We need a systematic theology large enough to match it and vital enough to back it."[3] Yet Rauschenbusch's challenge was not to write a work of systematic theology, but to provide a work that could serve as the basis

2. WR to Bishop Charles Williams, July 17, 1917, box 31; the dedication to Rauschenbusch appears in Williams's book, *The Christian Ministry and Social Problems* (New York: Macmillan, 1917).

3. *Theology for the Social Gospel,* 1.

for giving the social gospel a distinctive theological character that successive generations could flesh out and expand. "If theology stops growing or is unable to adjust to its modern environment and to meet its present tasks, it will die. . . . The social gospel needs a theology to make it effective; but theology needs the social gospel to vitalize it."[4]

Originally contemplating a dedication to his father, Rauschenbusch chose instead to dedicate the book to Augustus Strong. "You have been my teacher in theology, the president under whom I have worked in happiness and freedom for many years, my fatherly friend and the father of two of my friends."[5] Yet Strong, for all his love of Rauschenbusch, expressed a degree of ambivalence about his association with this newest project. When Rauschenbusch characterized him as "the last great systematizer of American Calvinism" in the book's original dedication, Strong was quick to retort. By this time in his life, Strong's career had traversed the spectrum of Protestant theological developments since the final third of the nineteenth century. He had followed a trajectory from an identity as one of American Protestantism's major Calvinist apologists to an individual who subtly modified his beliefs in the face of liberal ascendency by the end of the nineteenth century. Now in the twilight of his life, Strong was having second thoughts about his earlier toleration of liberalism, writing to Rauschenbusch that his theological position derived not from Calvin, but from the Reformation theology of Luther. "Luther indeed saw far more clearly than did Calvin the biological relation between Adam and his posterity, and between Christ and believers. The solidarity of the race, with Calvin, was legal and forensic; with Luther, it was vital and moral."[6] When Rauschenbusch changed the dedication to Strong to conclude, "A Theologian Whose Best Beloved Doctrine Has Been the Mystic Union with Christ," Strong was equally ambivalent. "I am a mystic only in the sense of the apostle Paul: 'This mystery, which is Christ in you' — a mystery, only in the sense that it is a secret known only to the believer, though a secret revealed to all who will receive the Lord Jesus."[7]

Strong's admonishments to Rauschenbusch probably had as

4. Ibid., 1.

5. WR to Augustus Strong, June 26, 1917, box 40.

6. Augustus Strong to WR, August 31, 1917, box 40.

7. Augustus Strong to WR, September 11, 1917, box 40.

much to do with the contents of Rauschenbusch's new book as they did with any concern Strong may have had to clarify his understanding of orthodox Protestant theology. Indeed, Strong probably took little comfort when Rauschenbusch wrote Strong his desire that his new book say something significant about the future of theology, not simply rehash older doctrines. ". . . whether we like it or dislike it, the times are changing theologically, and the formulations of the Reformation Age are no longer the natural expression of our religious life."[8]

At the end of the summer, Rauschenbusch had a draft of the new book complete and submitted a final draft to Macmillan in October. In November, the book was published and quickly received favorable reviews from church leaders, pastors, and periodicals sympathetic to the social gospel. Charles Clayton Morrison, a Disciples of Christ pastor and editor of the interdenominational Protestant journal *Christian Century,* praised the book in a review and in a personal letter to Rauschenbusch. "In my judgment you have rendered the cause both of evangelical religion and social reconstruction a very great service, one of the most important that has been rendered by any of our recent thinkers."[9] The New England Methodist periodical *Zion's Herald* noted a shared sentiment among many church and secular periodical reviews, believing that the book was "one of the determining works in the period of intellectual groping through which we are passing in connection with the social application of the religion of Jesus Christ."[10] An Ottumwa, Iowa, pastor wrote Rauschenbusch an enthusiastic appraisal of the work, noting how it invoked an effusive response from members of his congregation. "I am begging them here to begin to read your books." Although this pastor's congregation was slow to warm up to Rauschenbusch's theology, once they do, "They smile!"[11] Such positive assessments of his work from Christian laity no doubt brought satisfaction to Rauschenbusch.

Yet even some of his liberal colleagues couldn't help critiquing the book on several points. Vida Scudder, as she had done in response to his earlier works, chided Rauschenbusch's bias against the high church traditions, especially Anglicanism.[12] Gerald Birney Smith,

8. WR to Augustus Strong, September 6, 1917, box 40.
9. Charles Clayton Morrison to WR, February 15, 1918, box 40.
10. *Zion's Herald* (January 2, 1918), clipping in box 155.
11. Letter to WR, February 3, 1918, box 32.
12. Vida Scudder to WR, March 27, 1918, box 40.

dean of the University of Chicago Divinity School, while affirming that the book was "the main theological event of the year in Chicago," added his concern that Rauschenbusch was too "Ritschlian" in his theology. Smith noted that Rauschenbusch's insistence on focusing chiefly on Jesus' role as the initiator of the kingdom ignored how Christianity was "the outgrowth of a complex social situation, in which Hellenic as well as Judaic forces were positively present."[13]

Not surprisingly, Augustus Strong's tepid praise of the book was muted by his critique. Although he noted that Rauschenbusch wrote a "great book" for "an amateur in theology," he was dismayed by Rauschenbusch's continued departure from historical Christian doctrine, especially related to the doctrine of the atonement. "Your theology is one of love, but not of righteousness like that of Paul," he complained to Rauschenbusch.[14] "In seeking to make a new application of Christianity, are you not leaving out the only Christianity we have to apply? Are you not replacing Christianity by a man-made substitute, which furnishes neither explanation of man's universal sin nor dynamic whereby to cure it?"[15] Strong pleaded with Rauschenbusch to write his next book that would "show more clearly that you still hold 'the faith once for all delivered to the saints.'"[16]

Most of the book's severest critics accentuated Strong's concern about the book's slipshod interpretations of Christian doctrine. The *Presbyterian* dismissed the book as a poor attempt to synthesize a connection between historical Christian doctrine and contemporary Christian social action. "There is much that is suggestive about the book, but as a contribution to theology, it is hardly to be taken seriously."[17] The *Lutheran Quarterly* was even more dismissive, observing that "Men, like our author, fail to see that as far as society is in a wholesome and happy state, it has come to this state by the preaching of the old, everlasting truths of the Bible."[18]

Rauschenbusch's response to doctrinal criticisms of his book was almost cavalier. While noting to one colleague that he was sensitive to

13. Gerald Birney Smith to WR, April 30, 1918, box 40.
14. Augustus Strong to WR, December 28, 1917, box 31.
15. Augustus Strong to WR, March 4, 1918, box 155.
16. Augustus Strong to WR, December 28, 1917, box 31.
17. *The Presbyterian,* clipping in box 94.
18. *The Lutheran Quarterly,* January 1918, box 106.

the Hellenistic influences upon the New Testament, he stuck to his argument that these influences were largely destructive of the true intent of Jesus' teachings regarding the kingdom. "It seems plain that historically the Greek theology has been the basis for asceticism and otherworldliness, and that its dualism is alien to the original gospel and offers no basis for the social gospel." He candidly admitted his lack of interest in attending to many fine points of Christian doctrine, such as the Trinity. "The effort to establish some sort of social relation between the three Persons has never attracted me."[19]

In many respects, the verdict of future generations would be kinder in their assessment of *A Theology for the Social Gospel.* The book's language not only seemed less dated to successive generations compared to some of Rauschenbusch's earlier works but also the book served as a succinct summary of many of the mature theological beliefs of Walter Rauschenbusch and the social gospel movement at the climax of World War I. The mid-twentieth century liberal theologian Daniel Day Williams went as far as calling this book the classic expression of American theological liberalism.[20]

What many of the book's contemporary critics missed was that Rauschenbusch's purpose for writing *A Theology for the Social Gospel* was not only to pen a theological apologetic for the social gospel but also to provide a theological basis for Christian social action and social reconstruction after the world war. Although the book reiterates many of his core beliefs, the book's purpose was to make Christians meditate upon the meaning of salvation in ways that spoke to the conditions of modern twentieth-century society. While affirming the importance of individualistic salvation for the Christian, he argued that such a perspective alone "has not given us an adequate understanding of the sinfulness of the social order and its share in the sins of all individuals within it."[21] Perhaps acknowledging his own shortcomings as a theologian, Rauschenbusch noted that the discipline of theology was "not superior to the gospel. It exists to aid the preaching of salvation."[22] After arguing that the social gospel represented a vital development in

19. WR to John Wright Buckham, January 4, 1918, box 32.

20. Gary Dorrien, *The Making of American Liberal Theology,* Volume I (Louisville: Westminster John Knox Press, 2001), xix.

21. *Theology for the Social Gospel,* 5.

the history of Christian theology, Rauschenbusch examined the social gospel in relationship to human sin and evil. Unlike orthodox theologians like Strong, he rejected a belief that understanding sin and evil were "a kind of unvarying racial endowment, which is active in every new life and which can be overcome only by the grace offered in the Gospel and ministered by the Church."[23] He believed that such an orthodox belief in sin would blind men and women to the existence of evil that confronted people in everyday life, commenting wryly, "it is possible to hold the orthodox doctrine on the devil and not recognize him when we met him in a real estate office or at the stock exchange."[24] This assertion led Rauschenbusch into a lengthy exposition not only on the need for the social gospel to identify its mission with the kingdom of God, but to vigilantly oppose the existence of collective sin, what he called "the kingdom of evil."

Later polemical attacks against the social gospel from neo-orthodox theologians like Reinhold Niebuhr charged the tradition for lacking an adequate theology of sin and evil. Yet in 1917, Rauschenbusch's argument concerning the kingdom of evil anticipated the arguments that would be used by theologians like Niebuhr in the 1930s to debunk the liberalism of the social gospel. For Rauschenbusch, these "super-personal" forces formed a tapestry in which the actions of individuals took on a life of their own in the context of a community. "The apparently free and unrelated acts of individuals are also the acts of the social group. When the social group is evil, evil is over all."[25]

Rauschenbusch rejected the neo-Augustinian critique of original sin, central to later neo-orthodox theologians, that emphasized the corruptibility of human nature due to the doctrine of the fall. Even as he dealt with his own pain over events of the world war, Rauschenbusch showed no interest in confronting the possibilities that the nature of humanity was corrupted in the sense spoken of by Paul and Augustine. He believed rather that evil manifested itself "organically," and in biological fashion was transmitted from one group to another. Once these social evils manifested themselves collectively within society,

22. Ibid., 6.
23. Ibid., 43.
24. Ibid., 35.
25. Ibid., 81.

they were nearly impossible to overcome. "The life of humanity is infinitely interwoven, always renewing itself, yet always perpetuating what has been. The evils of one generation are caused by the wrongs of the generations that preceded, and will in turn condition the sufferings and temptations of those who come after."[26]

There is a tendency in the book to identify the kingdom of evil among the political and economic interests of nondemocratic-aristocratic "ruling classes" in the West. As the book reached its climax, he argued that many of these same upper-class interests were responsible for attempting to place Jesus' kingdom in the realm of an otherworldly eschatology. "My own conviction is that the professional theologians of Europe, who all belong by kinship and sympathy to the bourgeois classes and are constitutionally incapacitated for understanding any revolutionary ideas, past or present, have overemphasized the ascetic and eschatological elements in the teachings of Jesus."[27] As opposed to upholding the role of the church based upon its ecclesiastical status, its mission was grounded in the quest to build a just society. "In the last resort the issues of future history lie in the moral qualities and religious faith of nations. This is the substance of all Hebrew and Christian eschatology. . . . Our chief interest in any millennium is the desire for a social order in which the worth and freedom of every least human being will be honoured and protected."[28] While Rauschenbusch continued to see social progress as an evolutionary development, social progress was not inevitable, nor was it necessarily peaceful. "The coming of the Kingdom of God will not be by peaceful development only, but by conflict with the Kingdom of Evil. We should estimate the power of sin too lightly if we forecast a smooth road."[29] Rauschenbusch held out hope that social catastrophes, like the world war, would lead Christians to a greater awareness of the existence of evil in the world. Yet he also made it clear once again that working toward the kingdom was never a culmination realized in history, but had its consummation beyond history. In rhetoric similar to the conclusion of *Christianity and the Social Crisis,* he af-

26. Ibid., 79.
27. Ibid., 158.
28. Ibid., 224.
29. Ibid., 226.

firmed, "an eschatology which is expressed in terms of historic development has no final consummation. Its consummations are always the basis for further development. The Kingdom of God is always coming, but we can never say 'Lo here.'"[30]

As had been the case with *The Social Principles of Jesus, A Theology for the Social Gospel* ignored the rhetoric of "Christianizing" the social order, emphasizing instead the imperative that Christians engage in social struggle to build a just society. As Rauschenbusch noted in the book's final chapter, future generations of Christians needed to see in the doctrine of the atonement "the clearest and most conspicuous case of prophetic suffering." For those who love and follow Jesus, his death on the cross was a sign to "all who bore prophetic suffering by the consciousness that they were 'bearing the marks of the Lord Jesus' and were carrying on what he had borne."[31] For Rauschenbusch, as for others who would carry on the tradition of the social gospel after the war, the cross of Christ was a prophetic symbol of how the redemptive forces of the kingdom of God could speak to a war-torn world. He ended the book with the hopeful assertion, "The era of prophetic and democratic Christianity has just begun. This concerns the social gospel, for the social gospel is the voice of prophecy in modern life."[32]

Although *A Theology for the Social Gospel,* unlike his other major works on social Christianity, did not focus on specific ways that churches could engage in "social reconstruction," it signaled an emerging shift among some of Rauschenbusch's colleagues in the social gospel movement. By 1917, younger peers like Francis McConnell and Harry Ward, while supportive of the war, picked up Rauschenbusch's concerns related to how the dangers of capitalism and militarism jeopardized the church's mission to work for a just social order. Furthermore, a younger generation of clergy, many of whom were galvanized by the writings of Rauschenbusch, would pick up this theme and translate it into their own understanding of Christian socialism in the 1920s. Among these liberal leaders were Sherwood Eddy, Charles Clayton Morrison, and a young Detroit pastor named Reinhold Niebuhr.

30. Ibid., 227.
31. Ibid., 279.
32. Ibid., 279.

Rauschenbusch increasingly believed that social struggle was inevitable. In a reflection that he had written in 1915, he speculated about the state of America and of its churches in the postwar world. On one hand he predicted a boom for capitalism, regardless of whether America entered the war, noting that churches would need to develop new strategies for dealing with the vestiges of postwar capitalism and militarism. "The churches will continue to have a hard time in the midst of capitalistic industrialism," he asserted. "The country will drift into militaristic organization and ideas, and many ministers will then preach what they have been denouncing. Others will earnestly try to preach the gospel of peace as they did before the war, but the memory of the enthusiasm with which we made profit out of carnage will shame us and be cast in our face by sceptics." Rauschenbusch expressed his belief that the only way for the churches to counter these trends was to "urge the churches toward Christian union and consolidation of their forces."[33] Two years later, in late 1917, he expressed to Washington Gladden his doubts that an allied victory in the war would create lasting social or economic equality. Expressing his longstanding distrust of Woodrow Wilson's political motives, Rauschenbusch saw a postwar world of selfish capitalistic greed, where war industries would boom and government would do little to control these appetites. He argued, "all the people who have been hypnotized by the currents of hate and revenge, all the interests that have been making a thousand per cent . . . will hate to come down to eight per cent again." Rauschenbusch revealed that his long-standing faith in the eventual triumph of political democracy was shaken. As he noted to Gladden, any real global democratic social change that occurs because of the war would be largely superficial, "and the simple-minded public does not know enough about geography and international economics to see where it is being tricked."[34]

At the very moment that America entered the war, however, Rauschenbusch took an interest in the dramatic political events in Russia, when in February 1917, Czar Nicholas II was overthrown in a largely bloodless coup, leading to the establishment of a Provisional Socialist government under the head of Alexander Kerensky. "Tell me

33. WR, typed manuscript circa 1915, box 29.

34. WR to Washington Gladden, November 17, 1917, box 31.

more about the revolution in Russia when you come," he wrote to Hilmar eagerly that spring. "I wish it would hit us some too."[35] Rauschenbusch, like the majority of social gospelers, had a difficult time assimilating the events that unfolded in Russia in 1917. While these leaders took no pleasure in the overt atheism represented by Vladimir Lenin's "October Revolution" later in the year, many were nevertheless intrigued about the possibilities of economic change and the initiatives of state socialism proposed by Lenin's government. The "wait and see" attitude taken by many liberal clergy toward the Bolshevik Revolution was symptomatic of a larger debate that would engulf American Protestantism in the 1920s and 1930s over the extent to which the economic measures in the Soviet Union represented manifestations of the kingdom of God.

Yet Rauschenbusch kept affirming what had become one of his fundamental ethical assertions — that violence was antithetical to Christian teaching. In a letter to John Phillips written a few months after American entry in the war he dismissed the argument that Jesus could sanction violence as "theoretical twaddle," asserting that "in actual practice we do not love when we kill. Killing becomes unbearable when we love. . . . Now, when we no longer are in a state of love, we are no longer on a Christian basis of action."[36]

A VALEDICTORY WORD?

By the fall of 1917, Rauschenbusch's main objective was to interpret how the theological principles articulated in the new book related to his hopes for social reform in postwar America. As had frequently been the case in the past, more personal matters distracted him from this task. In part, he was worried over Hilmar, who after much soul searching had chosen to enlist in the army, where he was to serve as an ambulance driver on the western front. He was also dissatisfied with his teaching at Oberlin, and exhausted by his commute back and forth between his classes in Rochester and Oberlin. "My classes are quite large" with "many visitors," he noted to Winifred in October

35. WR to Hilmar Rauschenbusch, March 22, 1917, box 50.
36. WR to John Phillips, May 16, 1917, box 31.

about his teaching at Oberlin. Yet he also expressed his own frustration with his teaching. "I m rather dissatisfied with my work. Especially my historical course seems to me trite and poorly worked out."[37] Rauschenbusch was scheduled to make several addresses early in 1918, including a series of addresses at YMCA conferences in the Northeast. While he likely would have not addressed the specifics of his stance toward the war, it is probable that he would have emphasized the dangers of capitalism toward the creation of a just social order after the war, and discussed specific ways how the theological contours sketched out in his recent book could empower churches in a postwar world.

However, by the end of January 1918, Rauschenbusch canceled all of his upcoming speaking engagements. For months he had been complaining of fatigue, and efforts to isolate the problems medically were turning up no solutions. The first signs of trouble were indicated in a letter to Winifred in late October 1917, when he noted a concern about fatigue and a low blood count.[38] As his fatigue worsened he began to develop pains in his abdomen and a shakiness in his hands. Originally diagnosed with a bacteriological infection, Rauschenbusch had several teeth extracted in late 1917 and early 1918. In January, a series of scans on his liver, spleen, and kidneys turned up nothing conclusive. With both Clarence Barbour and Conrad Moehlmann on leave from the seminary for duty with the national YMCA, Rauschenbusch was determined to maintain his teaching obligations. He wrote a hopeful letter to Barbour that he desired to maintain some semblance of a normal schedule. "I only want you to understand that I am traveling an uphill road at present. Work and effort come hard and cost will power. . . . So I prod along like a Christian . . . looking to the Lord and taking all the sleep I can get as my only medicine."[39]

Yet Rauschenbusch's condition continued to worsen, and following a diagnosis of "pernicious anemia," on March 14 Rauschenbusch recorded in his calendar that he "closed up my work at the seminary."[40] With the support of President Barbour, Rauschenbusch took

37. WR to Winifred, October 26, 1917, box 143.

38. Ibid.

39. WR to Clarence Barbour, February 25, 1918, box 32.

40. WR calendar, box 106.

an indefinite leave of absence, a decision that likely pained him as much as his illness.

At the time he stopped teaching, Rauschenbusch wrote an addendum to his will that scholars would later interpret as an indication of Rauschenbusch's desire to die. "I have long prayed God not to let me be stranded in a lonesome and useless old age, and if this is the meaning of my present illness, I shall take it as a loving mercy of God toward his servant. Since 1914 the world is full of hate, and I cannot expect to be happy again in my lifetime. . . . The only pang is to part from my loved ones, and no longer to be able to stand by them and smooth their way. For the rest, I go gladly, for I have carried a heavy handicap for thirty years, and have worked hard."[41]

This statement appears to support a view that Rauschenbusch was left brokenhearted by the events of the war — an interpretation that his daughter, Winifred, and even Dores Sharpe, resisted. She believed her father to be full of life in his last years, and that his assertions were chiefly "private" reflections, "what you say to your best friend, to whom and to whom alone you confide."[42]

Rauschenbusch was clearly agonizing over the events of the last four years. Certainly, his perspective was influenced by the pain of his illness, and a frustration over the inability of his doctors to treat it. Yet it also reflected the tendency among social gospel liberals to embrace personal suffering as a sign of Christlike perseverance — a suffering that would ultimately be redemptive. As Rauschenbusch emphasized in his recent writings, to suffer as Christ suffered represented the essence of the prophet's purpose in contributing to the redemption of society. Rauschenbusch clearly felt that he had fulfilled the prophet's role in this regard.

In fact, frustrated by the inability of doctors to locate the cause of his illness, Rauschenbusch desperately wanted to get better and return to his former activity. His spirits were lifted by a resolution of affection sent by his students. "I need not tell you all how deeply this whole thing has affected me," he told a seminarian. "When I pulled down the roll-top of my desk . . . and locked up, I had all kinds of feelings. . . .

41. Copies of this "last will" can be found in boxes 39 and 180. See also Sharpe, 448-49.

42. Winifred R. Rorty to Dores Sharpe, December 17, 1938, boxes 50 and 155.

You can tell the boys that, from all the information I have been able to get, . . . there is a fair chance for me, and I may have a complete recovery. So we will keep the flag of hope flying and do what we can."[43] As spring dawned in Rochester, Rauschenbusch took some comfort in being able to do some gardening at Portsmouth Terrace, and even took time to have a photographic portrait taken for an upcoming seminary directory.

But even this momentary solace was interrupted by another controversy surrounding his position on the war. Through the prodding of Barbour and Rauschenbusch's former faculty colleague, Cornelius Woelfkin, Rauschenbusch reluctantly agreed to make a public statement in support of the allied war effort. The statement, which was reprinted in a number of religious and secular periodicals in the summer of 1918, had been viewed as a peculiar, and in some instances tragic, coda to Rauschenbusch's career. Winifred saw her father's decision to write this letter as the "one great mistake" in his life, noting that the letter displayed "a little lack of courage in a man who otherwise had much courage."[44] On one hand, Winifred's assertions are justified. Although Barbour and Woelkfin were likely motivated by their friendship with Rauschenbusch and a desire to preserve his good name, the fact that an old friend and colleague like Woelfkin had questioned Rauschenbusch's loyalty and patriotism in the first place had to be painful. Even after Rauschenbusch drafted the letter, Barbour suggested several editorial revisions that made clearer Rauschenbusch's condemnation of Germany.[45]

Woelfkin, who after leaving the seminary faculty became the senior minister at Fifth Avenue Baptist Church in New York City, had issued a public challenge to Rauschenbusch to clarify his position on the war. Although he privately professed his personal affection for Rauschenbusch, the attack hurt Rauschenbusch deeply, and the fact that Barbour had allied himself with Woelfkin likely gave him the impression that his two friends were ganging up on him. It is probable, however, that Woelfkin and Barbour feared for Rauschenbusch's personal safety. At a time when high-profile leftists like Eugene Debs

43. WR to Harlan Frost, March 30, 1918, box 50.

44. Winifred Rauschenbusch to Henry Robins, November 12, 1929, box 143.

45. Barbour to WR, May 1, 1918, box 91.

were imprisoned for violation of federal espionage acts, and with Rauschenbusch's outspokenness against the war in the past, Barbour and Woelfkin perhaps viewed a pro-war statement from Rauschenbusch as a way of protecting him from government persecution. When Rauschenbusch expressed his anxiety over writing a statement on the war, Woelfkin was quick to console his friend, affirming, "it was only my solicitation for the regard in which your friends have held you that made me write you at all."[46]

Rauschenbusch's statement can hardly be taken as an exuberant endorsement of the war. Even though it can be argued that Rauschenbusch's response to Woelfkin emerged from coercion (a view upheld by Winifred), a close reading of the response affirmed many of Rauschenbusch's major insights regarding Germany, the dangers of Western militarism, and his faith in the virility of American democracy. Noting his long-standing objection to the lack of a democratic tradition in Germany, and the dangers inherent within the legacy of German militarism, Rauschenbusch reflected a sentiment consistent throughout his public career: the need to export to the world the theoretical and practical models of American democracy.

> The American ideals of Democracy have dominated my intellectual life. My literary and professional work for years has been characterized by the consistent effort to work out democratic interpretations of history, religion and social life. My social point of view is at the farthest remove from the autocratic, imperialistic and militaristic philosophy, and my Christian social convictions are the direct negation of Nietzsche. . . . I am, therefore, not merely an American in sentiment, but have taken our democratic principles very seriously, and used my life to inculcate and spread them here and abroad.

While noting his hope that "the terrible education of the war has acted as an enforced repentance for all the nations," Rauschenbusch echoed a popular sentiment in the letter, asserting that allied victory would put America in a unique position of leadership in the postwar world. Compared to Europe, "we have fewer selfish interests at stake

46. Cornelius Woelfkin to WR, May 1, 1918, box 91.

than the other peoples; we have the great traditions of democracy; we can lift the whole contest above a fight for territory and trade privileges and make it a battle for the freedom of the nations and the achievement of international order and peace. . . . Whatever the outcome may be, President Wilson will have a tremendous task to translate his idealistic utterances into realities against the pressure of selfish interests at home and abroad. . . . Therefore the President deserves our earnest support in standing for the noblest ends to which he has given such remarkable expression."

In many respects, the Woelfkin letter highlights a reflective tone that discloses Rauschenbusch's continuing ambivalence about the war. "In these four years our nation has swung through many changes of thought and feeling. We have all passed through experiences shocking and unexpected for which no previous experience has prepared us. I have all along felt like a swimmer in a stormy sea, and have only been able to struggle with each impact as it came." Winifred, however, was likely accurate on one point of the letter. In its conclusion, Rauschenbusch spoke of Hilmar's service in France, noting his eldest son as an example of how "we best realize some things through our children."[47] Yet Rauschenbusch later told Winifred that he wished his son had chosen to become a conscientious objector.[48]

After Rauschenbusch finished the final draft of the letter, he and Pauline boarded a train for Baltimore to the Johns Hopkins Medical Center, in hopes of gaining further clarity on his illness. Treated by Dr. Louis Hamman at Hopkins, Rauschenbusch endured a series of tests that brought more questions than clarity to his condition. Hamman agreed with the diagnosis of Rochester physicians that Rauschenbusch was suffering from a form of anemia, yet conceded that there might be something else in Rauschenbusch's condition that was likely causing the anemia.[49] At the end of two frustrating weeks in the hospital, Rauschenbusch returned home with only recommendations on diet and the use of hydrochloric acid to alleviate his stomach pains. In a report to Rauschenbusch's physician in Rochester,

47. "A Clear Cut Statement on the War," typed manuscript, box 46.
48. Winifred Rauschenbusch to Henry Robins, November 12, 1929, box 143.
49. Physician's report, "Summary by Dr. Hamman," May 15, 1918, box 35.

Hamman expressed doubt that Rauschenbusch's problems were caused by "an obscure carcinoma."[50]

While at Hopkins, Rauschenbusch wrote a statement to be read to an upcoming meeting of the American Baptist Home Missionary Society. The tone of the letter reasserted Rauschenbusch's belief that personal faith and social transformation were interrelated. "My life would seem an empty shell if my personal religion were left out of it," he wrote. "It has been my deepest satisfaction to get evidence now and then that I have been able to help men to a new spiritual birth. I have always regarded my public work as a form of evangelism, which called for a deeper repentance and a new experience of God's salvation."[51] Yet it was apparent that Rauschenbusch was growing depressed over his condition. The day before leaving Hopkins, on May 19, he acknowledged, "I feel under obligation to do all I can to recover, but I am not enthusiastic about it." While acknowledging that there were several more books he would like to write, and how difficult he would find it to part with family and friends, he wondered "if God is not intending to be very kind to one of his servants who, for reasons known to Him, has carried a heavy load for 30 years and yet has done the day's work as well as the next man."[52]

A DISCIPLESHIP OF SUFFERING

By May 1918, Rauschenbusch's attention was focused on death. Yet it was not so much a matter of being brokenhearted as it was, in his mind, a reflection of his evangelical-liberal faith that in choosing the path that he followed, he was, in a sense, following the path of Christ to Calvary.

This evangelical-liberal dimension in Rauschenbusch's thought emerges in a poem he wrote that spring entitled "The Little Gate to God" (a title given by Pauline). The poem has been highlighted by many scholars as a testimony to Rauschenbusch's personal spiritual-

50. Louis Hamman to John Williams, May 28, 1918, box 35.
51. WR to L. Barnes, May 10, 1918, box 39. Quoted in Hudson, 46.
52. WR to Dores Sharpe, May 19, 1918, box 155. Quoted in Minus, 192.

ity, reflecting a deep faith that as he confronted the possibility of death, God's presence was with him:

> In the castle of my soul
> Is a little postern gate,
> Whereat, when I enter,
> I am in the presence of God.
> In a moment, in the turning of a thought,
> I am where God is.
> This is a fact.

The poem makes clear, however, that Rauschenbusch's personal sense of connection with God was cast in the context of his being God's prophet, who was attempting to affirm the goodness of life among those who both loved and despised him.

> When I am in the consciousness of God,
> My fellowmen are not far-off and forgotten,
> But close and strangely dear.
> Those whom I love
> Have a mystic value.
> They shine, as if a light were glowing within them.
> Even those who frown on me
> And love me not
> Seem part of the great scheme of good.
> (Or else they seem like stray bumble-bees
> Buzzing at a window,
> Headed the wrong way, yet seeking the light.)

Like Jeremiah who witnesses the fall of Judea, Rauschenbusch weeps for a creation that was committing social evils that caused civilizations to move further away from God.

> Is it strange that I love God?
> And when I come back through the gate,
> Do you wonder that I carry memories with me,
> And my eyes are hot with unshed tears for what I see,
> And I feel like a stranger and a homeless man

Where the poor are wasted for gain,
Where rivers run red,
And where God's sunlight is darkened by lies?[53]

As much as any hymn, sermon, article or book written in that era, "The Little Gate to God" captured the essence of Walter Rauschenbusch's understanding of the social gospel movement. For many social gospel leaders like Rauschenbusch, faithful living was inseparable from the reality of social struggle, and the inevitable consequence of social struggle was human suffering — even to the point where death was the inevitable consequence. The poem reflects Rauschenbusch's belief that he had done all he could to be God's servant.

After his return to Rochester, Rauschenbusch's spirits appeared to rally. While he struggled with eating solid food, he occasionally worked in his garden and answered correspondence, assisted by his son Paul. In early June, however, x-rays finally revealed a growth on Rauschenbusch's colon. As he prepared to go to the hospital, Rauschenbusch wrote a letter to an RTS student in response to several of the young man's queries, one of them concerning whether the student should enlist. Rauschenbusch's response indicates that he was willing to a point to offer hope that the war could be redemptive. While still suspicious of Wilson, he was encouraged by his "Fourteen Points" peace proposal. Rauschenbusch felt that "Wilson has put the war on far higher grounds, and if his highest utterances can be made effective, all the sufferings may not be an excessive price." While throwing in his critique of the war (with which this student was, no doubt, quite familiar) about how selfish economic and political interests could undermine a lasting peace, he counseled the student to think carefully about enlistment, but added that his decision was one of his own conscience, adding, "The life in camp and the personal contact with the men would be a new and great experience, which can not be replaced by anything else." Rauschenbusch's letter concluded with an affirmation that reflected how much he cherished the role of serving as a mentor to his students.

53. "The Little Gate to God"; various published versions of this poem can be found in the Rauschenbusch Family Collection. See also Hudson, 46-48.

> This is the way the matter now looks to me, but I stand at one side, and the instincts of young men are likely to be truer and better. You are fortunate in having the wise and loving mind of your friend to help you. Whatever you decide, I shall follow you with a great affection; feeling your moral integrity and sincerity, and your desire to hold to Christ at a time when all the world seems to accept him in a qualified sense.[54]

The next day, June 14, doctors' surgery on Rauschenbusch confirmed what the physicians at Hopkins couldn't uncover — Rauschenbusch had colon cancer and there was nothing that could be done medically to treat it. Part of the tragedy of this discovery is that doctors kept Pauline in the dark about the grave state of his health, giving her false hope that Walter would make at least a partial recovery. After his operation, Pauline wrote Dores Sharpe with the hopeful prognosis that "at least he has a fighting chance."[55] Yet two weeks later, she told Sharpe of her pain "to see Walter so weak — and note all his subconscious terrors — about the future — whether he'll be strong enough to do his work. . . . Keep on praying Dores — but there is hope."[56]

For several weeks, Rauschenbusch lingered between periods of lucidity and periods of dementia. He received visits from a few old friends like Edmund and Carolyn Lyon, as well as many letters from colleagues like Clarence Barbour. In early July, Winifred came to visit her father's bedside and Rauschenbusch rallied briefly. He spoke to her about some of his regrets, including what he had written about Hilmar in the Woelfkin letter, saying he wished his son had become a conscientious objector.[57]

Winifred later revealed that she was aware that this would be her final visit with her father. Yet the severity of his illness remained a secret kept from the family. Paul, who was himself soon to enlist in the army, traveled back to Chicago with his sister, and Hilmar, on the front lines in France, only knew that his father was recovering in the hospital and would soon be returning home. During this hospitalization,

54. WR to Harlan Frost, June 13, 1918, box 50.
55. Pauline Rauschenbusch to Dores Sharpe, June 14, 1918, box 65.
56. Pauline Rauschenbusch to Dores Sharpe, June 25, 1918, box 65.
57. Winifred R. Rorty to Henry Robins, November 12, 1929, box 143.

Walter was comforted by a short story that Hilmar had written in France, and after his surgery he commented to Pauline that "if Hilmar ever writes, he will go farther than I did."[58]

Although it appeared by early July that Rauschenbusch was well enough to return to Portsmouth Terrace, Pauline sensed that her husband's end was near. On July 14, she wrote a moving letter to him, affirming that he had indeed been responsible for leaving behind a wonderful legacy. "We have five fine children — who are all going to help make this old world of ours better — and you are going to see some of it at least — and you've given them of your spirit — you are their great inspiration and will be more and more. . . . There too you will some day (not too far in the future now) see Peace and goodwill on earth again. . . . remember dearest, always you will be loved and cherished by me — by the children — Dearest Walter I love you — I love you."[59] On July 23, Paul wrote a letter to his father expressing hope in their future relationship. "But I look forward still, father, to our walking and talking and working together some time in the not-too-distant future, when the world steadies to its keel again. It has listed far to port for a time, but life is still worth living, and there's a better time ahead, when the off-shore gust has been safely weathered."[60]

By the time Paul wrote this letter, Pauline finally learned the truth from doctors that her husband would not recover, and she expressed in a letter to Hilmar her hope that her husband would die peacefully.[61] On July 25, she sent a telegraph to Dores Sharpe that read simply, "Walter fell asleep quietly to-day his warfare is ended."[62] Word of Rauschenbusch's death generated numerous heartfelt public and private responses. On July 27, a simple funeral service was held at the Rauschenbusch home conducted by Clarence Barbour. Not all of the Rauschenbusch family attended the service, however. Hilmar did not learn of his father's death for almost a month. In a letter that Pauline wrote years later to Lincoln Steffens, she reported that Hilmar's army comrades kept word of Rauschenbusch's death from him, out of concern for his safety.[63]

58. Pauline to Lincoln Steffens, January 18, 1921, box 120.
59. Pauline to WR, July 14, 1918, box 37.
60. Paul Rauschenbusch to WR, July 24, 1918, box 120.
61. Pauline to Hilmar Rauschenbusch, July 24, 1918, box 123.
62. Telegraph message, Pauline to Dores Sharpe, box 155.
63. Pauline to Lincoln Steffens, January 18, 1921, box 120.

In the weeks following her husband's death, religious and secular periodicals commented on the significance of Rauschenbusch's ministry upon his times. "To lose Walter Rauschenbusch in the days of settlement and reconstruction that are before us is a heavy disaster for the cause of world-wide Christian democracy," lamented Harry F. Ward. "When the record of these times is measured it will be found that none exercised a greater influence than he upon the development of Christian thought and action."[64] Even the conservative Baptist periodical *Watchman-Examiner,* a paper that had raised repeated questions over the years related to Rauschenbusch's doctrinal soundness, took a conciliatory tone upon word of his death. "We have always recognized him as among the finest-spirited and ablest of the exponents of liberalism both in theology and ecclesiology. It is not too much to say that he is the most widely read of all the Baptist authors of our generation."[65] Pauline received hundreds of letters from many of her husband's colleagues, former students, and ministers influenced by his teaching. Many stressed the ways that his faith and teachings helped them make sense of religious beliefs in the context of the early twentieth century. Others spoke about how the strength of his character and example left an indelible mark on their ministries. Of all the personal condolences received by Pauline, one, written by a YMCA executive, captured the ethos of Walter Rauschenbusch's life for those who loved him:

> He was our admiration and our despair. We looked up to him, but none of us could climb to his height. I have never known a man who seemed so far to fulfill, or to have fulfilled in him the Saviour's promise "Blessed are the pure in heart for they shall see." He was pure, and he saw. His sufferings grew out of this. They are over. He sees now in a clearer light.[66]

64. "Rauschenbusch Number," *Rochester Theological Seminary Bulletin* (November 1918): 68.

65. Ibid., 69.

66. James Abrams to Pauline Rauschenbusch, August 15, 1918, box 91.

A LOST KINGDOM?

On March 3, 1919, Winifred wrote a lengthy letter to Hilmar, who was preparing to return home to America after the war. He had not seen his father for several months preceding his death, and would finally have a chance to journey home to reunite with his family and to scatter his father's ashes — a final closure for a family that had endured a prolonged and painful grief.

Writing from Washington, D.C., where she was doing research on that city's race relations for her mentor Robert Park in the University of Chicago sociology department, Winifred echoed the sentiment of a "lost generation" of American youth, who were picking up the pieces of their lives after the "Great War." Her words to Hilmar not only expressed her sense of disillusionment over the world they were inheriting from their elders but also expressed a sentiment that many of the values, visions, and dreams that had been espoused by men like Walter Rauschenbusch were already obsolete. Confronting Hilmar's fears that he would not be able to live up to his father's legacy, Winifred asserted that Hilmar's life was his to live, apart from his family's legacy. "I wish I knew how to tell you that you might as well perform a psychic operation and cut yourself clear of a lot of ties that your memory and imagination have created," she counseled. "Your role as Father's son has disappeared utterly. The memory of his gracious and exquisite personality lingers with a few gentle souls of the older generation; his ideas are remote as the mid-Victorian era. You and I as life goes on, will have more gripping wisdom, more force than he, less patience, less grief, and — less faith."[67]

Without her knowing it, Winifred's assertion spoke to a larger chasm that took place in American Protestantism in the decade following her father's death. By the mid-1920s, the confident stance of Protestant virility and unity that epitomized Rauschenbusch's coming of age in the late nineteenth century had given way to a religious landscape marked by division and discord. The squabbles over religious orthodoxy that Rauschenbusch engaged in during the late nineteenth century gave way to sharply contested and highly publi-

67. Winifred Rauschenbusch to Hilmar Rauschenbusch, March 3, 1919, box 123.

cized battles in the 1920s, resulting in the mass exodus of religious "fundamentalists" from rank-and-file Protestant denominations. On the surface, it may have appeared to the heirs of Rauschenbusch that their mentor was right, in terms of forecasting the demise of theological orthodoxy.

Yet the 1920s brought little solace for the heirs of liberal modernists, and for the heirs of the social gospel in particular. While some liberals continued to wax poetic about the possibilities of the coming kingdom, those who carried on the mantle of social Christianity in America were less clear about their message, their tactics, and, in particular, their audience. The 1920s saw the rise of many heirs to the legacy built by the likes of Josiah Strong, Washington Gladden, and Walter Rauschenbusch. Many of these leaders, including Francis McConnell and Harry Emerson Fosdick, attracted strong public followings through their writings and their public ministries. Yet none of these men shared the late Victorian optimism of the first generation of social gospelers in America or, more importantly, the sense that they, like their predecessors, were speaking on behalf of a Protestant theological and cultural hegemony that would witness in their lifetimes ever clearer signs of the kingdom of God in America. To be sure, the next generation of social gospelers addressed, sometimes boldly, a range of social issues that emerged in the aftermath of World War I, and increasingly the movement raised a number of issues related to racial justice and gender equality that went beyond the Victorian suppositions of the original social gospel movement. At the same time, many of these proponents frequently saw themselves under assault from the organized political resistence of conservative Protestant laymen who, ironically, had once been enthusiastic backers of the cause of Christianizing American society.

Idealism remained strong in American Protestantism after Walter Rauschenbusch's death. But it was chastened by the human and economic tyranny of the world war, and later by the specter of worldwide economic depression. Protestant leaders found themselves not just critiquing the shortcomings within the idealism of the earlier social gospel but, more importantly, how Protestants could arise out of the ashes of the social gospel. By the early 1930s, the efforts of a generational peer of Winifred Rauschenbusch, Reinhold Niebuhr, came to represent for many in American Protestantism a symbolic, if not literal, end of the social hopes and aspirations of Walter Rauschenbusch's Christian idealism.

And yet, as much as Winifred argued the case for a psychic distance between her generation and that of her father's, neither they nor the leaders of American Protestantism could escape his legacy. There was no escaping the fact that even as theological liberalism was debunked by neo-orthodox theologians like Reinhold Niebuhr, these were men who sought to do exactly what Rauschenbusch had done in his generation: to serve as the moral conscience of America, struggling, as Niebuhr often did, to believe that the Protestant hegemony envisioned by Rauschenbusch could somehow survive in the twentieth century. There was also no escaping the fact that future generations of Christians found in Rauschenbusch's writings the seeds to wage nonviolent campaigns for justice, in the name of causes that Rauschenbusch himself would have found difficult to conceive.

If historians are accurate in suggesting that religious great awakenings are followed by periods marked by the secular assimilation of these beliefs and ideals, then Walter Rauschenbusch's family never escaped his legacy, as Winifred had hoped. Pauline sought to preserve her husband's legacy for the rest of her life, living thirty-one more years before she died in 1949 at the age of 85. In the decades following Walter's death, she continued to live at 4 Portsmouth Terrace, her home serving as a place of symbolic power for those associated with Rochester Theological Seminary and for many liberal church leaders who saw her home as a place of pilgrimage. For Rauschenbusch's children, however, the pietistic faith of their father was replaced by a channeling of his social passion in distinctively secular ways. All three of his sons, Hilmar, Paul, and Karl, became associated with academia and New Deal economic practices of the 1930s. Seven years after his father's death, Paul married the daughter of Supreme Court Justice Louis Brandeis. The young couple pioneered in the drafting of the nation's first unemployment compensation legislation working with their mentor, John R. Commons, at the University of Wisconsin. Elizabeth became an actor and fine arts professor at the University of Rochester, and her interest in theater became her means of reaching out to inner-city youth in Rochester.[68]

68. The personal papers of all of Rauschenbusch's children are housed as

As his children disseminated the teachings of their father in disparate ways, it was Winifred who struggled in her adult years to synthesize a balanced view of her father's place in American history. In the 1920s, she embarked on a career as a writer and journalist and, like her siblings, embraced a variety of political causes befitting her father's legacy. At the same time, she emerged as the primary family spokesperson and defender of her father's legacy, asserting his significance for his historical era yet challenging the efforts of men like Dores Sharpe to deify him.[69] What Winifred saw, and what many overlooked, was an imperfect man who nevertheless strove in life for that which was perfect and unobtainable. As she wrote to her mother in the late 1920s, "He was perhaps the most incisive mind in the American Protestant church while he was alive." Yet, "in relationship to his own conception of himself he was both a success and a failure — I mean in the sense of failing to accomplish all that one hoped to accomplish." Yet Winifred concluded by noting something many historians overlook — that the attractiveness of a historical figure for later generations is often generated as much by one's failures as successes. "It is not a bad thing to be a failure. If one is a great enough failure, it sometimes means that one's place in history is secure."[70]

The truth of Winifred's assertion, however, would not be fully realized until the mid 1950s, when the tradition of prophetic Christianity that Walter Rauschenbusch helped spawn in the early twentieth century reached a point of national consciousness. In 1955, the Montgomery bus boycott signaled the emergence of Martin Luther King, Jr., as the major spokesperson of the civil rights movement and as the greatest exponent in the second half of the twentieth century for a prophetic vision that spoke to the moral conscience of the world. Beneath how King spoke to the contemporary historical context of his generation there emerged a deeply layered message of social redemption that revealed, in a somewhat altered idiom, the social hope of Walter Rau-

part of the Rauschenbusch Family Collection in the American Baptist–Samuel Colgate Library, Rochester, NY.

69. This tension is revealed in numerous letters between Winifred and Dores Sharpe during the time when the latter was writing his biography on Rauschenbusch. See various correspondences in box 155. The secular direction of Winifred's career was followed by her son, philosopher Richard Rorty.

70. Letter Winifred to Pauline, November 7, 1929, box 121.

schenbusch. As King wrote in his famous essay "Pilgrimage to Nonviolence," Rauschenbusch provided King much of the theological basis for his vision for nonviolent social change.

> Rauschenbusch had done a great service for the Christian Church by insisting that the gospel deals with the whole man, not only his soul but his body; not only his spiritual well-being but his material well-being. It has been my conviction ever since reading Rauschenbusch that any religion which professes to be concerned about the souls of men and is not concerned about the social and economic conditions that scar the soul, is a spiritually moribund religion only waiting for the day to be buried.[71]

In succinct fashion, King summarized the message of Walter Rauschenbusch and the theological movement he helped shape. Rauschenbusch unknowingly bequeathed to future generations of secular and religious leaders a compelling message of theological and social crisis in the West — a message that helped galvanize new movements for social change in twentieth-century America. Yet few, if any, of those who would be inspired by him after his death recognized that his theology emerged from Rauschenbusch's lifelong desire to preserve for the nation's Protestant churches the primary place of honor in the shaping of America's social-political destiny.

Walter Rauschenbusch symbolized an era within American religious history when many were struggling with competing visions of faith, and his death left many with a sense of ambiguity about the church's future role in shaping the nation's destiny. His evangelical-liberal theology was tied to a Protestant culture that yearned to maintain its grip of cultural domination upon the American middle class, a goal that receded from the agenda of even the staunchest defenders of Rauschenbusch's theological vision in the years following his death. Fragments of Rauschenbusch's social vision would be embraced and reappropriated by different audiences in the twentieth century, resurfacing among disparate religious and secular constituencies. While many secular and religious reformers were compelled by Rauschen-

71. Quoted in Martin Luther King, Jr., *Stride Toward Freedom* (New York: Harper & Row, 1958), 91.

busch's conviction that "the kingdom of God is always but coming," few dwelt on the way in which the prophetic language of his theology was tied to preserving a late nineteenth-century vision of Protestant cultural hegemony.

Winifred recognized that her father was devoted to the pursuit of the unobtainable goal to sanctify a model of American society that had largely vanished by the time of his death. Yet her father's idealism remained persistently infectious throughout the twentieth century, perhaps in part because no other movement of social transformation emerged out of the tradition of theological liberalism that has been as compelling. Walter Rauschenbusch may have spent his life chasing an unobtainable ideal. Yet this hasn't discouraged successive generations from engaging in the same quest.

Bibliography

The majority of primary sources consulted for this book came from the Rauschenbusch Family Manuscript Collection, housed in the American Baptist–Samuel Colgate Historical Library at Colgate Rochester Crozer Divinity School, Rochester, New York. The collection, totaling 180 boxes, contains thousands of letters and unpublished documents, as well as newspaper clippings, articles, personal papers, and other memorabilia of Walter Rauschenbusch and his family, including the papers of his five children. (The Historical Society collection also contains the only known extant voice recording of Rauschenbusch, a three-minute segment that Rauschenbusch recorded as part of a letter dictation, circa 1916.) Additional Rauschenbusch materials are available at the Ambrose Swasey Library of Colgate Rochester Crozer Divinity School.

The biography utilized a variety of Walter Rauschenbusch's writings, including published and unpublished articles, papers, sermons, and speeches. Most of Rauschenbusch's major books went through multiple editions since their original publication. These works include *The Righteousness of the Kingdom* written in the early 1890s and first published by Abingdon Press in 1968 (a revised edition was published by Edwin Mellen Press in 1999); *Christianity and the Social Crisis* (originally published in 1907; most recently reprinted by Westminster/John Knox Press in 1991); *Christianizing the Social Order* (originally published in 1912 and currently out of print); and *A Theology for the Social Gospel* (originally published in 1917 and recently reprinted by Westminster/John Knox Press, 1997). Rauschenbusch's shorter published volumes, *Prayers of the Social Awakening* (1910), *Unto Me* (1912), *Dare We Be Christians?* (1914), and *The Social Principles of Jesus* (1916), were widely disseminated in the years following Rauschenbusch's death. These books are supplemented by numerous articles and reviews that are cited in the biography.

I. SOURCES ON WALTER RAUSCHENBUSCH

Dores Sharpe's *Walter Rauschenbusch* (New York: Macmillan, 1942) and Paul Minus's *Walter Rauschenbusch: American Reformer* (New York: Macmillan, 1988) are the two previous full-length biographical treatments of Rauschenbusch's life. Sharpe provides useful insights, including extended quotes from Rauschenbusch's earlier, more obscure writings. However, the book contains numerous factual errors and his account is highly hagiographical. Minus's book made extensive use of the Rauschenbusch family papers and remains a valuable and important study.

While biographical accounts of Rauschenbusch are in short supply, anthologies and theological-ethical assessments of his thought are in abundance. The American Baptist–Samuel Colgate Library contains bibliographical listings of the numerous books, journal articles, and doctoral dissertations that have been written on Rauschenbusch since the 1920s. Anna Singer, *Walter Rauschenbusch and His Contribution to Social Christianity* (Boston: Richard G. Badger, 1926), Vernon Parker Bodein, "The Development of the Social Thought of Walter Rauschenbusch," in *Religion In Life* (Summer 1937), Bodein, *The Social Gospel of Walter Rauschenbusch and its Relation to Religious Education* (New York: Yale University Press, 1944), Benjamin E. Mays, ed., *A Gospel for the Social Awakening* (New York: Association Press, 1950), Benson Y. Landis, ed., *A Rauschenbusch Reader* (New York: Harper & Row, 1958), Robert T. Handy, ed., *The Social Gospel in America, 1870-1920* (New York: Oxford University Press, 1966), and Winthrop S. Hudson, ed., *Walter Rauschen-*

busch: Selected Writings (New York: Paulist Press, 1984), remain frequently cited anthologies and critical assessments of Rauschenbusch's theology. In particular, Hudson's volume contains numerous samples of Rauschenbusch's early writings, giving the reader an invaluable look into the development of his thought. Both the Handy and Hudson volumes provide excellent biographical information on Rauschenbusch's life. Donovan E. Smucker, *The Origins of Walter Rauschenbusch's Social Ethics* (Montreal and Kingston: McGill–Queen's University Press, 1994), a book originally written as Smucker's doctoral dissertation in the 1950s, remains an excellent source for understanding the disparate theological streams that influenced Rauschenbusch. Klaus Juergen Jaehn, *Rauschenbusch: The Formative Years* (Valley Forge: Judson, 1976), represents an excellent narrative of Rauschenbusch's early ministry in New York City and also provides a useful bibliography of Rauschenbusch's early publications in the 1880s. Reinhart Mueller, *Walter Rauschenbusch: Ein Beitrag zur Begegnung des deutschen und des amerikanischen Protestantismus* (Leiden: E. J. Brill, 1957), remains a significant assessment of Rauschenbusch's early ministry, especially his pietist heritage.

By far, the greatest focus on Rauschenbusch has come from scholars who have assessed his work in light of subsequent developments in twentieth century theology. Max Stackhouse, in his introductions to the original and revised editions of Rauschenbusch's *The Righteousness of the Kingdom* (Nashville: Abingdon, 1968; Lewiston: Edwin Mellen Press, 1999, revised), provides useful insights into understanding Rauschenbusch's theology, in relationship to the rise of neo-orthodoxy in the 1930s. Other works that discuss the twentieth-century significance of Rauschenbusch's theology at length include Gary Dorrien, *Reconstructing the Common Good* (Maryknoll: Orbis, 1990), Harlan Beckley, *Passion for Justice: Retrieving the Legacies of Walter Rauschenbusch, John A. Ryan, and Reinhold Niebuhr* (Louisville: Westminster/John Knox Press, 1992), and Dorrien, *The Making of American Liberal Theology*, Volume II (Louisville: Westminster/John Knox, 2003). Rauschenbusch's life has also been the subject of numerous doctoral dissertations; among those consulted for this biography include David Roy Harry, "Two Kingdoms: Walter Rauschenbusch's Concept of the Kingdom of God Contrasted with the Theology of Revivalism in Early Twentieth Century America" (Ph.D. dissertation, Southwestern Baptist Theological Seminary, 1993), and Heinz D. Rossol, "Walter Rauschenbusch as Preacher: The Development of His Social Thought as Expressed in His Sermons from 1886-1897" (Ph.D. dissertation, Marquette University, 1997). This latter study is a definitive account of the theological content of Rauschenbusch's sermons during his New York City ministry. One of the most vivid first-person accounts of Rauschenbusch's personality is provided by Edwin Dahlberg, one of his former student secretaries. A partial transcript of that interview appeared under the title, "Edwin Dahlberg in Conversation: Memories of Walter Rauschenbusch," in *Foundations* 18 (1975): 209-18 (excerpted from a recorded interview with Dahlberg that is available in the American Baptist–Samuel Colgate Library, Rochester). The November 1918 edition of the *Rochester Theological Seminary Bulletin* ("The Rauschenbusch Number") contains numerous excerpts from Rauschenbusch's writings, as well as several personal tributes.

The attention paid to Rauschenbusch as a theologian and ethicist has not been matched by extended treatments of him as a historical subject, especially critical assessments of his impact upon his era of American religious history. Nevertheless, significant work has been done on the relationship of his theology to the development of the social gospel in the United States. Jacob H. Dorn, "The Social Gospel and Socialism: A Comparison of the Thought of Francis Greenwood Peabody, Washington Gladden, and Walter Rauschenbusch," *Church History* 62 (March 1993): 82-100, and William McGuire King, "The Biblical Base of the Social Gospel," in *The Bible and Social Reform*, ed. Ernest Sandeen (Philadelphia: Fortress Press, 1982), are important studies that relate Rauschenbusch's theology to his understandings of Scripture and political socialism.

Recent historical scholarship has offered a reassessment of Rauschenbusch's thought in light of contemporary gender analysis. Janet F. Fishburn, *The Fatherhood of God and the Victorian Family: The Social Gospel in America* (Philadelphia: Fortress, 1981), and Fishburn, "Walter Rauschenbusch and 'The Woman Movement': a Gender Analysis," in *Gender and the Social Gospel*, ed. Wendy Deichmann Edwards and Carolyn DeSwarte Gifford (Urbana: University of Illinois Press, 2003), examine Rauschenbusch's conservative Victorian views on gender. Rauschenbusch's understanding of gender in relationship to his own family is discussed in Susan Curtis, *A Consuming Faith: The Social Gospel and Modern American Culture* (Baltimore: Johns Hopkins University Press, 1991), Casey Nelson Blake, "Private Life and Public Commitment: From Walter Rauschenbusch to Richard Rorty," in *A Pragmatist Progress? Richard Rorty and American Intellectual History,* ed. John Pettegrew (Lanham: Rowman & Littlefield, 2000), and Christopher H. Evans, "Gender and the Kingdom of God: The Family Values of Walter Rauschenbusch," in *The Social Gospel Today,* ed. Christopher H. Evans (Louisville: Westminster/John Knox Press, 2001). Carl E. Schneider, "Americanization of Karl August Rauschenbusch, 1816-1899," *Church History* 24 (March 1955): 3-14, remains one of the few critical engagements with the historical significance of Walter Rauschenbusch's father.

The role that Walter Rauschenbusch's understanding of church history had upon his theology has been explored by some excellent studies. See especially the work of Henry Warner Bowden in "Walter Rauschenbusch and American Church History," in *Foundations* 9 (July-September 1966): 234-50, and in a chapter, "Church History and the Social Gospel," from his book, *Church History in the Age of Science* (Chapel Hill: University of North Carolina Press, 1971). Charles R. Strain, "Toward a Generic Analysis of a Classic of the Social Gospel: An Essay-Review of Walter Rauschenbusch's *Christianity and the Social Crisis,*" in *Journal of the American Academy of Religion* 46/4 (1978): 525-43, discusses the enduring importance of this book in relationship to other social gospel writings of that time period.

II. THE SOCIAL GOSPEL

The social gospel is a well-researched topic and this study benefited from a large corpus of scholarship. An excellent overview of the historiography of the social gospel is Ralph E. Luker's "Interpreting the Social Gospel: Reflections on Two Generations of Historiography," in *Perspectives on the Social Gospel,* ed. Christopher H. Evans (Lewiston: Edwin Mellen Press, 1999). Luker's essay summarizes most of the major published articles and monographs that have been written on the social gospel since the 1930s. This biography benefited from the insights of many of these path-breaking studies, including Charles Howard Hopkins, *The Rise of the Social Gospel in American Protestantism, 1865-1915* (New Haven: Yale University Press, 1940), and Henry F.

May, *Protestant Churches and Industrial America* (New York: Harper & Row, 1949). May's work, in particular, remains very helpful toward understanding the varying responses to social reform undertaken by American Protestant churches in the late nineteenth century. Ronald C. White, Jr., and Charles Howard Hopkins, eds., *The Social Gospel: Religion and Reform in Changing America* (Philadelphia: Temple University Press, 1976), represented one of the first studies of the social gospel that examined sources other than mainline Protestant male clergy from the northeastern United States, and Paul T. Phillips, *A Kingdom on Earth: Anglo-American Social Christianity, 1880-1940* (University Park: Pennsylvania State University Press, 1995), looks at the social gospel as part of a transatlantic phenomenon, with significant roots in nineteenth-century British social Christianity. Phyllis Airhart, *Serving the Present Age: Revivalism, Progressivism, and the Methodist Tradition in Canada* (Montreal and Kingston: McGill–Queen's University Press, 1992), compares the Canadian religious context to the United States in relationship to the rise of the social gospel. Peter J. Frederick, *Knights of the Golden Rule: The Intellectual as Christian Social Reformer in the 1890s* (Lexington: University of Kentucky Press, 1976), highlights the relationship between numerous Christian reformers to the larger contours of turn-of-the-century Progressive Era America (including an excellent chapter on Rauschenbusch and George Herron). Institutional Protestantism's movement toward the social gospel is explored by Donald K. Gorrell in *The Age of Social Responsibility: The Social Gospel in the Progressive Era, 1900-1920* (Macon: Mercer University Press, 1988), and the social gospel's relationship to American racism in Ronald C. White, Jr., *Liberty and Justice for All: Racial Reform and the Social Gospel, 1875-1925* (San Francisco: Harper & Row, 1990), and Ralph E. Luker, *The Social Gospel in Black and White: American Racial Reform, 1885-1912* (Chapel Hill: University of North Carolina Press, 1991). Luker's work also includes a chapter dealing with Rauschenbusch's engagement with American racism.

If the reader is looking for one source that highlights vividly the popular context for understanding the social gospel, then one needs to read William T. Stead's now widely forgotten work *If Christ Came to Chicago!* (originally published in 1894). In many respects, this book is a nonfiction version of Charles Sheldon's immensely popular social gospel novel *In His Steps* (originally published in 1897 and still in print today). Ray Stannard Baker, *The Spiritual Unrest* (New York: Frederick H. Stokes Company, 1910), gives an interesting first-person look at the relationship of religion to Progressive Era America, written by one of its chief journalistic figures.

While studies on Walter Rauschenbusch have emphasized the importance of his theology and ethics, most of the scholarship on the social gospel has largely ignored the theological contributions of the movement. Willem Adolph Visser 't Hooft, *The Background of the Social Gospel in America* (Haarlem, 1928), represented one of the first (and still relevant) efforts to analyze the social gospel as a theological phenomenon, written by a prominent European leader of the twentieth-century ecumenical movement. William McGuire King gives a more contemporary assessment of the social gospel's theological legacy in "'History as Revelation' in the Theology of the Social Gospel," in *Harvard Theological Review* 76:1 (1983): 109-29, and "An Enthusiasm for Humanity: The Social Emphasis in Religion and Its Accommodation in Protestant Theology," in *Religion and Twentieth-Century American Intellectual Life*, ed. Michael J. Lacey (Cambridge: Cambridge University Press, 1989). Susan Hill Lindley's "Deciding Who Counts: Toward a Revised Definition of the Social Gospel," in *The Social Gospel Today*, also provides a useful way for one to understand the theological contours of the social gospel.

Despite the prominence of Rauschenbusch's social gospel colleagues such as Washington Gladden, Richard Ely, George Herron, and Josiah Strong, there have been few in-depth studies of these major figures of American religious history. Only Washington Gladden has been the subject of a full-length biography, by Jacob H. Dorn, *Washington Gladden: Prophet of the Social Gospel* (Columbus: Ohio State University Press, 1967). Gladden's autobiography *Recollections* (Boston: Houghton Mifflin, 1909) provides an insightful window into the development of the social gospel from the perspective of one of its seminal figures. Critical biographies of Richard Ely, George Herron, and Josiah Strong remain to be written.

The argument that the social gospel emerged as an outgrowth from earlier movements of nineteenth-century Protestant evangelicalism remains somewhat controversial. However, Timothy L. Smith's *Revivalism and Social Reform in Mid-Nineteenth Century America* (Nashville: Abingdon Press, 1957) and Ralph Luker's *Social Gospel in Black and White* present compelling arguments that highlight a continuity between Protestant postmillennialism of the early nineteenth century and the cultural and theological worldview of many representatives within the social gospel movement.

While most historical studies tend to see 1918 as the traditional end of the social gospel era, several works have examined the development of the social gospel impulse in American Protestantism after World War I. See Paul Carter, *The Decline and Revival of the Social Gospel: Social Political Liberalism in American Protestant Churches, 1920-1920* (Ithaca: Cornell University Press, 1954), Robert Moats Miller, *American Protestantism and Social Issues: 1919-1939* (Chapel Hill: University of North Carolina Press, 1958), Donald Meyer, *The Protestant Search for Political Realism: 1919-1941* (Berkeley: University of California Press, 1960), and William McGuire King, "The Emergence of Social Gospel Radicalism in American Methodism" (Ph.D. dissertation, Harvard University, 1978).

III. NINETEENTH- AND TWENTIETH-CENTURY AMERICAN PROTESTANTISM/RELIGION IN THE PROGRESSIVE ERA

Despite the large number of outstanding survey texts dealing with the general topic of American religious history, investigating the relationship of theological liberalism (and social Christianity / the social gospel in particular) to the larger historical and theological changes taking place in the second half of the nineteenth century remains a hotly contested and, in some ways, elusive topic. Texts that include significant discussion of this period in American religious history include Robert T. Handy, *A Christian America: Protestant Hopes and Historical Realities* (New York: Oxford University Press, 1971), Sydney Ahlstrom, *A Religious History of the American People* (New Haven: Yale University Press, 1972), William R. Hutchison, *The Modernist Impulse in American Protestantism* (Cambridge: Harvard University Press, 1976), Martin E. Marty, *Modern American Religion: The Irony of It All* (Chicago: University of Chicago Press, 1986), and William R. Hutchison, ed., *Between the Times: The Travail of the Protestant Establishment* (Cambridge: Cambridge University Press, 1989). Grant Wacker, "The Holy Spirit and the Spirit of the Age in American Protestantism, 1880-1910," in *Journal of*

American History 72 (June 1985): 45-62, represents a carefully nuanced essay that fleshes out the historical and theological terrain confronted by orthodox and liberal Protestants in late nineteenth-century America. Additionally, Wacker's book, *Augustus H. Strong and the Dilemma of Historical Consciousness* (Macon: Mercer University Press, 1985), represents a definitive study of Augustus Strong's theology, especially taking up the question of Strong's liberal turn during the years when Rauschenbusch's theological star was on the rise. Gaius Glenn Atkins, *Religion in Our Times* (New York: Round Table Press, Inc., 1932), is an interesting perspective on the theological changes in late nineteenth- and early twentieth-century American Protestantism, written by a church leader who lived through that era.

Kenneth Cauthen, *The Impact of American Religious Liberalism* (New York and Evanston: Harper & Row, 1962), develops useful theological and historical typologies for classifying twentieth-century theological liberalism (including to help popularize the label of Walter Rauschenbusch as an "evangelical-liberal"), as do numerous volumes by Gary J. Dorrien, most especially *Soul in Society: The Making and Renewal of Social Christianity* (Minneapolis: Fortress Press, 1995) and the first two volumes in his series, *The Making of American Liberal Theology* (Louisville: Westminster/John Knox, 2001, 2003).

Despite its popularity during the Progressive Era, few historians have written on the Open Forum movement, through which Walter Rauschenbusch spread many of his ideas across America. George W. Coleman's edited history of the forum's founding and early years, *Democracy in the Making: Ford Hall and the Open Forum Movement* (Boston: Little Brown, 1915), remains a fascinating source into a largely ignored chapter of Progressive Era America. Two excellent articles by Arthur S. Meyers carry the history of the open forum movement from the era of Walter Rauschenbusch into the 1920s and 1930s, "A Bridge to the Future: From the Boston Baptist Social Union to the Beth El Open Forum," in *American Baptist Quarterly* (September 1995): 225-40, and "'The Striking of Mind Upon Mind': The Open Forum and the Social Gospel," in *Baptist History and Heritage* (spring 2000): 20-36.

IV. ROCHESTER, NEW YORK, AND ROCHESTER THEOLOGICAL SEMINARY HISTORY

The religious history of Rochester and western New York occupies a major theme in several significant monographs. Paul Johnson, *A Shopkeeper's Millennium: Society and Revivals in Rochester, New York* (New York: Hill and Wang, 1978), reflects upon the distinctive religious and cultural context that characterized Rochester, just prior to the arrival in the city of August and Caroline Rauschenbusch in the 1850s. In terms of detailed accounts of the political and social history of the city of Rochester from its founding to the present day, one needs to turn to the writings of the late Blake McKelvey. As long-time city historian, McKelvey was editor and frequent contributor for the monthly *Rochester History,* with many of the articles written by McKelvey. In particular relation to this book his article "Walter Rauschenbusch's Rochester," *Rochester History* 14 (October 1952): 1-27, provides a vivid snapshot into the religious and cultural context of the city during Rauschenbusch's years on the Rochester Theological Seminary faculty. McKelvey's final book, co-authored with Ruth Rosenberg-Naparsteck, *Rochester: A Panoramic History* (Sun Valley: American Historical Press, 2001), provides the reader with a wonderful narrative and pictorial account of Rochester's rise as a major manufacturing and cultural city in the United States.

With all the attention paid to Rauschenbusch's career as a writer, speaker, and teacher, little effort has been made to explore his role as a social reformer in the city of Rochester. John R. Aiken, "Walter Rauschenbusch and Education for Reform," in *Church History* 36 (December 1967): 456-69, remains a significant study, providing a critical look into this dimension of Rauschenbusch's public life. LeRoy Moore, Jr., "The Rise of American Religious Liberalism at the Rochester Theological Seminary, 1872-1928" (Ph.D. dissertation, Claremont Graduate School, 1966), is a definitive study of the history and subsequent liberal theological turn of Rochester Theological Seminary in the early twentieth century. Moore's account gives an excellent overview of the presidential administration of Augustus Strong and discusses Rauschenbusch's role on the faculty at length. Albert John Ramaker, a former classmate and faculty colleague of Rauschenbusch, provided a brief history of the seminary's German department in "The Story of the German Department," *Rochester Theological Seminary Bulletin* (October 1927): 30-43. A pamphlet by Conrad Henry Moehlman, "The Ambrose Swasey Library," published by the Rochester Historical Society (1937), provides a vivid account of the fledgling years of the seminary and that school's relationship with its sister institution, the University of Rochester.

Index

Throughout, WR = Walter Rauschenbusch